MAGILL'S
SURVEY
OF
AMERICAN
LITERATURE

MAGILL'S SURVEY OF AMERICAN LITERATURE

Volume 5

Olsen–Snyder

REFERENCE

Edited by
FRANK N. MAGILL

Marshall Cavendish Corporation
New York • London • Toronto • Sydney • Singapore

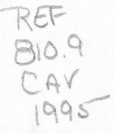

Published By
Marshall Cavendish Corporation
2415 Jerusalem Avenue
P.O. Box 587
North Bellmore, New York 11710
United States of America

∞ The paper used in these volumes conforms to the American National Standard for Permanence of Paper for Printed Library Materials, Z39.48-1984.

Library of Congress Cataloging-in-Publication Data
Magill's survey of American literature. Edited by Frank N. Magill.
    p. cm.
  Includes bibliographical references and index.
  1. American literature—Dictionaries. 2. American literature—Bio-bibliography. 3. Authors, American—Biography—Dictionaries. I. Magill, Frank Northen, 1907.
PS21.M34 1991
810.9′0003—dc20
ISBN 1-85435-437-X (set)   91-28113
ISBN 1-85435-442-6 (volume 5)   CIP

Second Printing

PRINTED IN THE UNITED STATES OF AMERICA

CONTENTS

MAGILL'S
SURVEY
OF
AMERICAN
LITERATURE

TILLIE OLSEN

Born: Omaha, Nebraska
January 14, 1913

Principal Literary Achievement

Olsen's fiction affirms the individuality and complexity of women; it led to a wider recognition of the contributions of women writers in literary history.

Biography

Tillie Olsen, the second of six children, was the daughter of Samuel and Ida Lerner. Her parents, Russian Jews, immigrated to America after the 1905 rebellion. Her father was a laborer, and he served for many years as secretary to Nebraska's Socialist Party.

Olsen knew she wanted to become a writer when she was fifteen. She bought a number of issues of *The Atlantic Monthly* in an Omaha junkshop. In those volumes she read in serialized form the novel *Life in the Iron Mills*. At that time *The Atlantic Monthly* did not publish the names of contributors. For many years Olsen did not realize that the author of the novel was a woman, Rebecca Harding Davis. Olsen was impressed by the realism of this story and realized that literature could be made from the lives of ordinary people who struggled to eke out a living and raise a family. Olsen left high school during her senior year in order to find work and help her family. Shortly thereafter she was jailed after helping to organize packing-house workers in Kansas City. That experience inspired her to begin a novel, *Yonnondio: From the Thirties* (1974), about the experiences of a working-class family whose hopes for a better life are dashed by a cruel capitalist economic system.

Olsen began to write this novel in 1932. Despite a battle with pleurisy, she continued to work on the manuscript. She moved to California and settled in San Francisco, where she worked closely with labor unions, was arrested for organizing, and was an active member of the Young Communist League. She published two poems and "The Iron Throat," a small section of the manuscript of the novel in progress in *Partisan Review* in 1934.

In later issues of *Partisan Review* in 1934, she contributed an essay on the warehouse strike in San Francisco called "The Strike," and she wrote a first-person account of being arrested and brutally questioned with other Communist sympathizers in "The Thousand Dollar Vagrant." "The Iron Throat" was enthusiastically received by critics. Bennett Cerf and Donald Klopfer, editors with Random House, offered

her a monthly stipend if she would complete a chapter each month. She signed a contract and moved to Los Angeles to begin the project, but she was unable to concentrate on the writing. After canceling the contract, she returned to San Francisco. She never finished *Yonnondio: From the Thirties.*

In 1936 she married Jack Olsen, a union printer. They had four daughters, Karla, Julie, Katherine, and Laurie. She contributed no further stories, poems, or essays to *Partisan Review.* Instead, she worked as a transcriber in a dairy equipment company and worked at various part-time jobs; she produced no further published writings for twenty years.

Between 1953 and 1954, she composed "Help Her to Believe," a short story about a mother's reminiscences of her daughter. This story was published in 1956 in the *Pacific Spectator* and reprinted in 1961 under the title "I Stand Here Ironing" in her collection of four stories, *Tell Me a Riddle.* Other stories in the collection included "O Yes," the title story, and "Hey Sailor, What Ship?" With the publication of this book, Tillie Olsen broke her silence. The stories in the collection have been anthologized more than fifty times, and the book has been translated into several languages. Critical response to the book was enthusiastic, and her reputation as a writer and a spokesperson for the feminist literary tradition was assured with its publication.

Between 1961 and 1972, Olsen published three articles that arose from her involvement in grants and fellowships received after publication of *Tell Me a Riddle.* "Silences: When Writers Don't Write" appeared in *Harper's* in 1965. It was based on a 1964 seminar, "Death of the Creative Process." A second article, "One Out of Twelve: Writers Who Are Women in Our Century" (1972), was developed from notes from a 1971 address to the Modern Language Association Forum on Women Writers. In 1972, Olsen contributed the afterword to the Feminist Press reprint of Rebecca Harding Davis' 1861 classic novel, *Life in the Iron Mills.* This substantial essay was important both professionally and personally to Olsen. The fifteen-year-old girl who had read the novel in *The Atlantic Monthly* was now a highly regarded author. Having the opportunity to write the afterword to this novel closed an important circle in her life.

Another closing of a circle was the 1974 publication of her unfinished novel *Yonnondio: From the Thirties.* Her husband had discovered the manuscript while looking for other papers. Rather than try to add to the manuscript or revise it, she organized it from many drafts and versions of the text. After eight chapters the text ends suddenly, and the author adds a note commenting on its incomplete state. Critics hailed this unfinished novel as a great work of fiction.

During the 1970's, Tillie Olsen taught courses in literature and in women's studies at several universities in the United States and abroad, and she became well known as a lecturer to women's groups, university students, and writers' organizations. In 1978, her book *Silences* was published. The book includes the two previously published essays noted above, the afterword from *Life in the Iron Mills,* and a compendium of quotations, excerpts, and comments by and about famous men and women writers who were "silenced" at some time in their creative lives.

Olsen became a mentor for young writers and a spokesperson for feminist concerns. She developed reading lists of works by women, and she promoted the reprinting of significant literary classics written by women. In 1979, she was awarded
an honorary doctorate from the University of Nebraska. Olsen's *Mother to Daughter,
Daughter to Mother: Mothers on Mothering* was published in 1984. The text includes a calendar of months, a series of excerpts from women's writings arranged
according to topic based on mother-daughter relationships, and a list of titles of
works by women.

Analysis

Readers of Tillie Olsen's fiction may come away with a heightened understanding
of the complexities inherent in being a woman in a society that values predominantly
the male perspective on things. Olsen challenges readers to empathize with the wom-
en's point of view. Whether she is speaking through a character in her fiction or
speaking directly to teachers, writers, or readers of fiction, Olsen always seeks to
redress the balance between the male and the female points of view.

What does Olsen want her reader to know about women? She invites readers to
consider their various strengths, the history of their being an oppressed class of people, the limited roles they were offered in Western society, the abusive relationships
they were forced to suffer, the powerful alliances they made with other women, the
tolerance and patience they exhibited toward their husbands, the silences and soli-
tudes they experienced at different times of their lives, their being expected to live
"for" others instead of "with" others, and their capacity for insight and wisdom
into the heart of life. In short, Olsen wants readers to know of the richness, depths,
and diversity of the inner lives of women. She wants readers to view life through a
woman's eyes—and see women as individuals.

Whether she tells a story from the point of view of the child Mazie in *Yonnondio:
From the Thirties* or from the point of view of an old woman in "Tell Me a Riddle"
(1961), Olsen uses the technique of interior monologue to great advantage. Olsen
organizes the thoughts of the character directly on the page; readers, in effect, over-
hear what the character is thinking. This approach requires close reading and active
participation on the part of the reader. It is impossible to skim these sections. Another aspect of style in Olsen's writing is her use of lengthy descriptive passages
within the narrative. At times, her writing in *Yonnondio: From the Thirties* appears
to be as lyrical as the poems of Walt Whitman or E. E. Cummings. At other times,
the writing is graphic and detailed in its realism, with the density of phrasing similar
to the fiction of William Faulkner. What stands out in all of her writings, however, is
that Olsen's voice and style are unique. That she found her own voice and expressed
themes of importance to her own life matters most in any assessment of her contributions as a writer.

Although her fiction emphasizes a woman's point of view, her characters and
plots are universal ones, of importance to the lives of both men and women. Olsen's

fiction is committed to the lives of the poor, the uneducated, the despised, and the downtrodden. Her mother's resistance against oppression in czarist Russia and her father's long membership in the Socialist party contributed to her own commitment to socialist ideals in the 1930's. To some extent, Olsen sees herself as a spokesperson for those who do not have speech—for those who are silenced by governments, by societal attitudes, by economic systems. "The Strike" is a protest against unfair labor practices. *Yonnondio: From the Thirties* is a novel of protest about the evils of the capitalist economic system. "Tell Me a Riddle" is a protest about American society's tendency to patronize the elderly. *Silences* is largely a protest against a literary tradition in America that excludes an equal representation of women.

Since Olsen's fiction emphasizes the woman's point of view, it necessarily depicts women's roles within the family and women's place in generational conflicts. Her fiction contains stories that reveal dimensions of mother-daughter relationships, father-daughter relationships, and sibling relationships. "Tell Me a Riddle" is one of the few honest portrayals of a relationship between an old couple, married forty-seven years. That story also realistically depicts three generations in conflict. In her portrayal of women's experience, Olsen seeks to communicate the importance of choice in a woman's life. Without choices, women are reduced to stereotypes and offered few viable roles in life. With choices, women become equal to men, able to articulate individual goals, fully capable of a wide range of emotions and ideas.

Olsen's contributions as a writer are matched by her contributions as a spokesperson for the feminist literary tradition and as a role model for women (and men) who are writers. *Silences* is a rallying cry for teachers and critics to study at length the contributions of women writers. It is also an appeal for understanding how and why women writers, including Olsen herself, have been silenced through history. Olsen's own life and writings have inspired writers to sustain themselves through hard times and not yield to pressures or circumstances that would silence them.

YONNONDIO

First published: 1974
Type of work: Novel

A family in the 1920's barely survives a series of financial and family crises as the father ekes out a living as a common laborer.

The manuscript of *Yonnondio: From the Thirties* was lost to Tillie Olsen for more than thirty years before being accidentally discovered by her husband, who was looking for other papers. A portion of the novel had been published in 1934 in *The Partisan Review*, a journal devoted to socialist writing. Although the story was well received by critics, Olsen never completed the novel. Instead, she reared a family of four children and worked at part-time jobs for most of her adult life until the 1961 publication of *Tell Me a Riddle*. This collection of stories led to the discovery of

Tillie Olsen as a major literary talent, and it made the publication of *Yonnondio* an important addition to her works. Olsen decided not to add to or substantially revise the manuscript. At the conclusion of the eight chapters of this unfinished novel, Olsen adds the following note: "Reader, it was not to have ended here, but it is nearly forty years since this book had to be set aside, never to come to completion."

The title is taken from a poem by Walt Whitman called "Yonnondio." In the poem, Whitman laments the passing of the great American Indian nations in the face of the white man's advance. After recalling the contributions of these peoples, Whitman concludes the poem, "Then blank and gone and still, and utterly lost." That line could serve as a description of the middle years of Olsen's career: Although she began to develop her art in the 1930's, circumstances led to her being silenced as a writer for more than twenty years.

The novel depicts the experiences of Jim and Anna Holbrook and their family. Jim is an itinerant laborer who struggles to find a decent job, first in a coal mine in Wyoming, then on a tenant farm in North Dakota, and finally in a meat packing house in Omaha, Nebraska. No matter where Jim works, he never earns enough to make ends meet. He feels trapped in a recurring cycle of poverty and desperation. He loves his wife and children but he feels trapped by them because they represent a limit to his freedom as a man and an insurmountable financial burden. He begins to drink excessively, he abuses his wife, and he neglects his children.

Anna tries to be responsive to his misery, but she is overwhelmed with the duties of homemaking and child care, and she often faces bouts of depression. She suffers from physical exhaustion and experiences a miscarriage. Anna wants her children to have a better life than Jim and she have had, and she values education as one way the children might improve their lot in life. The children, however, have few opportunities for education. Anna often experiences stress over the narrow limitations of her role as a woman. An old man in the novel characterizes her as a woman who "has had everything to grind out life and yet has kept life." Anna experiences a major victory in the novel when she asserts her independence in the face of Jim's restrictive attitudes.

The politics of the novel are clearly on the side of the proletariat, that class of people who have the lowest status—the working-class in an industrialist society. Everyone who hires Jack Holbrook takes advantage of him. The coal mining company compels him to do work that is physically demanding and dangerous. The wage he earns is insufficient for his family's basic needs. After working one season on a tenant farm in North Dakota, Jack is deeper in debt than when he started at the beginning of the season. When he works as a laborer in Omaha, his wage never keeps pace with the family's expenses. Jack's plight underscores a common theme in Marxist-socialist politics: The worker has "nothing to sell but his labor power."

Consequently, the worker is stripped of his identity and becomes a tool of the economic forces that control his destiny. At one point, Olsen explains that if workers were to revolt, they "could wipe out the whole thing, the whole god-damn thing, and a human could be a human for the first time on earth." Both Jack and Anna, then, are victims of complex economic forces that exclude a number of people from the opportunities of attaining the American Dream.

Olsen portrays this economic exploitation symbolically throughout the novel. The coal becomes a symbol of the domination of the workers' lives: "Earth sucks you in, to spew out the coal, to make a few fat bellies fatter." The stench of the meat-packing houses in Omaha also dominated the landscape of the people who live there. Olsen writes, "That is a reminder—a proclamation—*I rule here.*" Wherever the family turns, they are rendered powerless by a harsh and unsympathetic economic system.

At times Olsen's writing style appears to be a combination of the graphic realism of Upton Sinclair's *The Jungle* (1906) and John Steinbeck's *The Grapes of Wrath* (1939) with the lyrical poetry of Walt Whitman's *Song of Myself* (1855). The latter style is most evident in Olsen's emulation of the lengthy descriptive passages common to Whitman's poetry. In one scene, she summarizes what is lost when an individual realizes his lot in life: "the little things gone: shoeshine and tailormades, tickets to a baseball game, and a girl, a girl to love up, whiskey down your gullet, and laughter, the happy belch of a full stomach, and walking with your shoulders back, tall and proud." Such passages reveal both an eye for detail and a sensitivity to the suffering of impoverished human beings.

Most of the story is told from the point of view of Mazie, Jack and Anna Holbrook's oldest child. Mazie is in a position to witness the terrible deprivation experienced by the family and the growing sense of desperation felt by her parents. In some scenes Mazie is called upon to become a "parent" to her parents as well as to her siblings. Readers gain insights into Mazie's character directly, through the technique of interior monologues; they portray the thoughts of a character in richly descriptive passages. This technique helps readers identify with Mazie's experiences.

In other cases, Olsen introduces the points of view of the parents and many minor characters. Late in the novel, Anna's point of view begins to predominate as she recovers a sense of purpose in her life and asserts herself in her relationship with Jack. On several occasions, Olsen directly addresses the readers in order to involve them in the political messages inherent in her work and in the lives of the characters she portrays. More than anything, Olsen wants readers to know that people such as Mazie and her parents suffer; she wants to give voice to the silent and the oppressed so that others can listen to what they have to say.

I STAND HERE IRONING

First published: 1956
Type of work: Short story

Prompted by a counselor's inquiry, a mother reviews her nineteen-year-old daughter's childhood and examines the basis of their relationship.

The first sentence in "I Stand Here Ironing" sets the tone and establishes the mood of the entire story: "I stand here ironing, and what you asked me moves tormented back and forth with the iron." Prompted by the counselor's concern for her daughter's future development, the mother responds with a tone of resignation, even despair, as she tries to explain to her visitor the nature of her circumscribed life and the nature of her daughter's desperate attempts to find her own identity within a self-limiting environment. Like the iron to which she refers, her daughter's life has moved in a cycle of progression and retrogression, between moments of joy and satisfaction and moments of isolation and despair. Ironing is also a perfect metaphor for the limited roles imposed upon women—of wife, homemaker, and mother—and all that is lost to women because of those narrow roles.

The mother tells a story of self-denial, deprivation, and loss. Emily, the subject of the counselor's inquiry, is the oldest of five children. The mother recalls a special memory of Emily as a baby—beautiful, joyous, full of life. "She was a miracle to me." After eight months of bliss, however, her husband leaves them suddenly, and she is forced to find work to rear her child. She is even compelled to leave the child with her former husband's family for a year. The mother remarries, and soon is pregnant with her second child. For a time, she has to send Emily to a convalescent home because of her ill health. The effect of these separations on Emily is devastating: She becomes a remote, isolated girl who has few friends and does poorly in school. The mother concludes, "I was working, there were four smaller ones now, there was not time for her."

Somehow Emily survives these deprivations and develops a talent for mimicry. Although her mother is encouraged to help Emily refine that gift, she contends, "but without money or knowing how, what does one do? We have left it all to her, and the fight has as often eddied inside, clogged and clotted, as been used and growing."

One of the central themes in the story is that Emily's individuality and uniqueness of character are realized through her mother's reminiscences. The mother does not view Emily with the same limited perspective that society applied to her as a young woman. In fact, one of the ironies of the story is that Emily, who is nineteen, was born when her mother was nineteen. It is clear that the mother's reminiscences of Emily's childhood are meant as a comparison between constraints placed upon the mother's life when she was nineteen and the possibilities open to her daughter's life at the same age. In effect, Emily has choices, whereas her mother had none.

Another important aspect of the story is that readers gain insights into the complexities of mother-daughter relationships. Although the mother may have made mistakes in rearing her daughter, she refuses to accept all the responsibility for what her child has become. The details of her reminiscences help readers become sensitive to all that was lost, and yet all that was preserved, in this relationship. At the end of the story, the mother concludes, "Let her be. So all that is in her will not bloom—but in how many does it? There is still enough left to live by." Despite having grown up under harsh and impoverished living conditions, this young woman is a survivor and has the capacity to meet life on her own terms.

TELL ME A RIDDLE

First published: 1961
Type of work: Novella

An old woman defies her domineering husband's retirement plans and then undertakes a personal struggle against cancer.

Tell Me a Riddle is Tillie Olsen's greatest achievement as a writer of fiction. This novella expands upon themes that Olsen developed in her earlier stories and adds new insights into relationships between married couples and the experiences of women.

The initial conflict in the novella is between Eva and her husband. Now that they have reared their family and all the children have established their own homes all over the country, their forty-seven-year marriage reaches a point of crisis. Eva's husband wants to sell the house and move into a retirement home, the Haven (a particularly appropriate metaphor for his need for a safe harbor from the lifetime of poverty and crushed expectations). His desire for freedom is really a desire for security. Eva seeks freedom too, but she defines freedom as "*never again to be forced to move to the rhythms of others.*" She wishes "at last to live within." She perceives her husband's plan to sell the house as another in a long list of decisions that will continue her subservience to his will. Now, in old age, she makes a final stand against that form of bondage.

Their children are shocked at the dispute, and they have little sympathy for Eva's need to develop her inner life. When she becomes ill, they attribute it to lethargy and psychosomatic causes; then her illness is diagnosed as a malignant cancer, and she is given only a year to live. Her children rally around her and suggest that David take her to visit the various children and grandchildren. Although he is dismayed at the expenses required by these travels, he acquiesces and tries to be a cheerful and helpful companion.

Eva wants more than anything to find the solitude that will reconcile her to the deprivations of the past. She finds that inner peace partly through her interactions with a granddaughter, Jeannie, who is to some extent Eva's alter ego; that is, she is a young woman who believes that she has the power of choice in her life. Her self-fulfillment will not be thwarted by submission to male choices. She is the perfect attendant for Eva's last days. She takes care of Eva's physical needs, records the old woman's beauty through a series of sketches, and assists David in staying with his wife to the end.

Eva's truest inner peace and most perfect expression of solitude, however, comes as her mind returns to her roots as a child and young woman in Russia during the turbulent years at the turn of the century, when czarist oppression was felt by the peasant classes. She has two key memories that sustain her: One is of herself as a young woman. At that time she was a member of the resistance, fighting the czarists. She shared a cell with Lisa, who was a patriot for the anti-czarist forces. Lisa killed an informer in order to save the lives of many of her comrades, even though that action led to her own death. Lisa was Eva's hero; she inspired Eva to consider larger social and political issues. To Eva, Jeannie is a modern-day version of Lisa.

Eva's other memory, which sustains her in the face of death, is a memory of being a child in Russia and dancing joyously at a country wedding. That image of a dancing child suggests a moment of perfect freedom before the girl child becomes a woman and is compelled to submit to social forces that require her to fulfill narrow roles. In a sense, then, Eva goes back to her childhood in order to reconcile the lifelong compromises she made with her own needs of identity and self-fulfillment. The novella ends with a hopeful tone, because even in death there is an affirmation of the beauty and timelessness of that inner peace that Eva sought so courageously in the last year of her life.

At one point in the novella, Eva notes that when her husband played with the grandchildren he "knew how to tickle, chuck, lift, toss, do tricks, tell secrets, make jokes, match riddle for riddle." When the children asked Eva, "Tell me a riddle," however, her answer was always, "I know no riddles, child." To some extent her response reinforces the difference—the conflict—between Eva and her husband, between all men and women. On another level, Eva's response is ironic, for her life has been a mystery to which she cannot give voice. So much is inside, and she seeks the answer to the riddle of her own life.

One of the main themes in the novella is that a woman's life must be her own, and not the lives of her children or of her husband. It is inappropriate for a woman to live her life "for" others. Instead, she needs to find the same measure of self-fulfillment that men expect to find in their lives. Another theme is that women have as many insights into the human condition as men do. The woman in *Tell Me a Riddle* has a profound capacity for courage, an empathy for those who are impoverished and oppressed, and insights into the social and political ills that foster human oppression.

SILENCES

First published: 1974
Type of work: Essays

In this collection of essays, Olsen writes of the circumstances that can block writers' (especially women writers') abilities to create.

Written to "re-dedicate and encourage" writers, *Silences* is a compendium of essays, quotations, and commentaries devoted to the reasons various writers either have not written more or have not written at all. It includes two essays written by Tillie Olsen, her afterword to a reprinting of Rebecca Harding Davis' 1861 novel *Life in the Iron Mills*, and more than 150 pages of commentary and original source material relating to the "silences" of many well-known authors, such as Thomas Hardy, Gerard Manley Hopkins, Virginia Woolf, and Herman Melville. Olsen calls this long section "Acerbs, Asides, Amulets, Exhumations, Sources, Deepenings, Roundings, Expansions." Each entry is keyed to the two essays that begin the text.

Of major importance in *Silences* are the two essays that begin the text. The first, "Silences in Literature," was first published in 1965. In this essay Olsen decries the silences that have stopped great literary talents from producing to their full potential. Olsen assigns the term "silences" various categories: "some the silences for years by our acknowledged great; some silences hidden; some the ceasing to publish after one work appears; some the never coming to book form at all." Other silences are caused by censorship, restrictive governments, or narrow societal roles. She concludes, "Where the gifted among women (*and men*) have remained mute, or have never attained full capacity, it is because of circumstances, inner or outer, which oppose the needs of creation." Her central example is her own story. For twenty years (from 1934 to 1954) she did not publish. She writes, "The simplest circumstances for creation did not exist." Although she kept alive in herself her love for writing, she was unable to bring any work to fruition. This essay is a lament for what she and other great writers have lost by not fulfilling their artistic potential.

The second essay, "One Out of Twelve: Writers Who Are Women in Our Century," was first published in 1972. Olsen contends that of all writers cited in anthologies, listed on syllabi of modern literature courses, noted in the year's best (or decade's best) collections, listed on required reading lists, or considered in book review sections, only one in twelve writers is a woman. Beginning with this simple but devastating statistic, Olsen goes on to cite many of the ways in which women have been rendered secondary or inferior to men in many cultures. She lists stereotypes, taboos, religious characterizations, and narrow and confining roles. She also places her own experience in the context of other women who were "silenced" and devalued. She concludes, "You who teach, read writers who are women. There is a whole literature to be re-estimated, revalued. . . . Read, listen to, living women writers. . . . Not to have audience is a kind of death." Both essays are an appeal for understanding that writers fail to create because of the "unnatural silences" that plague them.

Summary

It is unusual for readers to look upon a writer as a role model, but that is the case for many readers of the works of Tillie Olsen. They have been inspired by this woman's long and difficult struggle to sustain her writing, and they have been moved by her commitment to the realization of women as individuals in her writing. Olsen's literary reputation is based primarily on an unfinished novel and a book of four stories, but her gifts as a writer have encouraged other writers and stimulated a new interest in feminist literary classics.

Bibliography

Boucher, Sandy. "Tillie Olsen: The Weight of Things Unsaid." *Ms.* 3 (September, 1974): 26-30.

Cuneen, Sally. "Tillie Olsen: Storyteller of Working America." *Christian Century* 21 (May, 1980): 570-574.

McElheny, Annette Bennington. "Alternative Responses to Life in Tillie Olsen's Work." *Frontiers* 2 (Spring, 1977): 76-91.

Martin, Abigail. *Tillie Olsen.* Boise, Idaho: Boise State University Press, 1984.

Orr, Elaine Neil. *Tillie Olsen and a Feminist Spiritual Vision.* Jackson: University Press of Mississippi, 1987.

Schwartz, Helen J. "Tillie Olsen." *American Women Writers.* Vol. 3, edited by Lina Mainiero and Langdon Lynne Faust. New York: Frederick Ungar, 1981.

Shulman, Alix Kates. "Overcoming Silences: Teaching Writing to Women." *Harvard Educational Review* 49 (November, 1979): 527-533.

Robert E. Yahnke

CHARLES OLSON

Born: Worcester, Massachusetts
December 27, 1910
Died: New York, New York
January 10, 1970

Principal Literary Achievement

Olson was an influential poet and essayist during the post-World War II period; his long work, *The Maximus Poems*, develops and experiments with the form of the long poem.

Biography

Charles Olson was born on December 27, 1910, in Worcester, Massachusetts. His father, Charles Joseph Olson, was a letter carrier of Swedish descent, and his mother, Mary Theresa Hines, came from an Irish-American background. The family was poor and lived in a lower-middle-class neighborhood in Worcester. Although the young Charles had the usual father-son conflicts during his youth, he greatly admired his father for the force of his personality and his fortitude in standing up to the high-handed political scheming of his supervisors in the postal service. His relationship with his mother was extremely close, and a number of his finest poems are laments and elegies over her death in 1950. Both Olson and his father stood more than 6 feet, 7 inches tall and towered over Mrs. Olson, as family photographs show.

Olson's career as a student was earmarked by success at every step. He qualified for entrance into the Worcester Classical High School, where he earned the highest grades. He also began winning prestigious awards in oratorical contests, taking third place in a national oratory contest in Washington, D.C., in 1928. His prize was a ten-week tour of Europe, where he began his first personal contact with world history, especially Greek and Roman history. Returning from Europe, he entered Wesleyan University as a scholarship student, qualifying as a member of Phi Beta Kappa. During his years at Wesleyan, he participated in many theatrical productions, wrote for the school newspaper, played soccer (as a goalie), and became a candidate for a Rhodes Scholarship. During his summers, he performed in little theater productions in and around Gloucester, Massachusetts, his family's permanent summer residence during most of his younger years. Gloucester became the central subject matter and focus for Charles Olson's major long poem, *The Maximus Poems* (1960), which he began writing in 1947.

After graduation from Wesleyan, Olson attended Yale University on an Olin scholarship and began work on a master's degree, but he decided to return to his undergraduate school instead. He earned his master's degree at Wesleyan in 1932 with a thesis on nineteenth century American novelist Herman Melville. After some intense research in the papers and books of Herman Melville's personal library, he began teaching at Clark University in Worcester. At this time he met a writer who became for him a mentor and close friend, Edward Dahlberg. Dahlberg's commitment to scholarship and his standards of excellence influenced Olson to pursue further graduate studies at Harvard University, where he became one of the first three candidates for the newly formed Ph.D. program in American civilization. After some intermittent sailing trips on a schooner and a hitch-hiking trip across the country, Olson took a variety of interdisciplinary courses at Harvard and started a dissertation comparing William Shakespeare's *King Lear* (1605) to Melville's *Moby-Dick* (1851), to be supervised by the renowned scholar of American literature, F. O. Matthiessen.

For a variety of complex reasons, Olson decided not to finish his Ph.D. dissertation. He received a Guggenheim Fellowship and finished his book on Melville, which Edward Dahlberg advised him not to publish. He then worked in a variety of jobs in the Franklin D. Roosevelt administration and for the Democratic party; he resigned after Roosevelt's death in 1945, even though he had been offered the job of assistant secretary of the treasury and the position of postmaster general. He had become thoroughly disillusioned by his experience in politics and began a series of visits to his poetic mentor, American poet Ezra Pound, at St. Elizabeth's Hospital, where Pound had been confined for mental incompetence.

It was during this transitional period that Olson began writing poems and publishing them in such journals as *The Atlantic Monthly, Harper's*, and *Harper's Bazaar*. It was with the help and encouragement of Pound that Olson published his first book, called *Call Me Ishmael* (1947), which had come out of a major re-visioning of his earlier work on Melville. After a trip to the West Coast, where he met the poet Robert Duncan and the geographer Carl Sauer, he was invited to Black Mountain College in North Carolina by its rector, Josef Albers, to lecture. He so impressed the faculty and staff there that he was invited to become its new rector; he remained until the school closed in 1956. He also began a friendship there with the poet Robert Creeley that continued throughout his life and was perhaps his most crucial poetic and spiritual contact.

Two major works were published in 1950 that eventually made Olson well known and led to him being considered the leader of a school of writers called "the Black Mountain poets." They included a number of Black Mountain faculty and students: Robert Creeley, Robert Duncan, Edward Dorn, Jonathan Williams, Denise Levertov, Joel Oppenheimer, and the fiction writers Fielding Dawson and Michael Rumacker. The first work for which he became famous was his revolutionary essay entitled "Projective Verse" (1950), published in *Poetry New York*, and a poem called "I, Maximus of Gloucester, to You." This poem became the first of a long series of poems which would eventually become *The Maximus Poems*. In 1952, Olson received a grant to study Mayan culture in the Yucatán peninsula, the results of which were later published as *Mayan Letters* (1953). In 1960, two other major publications emerged besides *The Maximus Poems*. Donald Allen edited and published an anthology that included Olson's famous essay "Projective Verse" and several of his notable poems, such as "In Cold Hell, in Thicket," "As the Dead Prey upon Us," and his response to T. S. Eliot's *The Waste Land* (1922), "The Kingfishers." His first collection of shorter poems was also published, under the title *The Distances* (1960).

With the demise of Black Mountain College in 1956, Olson returned to Gloucester and worked steadily on the next major section of Maximus poems, called *The Maximus Poems, IV, V, VI* (1968). Although he taught periodically at the State University of New York at Buffalo and the University of Connecticut, he also lectured and gave poetry readings throughout America and Europe. He published a collection of his essays called *Human Universe and Other Essays* in 1965; the title essay is the most comprehensive summary of his poetic and philosophical beliefs and is a vivid demonstration of his piercing intellectual insights. His career ended prematurely when he became terminally ill with cancer of the liver; he died in New York City on January 10, 1970.

Analysis

One of the important keys to understanding Charles Olson's highly complex prose and poetry is the fact that he was also one of the greatest and most effective teachers in the history of American pedagogy. The success of his students as writers and artists attests his powerful classroom presence. His essays and poetry also consistently teach his readers the most important lesson: learning how to learn on their own. His advice to the young poet Edward Dorn at Black Mountain College in 1955 is a case in point. Dorn had asked him for a list of required readings, and Olson showed him how to use it: "Best thing to do is *to dig one thing or place or man* until you yourself know more about that than is possible to any other man. It doesn't matter whether it's Barbed Wire or Pemmican or Paterson or Iowa. But *exhaust* it. Saturate it. Beat it. And then U KNOW everything else very fast: one saturation job (it might take 14 years). And you're in, forever." Edward Dorn did exactly that after leaving Black Mountain: He devoted years of research to the American West and specifically to the Shoshone tribe. Olson had taken his own advice and began gathering information of all kinds on his own hometown, Gloucester, Massachusetts, which eventually became the subject matter for his monumental *Maximus* poems.

Olson had published a radically new book on Melville's *Moby-Dick* in 1947 called *Call Me Ishmael*, which he had abstracted from his proposed doctoral dissertation at Harvard on the affinities between Shakespeare's *King Lear* and *Moby-Dick*. He had submitted the original to his mentor, Edward Dahlberg, who deleted half the text and urged him to rewrite it completely. Not only did Olson follow his teacher's advice, he also refocused his entire thesis. *Call Me Ishmael* departs from the usual symbolic interpretations of the novel in terms of "good versus evil" or viewing the sea as the existential void. Olson reinterprets *Moby-Dick* as an economic blueprint of the relationship of various classes in society; that is, economic factors lie beneath everything and are the key to understanding the real themes of the novel and the history of that period. He viewed *Moby-Dick* as one of the most compelling documents to date of America's perennial attempt to conquer nature by the sheer force of its will as expressed in destructive patterns of industrialization and mechanization.

Man's obsessive attempt to control the powers of nature and the resulting chaos that such self-destructive behavior produces became one of Olson's principal themes throughout his poetry and prose. Olson perpetually used various versions of the mythic motif of the Fall, disengaging it from any specifically Christian contexts, and traced it back to man's fatal separation from his condition of oneness with nature that resulted from his fall into consciousness. In his next prose work, "Projective Verse" (1950), Olson addressed man's fallen condition as it manifests itself in the kind of overly self-conscious, totally subjective poetry that practitioners of the poetics of the New Criticism were writing during the 1930's and 1940's. Such anti-Romantic poets often described their mental anguish in traditional rhyme and meter and lamented a world completely cut off from anything but a subjective reality. Olson proposed that the spirit of Romanticism reassert itself in what he called "objectism" (a term he created) as a more radical alternative to William Carlos Williams' and Ezra Pound's "objectivism":

> Objectism is the getting rid of the lyrical interference of the individual as ego, of the "subject" and his soul, that peculiar presumption by which western man has interposed himself between what he is as a creature of nature (with certain instructions to carry out) and those other creatures of nature which we may, with no derogation, call objects. For man is himself an object.

He further exhorts man to recognize himself as an object among the other objects in nature and to do so with an attitude of humility. Only when man becomes conscious of his proper position within nature's laws will he be able to stop destroying it as well as himself; he may even become of use.

Part of Olson's project to re-energize American poetry was very much connected to man's humble recognition of his place in nature, which, Olson hoped, would constitute a radical modification in his stance toward reality. Since reality as viewed from a Romantic perspective is always a "process," then poetry itself must engage in that process. For Olson, poetry was not the "mirror held up to nature" that the pre-Romantics had proposed, but a physical engagement with life's very energies and, therefore, an enactment of life itself. Olson redefines what poetry is in "Projective Verse": "A poem is energy transferred from where the poet got it . . . by way of the poem itself to, all the way over to, the reader. Okay."

For many modern artists and philosophers in the early twentieth century, knowledge had become an open field in which an observer recognizes patterns rather than creating them. Olson believed that the poet must follow suit and must work in the open; he must avoid the old rules of the inherited iambic pentameter line, regular rhythm, and rhyme. "He can go by no track other than the one the poem under hand declares, for itself . . . FORM IS NEVER MORE THAN AN EXTENSION OF CONTENT." The rhythm should be established by the "musical phrase" that Pound exhorted and not by the stultifying regularity of the metronome that traditionalists follow. The length of the line should be determined "from the breath, from the breathing of the man who writes, at the moment that he writes." His evidence for what more conservative critics saw as an outrageous oversimplification of the rules of prosody was to go back to the etymological root of the word "is" and point out that the Aryan root "as" meant "to breathe."

Olson, true to his philosophical belief that "things" precede theory, had written one of his greatest poems the previous year, "The Kingfishers" (1949), from which he had derived the principles of his new poetics. This poem's form is indeed an extension of its content, thereby fulfilling the major requirement of an open-field composition. The poem refocuses T. S. Eliot's "wasteland" motif by including natural cyclicity as redemptive rather than relentlessly mechanistic. It also proposes a major reorientation away from the despair and ennui of the last stages of the Austro-Hungarian Empire, which Eliot's *The Waste Land* documents, toward a revaluation of the ancient civilizations of the West as Olson explores the Mayan ruins of Yucatán. Olson consciously moved away from his Greco-Roman academic orientation and found a more viable path in pre-Socratic ideas, particularly in Heraclitus' proposition that reality is in constant flux and that any attempt to categorize or systematize flux is doomed from its inception. Olson visited the great Mayan ruins to see for himself the destruction that the "civilized" Europeans had brought with them. Olson embraced change in all its fluidity and found his vocation as a poet and archeologist in his commitment to hunting among its stones. Although Olson was disturbed by the Mayan ruins, he perceived himself as an object among other objects within nature, and he dug even deeper into nature's endless change. Salvation consists of probing more deeply into the actual earth rather than resorting to Eliot's retreat into the comfort and security of English history and the Anglo-Catholic church.

Olson published many poems and essays during the 1950's, the most notable of which were *In Cold Hell, in Thicket* (1953), *Mayan Letters*, "As the Dead Prey upon Us" (1956), and *The Maximus Poems 11-12* (1956). "As the Dead Prey upon Us" expresses his anguish over the death of his mother as she appeared to him in recurring dreams. The ultimate fear that a soul must face in a demythologized world is the necessary descent into hell: "What a man has to do, he has to do, he has to/ meet his mother in hell." Olson demonstrates exactly how projective verse works by using the raw material of his own dreams and then juxtaposing images of his broken-down car with a next-door neighbor and a mysterious "Blue Deer"; he lyricizes all these disparate elements, thereby fusing them into his own surrealist but lucid narrative.

Two major volumes of poetry appeared in 1960: *The Maximus Poems* and *The Distances*. His collected essays, entitled *Human Universe and Other Essays*, were published in 1965. *The Distances* encapsulates perfectly in its title the themes that

Olson addressed throughout the remainder of his writing career: the sense of loss of a common consciousness and the disengagement of man from a direct experience of reality. Many of the poems in this volume lament man's fall into consciousness, a condition that automatically induces feelings of isolation and alienation from a primordial center. The poet alone possesses the power to enact a consciousness that can rediscover what "science has run away with . . . discovering this discarded thing nature." Olson's enemy is the same one that troubled Ezra Pound, the penchant of the mind to abstract itself from the body, to systemize and categorize the essential wholeness of experience into endless classifications which man then mistakes for life itself. His definition of "the absolute" in "Human Universe" is uncompromisingly existential: "If there is any absolute, it is never more than this one, you, this instant, in action."

It is this very disengagement of man from a direct experience of reality that becomes the principal subject for the massive work he began to publish in 1960, *The Maximus Poems*. Only a restoration of man to the energies of the local could begin to mend the split, the "iron-dealt cleavage" that Hart Crane hoped to heal in his long poem *The Bridge* (1930). There is little doubt that Olson saw his epic poem as a timely successor not only to Crane's huge work but also to other large efforts, such as Pound's *Cantos* (1917-1970) and Walt Whitman's *Leaves of Grass* (1855). Most important, perhaps, he saw it standing beside William Carlos Williams' *Paterson* (1946-1958).

THE MAXIMUS POEMS

First published: 1960
Type of work: Long poem

The voice of "Maximus" awakens the citizens of Gloucester, Massachusetts, to their own potential.

The first volume of what eventually became a three-volume, six-hundred-page poem was called *The Maximus Poems*. It was published by the Jargon Society, a press which had been created by poet (and former student of Olson) Jonathan Williams. The keys to an understanding of the entire Maximus project are the specific maps that Olson placed on the covers of the first two volumes. A U.S. Coast and Geodetic Survey map of Gloucester, Massachusetts, appears on the cover of the first volume, immediately grounding the reader in the specific geography of the place where Olson spent his childhood summers and was to live the last ten years of his life. Olson's major models for *The Maximus Poems* were Whitman's *Leaves of Grass*, Pound's *Cantos*, and (especially) Williams' *Paterson*. Williams' poem was an unequivocal reaction to the gloomy abstractions of Eliot's apocalyptic *The Waste Land*, which lamented, by means of literary fragments, the fractured consciousness of a European civilization that had lost its religious center. Williams proposed his own hometown, Paterson, New Jersey, as the subject of his epic poem, insisting that an authentic American poet, following the lead of Whitman, must begin with an activitation of the energies of the local. Olson thoroughly agreed, and though both poets admired Pound's *Cantos*, they found them, Williams said, "too perversely individual to achieve the universal understanding required."

Williams, however, envisioned the American epic as a kind of newspaper: "It must be a concise sharpshooting epic style. Machine gun style. Facts, facts, facts, tearing into us to blast away our stinking flesh of news. Bullets." Nothing could describe Olson's style more precisely than Williams' words. If the theme of much of Olson's poetry in *The Distances* concerns what Heraclitus described as "man's estrangement from that with which he is most familiar"—his own body—then *The Maximus Poems* by the sheer weight of its geographical and historical information, puts man back into contact with his origins: nature as manifested in the literal ground upon which he stands. Olson was an authentic Romantic in that he believed redemption would come not from some remote, quasi-mystical center, but from a proper reintroduction to nature itself on the most specific level.

Much of this first Maximus volume is organized in the form of letters from a fictive persona that Olson borrowed from ancient Greek literature. Maximus of Tyre was a philosopher and a dialectician who wandered about Mediterranean communities continually lecturing on Homer's *Odyssey*. The figure is also a version of psychologist Carl Jung's archetypal "homo maximus" or "greatest man." Olson begins by identifying himself with the figure of Maximus in the title of the first poem, which is also the first line of the poem: "I, Maximus of Gloucester, to you . . . a metal hot from boiling water, tell you/ what is a lance, who obeys the figures of the present dance." The reference to the dance is a direct connection with one of the principal metaphors that Williams used throughout *Paterson* to signify man's total physical and spiritual involvement with the energies of life itself.

Olson, therefore, locates his task in awakening the citizens of Gloucester to the experience of natural life in spite of being cut off from its healing powers: "when all is become billboards, when, all, even silence, is spray-gunned?" Maximus continues to exhort his citizens to take drastic action against the commercialization and modernization of their soil: "o kill kill kill kill kill/ those/ who advertise you/ out." Much of this first volume laments the loss of traditional local values, beliefs, and practices that are being destroyed by a nation corrupted by blatant materialism. He renames Muzak "mu-sick" and decries the damage done to man's instinctual life: "No eyes or ears left/ to their own doings (all invaded, appropriated, outraged, all senses/ including the mind . . . lulled."

The Maximus Poems, then, can be viewed as an extended meditation of the ruins of his own origins by a civilization whose arrogance has blinded it to its obligations to both the physical and spiritual ecology. Much of the remainder of this first volume is a painstaking reconstruction of the actual history of Gloucester, using information from archival documents and early historical sources and juxtaposing its data to reveal the subtexts of greed and power that drove the original European settlers to

America. Olson refuses to create fictive structures of "versions" of history and strives more than any other American poet to permit the "facts" to speak for themselves; he wants, as far as possible, an unmediated vision whose primary content consists of historical and anecdotal records and even statistical facts. He demands an empirical myth whose origins and energies are grounded in a specific locale. Olson's task is to arrange and organize these unconnected fragments of history in such a way that a continuity between the past and the present will become evident. His readers will, he hopes, learn from the past and improve their future. Olson firmly believed in his redemptive role as a historian when he declaimed: "My memory is/ the history of time." For without memory, there remains nothing but the disconnected segments of an exhausted civilization that Eliot documented in *The Waste Land*.

THE MAXIMUS POEMS, IV, V, VI

First published: 1968
Type of work: Long poem

This volume deepens and extends Olson's attentions beyond the local and into the mythic origins of Western civilization.

The key to this second volume of *The Maximus Poems*, sometimes called *Maximus II*, is the map that Olson placed on the cover. It is a map of Gondwanaland, the name by which many geographers call the primordial or unified continent that existed before, as Olson put it: "Earth started to come apart at the seams, some 125 million years awhile back and India took off from Africa & migrated to Asia." In this volume, Olson continues to probe the specific historical information of Gloucester but also moves inland to explore the history and origins of a section of Gloucester called Dogtown. Working, however, in an "open field" forced Olson to delve even more deeply into what preceded history, and he found himself confronting the nature and function of prehistorical forms of consciousness called myth. Much of this volume examines systems of mythic consciousness and attempts to understand how myths are encoded with essential human information and become permanent forms of human experience. Olson, an avowed believer in the theories of psychologist Carl Jung, also viewed myths as archetypes of the collective unconscious.

Olson's advice to Edward Dorn to "exhaust" or "saturate" one place until he knew more about it than anyone else ever could became a reality for Olson in his years of examining Gloucester. It also, however, necessitated a rearrangement of the rest of the world in the light of what he learned about his origins. Immediately after declaring that his memory is "the history of time" in *The Maximus Poems IV, V, VI* he locates another, more onerous task: "I am making a mappemunde [a map of the world]. It is to include my being." Such an obligation demanded that Olson explore not only history and myth but also other associated subfields such as archaeology, paleontology, geography, geology, and anthropology. What *The Maximus Poems, IV,*

V, VI became, then, was a recapitulation of the origin and development of human consciousness, a task so demanding that the structure of the poem almost collapses beneath the burden. Few literary conventions are observed as the language becomes more dense and private. Transitions between sections are either nonexistent or so personal that understanding it is impossible. The influence of Alfred North White-head's *Process and Reality* (1929) is evident throughout, particularly in the in-process appearance of many of the poems. Olson himself suggested that the arrangement of the material was closer to that of a mosaic taking shape than to any kind of finished narrative product.

Many of the earlier characteristics of the fictive voice of Maximus are missing from this volume because Olson, following his own advice in "Projective Verse," removed "the lyrical interference of the individual as ego." This volume can be viewed as a prime example of what he called "objectism," since his control and arrangement of the mythological, historical, and geographical data are virtually un-detectable. The "facts" do, indeed, "speak for themselves," and the structure suffers accordingly. What Olson was rigorously trying to avoid, however, was the appear-ance of any kind of tidy synthesis of myth and history, such as that which Joseph Campbell proposed in *The Hero with a Thousand Faces* (1949). Olson adamantly opposed any synthesizing structure that even remotely resembled an imaginative or fictive arrangement of "facts." Although he read and heavily annotated all of the fourteen volumes of Jung's works in his personal library, he refused to impose any kind of limiting interpretive structure on the materials of history and was much closer to the structuralism of French anthropologist Claude Lévi-Strauss than to Camp-bell's Jungian archetypes.

Olson defined an American as "a complex of occasions,/ themselves a geometry/ of spatial nature" and added that this definition explained his feeling of oneness with the world: "I have this sense,/ that I am one/ with my skin." He kept coming back to the geographical, the local, and feared involvement with intellectual classifications of any kind. His grounding in Gloucester became a position from which he could measure the world.

THE MAXIMUS POEMS, VOLUME THREE

First published: 1975
Type of work: Long poem

The Maximus Poems, Volume Three continues with the omniscient voice of "Maximus," but the personal crises of Olson himself are evident throughout.

Volume 3 of *The Maximus Poems* was never completed by Olson, who died in 1970, but among the mass of material left after his death were indications of certain directions that later scholars followed in gathering the material and organizing it into a coherent form. University of Connecticut professors George Butterick and Charles

Boer devoted many years to a thoughtful arrangement of the materials for volume 3. Olson had determined the first and last poems in the collection, and Butterick and Boer followed the same order that Olson had used in the first two volumes—essentially a chronological one—in their edition. Many of the poems included were left in an unrevised form.

Olson's attentions had changed dramatically in this volume, and many of the poems became quite personal, reflecting the private crises that he was undergoing, specifically the tragic death of his wife in an automobile accident in 1964. The "Maximus" of this volume continues to dig into the local history and geological data of Gloucester, but he finds himself repeatedly confronting the bare earth itself. Unlike Wallace Stevens and Robert Duncan, whose imaginations found satisfaction in fictive certainties, Olson's inability to trust the powers of the imagination drove him to search for the divine in the physical. He stated it quite directly: "I believe in God/ as fully physical." In poem 143, "The Festival Aspects," he rehearses the various stages of man's Fall and his division from sacred consciousness but suggests that the continued force of his attentions would eventually redeem the fallen world and unify it by the almost telekinetic power of his consciousness.

Though Olson still raged against the dehumanizing encroachments of progress, he comes closer to a deeper understanding and acceptance of the essential mystery at the heart of existence. "Praise the mystery/ of creation, that in matter alone." By the conclusion of the volume, his concerns have become completely personal. He knows that he is dying of cancer of the liver and imagines that he is a stone. He also locates himself, finally, in both his origin and destiny in the next-to-last poem of the book, "Mother Earth Alone." The very last Maximus poem consists of only eight words that brutally summarize the attenuated range of his awareness in the final days of his illness: "my wife my car my color and myself." Haunted by the death of his wife and jaundiced by cancer, he returned to the source of his life as a poet—his own personal consciousness, from which an entire mythic world had emerged.

Summary

In many ways *The Maximus Poems* constitute the postmodern equivalent of William Carlos Williams' *Paterson* and Ezra Pound's *Cantos*. Charles Olson saw his own effort as an attempt to find a middle ground between Pound's over-inflated "EGO AS BEAK" and its disastrous results in the *Cantos*, and Williams' inability to forge a mythic persona powerful enough to keep *Paterson* from collapsing under the weight of its own historical data. Olson's "Maximus" is a hero of consciousness who recognizes the poem as the one area in which man may be totally himself. The poem as both art and historical document, which *The Maximus Poems* purports to synthesize, also makes the voice of the poet immortal. Olson combined the consciousness of the individual with the mythic energies of the local and became, as Maximus, a spokesman for the earth itself.

Bibliography

Boer, Charles. *Charles Olson in Connecticut*. Chicago: Swallow Press, 1975.

Boundary 2 (Fall, 1973/Winter, 1974). Special Olson issue.

Butterick, George. *A Guide to "The Maximus Poems" of Charles Olson*. Berkeley: University of California Press, 1978.

Byrd, Don. *Charles Olson's Maximus*. Urbana: University of Illinois Press, 1980.

Charters, Ann. *Olson/Melville: A Study in Affinity*. Berkeley: Oyez Press, 1968.

Christensen, Paul. *Charles Olson: Call Him Ishmael*. Austin: University of Texas Press, 1978.

Duberman, Martin. *Black Mountain: An Exploration in Community*. New York: E. P. Dutton, 1972.

Paul, Sherman. *Olson's Push*. Baton Rouge: Louisiana State University Press, 1978.

Von Hallberg, Robert. *Charles Olson: The Scholar's Art*. Cambridge, Mass.: Harvard University Press, 1978.

Patrick Meanor

EUGENE O'NEILL

Born: New York, New York
October 16, 1888
Died: Boston, Massachusetts
November 27, 1953

Principal Literary Achievement

Often considered the greatest American dramatist of the twentieth century, O'Neill transformed the American theater from artifice into art through ceaseless experimentation and uncompromising psychological realism.

Biography

Eugene Gladstone O'Neill was born in the Barrett Hotel in New York City in 1888, son of James O'Neill, an actor celebrated for his portrayal of the Count of Monte Cristo, and Ella Quinlan O'Neill, a sensitive woman who became a narcotics addict shortly after his birth. His older brother Jamie was an early idol; another brother, Edmund, had died in infancy, evoking a great guilt in his mother. As a child, Eugene toured much of the year with his parents and spent the summers in New London, Connecticut; at the age of seven, partly to protect him from knowledge of his mother's addiction, he was sent to a boarding school outside New York City. Lonely and frightened, he retreated to his imagination and into the world of books. The discovery of his mother's addiction, when he was almost fifteen, was traumatic; it resulted in his rejection of the Catholic faith and infused his life thereafter with grief for her suffering and guilt for his part in it.

After a year at Princeton University, O'Neill prospected for gold in Honduras, leaving behind a pregnant wife, Kathleen Jenkins, who bore him a son, Eugene, Jr. Shortly after his return, he shipped out to Buenos Aires on the *Charles Racine*, one of the last sailing ships. The two-month voyage was a high point in his life, and the sea figures prominently in many of his plays, from *Bound East for Cardiff* (1916) to *Long Day's Journey into Night* (1956). Back in New York, he drifted aimlessly, drinking and loafing in saloons such as Jimmy-the-Priest's, which became the setting for *Anna Christie* (1921) and *The Iceman Cometh* (1946). Eventually, after cooperatively providing Kathleen with grounds for a divorce, he fell into a deep depression, culminating in a suicide attempt.

When he recovered, his father found him a job as a reporter on the New London *Telegraph*, but after a few months O'Neill contracted tuberculosis and spent the first

1567

half of 1913 at Gaylord Farm Sanatorium in Wallingford, Connecticut. Perhaps it was this confrontation with mortality that encouraged him to focus his literary talents; he wrote several one-act plays and in the fall of 1914 enrolled in George Pierce Baker's famous playwriting course at Harvard University, a serious step for a young man now determined to be "an artist or nothing."

When financial concerns made a second year with Baker impossible, O'Neill became acquainted with a group of Greenwich Village artists and intellectuals who, in the summer of 1915, had founded the Provincetown Players. Recognizing O'Neill's talent, they were happy to produce his play *Bound East for Cardiff* and a number of his plays thereafter, both in Provincetown and in New York.

His first Broadway production, *Beyond the Horizon* (1920), was a starkly realistic drama set in rural New England, in which two brothers live out each other's dreams. The play earned for O'Neill a Pulitzer Prize and critical recognition as a serious dramatist. The 1920's were productive years for O'Neill. He wrote constantly, saw productions on and off Broadway of eighteen of his plays, and was awarded two more Pulitzer Prizes: for *Anna Christie*, a somewhat romantic play about a prostitute who is reformed by the sea and the love of a good man, and for *Strange Interlude* (1928), an experimental effort utilizing stream-of-consciousness techniques. Although a second marriage in 1918, to Agnes Boulton, had produced two children, Shane and Oona, the union was not a happy one, and as the decade ended, O'Neill divorced Agnes and took a third wife, Carlotta Monterey. Theirs was a stormy and passionate relationship, which endured until his death.

The 1930's began with successful productions of the monumental *Mourning Becomes Electra* (1931) and *Ah, Wilderness!* (1933), the only light-hearted comedy O'Neill ever wrote, but *Days Without End* (1934), a somewhat autobiographical story of a struggle with faith, was harshly criticized and twelve years passed before another O'Neill play was seen on Broadway. In 1935, O'Neill began working on a cycle of eleven plays that would follow the history of an American family from the Revolution to the twentieth century. Entitled *A Tale of Possessors Self-Dispossessed*, the plays were to focus on American materialism and greed through the generations, played against a background of national events. Unfortunately, only *A Touch of the Poet* (produced posthumously in 1957) was completed.

When the Nobel Prize in Literature was awarded him in 1936, O'Neill was already in the grip of a degenerative nerve disease. Since he was accustomed to writing his plays in a minuscule longhand, the tremors of the progressive disease made him increasingly unable to hold a pencil, and thus to pursue his profession.

Forced to abandon the cycle, from 1939 to 1941 he struggled with the creation of several plays, among them his two masterpieces, *The Iceman Cometh* and *Long Day's Journey into Night* (produced and published posthumously in 1956 and awarded a fourth Pulitzer Prize. When the Broadway production of *The Iceman Cometh* was not particularly successful, O'Neill retired into seclusion; his final days were spent under the care of his wife in Boston's Hotel Shelton. Shortly before he died, he noted, "Born in a hotel room—and God damn it—died in a hotel room!" Death came on November 27, 1953.

In tribute, *The New York Times* critic Brooks Atkinson wrote, "A great spirit and our greatest dramatist have left us, and our theater world is now a smaller, more ordinary place."

Analysis

Like William Shakespeare, Eugene O'Neill was a man of the theater: He was born into it, grew up in it, worked in it, and wrote for it. He knew his craft, and he hated the artificiality and pretense of the commercial theater. He said, "The theatre to me *is* life—the substance and interpretation of life . . . [And] life is struggle, often, if not usually, unsuccessful struggle."

O'Neill was an artist of integrity and courage; he was constantly exploring, expanding, experimenting. Although he tended toward realism in his work, rejecting material that could not be verified by the senses, at times he played with nonrealistic, expressionistic devices, externalizing the interior state of a character with sound or light or language: the throbbing tom-toms in *The Emperor Jones* (1920), to signify Jones's increasing hysteria; the masks in *The Great God Brown* (1926), to portray the multifaceted nature of the characters; the foghorn in *Long Day's Journey into Night*, to parallel Mary's increasing confusion. At other times, his characters seem to have sprung from a Darwinian naturalism, helpless in the grip of forces beyond their control.

O'Neill also experimented with content and structure. When Eugene, Jr., became a classical scholar, the playwright sought to share these interests and grew fascinated by the powerful material of Greek tragedy: incest, infanticide, matricide, and the accompanying burden of guilt and atonement. He shared the Greeks' view of the individual in conflict with the universe and with whatever God or gods inhabit it, and he was further concerned with the dearth of tragedy in the modern theater. *Desire Under the Elms* (1924), which includes infanticide, and *Mourning Becomes Electra*, which derives from Aeschylus' *Oresteia* (from the fifth century B.C.) were efforts to create modern tragedies exploring the agonies suffered by those who behave against law and conscience.

The structure varies from play to play. O'Neill could use a traditional brief one-act structure, as in the early sea plays, but both *The Hairy Ape* and *The Emperor Jones* are long one-acts with a number of scenes. *Desire Under the Elms* is a traditional length three-act play, but *Strange Interlude* is a very long play in two parts with fourteen scenes and a break for dinner. *Mourning Becomes Electra* is perhaps the longest, essentially consisting of three full-length plays, with a total of thirteen acts. *The Iceman Cometh* and *Long Day's Journey into Night*, with four acts each, run between four and five hours in the theater. At times both audiences and critics complained, but O'Neill insisted that the length was appropriate and necessary for his ideas.

Yet, even at his most experimental, there is an unerring psychological validity to his characters. The ideas of Freudian psychoanalysis were current through O'Neill's career, and the power of the unconscious suited his characters well. They may openly express a longing for the sea or for a farm or for a place in the universe, but the conflict with the father or the longing for love from the mother rages not far below the surface. Working from his own unconscious, O'Neill created plays that were disguised attempts to work through his personal conflicts with his mother, father, and brother, and with his own quest for identity. Travis Bogard claims that "the sum of his work comprises an autobiography."

Although O'Neill's view of humanity was despairing and nearly tragic, there are no moral messages in his plays. He does not preach or promote causes. There are few villains in his works; instead there are characters of enormous energy, driven by huge passions—lust, greed, ambition, and love. A major thematic concern with O'Neill is obsessive love, love that drives a person without reason and beyond conscience, love that does not heal but smothers and destroys. Although Christine and Lavinia Mannon in *Mourning Becomes Electra* are prime examples of this obsession, characters in *Beyond the Horizon*, *The Great God Brown*, *Desire Under the Elms*, and *Strange Interlude* are also consumed by their passions.

O'Neill explored the notion that there are many facets of personality and that people rarely reveal themselves unmasked to others—or even to themselves. When they do, they discover that others are presenting only masks in return, a response that can be disappointing and even frightening. While Shakespeare could use asides and soliloquies, O'Neill sought other methods to reveal the psyche. In *The Great God Brown*, he uses actual masks, which actors don and remove; in *Strange Interlude*, he uses interior monologues. Somewhat controversial, these theatrical devices underscore the theme of the evasive nature of humanity.

A corollary theme concerns the need for illusion. O'Neill states that human beings often behave from a network of illusions that they have created about themselves and about others. In *Anna Christie*, Chris Christopherson believes that he hates "dat ole davil, sea"; his daughter Anna insists that all men are worthless. These illusions are shattered by events in the play and replaced by a better reality. In *The Iceman Cometh*, written twenty years later, O'Neill draws characters surviving upon their "pipedreams": They believe that they will leave Harry Hope's saloon in the near future and lead productive lives. When they are forced to face their illusions, they seek death.

As might be expected, O'Neill is not universally admired. His principal detractors find his style crude, his language clumsy, and his plays in need of editing. Concerning style, one must remember that O'Neill was blazing a path separate from the contrivances of the romantic "well-made play." Aside from the early *The Hairy Ape* (1922), there are few overheard or misinterpreted conversations and few traditional happy endings with all threads resolved. As for language, on the printed page the dialogue may look stilted and unbelievable, but in the mouths of talented stage professionals, it rings true. Finally, as with the works of Shakespeare, judicious editing may be desirable, but the powerful experience provided by the plays in performance is undeniable.

THE EMPEROR JONES

First produced: 1920 (first published, 1921)
Type of work: Play

A greedy, materialistic ruler is stripped of his pretensions and pursued to his death.

The Emperor Jones, which ran for 204 performances at the Provincetown Playhouse in Greenwich Village, represented the first major success by a black actor on the American stage; it also made O'Neill famous.

Almost medieval in structure, this long one-act play in eight scenes details the fall from power of a corrupt ruler, former Pullman porter Brutus Jones, who has made himself emperor of a West Indian island and greedily exploited the natives. As the play opens, the populace has revolted, and Jones realizes he must flee. In his egocentricity, he believes that the legend he has created—that he can be killed only with a silver bullet—will protect him and that his planned escape route through the forest will take him to a waiting ship and safety with the riches intact that he has extorted from the people.

As Jones travels through the forest he is stripped physically, mentally, and emotionally of the trappings of civilization and forced back through his racial memory to a tribal past, where, naked and hysterical before the Crocodile God, he uses his silver bullet to reject the possessive god as the natives approach to kill him, ironically, with their own silver bullets. The play permits several levels of interpretation. Socially, a proud, greedy, corrupt ruler is deposed by his downtrodden people. Psychologically, man regresses through individual memory to his racial unconscious. Philosophically, man fights his inevitable losing battle with the forces of the universe. Theologically, man denies a possessive god and is sacrificed to him.

Equally significant are the expressionistic devices that O'Neill has incorporated. In the middle of the first scene a tom-tom "exactly corresponding to normal pulse beat—72 to the minute—[begins] and continues at a gradually accelerating rate from this point uninterruptedly to the very end of the play." Realistically, the drumbeats represent the natives communicating with one another as they pursue Jones. On the nonrealistic expressionistic level, they represent Jones's heartbeats as his anxiety increases and he regresses to a tribal past. When the drums stop, the audience knows that Jones is dead.

Another device is the gradual stripping of clothes, which is both physical and psychological: Jones begins in his emperor's robes and ends in a tattered loincloth, as he regresses from a civilized to a savage state. Finally, daylight contrasts with moonlight (a device O'Neill also uses in *Long Day's Journey* and *The Iceman Cometh*). Day represents harsh reality where no illusions can survive; moonlight is illusion. The play begins at 3:30 in the afternoon, when the sun "still blazes yellowly."

The scenes pass through nightfall into darkness, at nine, eleven, one, three, and five o'clock, ending at dawn, and they parallel Jones's progress through the increasing darkness of his mind to his death in the bright light of day.

The play prefigures the basic theme of O'Neill's last plays, which is that man cannot live without illusions. Jones believes that he has done this, that he has manipulated and outwitted the natives' superstitions for his own ends. His great illusion is that he can deny his illusionary past, his humanity, and his need for a god force stronger than himself.

DESIRE UNDER THE ELMS

First produced: 1924 (first published, 1925)
Type of work: Play

The passionate desires of father, wife (and stepmother), and son result in a triangle of tragedy and retribution.

Banned in Boston and England, narrowly escaping a ban in New York, and its Los Angeles cast arrested for obscenity, *Desire Under the Elms*, with incest, adultery, and infanticide openly treated, brought O'Neill into conflict with various censors and brought much of the public to the box office. It ran for 208 performances on and off Broadway and may be the first important American tragedy.

The play demonstrates O'Neill's exploration of Greek theater. It does not derive directly from any particular play, but its material echoes *Hippolytus* and *Medea*, which contain incest and infanticide. The inhibited, puritanical society of New England in 1850 seemed to O'Neill appropriate for the epic Greek quality he sought. A further debt to the Greeks occurs in the sense of an inevitable fate awaiting the participants, Ephraim Cabot, his son Eben, and Ephraim's new wife, Abby Putnam.

The desire of Eben and Abby for each other is apparent from the moment she steps into the house, although it is masked by Eben's antagonism and her caution. He is loyal to the memory of his dead mother, whom he feels was robbed of her land and worked to death by Ephraim. The farm is his, he believes, and Abby is an intruder, seeking to steal his inheritance. She, in turn, has learned to fight for what she wants, and now she seeks security and a place of her own.

If Eben were not there, quite likely Abby would have made a good wife for Ephraim as long as he lived; however, the mutual physical attraction of Abby and Eben cannot be resisted. In a powerful scene in which Abby lures Eben into the parlor and declares her love, promising that she will take the dead mother's place, "with a horribly frank mixture of lust and mother love," the adultery is consummated.

One psychoanalytic critic noted that the play seems to have been written by someone in "intense mourning for his mother" (O'Neill had lost both his mother and brother in the previous two years). Certainly the yearning for the nurturing protective mother permeates the work, not only in Eben's speeches about his love for his mother and in his incestuous love for the wife of his father, but also in Abby's speeches about her willingness to substitute for the mother. Further, both Abby and Eben strongly desire the land, which belonged to the mother, and which represents the same nurturing, protective qualities. This motif is further emphasized in O'Neill's specific directions for the visual effects of the setting, in which he calls for two elms on either side of the house with "a sinister maternity . . . like exhausted women resting their sagging breasts and hands and hair on its roof."

The Oedipal conflict of father and son for superiority, through possession of the woman, underlies the action of the play. Ephraim's superior maleness will be demonstrated unequivocally with the birth of a son by Abby. Eben's secret knowledge that Abby's son is his secures his male superiority as well as his claim to the farm. When Eben becomes jealous of Ephraim's possessiveness of the baby, Abby, literally accepting his cry that he wishes the baby had never been born, murders the child to prove her love. She readily acknowledges her crime, Eben accepts his responsibility, and both resign themselves to punishment. Ephraim must remain on the farm. "God's hard," he says, believing that a force beyond himself has guided events.

The structure of the play is one of O'Neill's tightest; its three acts are economical and swiftly moving. O'Neill's innovative set design of the original production made use of a house exterior and interior: When a scene occurred in one room, the exterior wall could be removed, and scenes set in different rooms could be viewed simultaneously. This allowed for an easy flow from one scene to another. The lighting also contributed, providing a contrast between the brightly lit exterior and the dim shadowy interior.

O'Neill's use of language is masterful; the Yankee words and phrases such as "Ay-eh," "purty," "I love ye, Abby," and the biblical passages recited by Ephraim arise naturally but effectively from the characters. yet the character of Eben is the key to the essence of the play. Of a sensitive nature, like the author himself, the weak questing son is a figure O'Neill used many times. Here his love of the land, his awareness of its beauty, and his need for love infuse the play with poetry and elevate it above the level of simple realism into poignant tragedy.

THE GREAT GOD BROWN

First produced: 1926 (first published, 1926)
Type of work: Play

The rivalry of the artist in conflict with himself and a materialistic society results in his self-destruction.

"I love that play," O'Neill declared of *The Great God Brown*, which remained one of his favorites. Perhaps his fondness derived from the subjective, autobiographical nature of Dion Anthony, one of the characters, who expresses O'Neill's search for spiritual certainty, as well as his physical qualities and his bitterness; perhaps his liking sprang from the expressionistic device of the masks, which makes the play one of his strangest and most experimental. Although the critics did not share O'Neill's feeling, the public was fascinated by the play, which ran for more than 280 performances.

The plot, which is somewhat obscure, involves two young men, friendly rivals from childhood, Dion Anthony and Billy Brown. Dion, an artist, should become a painter, but his father refuses to send him to college; Billy, the stereotypical, ideal American boy, goes to college, becomes an architect, and joins his father's firm. It is Dion who wins the girl, Margaret, despite Billy's love for her.

Seven years pass. The marriage of Dion and Margaret is unsuccessful: "We communicate in code—when neither has the other's key!" says Dion, drinking and gambling his inheritance away. Billy, now successful, employs Dion at Margaret's request, and uses Dion's creativity to enhance his own designs. Their career rivalry extends to Dion's friend, the prostitute Cybel, whom Billy keeps as a mistress. These events are understandable, almost banal, until the end of act 2, when Dion suddenly accuses Billy of being unable to love and trying to steal Margaret and Cybel out of envy. Brown admits his love for Margaret; Dion replies, "with a terrible composure":

No! . . . Brown loves me! He loves me because I have always possessed the power he needed for love, because I am love!

Dion then dies of his alcoholism, but his final wish is for Brown to assume the Dion Anthony identity through the device of the mask. Brown accedes, even playing husband to Margaret. The masquerade cannot be maintained, however, and he is shot as the supposed murderer of Dion.

The interest of the play lies not in the plot outline, but in the way O'Neill has developed the characters and themes. The principal device is the use of the mask, a legacy from the Greek theater, which forcefully makes the statement that humans present images to one another, that they rarely expose the truth of themselves. Characters don and remove masks at significant moments: When Dion in desperation drops his mask before Margaret to beg for her love, she is so frightened she faints. Billy also drops his mask before Margaret to declare his love for her; she remains masked and rejects him. The expression of the masks changes as the characters alter, age, experience emotion. The only relationship presented in which the participants are unmasked is that of Dion and Cybel. They are honest together. A masked drama is valuable, according to O'Neill, because it provides "a fresh insight into the inner forces motivating the actions and reactions of men and women."

Yet the statement of the play is not clear. As representative of American greed and materialism, Billy Brown is an unusually sympathetic character. He is a "good loser" with Margaret, and his success has fallen upon him without aggression on his part. Billy's assumption of Dion's identity in the third act, which apparently O'Neill intended to demonstrate the isolation and torment of the artistic psyche, leads to a confusing, almost farcical switching of masks. At one moment Billy, in his own mask, speaks to his employees as "Mr. Brown," then he runs offstage, returning almost immediately in Dion's mask to encounter Margaret.

Finally, the interest of the audience lies not with Billy, who hardly seems the "great god" of the title, but with Dion, O'Neill's artist surrogate, whose dark passion is sometimes narcissistic and self-pitying, sometimes poetic and touching. His torment results from his inability to be an artist and to win the approval of God; instead, he must relinquish his creative ideas to another man and remain anonymous. Those familiar with O'Neill's history will recognize both the determined "I want to be an artist or nothing" that informs much of his work and the pain accompanying that desire. *The Great God Brown* is a flawed play, infrequently revived, but it merits study for its use of the masks and for its exploration of identity.

MOURNING BECOMES ELECTRA

First produced: 1931 (first published, 1931)
Type of work: Play

The Mannon family, seemingly cursed in its relationships of love and hate, commits adultery, murder, and incest through three generations.

The idea of creating a modern psychological drama rooted in Greek legend germinated in the spring of 1926, but *Mourning Becomes Electra* was not completed until the spring of 1931; it opened in October and was deemed a masterpiece by more than one critic. O'Neill said: "By the title *Mourning Becomes Electra* I sought to convey that mourning befits Electra; it becomes Electra to mourn; it is her fate; black is becoming to her and it is the color that becomes her destiny."

The Greek source for O'Neill was the *Oresteia* of Aeschylus, from the fifth century B.C., the trilogy detailing the relationships of the house of Atreus. In the first play, after the siege of Troy, Clytemnestra murders her husband, the victorious Agamemnon; in the second, their son Orestes, with his sister Electra, murders his mother and her lover Aegisthus; in the third, Orestes is hounded by the Furies for matricide but is eventually freed from his guilt and acquitted of the crime. O'Neill reworked much of this story; he also drew upon the versions of *Electra* by Sophocles and Euripides, which focus upon the daughter, a haunted woman, torn by hate and love and never at peace.

The Mannon family (the name may be associated with "mammon" and the family's materialism) is the center of O'Neill's play, which is set in New England immediately after the Civil War. The house is described in the stage directions as resembling a white Greek temple, with six columns across the front porch. In the first part, "The Homecoming," Christine Mannon (Clytemnestra) has taken a lover, Adam Brant (Aegisthus), while her husband Ezra (Agamemnon) has been fighting in the war. Daughter Lavinia (Electra) is jealously aware of the affair and threatens her mother with exposure. In this section, mother and daughter are rivals for the love of Ezra and Adam. When Ezra returns, while Lavinia desperately tries to win his love and attention from her mother, he makes an impassioned effort to communicate with Christine, begging her to love him. Thinking only of her lover, she rejects him, and when he has a heart attack, she administers poison rather than medicine. In his death throes, he reveals Christine's crime to Lavinia.

The triangular structure of the second section, "The Hunted," includes Lavinia, Christine, and the newly returned battle-scarred Orin (Orestes). Each woman is seductive and persuasive with him, but Lavinia is victorious in convincing him that Christine killed Ezra and that he should avenge their father's murder by killing Adam Brant. He accomplishes the act, which drives Christine to commit suicide and leads to Orin's mental deterioration through his burden of guilt. In the final section, "The Haunted," both Lavinia and Orin struggle to transcend their past crimes, first through incestuous love of each other, then through relationships outside the family. When this is impossible, Orin commits suicide and Lavinia secludes herself in the Mannon mansion.

Although the plot represents another reworking of the O'Neill family drama, with the author infusing autobiography into both Lavinia and Orin, it is also faithful to the Greek legend. In addition, O'Neill borrowed other elements from the Greeks. He adopted the form of the trilogy (*Mourning Becomes Electra* contains three full-length plays), he created the character of Seth to function as the leader of the chorus and townspeople to act as the chorus itself. Most important, he sought to find an equivalent to the Greek sense of fate, the inescapable destiny toward which the characters rush, which the Greeks achieved through their culture's belief in gods and goddesses and in their shared morality. This was difficult to approximate in a modern culture that does not believe in such external forces.

To solve the problem, O'Neill set the play in a Puritan-derived New England culture, similar to that of *Desire Under the Elms*, a culture which insisted upon personal responsibility and which offered no easy absolution or forgiveness. The sense of fate surrounds the past, present, and future of the family, as the past sins of the father (and mother) are redressed by the children with greater sins, for which they in turn must suffer in the future. "I'm the last Mannon," says Lavinia as she imprisons herself in the mansion. "I've got to punish myself." The tragic destiny of the Mannon family is oblivion.

The sense of fate is further reinforced by the use of the mask concept. O'Neill, still fascinated by the device, wrote one draft of the play with characters donning and removing masks, as in *The Great God Brown*; he soon rejected the device, although not its significance. Instead, he enlisted the actors' skills to create expressions on the faces of the Mannon family like "life-like masks." These emphasize the family similarity and the ties of blood that bind them together inextricably. In the final section, both Lavinia and Orin are altered in appearance and resemble their parents even more closely, a reminder that despite all resistance, heredity is destiny.

This view corresponds to that of the Darwinian naturalists, who describe humanity as the product of heredity and environment; thus, human beings are victims of forces beyond their control. Indeed, the play has links with the naturalistic theater. Where the naturalists claim that because of these forces people are not responsible for their actions, however, the Puritan mind claims that people should suffer guilt and be punished. Perhaps it is significant that in the Greek play Orestes is forgiven by the Eumenides and Electra is married to Pylades, a prince of Phocis, but in O'Neill's puritanical play there is no such mercy.

Once again, in *Mourning Becomes Electra* there is no moral message, only intense experience. The family is depicted in a tortured web of dependencies, jealousies, hatreds, and loves, which O'Neill describes without judgment. Reading the play later, he declared himself satisfied with its "strange quality of unreal reality." Finally, if *Mourning Becomes Electra* is not the artistic equivalent of the *Oresteia*, it is the closest example that twenty-five hundred years of theater have produced.

THE ICEMAN COMETH

First produced: 1946 (first published, 1946)
Type of work: Play

The salesman Hickey tries to shatter the "pipe dreams" of his friends in Harry Hope's saloon, but he succeeds only in proving that pipe dreams are necessary, even for himself.

With *The Iceman Cometh*, O'Neill discarded the literary sources and devices with which he had been experimenting for so long, as if they were pipe dreams of his own that protected him from the pain of reality, to concentrate upon realistic material and characters whom he had known firsthand. He set the action of the play in 1912, probably the most important year of his life, when he returned from South America, penniless and despondent, and landed at Jimmy-the-Priest's in New York.

In the play, Jimmy-the-Priest's becomes Harry Hope's saloon, where whiskey costs five cents a shot and a month's room and board, including a cup of soup, is three dollars. Of the nineteen characters O'Neill has shaped—bartenders, pimps, whores, ne'er-do-wells, retirees—most are based on the assorted derelicts and bums O'Neill encountered at that low period of his life. *The Iceman Cometh* is a naturalistic drama of "the lower depths," a genre displaying life at the extremities as more real, elemental, and meaningful than that of the pretentious, artificial middle class. Thus, the characters are the dregs of society, with few resources and fewer opportunities. Their heredity and the environment have victimized them.

Almost classical in its adherence to the unities of time and place, the play is structured like a musical theme and variations. Each character seeks an escape through alcohol from the pain of living. Each maintains an existence through a "pipe dream" he or she has created, an illusion surrounding the self that allows a continuance of the life-style cultivated at Harry Hope's. This motif is announced early in Larry

Slade's response to Rocky's joking remarks that Harry is going to demand payment from everyone—tomorrow. Larry says:

> I'll be glad to pay up—tomorrow. And I know my fellow inmates will promise the same. They've all a touching credulity concerning tomorrows. Their ships will come in, loaded to the gunwales with cancelled regrets and promises fulfilled and clean slates and new leases!

The theme is developed through repetition by each character of a particular dream—some comic, some serious, but all illusory.

Into this milieu of fantasy comes Hickey, the charismatic drummer (salesman), on his annual birthday visit. He is eagerly awaited by Harry's denizens, but this year he is somehow different; instead of settling down to his customary binge, he refuses alcohol, and he talks strangely about ridding himself of pipe dreams and helping Harry's regulars to rid themselves of theirs and find peace.

At first they think he is joking, that he is initiating a new game, but as he continues to goad, taunt, and ridicule, they become uneasy, irritated, and finally hostile. One by one he forces them to act upon their pipe dreams, to leave the comfort and security of their womblike existence, and to face for an instant their fantasy in the world beyond. These encounters with reality, however, do not bring peace. As the fourth act begins, the characters have returned to their former places and seek oblivion in alcohol with even greater determination. The atmosphere is funereal, and O'Neill's principal statement, that human beings cannot survive without illusions, is underscored.

The only two characters who remain in the saloon are Larry Slade, who manages to withstand Hickey's campaign, and his young acquaintance Don Parritt, a newcomer from the West Coast, whose illusion is that he betrayed his anarchist mother to the police out of patriotism and love. Hickey recognizes that somehow he and Parritt are "members of the same lodge." Their similarities become evident as the play progresses.

The climax of the play is reached not only through action but also through revelation, as each act brings new information about Hickey: the first, that he wants to bring peace to his friends; the second, that his wife Evelyn is dead; the third, that she was murdered; and the fourth, that he is her murderer. Hickey's illusion parallels Parritt's, that he killed out of love—to bring his wife peace—but Parritt interrupts Hickey's confession to blurt out the truth about the betrayal of his mother. "It was because I hated her." Hickey, reliving his speech to the body of Evelyn, virtually echoes him: "Well, you know what you can do with your pipe dream now, you damned bitch!" Evelyn's pipe dream was a faith in Hickey's reform, a faith which resulted in his guilt and resentment, but the reality of his hatred of Evelyn can be faced only for an instant; Hickey immediately insists that since he loved Evelyn, he must have been insane when he killed her; this is a new illusion, and it reinforces the illusions of the others: If Hickey is insane, all his urgings of their finding peace through discarding their pipe dreams must be false. They can comfortably return to their fantasy lives.

For Parritt, however, a return to fantasy is not possible; the guilt that his confession evoked cannot be denied, and he seeks punishment. Led away by officers Lieb and Moran, whose names bring associations with love and death, Hickey also seeks punishment. Parritt, with Larry's encouragement, commits suicide, and Larry is left without illusion, resigned to his humanity and his sympathy for both Hickey and Parritt, awaiting death.

A complex and disturbing play that runs about four and a half hours in performance, its greatness lies not in theatrical innovation but in psychological truth. Sharing the tedium and pain of this existence, the audience is also forced to face the necessity for illusion in their own lives. Not successful in its original Broadway production in 1946, the off-Broadway revival at the Circle-in-the-Square ten years later drew audiences for almost two years and sparked renewed interest in the O'Neill canon.

LONG DAY'S JOURNEY INTO NIGHT

First produced: 1956 (first published, 1956)
Type of work: Play

The Tyrone family struggles to cope with the mother's drug addiction, the father's miserliness, one son's tuberculosis, the other's profligacy, and, above all, the complexity of their feelings for one another.

By 1940, O'Neill had won three Pulitzer Prizes and the Nobel Prize in Literature, but the work for which he is remembered and praised and revered as America's foremost dramatist is *Long Day's Journey into Night*, his autobiographical work dealing with the torment of his own family. It earned for him a final Pulitzer Prize posthumously in 1956. In the dedication of the play to Carlotta, O'Neill says,

I mean it as a tribute to your love and tenderness which gave me the faith in love that enabled me to face my dead at last and write this play—write it with deep pity and understanding and forgiveness for all the four haunted Tyrones.

O'Neill was fascinated with the family unit and with the effects of heredity as well as relationships upon the generations. If one generation is poor, the second becomes miserly, and the third contemptuous, what remains for the fourth generation? O'Neill's outlined cycle of plays, which he was never to complete, explored the past and future of a single family through three hundred years and many generations. *Long Day's Journey into Night* also expresses the idea that bonds of blood are inextricable; each of the characters is in conflict over the role of the independent self and the role of dependent family member. In their ambivalence, feelings of love and hate surface and clash. The family unit is confined, a self-contained universe, and beyond is only the void.

In this family drama the O'Neill's become the Tyrones: father James, a famous actor known for his role as the Count of Monte Cristo; mother Mary, a thinly disguised portrait of Ellen Quinlan O'Neill; the two sons Jamie and Edmund, mirrors of Eugene's brother Jamie and the playwright himself. Set in New London, Connecticut, the time is 1912, the year of O'Neill's suicide attempt, and his brush with tuberculosis.

Like *The Iceman Cometh*, the structure is classical; the events are compressed into one August day. The first act occurs in the morning, the second before and after lunch, the third at 6:30 P.M., and the fourth at midnight. There are five characters (including the maid Cathleen), a shared past, and individual guilt. The action unfolds through psychological revelation; the past is revealed through the dialogue, the guilt through the relationships of the four family members.

The catalytic agent is Mary's morphine addiction, which she believes occurred after Edmund's birth when James hired a "quack doctor" to treat her, a belief that arouses guilt in both Edmund and James and encourages resentment in Jamie. In the first act she is supposedly "well" again, and the façade of a happy family can be maintained. Edmund is ill, however, probably with tuberculosis (in that period usually fatal), and concern for him provides Mary an excuse to return to her habit. The first to perceive that her latest cure is not successful is Jamie, who reveals his suspicions to Edmund. Soon all three men recognize that Mary's rambling complaints about their home, the servants, James's frugality, and Edmund's drinking are signs of her addiction. Each tries to persuade her not to succumb. Tyrone pleads brokenly, "Dear Mary! For the love of God, for my sake and the boys' sake and your own, won't you stop now?" She responds vaguely that they should not "try to understand what we cannot understand, or help things that cannot be helped—the things life has done to us we cannot excuse or explain."

After lunch, the men escape into town, leaving Mary alone. She begins to return to the past, or the past returns to her. With Cathleen imbibing Tyrone's liquor freely, Mary recalls her early days in the convent, her first meeting with James Tyrone, and her lost faith. When Edmund returns with confirmation of his tuberculosis, Mary refuses to listen and angrily cries, "I hate you when you become gloomy and morbid." Edmund bitterly retorts, "it's pretty hard to take at times, having a dope fiend for a mother!"

The last act unites the three men at midnight in drunken misery around the dining room table. First, James and Edmund alternate between bickering over the use of electricity and accusations of each other's culpability in Mary's addiction. Then each reveals a part of his real self: Tyrone's regrets about his wasted career; Edmund's love of the sea. Jamie arrives home, extremely drunk, to express in a moment of truth his hatred of Edmund. In the final moments, with the foghorn sounding in the background, the men in a drunken fog, Mary descends the stairs, in the deepest fog of all, trailing her wedding dress, and remembering how happy she had once been. Little hope remains.

The play is not totally autobiographical. O'Neill has exaggerated some aspects of his situations and omitted others. His father was not so miserly, nor his mother so emotionally dependent, nor he quite so blameless. Nevertheless, the skill with which complex relationships are developed and projected is masterful, and the truth of the family's conflicts is shattering.

Summary

In both his personal relationships and in his work, Eugene O'Neill embodies the flawed American character: alienated, isolated, guilty, and unable to separate from the family. Although he expresses concern with American greed, materialism, extravagance, and hypocrisy, he also probes deep into his own family romance, and by revealing himself, he reveals theatergoers to themselves.

Sometimes called the father of American drama, O'Neill demonstrated to the world that the American theater could be serious, moving, artistic, and truthful. Many critics believe that the O'Neill canon towers above all other twentieth century dramatists.

Bibliography

Berlin, Norman. *Eugene O'Neill*. New York: Grove Press, 1982.

Bogard, Travis. *Contour in Time: The Plays of Eugene O'Neill*. Rev. ed. New York: Oxford University Press, 1988.

Cargill, Oscar, N. Bryllion Fagin, and William J. Fisher, eds. *O'Neill and His Plays: Four Decades of Criticism*. New York: New York University Press, 1961.

Gelb, Arthur, and Barbara Gelb. *O'Neill*. New York: Harper, 1962.

Martine, James J., ed. *Critical Essays on Eugene O'Neill*. Boston: G. K. Hall, 1984.

Porter, Laurin. *The Banished Prince: Time, Memory, and Ritual in the Late Plays of Eugene O'Neill*. Ann Arbor: University of Michigan Research Press, 1988.

Sheaffer, Louis. *O'Neill: Son and Artist*. Boston: Little, Brown, 1973.

_____. *O'Neill: Son and Playwright*. Boston: Little, Brown, 1968.

Stroupe, John J., ed. *Critical Approaches to O'Neill*. New York: AMS Press, 1988.

Joyce E. Henry

CYNTHIA OZICK

Born: New York, New York
April 17, 1928

Principal Literary Achievement

Ozick, a highly acclaimed contemporary Jewish author, is best known for her concern with Jewish culture and morals in a secular, post-Holocaust society.

Biography

Cynthia Ozick was born in New York City on April 17, 1928, the second child of pharmacist William Ozick and Celia Regelson Ozick. She was reared in the Pelham Bay section of the Bronx, a middle-class neighborhood, where she attended Public School 71. "At P.S. 71," Ozick once remarked in an interview, "I was dumb, cross-eyed, and couldn't do arithmetic." Remembering encounters with anti-Semitic teachers and peers, she vividly recalls "teachers who hurt me, who made me believe I was stupid and inferior."

Regardless of her negative early educational experiences, Ozick emerged as a gifted academic. Her youth was spent devouring books, sometimes for eighteen hours a day. She attended Hunter College High School in Manhattan and New York University, where she was inducted into Phi Beta Kappa and was graduated cum laude with a bachelor's degree in English. She then taught from 1949 to 1951 at Ohio State University, where she earned an M.A. Her thesis, "Parable in the Later Novels of Henry James," revealed an early reverence for that late nineteenth and early twentieth century American novelist. In fact, throughout much of Ozick's early fiction rings a distinctive Jamesian tone.

Although she knew her destiny was to be a novelist, Ozick began her literary career by composing poetry, a pursuit she interspersed with fiction and essay writing until age thirty-six but then dropped. Her primary goal, writing a great modern novel, she began immediately after acquiring her graduate degree and marrying Bernard Hollote, a lawyer. She ambitiously began writing a "philosophical" novel, taking seven years to compose some 300,000 words of an incomplete tome. "Mippel," as she calls the unfinished work, in reference to mythical poet and visionary William Blake's "Mercy, Pity, Peace, and Love" (1789), is a typically erudite allusion.

Seven years into writing "Mippel," Ozick entered herself in a novella contest of sorts, assuming that she could complete a short piece of fiction in six weeks, then return to her novel. The novella project grew longer, however, consuming another

1583

seven years of her life, and eventually evolved into Ozick's first published work, *Trust* (1966). Coinciding with its publication, Ozick gave birth to her only child, Rachel, at the age of thirty-seven. Although Ozick continued to read and write, activities she believes she does out of necessity, rearing her daughter was distracting enough that she had little time to enjoy her new status as a published author.

Having always suffered from what she calls "age-sorrow," Ozick has measured the scale of her achievements on a chronological basis. Because she assumed that she would have published something of "literary merit" by the time she was twenty-five, and because she is highly self-critical, Ozick was not then unduly impressed with her literary achievement, and she has continued to doubt the mass appeal of her writing. Although her first novel met with widespread acclaim, it occurred twelve years later than she expected, thus diminishing her personal satisfaction.

After producing only one published work after fourteen years of novel writing, Ozick turned to short stories and novellas. In 1971, she published a volume of well-received short fiction, *The Pagan Rabbi and Other Stories*, in which she illustrated the fact that profound subject matter can exist in the shorter fiction genres. Five years later, Ozick followed with more short fiction, *Bloodshed and Three Novellas* (1976). She did not attempt another novel until the mid-1980's, when she published two novels, both considerably shorter than *Trust*: *The Cannibal Galaxy* (1983) and *The Messiah of Stockholm* (1987).

Ozick's numerous awards and grants, received over several decades, give testimony to her acknowledgment as a significant literary figure. In 1966, she taught at the Chautauqua Writers' Conference; two years later, she was one of two novelists awarded a fellowship by the National Endowment for the Arts. She was selected as a lecturer in the American-Israel Dialogue on Culture and the Arts at the Weizmann Institute in Israel in 1970, and in 1973, she served as O'Connor Professor at Colgate University and won the prestigious O. Henry Prize Stories competition. She won the Epstein Fiction Award in 1977 and was a Guggenheim Fellow in 1982. In 1983, Ozick was chosen by the American Academy and Institute of Arts and Letters to receive one of the Mildred and Harold Strauss Living Awards, an annual tax-free award of $35,000 for a minimum of five years.

Cynthia Ozick, a gentle person and a somewhat insecure writer, believes that her writing's lack of popularity is her greatest downfall. She is not convinced that she is being read widely, even though she has been translated into no less than eleven languages, and she thinks that the printing of her work in paperback was an act of philanthropy on the part of her publisher. Pursuits other than writing fiction and essays include writing literary criticism, translating Yiddish poetry, meeting occasionally with an informal group of writer friends, continuing her diary (kept since 1953), and answering every letter she receives.

Analysis

In her essays, as well as her fiction, Cynthia Ozick has repeatedly returned to a handful of themes connected with problems created by being Jewish in a secular society. In the earlier works *Trust* and *The Pagan Rabbi and Other Stories*, the Jewish connection is most obvious. In later works, the moral burden placed on post-Holocaust Jewish generations, while it might be less pronounced, remains indigenous to the characters' psyches. Ozick's work serves as a reminder that it is impossible to separate modern Judaism from the devastation that Jewish culture endured as a result of World War II, because Judaism in a vast majority of the civilized world was directly affected. As a result of Adolf Hitler's "final solution" (his attempted extermination of the Jews), the Jewish community in the United States burgeoned, the state of Israel was formed, and European Jewish culture, developed over centuries, was decimated.

Cynthia Ozick chose a career as a storyteller, yet she has remained unsure of the morality of telling stories. Whether the creativity that inspires storytelling is in conflict with the Second Commandment prohibiting idol worship, and whether the human creativity required to enter an author's make-believe world competes with the world of the Creator of the Universe are common themes in Ozick's fiction. Yet her assertion that people become what they most desire to contend with is how Ozick has justified the apparent moral conflict with her career choice. "Usurpation (Other People's Stories)" warns against this bending of the Mosaic rule, while "The Pagan Rabbi" illustrates the dangerous results when the creative imagination is allowed to overtake the Jewish mind-set.

Another of her interests that recurs in several Ozick works is the nature of language and its influence upon human culture. Because Ozick is a highly articulate writer who manipulates language with enormous precision and artistry, this latter curiosity is not surprising. Not only is Ozick a master of English, the secular language, she also reveals her deep affection for Yiddish, the *mamaloshen*, or mother tongue, in stories such as "Envy: Or, Yiddish in America."

This interest in language has fueled Ozick's desire to plow through her vast and ever-growing reading list. Although she has read widely and broadly, Ozick has "collected" twentieth century writers, most of whom are either Jewish or female (Bernard Malamud and Virginia Woolf, to name two). Ozick has used reading to prime herself for writing, and much of her fiction has been inspired by writers whose work she has read. In an interview, she commented, "I read in order to write." *The Messiah of Stockholm* illustrates what Ozick meant by this. This title is borrowed from Polish writer Bruno Schulz's lost manuscript, "The Messiah," and the plot is about the pursuit of the vanished masterwork. "Envy: Or, Yiddish in America" incorporates a caricature of another Jewish writer, Nobel laureate Isaac Bashevis Singer.

Other than reading, a main source of Ozick's inspiration has been her well-grounded Jewish knowledge. Her familiarity with the Talmud (the authoritative body of Jewish tradition and laws) and Cabala (Jewish mysticism) has often been the foundation upon which Ozick has built her prose. This knowledge has allowed Ozick to write about Jewish matters with authority and authenticity, whether her characters be observant or assimilated Jews.

One drawback with being an intellectual and a writer of ideas is that Ozick's characterizations tend to lack warmth, often making it difficult for the average reader to identify with her characters. This probably has led to what Ozick has seen to be her greatest shortcoming as a writer of fiction, her perceived lack of popularity. Protagonists such as Lars Andemening in *The Messiah of Stockholm* contribute to this perception of Ozick as a writer of ideas rather than as a window on the human condition. Lars, although an interesting character, has no ability to form lasting relationships and has all but cut himself off from society, even to the point of sleeping while everyone else is at work and working while everyone else is asleep. Edelshtein, the protagonist in "Envy: Or, Yiddish in America," is characterized as pitiable but basically unlikable—he too is unable to have a successful marriage or trust even his closest friends. Again, Rabbi Kornfeld in "The Pagan Rabbi," a character the reader knows only posthumously, lives in a world completely removed from reality.

Ozick, opposing the generally accepted rule that writers should write about that with which they already are familiar, has taught that writers should write about what they do not know, thereby removing the tendency toward insulation and forcing them to broaden their imaginations. Ozick has followed her own rule, especially when choosing settings for much of her fiction. A native New Yorker who has lived almost her entire life in that state, Ozick has written novels and short stories set in places as varied as Paris, Sweden, Canada, the Midwestern United States, Jerusalem, and Germany.

A novelist who discounts classification as a feminist writer as meaningless and essentially discriminatory, Ozick embraces her designation as part of the Jewish intellectual establishment. She has offered her audience prose for thought. Often complex, her writing rewards the reader in equal measure to the effort spent reading it.

THE CANNIBAL GALAXY

First published: 1983
Type of work: Novel

> A middle-aged school principal who has spent his life seeking out a child prodigy is blind to the brilliance of one of his own pupils.

In a story rich with metaphor, even the title of Cynthia Ozick's first novel in seventeen years, *The Cannibal Galaxy*, is pregnant with meaning. An astronomical term, a cannibal galaxy is a huge galaxy that swallows another until the smaller becomes an insignificant component of the larger; Western culture is the cannibal galaxy that devours Jewish culture. This story is about the struggle against having Judaism devoured by the modern world, yet the characters' particularly Jewish struggles parallel and reflect the struggles of many people, regardless of religious or cultural background. Many unique cultures, while they attempt to emulate the West, paradoxically fear the loss of identity in becoming Westernized.

The protagonist, Principal Brill, is caught between two worlds—his native Parisian Jewish ghetto, where he studied the centuries-old traditions of his ancestors, and modern-day Paris, complete with arguably the world's best museum, the Louvre, and the world-renowned university, the Sorbonne. In order to fulfill his destiny, Brill founds an American school based upon what he considers to be his unique inspiration, a dual curriculum. Brill theorizes that this combined method of learning will bridge the gap between the secular and the Jewish, thereby improving both teaching methodologies. As in numerous Jewish day schools, Brill plans that students will learn traditional Hebraic subjects, the Talmud and Gemara, half the day, and modern secular subjects, science and mathematics, during the other half. Brill devotes his adult life to this pedagogical pursuit, waiting for an exceptional child to work through his dual curriculum and to prove the worth of his life's work. Brill, however, is so fully absorbed in his preconception of the exceptional child that he overlooks her when she emerges. It is not until the child, Beulah Lilt, reaches adulthood and makes her significant contribution to society that Brill is at last able to see her brilliance, which has been discovered by others. Not surprising to the reader, but an agonizing shock to Brill, Beulah never mentions her childhood education except to note its lack of exception.

The way in which Ozick belittles Brill's entire life's work is severe, but her point, that compromise merely encourages mediocrity, is well taken. Rather than combining the best of both the traditional and modern worlds, Brill is left with a mediocre mixture of the two, which produces neither Jewish nor secular scholars of merit. Everything in middle-aged Brill's life is middling. Even his school is geographically located in the middle of America.

For much of his life, Brill sees himself as a creator and an original thinker. Yet when he meets the linguist Hester Lilt, a true intellectual, he cannot even hold a conversation with her without constantly being reminded of his ineptitude. Hester does not accept Brill's compliment that she is an original thinker. Rather, by way of his compliment, Hester forces Brill to realize how incredibly ordinary he is. Principal Brill acts as a reminder to many who think of themselves as original, creative, and maybe even brilliant. True brilliance is rare, and the last original thinking, Hester Lilt humblingly reminds him, occurred with Plato.

THE MESSIAH OF STOCKHOLM

First published: 1987
Type of work: Novel

An adult orphan pursues a lost masterpiece manuscript written by the man he imagines to have been his father.

The Messiah of Stockholm has a dual purpose: It is Cynthia Ozick's tribute to Bruno Schulz, the legendary Polish author of *Sklepy Cynamonowe* (1934; *Cinnamon Shops and Other Stories*, 1963) killed by the Nazis in a mass slaying. *The Messiah of*

Stockholm also focuses on the aspect of human nature that craves knowledge of the past in order to have a basis upon which to mold a perception of the present. The deeply human need to have a personal, as well as a cultural, history is one theme winding through this complex novel; this need for a self-history directs the path that orphaned Lars Andemening's life follows.

Ozick's third novel, set in the frigid city of Stockholm, Sweden, is a chilling story of one man's desperate search and struggle to create a rational past for himself. Lars, who selected his name from a dictionary, seeks help from a cast of other World War II refugees who also have public identities of their own choosing. Not all the secondary characters are refugees, however; those in Lars's world fall into two distinct categories: colleagues with factual pasts from the "stewpot" where he works, and refugees from the bookstore with fictional histories. Lars seeks out members of the latter group to help him discover his own indeterminable origins. Obsessed with his search for verification of something impossible to verify, Lars is incapable of establishing lasting relationships with anyone from either category.

His lack of any family history is considered cause, at least by one of his former mothers-in-law, for Lars's lack of success in both his personal and professional life. His daughter lives in America; a dried-up childhood paint set is Lars's only remaining connection with her. He only chose to keep the paints because of Schulz, who had been an art teacher as well as a writer; Lars hoped to see some of his "father's" talent genetically passed on to his daughter.

Lars's obsession with Schulz invades his consciousness awake or asleep, the latter being when Lars sees "as if he lets me have his [Schulz's] own eye to look through." In his fixation with discovering his past, he searches relentlessly for photographs, letters, reviews—any tangible connection with the dead author.

Reading Ozick's intricate fiction, one wonders where history ends and invention begins. Ozick's deep interest in World War II refugees underlies the plot of *The Messiah of Stockholm*, whereas Judaism plays a far less direct role than in her previous fictional works. Lars presumes himself to be the son of Schulz, a Jew, but he never acknowledges any connection with Judaism, probably because Schulz wrote in Polish rather than in Yiddish. Lars chooses to connect with Schulz by becoming extraordinarily literary, hoping to establish his paternity by sheer force of intellectual achievement.

Lars's made-up world of presumed identities and a lost masterpiece is bound to crumble. His tangible connection with his "father" has been primarily through the findings of obscure Schulz memorabilia that Mrs. Eklund imports from Poland to Sweden on his behalf. After she delivers what she claims to be the missing manuscript, Lars does some of his most profound thinking and realizes the absurdity of his pursuit: He cannot prove the unprovable. In a sudden metamorphosis, Lars leaves behind his belles lettres and becomes not merely part of the "stewpot" but a success in his everyday world.

THE PAGAN RABBI

First published: 1966
Type of work: Short story

A modern rabbi struggles between the religion he teaches and a forbidden world for which he yearns.

"The Pagan Rabbi" explores a modern Jewish problem, the overwhelming appeal of things non-Jewish, or "pagan." The title piece in Cynthia Ozick's first short fiction collection, "The Pagan Rabbi," is a mythical tale set in the modern world. There are three voices in the story: the intense dialogue controlled by the widow, the information provided by the narrator, and the reading of the deceased's suicide note.

Rabbi Isaac Kornfeld, a gifted and renowned intellectual, teacher, and writer, has hanged himself in the public park. The narrator, a childhood friend of the deceased, seeks to discover why a pious man, about to reach his intellectual peak at age thirty-six, would choose to end his life. Ozick was thirty-six years of age two years before "The Pagan Rabbi" was first published; she created a character similar to herself in age and talent. Kornfeld's mythical world exists in a modern city filled with parks bisected by filthy rivers rather than in an idyllic, nonpopulated nature reserve. In this unlikely setting, with his unique vision, Rabbi Kornfeld dares to experience the excruciating beauty, as well as the horrifying ugliness, of the pagan world forbidden to him.

In trying to unravel the mystery of his friend's death, the unnamed narrator pays condolences to Kornfeld's widow, Sheindel, a very clever mother of seven daughters, who as an infant miraculously survived a Nazi concentration camp. The widow reveals a letter left in her husband's coat to explain his fatal action posthumously. Sheindel describes it as a "love letter," but it does not confess any earthly infidelity. Kornfeld confesses that he has fallen in love with a free-spirited dryad. As a result of being unable to release what must be free, Kornfeld loses his own soul—revealed, to Kornfeld's horror, as an ugly, old man oblivious to anything of natural beauty around him, aware only of the worn Tractate of Mishna he is intently studying.

The three characters—the narrator, the widow, and the Rabbi—all approach Judaism differently. The narrator attempts to assimilate—he married out of the religion to a tall, blonde, frigid Puritan named Jane. His approach does not work because he is secretly in love with Sheindel, who with her seven female offspring, represents the survival of Judaism, a maternal religion. Sheindel stays within her Jewish world, accepting that she is different from those outside it. The third approach, a purely intellectual one, is Kornfeld's path. He questions and challenges everything, which has the paradoxical effect of strengthening his faith while he becomes enamored of all that is forbidden by it. His duplicity, living publicly as a Jew and privately as a Hellenist, leaves the Rabbi no alternative to suicide.

ENVY

First published: 1969
Type of work: Novella

An unknown Yiddish poet envies a fellow Yiddish writer's success and blames his own failure on his lack of a translator.

"Envy: Or, Yiddish in America" first appeared in *Commentary*, then was published as part of Ozick's first short story collection two years later. The connection between language and culture is explored as an aging Yiddish poet, a fictionalized Joseph Glatstein, centers his life on his all-encompassing jealousy of Yankel Ostrover, a thinly disguised Isaac Bashevis Singer.

True to Ozick's belief that large themes can be explored in short fiction, she expresses her concern with the nature of language while entertaining her audience with a comically wry story. It takes place in New York City, where Hershele Edelshtein, son of a Polish Hebraic tutor, has lived for forty years. Edelshtein writes Yiddish poetry for an obscure publication edited by his friend, fellow Yiddish poet and Ostrover envier Baumzweig. Baumzweig and Edelshtein are "secret enemies" (a concept that recurs in "The Pagan Rabbi" as well as in "The Shawl"). Their shared obsessive hatred of Ostrover, however, is the force that binds their tenuous friendship.

Ozick's treatment of the demise of Yiddish, the mother tongue of European Jews, reveals her fondness for the language of her forebears. Yet the death of Yiddish lacks sentimentality; in fact, it faces a brutal rejection from an educated young Jewish writer, Hannah. She represents the first generation of English-speaking secularized American Jews, those who have reduced the richness of Yiddish to a smattering of commonly used exclamations and insults.

Ironically, Edelshtein earns his meager living lecturing—in English—on the death of Yiddish. He is also forced to reduce Yiddish to a medium for telling jokes in order to hold the interest of his waning audiences. Edelshtein tells two of his jokes to the reader, one about a funeral, but Edelshtein, never able to read people well enough to mesh with current trends, realizes too late that the jokes "were not the right kind." Envy has kept Edelshtein in the pitiable position of being on the outside looking in since his boyhood in Minsk. In his dotage, Edelshtein daydreams about the past, when he was taken as a boy to Kiev, where his father taught the wealthy young boy with the beautiful face and the intricate German toys that Edelshtein could never play with.

Several decades later, Edelshtein remains outside, watching his Yiddish universe modernize without him. He makes a fool of himself by sending pathetic letters that display his desperation, then blames his utter failure on everything he can think of: lack of a translator, the Nazi extermination of six million Yiddish speakers, and anti-

Semitism. Edelshtein blames everyone but himself. His fury is twofold: He sees his beloved culture dying and he craves Ostrover's success.

Ozick endows her fictionalized Isaac Bashevis Singer with popular appeal and a quick wit. Ostrover goes so far as to use Edelshtein's failure as the basis for his latest successful fable, told as a story within the novella. Years earlier, Ostrover had done the same thing; after Ostrover's affair with Edelshtein's wife, he had written another successful story inspired by yet another of Edelshtein's failures.

"Envy: Or, Yiddish in America," while about a petty, narrow man with frustrated ambitions, also depicts, with a feeling of great loss, the deterioration of a culture as it disappears into the melting pot. While some, Ozick seems to say, can adapt and be translated, others, who are less flexible, can only look in from the outside, knowing the obscurity of death is imminent.

THE SHAWL

First published: 1981
Type of work: Short story

A magical shawl sustains the life of a hidden infant in a Nazi concentration camp.

"The Shawl" is a brief story that has a lasting impact upon its reader. Ozick's most anthologized work condenses within seven pages the horrors of the infamous Nazi concentration camps. This prize-winning fiction reverberates with images and themes common in Ozick's work: the Holocaust, World War II refugees, and secret enmity. Chilling imagery leaves the reader's senses buzzing like the electrified fence against which Rosa's fifteen-month-old child, Magda, is thrown. Through Ozick's powerful, yet uncharacteristically simple language, the reader shares the spiritually elevating love that Rosa, a young mother, has for her infant daughter, as well as her forbidden despair over Magda's barbaric murder.

Initially, the shawl provides warmth and protection as it hides the secret child. When Rosa can no longer suckle, the shawl magically nourishes Magda with the "milk of linen." In its third life-giving role, the shawl provides companionship, as Magda silently laughs with it as if it were the sister she never had. Without the shawl, Magda, separated from her source of life, is completely vulnerable. Her secret existence is instantly discovered and her brief life brutally extinguished.

The central metaphor, the shawl, wraps baby Magda and the story in many layers of interpretation. Ozick has crafted her three characters in the fashion of a fifteenth century morality play. In a morality play, each character represents moral qualities or abstractions. Similarly, Ozick's characters represent three states of existence. Magda, wound in the magical shawl, is Life, full of warmth and imagination. Rosa, who no longer experiences hunger, "a floating angel," is Spirit. Stella, always so cold that it has seeped into her hardened heart, is Death. Metaphorically, when Spirit looks away, Death, jealous of the warmth of Life, takes the life-source away, thus killing Life. The secret hatred that Stella harbors toward Magda is only surpassed by the disturbing images Rosa has of starving Stella cannibalizing the delicious looking infant.

A powerful story, whether read literally or interpreted metaphorically, "The Shawl" offers a private insight into the chillingly painful world created by World War II Germany. Rosa's loss is humankind's loss, and the gut-wrenching pain she experiences as she sucks out what little taste of Magda's life remains in the shawl is the pain of the modern world, gagged and left speechless by inhumanity.

Summary

Among her contemporaries, Cynthia Ozick has been distinguished by her devotion to literature; she does not go on to the next sentence until she has perfected the first. Although her fiction has universal relevance, Ozick's stories are rooted in her Jewish conscience, along with the moral, ethical, and cultural questions accompanying that often burdensome state of mind.

A recipient of numerous literary awards, Ozick's toughest critic is herself. A shy individual who is deeply concerned with contemporary Jewish culture and morals, Ozick's true personality can only be discovered through careful reading of her work.

Bibliography

Bell, Pearl K. "Idylls of the Tribe." *The New Leader* 59 (April 12, 1976): 18-19.

Blake, Patricia. "A New Triumph for Idiosyncrasy." Review of *The Cannibal Galaxy*. *Time*, September 5, 1983, 64, 66.

Cohen, Sarah Blacher, ed. "The Jewish Literary Comediennes." In *Comic Relief: Humor in Contemporary American Literature*. Urbana: University of Illinois Press, 1978.

Cole, Diane. "Cynthia Ozick." In *Twentieth Century American Jewish Writers*, edited by Daniel Waldman. Vol. 28 in *Dictionary of Literary Biography*. Detroit: Gale Research, 1984.

Kirkpatrick, D. L., ed. *Contemporary Novelists*. 4th ed. London: St. James Press, 1986.

Lowin, Joseph. *Cynthia Ozick*. Boston: Twayne, 1988.

Teicholz, Tom. "The Art of Fiction: Cynthia Ozick." *The Paris Review* 29 (Spring, 1987): 154-190.

Leslie Pearl

GRACE PALEY

Born: New York, New York
December 11, 1922

Principal Literary Achievement

Through the unique and very personal voice of her short stories, Paley has vividly, humorously, and empathetically depicted the characters and social concerns of her time.

Biography

Grace Paley was born in the Bronx, New York, on December 11, 1922. Her parents, Isaac and Manya (Ridnyk) Goodside, Ukrainian-born Jews, had been sentenced to exile as outspoken opponents of Russia's Czar Nicholas II—he to Siberia and she to Germany—before being released from imprisonment and emigrating to New York in 1905. Isaac learned English quickly and became a physician, and the Goodsides lived first on Manhattan's Lower East Side and then in the East Bronx.

Listening to the stories of the old country and the struggles endured there, told in Russian and Yiddish as well as English, their daughter Grace inherited an interest in political issues, a progressive belief system, and a willingness to speak her mind. A good student, she graduated from high school at the age of fifteen. In 1938, she entered Hunter College in New York City, but she was expelled for poor attendance; she also enrolled at New York University but left without a degree. She loved and wrote poetry on her own, and in the early 1940's, studied with poet W. H. Auden at New York's New School for Social Research.

In 1942, Grace Goodside married Jess Paley, a motion picture cameraman, by whom she had two children, Nora and Daniel. The Paleys lived in Greenwich Village in New York City, where the young mother did occasional office work and became involved in community activism, including Parent-Teacher Association demonstrations against civil defense and opposition to disruptive redevelopment of Washington Square Park.

Into the mid-1950's she continued writing poetry, mostly traditional and literary in style, but gradually recognizing the limits of the genre for expression of social and political concerns, she turned to prose. Her first collection of stories, *The Little Disturbances of Man*, appeared in 1959 to enthusiastic response. Following the book's success, at the urging of friends and colleagues, Paley set out to write a novel; though never completed, sections of it appeared in *The Noble Savage*

and *New American Review.*

In the early 1960's, she began teaching courses in writing at Columbia and Syracuse universities, and in 1966 she became a member of the faculty of Sarah Lawrence College, outside New York City. Still living in Greenwich Village and writing stories for occasional publication in magazines, Paley gained visibility speaking out on political issues. A fervent opponent of the American war effort in Vietnam, she went in 1968 on a fact-finding mission to visit draft-dodgers in France and Sweden, and the following year was among a group of pacifists that traveled to Hanoi for the liberation of three American prisoners of war. Her account of the Asian trip, "Report from the Democratic Republic of Vietnam," appeared in *WIN*, the newspaper of the War Resister's League.

Having divorced her first husband in the early 1960's, she married Robert Nichols, a writer and landscape architect, in 1972. Paley's second volume of stories, *Enormous Changes at the Last Minute*, was published in 1974, the same year she traveled to Moscow as a delegate of the War Resisters' League at the World Peace Congress. With the end of the Vietnam conflict, her activism focused on other issues, including women's rights, prison reform, the environment, and nuclear weapons. Her activities ranged from distributing leaflets on street corners to unfurling an antinuclear banner on the White House lawn in December of 1978, for which she and the other "White House Eleven" were arrested, convicted, fined one hundred dollars, and given six-month suspended jail terms.

In 1980, Paley was elected to the American Academy and Institute of Arts and Letters. A film version of *Enormous Changes at the Last Minute*, adapted by filmmaker John Sayles, was shown at the Film Forum in New York in the spring of 1985. Also that year, Paley published her third collection of stories, *Later the Same Day*, and her first collection of poems, *Leaning Forward*, and her opposition to American policies in Central America led to a trip to Nicaragua and El Salvador. Paley has lived in Greenwich Village for most of her life. Through the decades, her awareness of the plight of others and the needs of society as a whole have informed her writing, teaching, and political activities and have earned her a devoted following.

Analysis

On the dust jacket of *Enormous Changes at the Last Minute*, Paley commented that she "writes stories because art is too long and life is too short." Hers is an unusual accomplishment, for though the short story has earned its position as a respectable genre, few authors have achieved repute without venturing beyond its limits. The acclaimed masters of the short story—James Joyce, Ernest Hemingway, Honoré de Balzac, and Anton Chekhov—all wrote novels or plays as well. Moreover, Paley's reputation is based on three relatively slim collections. Nevertheless, the first, *The Little Disturbances of Man*, was reissued by a different publisher nine years after its original appearance, a rare event in the history of the short story.

Paley's early interest in poetry inculcated in her art the values of verbal economy and the layering of meaning; her prose style is highly poetic—compact, full of imagery, and less reasoned than sensed or felt. Some of the pieces in *Later the Same Day*, such as "Mother," "This Is a Story About My Friend George, the Toy Inventor," and "In This Country, but in Another Language, My Aunt Refuses to Marry the Men Everyone Wants Her To," are so brief that they seem less stories than sketches or impressions.

Even in structuring her longer stories, Paley rarely accepts conventional formulae, choosing instead an often meandering movement with loose shifts in time, tone, or point of view. A glimpse into Paley's technique may be found in "A Conversation with My Father" (1974), where the narrator, a writer, is asked by her father to compose a traditional story but finds it impossible to write that type of "plot, the absolute line between two points . . . [B]ecause it takes all hope away. Everyone, real or imagined, deserves the open destiny of life." Such apparent plotlessness demands an equal openness of the reader, for very few standard expectations will be fulfilled. Occasionally she ventures into more fantastic or artificially stylized ground, as in the seemingly absurdist "The Floating Truth" (1959) or the whimsically postured "At That Time: Or, The History of a Joke" (1985).

For the most part, Paley's stories, like poems, ask to be read aloud. They have a conversational tone, and the often awkward precision of meaning, jarring usages, and odd logic create an immediacy of communication. This very particular language traces back to a polyglot family tradition. Paley's immigrant parents and relatives spoke Russian, Yiddish, and English, and her own Bronx vernacular was influenced by their very different syntax and rhythms. Certain of her stories, such as "Goodbye and Good Luck" (1959) and "Faith in the Afternoon" (1960), delightfully convey distinct voices from the Jewish-American immigrant community.

Though seldom explicitly autobiographical, Paley's stories contain elements of her personal history. They often focus on Jews, mothers, and activists, and are generally set in New York City. A number of them are connected by common characters, centered around Faith, a wryly self-mocking divorcée, her parents, her friends Ruth and Edie, her sons Richard and Tonto, and her husbands and neighbors. Faith (the name suggests Grace) is generally considered Paley's fictional alter ego; her presence gives the individual stories personal reverberations and gives the collections overall a sense of unity.

Faith, like Paley, is a single mother concerned equally with the quality of life in Greenwich Village and in the future of the human race. Progressive social and political issues, though never completely eclipsing the portrayal of character and relationship, are important to Paley. Her treatment of women, their problems, their ambitions, and their relations with men, have earned her the admiration of feminist readers. Some stories feature immigrants, minorities, and the poor—such as the Puerto Rican family in "In the Garden" (1985) or the black mother in "Lavinia: An Old Story" (1985)—or candidly portray the brutality of city life, as in "Samuel" (1968) and "Little Girl" (1974). In the light of the poverty, violence, and disease that Paley's characters witness and endure, there is no choice but to have opinions, to voice them shamelessly, and to act upon them with courage.

Paley's writing, though political, is very rarely didactic, pessimistic, or angry. As a writer, she is attuned to the subtle signals and meanings of human emotion and communication, whatever the situation or backdrop, and this sensitivity provides a foundation of warmth and humor. Her satire, applied to old gossips or overzealous activists, is never malicious, and her overriding concern is ultimately to amuse, to touch, and to remind her reader of the wonderful joy and variety of being alive.

THE LOUDEST VOICE

First published: 1959
Type of work: Short story

An outspoken and strong-willed little Jewish girl is chosen to narrate her school's Christmas play.

"The Loudest Voice" is the first-person recollection of Shirley Abramowitz, who remembers her childhood as a place where "every window is a mother's mouth bidding the street shut up" and where her "voice is the loudest." Shirley is the daughter of Jewish immigrants, a bright and uninhibited child who talks loudly and incessantly and, like her father, fearlessly speaks her mind.

On a cold November morning, Shirley is summoned by the teacher organizing the school's Christmas play. Knowing that she has a loud and clear voice, he asks her to be his narrator. The Christmas play, and the involvement in it of Jewish children such as Shirley, occasions debate and commentary throughout the Jewish community, where some embrace assimilation into primarily Christian America while others firmly safeguard the integrity of ethnic and religious identity. In the Abramowitz home, Shirley's mother disapproves but her father counters with the argument, "In Palestine the Arabs would be eating you alive. Europe you had pogroms. Argentina is full of Indians. Here you got Christmas."

Shirley herself is proud of her voice and eager to perform; during the month of rehearsals her excitement focuses her usually dispersed energies and she becomes the director's efficient and trusted assistant. The day of the play arrives, Shirley narrates sensitively and admirably, giving an objective and amusing account of her classmates' earnest presentation. The story concludes later that night as the Abramowitzes and a neighbor discuss the day's events in their characteristically opinionated fashion, and Shirley, lying in bed, silently says her prayers and then loudly yells to quiet her parents' arguments.

In "The Loudest Voice," Paley creates a delightful and very immediate protagonist. Shirley's personality is defined by her comments—her perception of the loneliness of unpopular people, her innocent fusion of the Christmas play with the very Jewish world in which it is performed, and the overheard conversations and repartee that have remained in her memory. The story's title signals an affirmation of personal freedom, for Shirley, who is constantly being silenced in her day-to-day life, proudly believes that a voice worthy of the Christmas play must also have the power to make both its opinions and prayers heard. The story contrasts loud voices with the silence of death, memory, and contemplation, and implicit in Shirley's pride is Paley's own valuation of the freedom of self-expression.

As she tells her story, Shirley makes a few simple comments that establish the distance of passed time, the death of her parents, and the warmth with which she views the past. The incident of the Christmas play, though simple and basically undramatic, is like a prism reflecting many facets of her childhood and the life of that remembered community. Her father's assertion, "What belongs to history, belongs to all men," informs Shirley's own generous feeling toward the municipal Christmas tree which, like the Jews, "was a stranger in Egypt," and defines her open attitude toward life. Through many such touches, Paley portrays with empathetic lightness the ghetto mentality as it makes the transition to acceptance and comfort, and, in a larger view, distills centuries of Jewish exile and accommodation into the experience of a single child.

AN INTEREST IN LIFE

First published: 1959
Type of work: Short story

A young woman, deserted by her husband to rear four children alone, learns to find happiness in her simple life.

"An Interest in Life" holds nothing of the bizarre or extraordinary: It is a story about an ordinary woman named Virginia, her ordinary children, and the ordinary problems she faces making ends meet and finding happiness and love in a very imperfect world.

The story begins as Virginia's husband deserts her, ostensibly to join the Army, after giving her a broom and dustpan for Christmas. The gift is not a kind one; the relations between Virginia and her husband have been bitter and sarcastic. Once he departs, Virginia begins adjusting to the life of a single twenty-six-year-old woman rearing four young children—dealing not only with social service agencies, schools, and bills, but also with loneliness, anger, and the lingering mystery of where her husband went and whether he will ever return.

Into Virginia's misery and bitterness comes John Raftery, the married son of her widowed neighbor, as if, it seems, to "rescue" her. John offers her his devotion and comfort, but Virginia is hesitant to accept it fully. Still, he comes to see her faithfully every Thursday night, and his openheartedness and lightness of spirit bring life into her home, effecting subtle changes in the children's and Virginia's own outlooks. In the comfort of John's undemanding affection, she recalls the wildness of her passion for her husband and their tumultuous marriage, poisoned by his arrogance and cruelty, culminating in the broom and the desertion.

Then one Thursday, suddenly, without explanation, John stops coming. After two weeks' absence, Virginia abandons hope of his return. Dejected, she decides to go on a television game show called "Strike it Rich" and makes the requisite list of personal troubles. "The list when complete could have brought tears to the eye of God if He had a minute." It somehow cheers her up, however, and she realizes that all a person really needs "is an interest in life, good, bad, or peculiar."

Once she realizes this, the doorbell rings. It is John, returning to say goodbye forever, but Virginia's list and John's mocking response to her troubles—"They'd laugh you out of the studio. Those people really suffer"—impels her to act on another decision, and she finally accepts John as her lover. They settle into a steady situation that brings Virginia happiness and emotional stability and in which she still sometimes imagines, at the story's end, her husband's late-night return and a rediscovery of their lost passion.

"An Interest in Life" is told in the first person, so Paley brings the reader into Virginia's mind and perceptions. A sharp and economical use of language potently portrays the character's emotional life, as when she remembers a domestic climate where "[f]ire may break out from a nasty remark" or says that after her husband's desertion "sadness was stretched world wide across my face." The story's recurring images are of burning, shriveling, consumption, and deterioration. These images express the volatility of Virginia's marriage as well as her own protective, even paranoid, attitude toward other people and new experiences. Rather than be honest with her children, she feels the need to keep the truth from them and responds to their queries with evasive proverbs. In fact, she is generally critical of them, sardonic about her neighbors, and pessimistic about the system and her survival within it; only when John enters her life does she begin to open up to the possibilities of change in herself and others and to accept life without suspicion or fear. The progress of the story is a movement toward a more positive perception of life.

Characteristically, Paley employs comedy to achieve a balance in what would otherwise be a rather depressing tale. Virginia's bitterness does not nullify the comic elements in the portraits she creates of her children or Mrs. Raftery; the devices of the gift broom and the television game show, full as they are with the power of "sweeping clean" and "Striking it Rich," infuse the critical moments of Virginia's life with a clumsy domesticity. In the ordinary world, Paley seems to be saying, there is little that is truly profound or timeless, yet there is always the potential for happiness, for meaning, and for love.

FAITH IN A TREE
First published: 1974
Type of work: Short story

During an afternoon in the park, a woman's detachment and cynicism are converted into a commitment to action.

"Faith in a Tree," as the title suggests, is about a woman named Faith, the protagonist of many a Paley story, sitting in a tree. It is a Saturday afternoon, and Faith has brought her two young sons, Richard and Tonto, to their New York neighborhood park to play and pass the time, among other parents and children and passersby doing the same.

Unlike those around her, however, Faith feels subtly trapped in her life as a single mother; she senses an unidentifiable longing, both carnal and intellectual, to make a more meaningful connection with the world. Bored with the mundane pretensions of the park's social scene, she withdraws, retreats into herself and climbs into a sycamore to establish the distance and detachment she needs. From her post, she muses flippantly on the scene below her and its position in the universe—"What a place in democratic time!" She answers the queries of casual acquaintances passionately, but her cryptic answers are enigmatic and senseless; she describes and lampoons the other mothers, such as the self-righteous Mrs. Junius Finn, who "always is more in charge of word meanings than I am" and "is especially in charge of Good and Bad." She responds to the various stimuli of passersby, such as a pair of men listening to Bach on a transistor radio; she alternately ignores and wrangles with her clever and disapproving older son Richard; she jumps down from the tree for some competitive flirtation with a likable and considerate man named Phillip Mazzano. She later considers climbing back up for oxygen when another woman seems to be prevailing in the contest for his attention. These and other comments and encounters are reported through Faith's ironic and imaginative eyes.

After flowing timelessly and haphazardly in a manner thus reflective of Faith's inner diffuseness, the story ends with a twist reminiscent of an O. Henry tale—and not at all typical of Paley's style. A group of parents and children approach, wielding signs and clanging pots in protest against the American use of napalm in Vietnam, and they are dispersed by a local conservative-minded policeman. In the aftermath of the incident, Richard chastises Faith and her friends for their failure to confront the policeman and impulsively emblazons the protesters' message—"WOULD YOU BURN A CHILD? and under it, a little taller, the red reply, WHEN NECESSARY"—across the sidewalk. The apathy and restraint of the afternoon combine with the sudden excitement of the protesters' expulsion and Richard's spontaneous anger to affect Faith's view of her life dramatically, and, in the story's final paragraph, she traces to that specific moment her subsequent changes in appearance, employment, social life, communication, and awareness of and involvement in the world.

The impact of "Faith in a Tree" derives from the care and leisure with which Paley establishes Faith's sense of detachment. This is accomplished not only through the imagery—for example, comparing the other mothers to naval vessels—and acutely facetious tone, but also through Faith's attitude toward the reader, for she acknowledges the subjective posture she has taken to the world around her and on two occasions even includes footnotes that acknowledge the physical manifestation of her storytelling—the page—and refer beyond the internal context of the story to the reader's world as well. The detachment, mentally and stylistically, is thus complete;

it is its completeness which lulls the reader into an equal complacency, only to disrupt it again with Faith's sudden emergence from spiritual withdrawal into an active participation in the world. Paley is rarely didactic, but in "Faith in a Tree" her purpose is not only to entertain but also to motivate: Just as Faith is somehow tricked by circumstance into a meaningful new awareness and acceptance of responsibility, so is the reader (by implication) left, seemingly alone at the conclusion, to ponder the nature of complacency and determination and the small ways in which an individual may be driven to action.

ZAGROWSKY TELLS

First published: 1985
Type of work: Short story

In an encounter with a former customer and antagonist, an old Jewish man recounts the ordeals that forced him to confront his racism.

In "Zagrowsky Tells," Paley's recurring character Faith appears again, but in a secondary and not necessarily flattering role. The focus is on Zagrowsky, a retired Jewish pharmacist, as he sits in the park with his grandson, a black child named Emanuel.

Faith, a former customer whom Zagrowsky has not seen in years, approaches him and asks him about the boy. He begins to explain how he has come to have a black grandson, and as they reminisce about their shared past in the community he confronts her for having led a protest against him for supposedly racist practices. He denies having been racist, but Faith insists that he subtly mistreated his black customers. Faith then presses him to talk about Emanuel, and he tells the story: His daughter Cissy became mentally unbalanced, suffering attacks and even protesting his racism herself; she was committed to an institution north of the city where she became pregnant by a black gardener. Now she lives at home, still nervous and dependent, and Zagrowsky and his wife rear her son Emanuel.

Having heard his story, Faith begins to offer advice about providing for the child's racial identity, but Zagrowsky interrupts and angrily sends her off. Now confused and frustrated, he vents his anger on another stranger, an innocent man who approaches him to praise and ask about Emanuel. Faith quickly returns with a group of her friends and saves Zagrowsky from the bothersome stranger, then they warmly say goodbye, leaving Zagrowsky alone with Emanuel and uncertain as to what exactly has transpired.

"Zagrowsky Tells" really concerns two separate stories told by Zagrowsky. One is the story of his and Emanuel's history, a sad tale in which much of the pain and the meaning is left between the lines. Zagrowsky is a proud and bitter man who must work hard to face the difficult truths of his life: his bigotry, his failures as a father and husband, his inability to trust or communicate with others. Thus, his story is easiest told when he relies on facts.

The other story, however, is the story he tells the reader. This account, given in the immediate first-person present, weaves together the external reality of the encounters in the park with the internal monologue of Zagrowsky's mind. As he talks to Faith and looks after Emanuel, he is constantly digressing—observing, judging, evaluating, speculating, anticipating, imagining, and above all, remembering—and it is through his observations, thoughts, and memories that a true view of his life and his personality emerges. Paley thus portrays from within the fears, anxieties, and longing of a confused and repressed old man upon whom life has played an ironic joke.

As in so many of her stories, Paley's prevalent attitude toward her subject is one of generosity. The case against Zagrowsky is not a clear one, for his bigotry is subtle and not malicious; he elicits empathy, comparing the histories of the black and Jewish peoples, communicating his desire to act fairly and honestly, and acknowledging, in spite of the accumulated years of guilt and shame, the incontrovertibility of the past and the life-affirming value of expressing oneself. "Tell!" he says, "That opens up the congestion a little—the lungs are for breathing, not secrets."

The ultimate redemption, however, as well as the story's emotional power, lies not in a reasoned defense of past bigotry but in the compassionate reality of Zagrowsky's present situation, as intimated throughout the story. Given Cissy's illness and Mrs. Zagrowsky's limitations, Zagrowsky has willingly become Emanuel's primary parent, teacher, and friend. The two are constant companions, and the old man's devotion to the boy is absolute. Thus, during the course of the story the reader develops compassion—the same compassion that in the end motivates Faith to protect Zagrowsky—by recognizing the miraculous transformation that has been achieved in the heart of a bitter old man by the presence of an innocent little black boy.

THE EXPENSIVE MOMENT

First published: 1985
Type of work: Short story

An activist, in her later years, meditates on the choices she has made and on the political legacy left by her generation.

"The Expensive Moment" is a complex and textured fabric of moments, observations, encounters, emotions, and ideas in a particular period of Faith's life. Presumably the same character of Paley's other stories, she here inhabits a world of overtly political discussions and deeper, mellower wisdom.

The people in Faith's life are all vigorously engaged in political and emotional pursuits. Her sons are grown: Tonto is in love and Richard is an active member of the League for Revolutionary Youth. Faith is in a solid but stale marriage to a furniture store salesman named Jack and is having an intellectually and sexually stimulating affair with an attractive, mercurial China scholar named Nick. Her best friend Ruth meets her for lunch at the Art Foods Deli and laments the absence and uncertain future of her daughter Rachel, an errant political revolutionary. Faith reminisces about her own activist past and debates trade and political theory with her son Richard. Along with Ruth and Nick, she attends meetings and dinners where she meets exiled Chinese artists and writers.

At such a meeting, Faith meets Xie Fing, a Chinese poet, "a woman from half the world away who'd lived a life beyond foreignness and had experienced extreme history." The two women become acquainted, and Xie Fing invites herself to see Faith's home, a request which delights and flatters Faith. They spend the next day drinking tea in Faith's kitchen, touring the house and the neighborhood, discussing themselves, their children, their political activities, and the future. The story ends simply on a shared note of wistful regret, both women acknowledging in retrospect how little they knew about preparing their children for the real world.

Throughout the story are a variety of interrelated themes: the disparity between the depth of the individual's concern and his or her limited power to affect the world, the passage of time and the wisdom that comes with it, the burdensome responsibility of rearing children and then the painful necessity of letting them go, the contrast between the social and political ideals of the mind and the emotional and physical needs of the body. These themes come together at various moments; one of the most potent is when Faith thinks back on her anti-draft activities in the 1960's and contemplates the sacrifices that young people sometimes must make for their country or their ideals. Thinking about such sacrifices in the context of Rachel's revolutionary activities, and about the possibility that Richard too could someday disappear and never be heard from again, Faith recognizes that there sometimes comes "a moment in history, the expensive moment when everyone his age is called but just a few are chosen by conscience or passion. . . . Then you think sadly, I could have worked harder at raising that child, the one that was once mine."

"The Expensive Moment" is a very thoughtful story that, in examining the difficult choices that history forces an individual to make, by extension examines the cost of all choices. The tone, though relentlessly questioning and sometimes regretful, is never maudlin or angry—those do not seem to be colors on Paley's emotional palette. Rather, she gently mocks political convictions—mentioning the "L.R.Y.'s regular beep-the-horn-if-you-support-Mao meeting" and envisioning John Keats writing verses in a rice paddy in provincial China—even as she portrays a world in which ideas have weight and magnetism. In such a world, convictions—or, for that matter, a healthy and reasoned cynicism—are dramatic and sensual; they establish the connections between people and help Faith and those around her to make sense of their complex lives and find things to value as they travel across the ugly map of contemporary political reality. Such a world is not to be dismissed and avoided; rather, like Faith and Xie Fing, one can only earnestly strive to do one's best and forgive, though never forget, the past.

Summary

In proclaiming herself "a somewhat combative pacifist and cooperative anarchist," Grace Paley brings together the intelligence, awareness, empathy, and self-mockery that illuminate her writing. The saying goes, "actions speak louder than words," and Paley's decades of involvement in social and political issues fill the silences between the infrequent publication of her stories. On their own as well, the stories stand as a delightful, provocative, and moving vision of a segment of society, a collection of unique individuals striving to improve their lives and their world.

Bibliography

Cevoli, Cathy. "These Four Women Could Save Your Life." *Mademoiselle* 89 (January, 1983): 104-107.

Harrington, Stephanie. "The Passionate Rebels." *Vogue* 153 (May, 1969): 151.

Iannone, Carol. "A Dissent on Grace Paley." *Commentary* 80 (August, 1985): 54-58.

McMurran, Kristin. "Even Admiring Peers Worry That Grace Paley Writes Too Little and Protests Too Much." *People* 11 (February 26, 1979): 22-23.

Paley, Grace. "The Seneca Stories: Tales from the Women's Peace Encampment." *Ms.* 12 (December, 1983): 54-58.

Smith, Wendy. "Grace Paley." *Publishers Weekly* 227 (April 5, 1985): 71-72.

Barry Mann

WALKER PERCY

Born: Birmingham, Alabama
May 28, 1916
Died: Covington, Louisiana
May 10, 1990

Principal Literary Achievement

Widely recognized as the preeminent Christian "novelist of ideas" in the second half of the twentieth century, Percy created the American existentialist novel.

Biography

Walker Percy was born in Birmingham, Alabama, on May 28, 1916, living a basically idyllic Southern childhood until the suicide of his father, who was eloquently portrayed in the character of Will Barrett, protagonist of Percy's 1980 novel, *The Second Coming*. After his widowed mother's death, the teenaged Percy and his two brothers moved to Greenville, Mississippi, where they were subsequently reared to manhood by their father's first cousin, William Alexander "Uncle Will" Percy, a lifelong bachelor, whose autobiography *Lanterns on the Levee* (1942), was itself a Southern classic, portraying the proud South emerging from the ravages of the Civil War.

Walker Percy had no intention of becoming a writer, making his way instead to New York's Columbia College of Physicians and Surgeons in 1938 to become a psychiatrist after finishing his B.A. in chemistry at the University of North Carolina at Chapel Hill. During this time, Percy himself underwent psychoanalysis, whiling away his little free time as a medical student going to films and observing the behavior of other filmgoers, a habit that would profoundly influence his literary career.

After earning the M.D. in 1941, he attempted to complete his internship at Bellevue Hospital in New York City, and there contracted tuberculosis while performing autopsies on cadavers. This illness became pivotal in his career and in his life; while recovering in a sanatorium in upstate New York, he read voraciously, particularly existentialist philosophy, including the works of Swedish philosopher Søren Kierkegaard. The result was an improbable conversion to Christianity in 1943 and a decision to abandon medicine as a career and seek a vocation as a full-time writer.

Between 1943 and 1946, Percy attempted two forgettable novels, and he eventually turned instead to studying language acquisition theory and linguistics, devel-

oping themes that would later undergird the thematic concerns of his novels. After he married Mary Townsend in 1946, they both converted to Catholicism and relocated to the South, to Covington, Louisiana, near the quintessential Southern city of New Orleans. There they subsisted on Percy's inheritance from his uncle's estate. During the 1950's, Percy published a number of learned essays in scholarly journals on linguistics and its connections with psychology, and he continued to dabble in fiction.

When he finally settled on a set of characters and an appropriate theme, he deliberately steered his narrative craft away from the towering figure of William Faulkner and his convoluted regionalism toward a more direct, post-Southern genre of fiction. The result was Percy's first published novel, at the age of forty-five, *The Moviegoer* (1961), a National Book Award winner clearly patterned after the intense, philosophical "novel of ideas" written by French writers Jean-Paul Sartre and Albert Camus, whom Percy had discovered during his convalescence from tuberculosis. In essence, Percy created a peculiarly American genre of existential fiction, but with this difference: Percy wrote as an orthodox Christian whose characters were haunted as much by the presence as the absence of God in the modern world.

Percy followed *The Moviegoer* with a longer, even more philosophical novel in 1966, *The Last Gentleman*, whose plot introduces Will Barrett, a troubled, confused young man in search of himself; Barrett eventually finds meaning in laying down his life for others. As Percy's reputation as a formidable novelist of ideas grew, he upset expectations with his third novel, published in 1971, *Love in the Ruins*: It is a hilarious satire of modern technological life and the sham of modern psychiatry. Its protagonist, Dr. Tom More, is a thinly disguised evocation of Sir Thomas More who dutifully skewers the false utopias of Eastern religion, consumer capitalism, and errant liberal Catholicism.

As Percy continued to reap critical plaudits for his fiction, his nonfiction essays were collected and published in *The Message in the Bottle* in 1975, astonishing his readers with their variety and their expertise in arcane linguistic and psychological theory. Percy's fourth novel, the dark, disturbing *Lancelot* (1977), is the story of a vengeful husband who murders his wife and her lover.

Attempting to write his first "nonalienated," or optimistic, novel, Percy revived the character of Will Barrett for his 1980 book, *The Second Coming*. The now widowed Barrett finds true love—and God—in a densely plotted, comic work that revealed a new emphasis of affirmation in Percy that earned him back the critical respect he seemed to have lost with *Lancelot*. The critical and financial success of *The Second Coming* was rewarded by Percy's publisher by bringing out his quirky nonfiction book, *Lost in the Cosmos: Or, The Last Self-Helf Book*, in 1983. *Lost in the Cosmos* was at once a satire of television talk-show hosts, a serious monograph on language and semiotics, and a brief for Christianity—delighting some critics and readers and confusing others.

In 1987, Percy published what many regard as his greatest achievement, *The Thanatos Syndrome*. This novel also revives a past Percy character, Dr. Tom More; fresh from a prison sentence for selling drugs to truck drivers, he discovers and thwarts a fiendish plot—engineered by a coterie of prominent and respectable lawyers and doctors—to anesthetize the populace by drugging the drinking water of Feliciana Parish in Louisiana.

Percy's death on May 10, 1990, after a battle with cancer, left orthodox Christianity with nearly no legitimate representative in modern letters. He will long be remembered for his poignant warnings against a potential holocaust in Western culture because of its creeping acceptance of situational ethics at the expense of an eternal moral standard that regards human life as meaningful and precious.

Analysis

Like fellow Southern Catholic writer Flannery O'Connor before him, Percy saw through the pious pretensions of an irreligious age. His southernness may have cleared his vision, but it was his sweeping grasp of Western civilization and its foundations that gave his fiction its substance.

The twentieth century, Percy declared in the words of Father Smith, hero of *The Thanatos Syndrome*, is that period of history in which God "has agreed to let the Great Prince Satan have his way with men for a hundred years—this one hundred years." Percy's protagonists—from Binx Bolling in *The Moviegoer* and Tom More in *Love in the Ruins* to Will Barrett in *The Second Coming*—are all, in their own unique ways, refugees from that century, one in which, Percy notes, "more people have been killed . . . by tender-hearted souls than by cruel barbarians in all other centuries put together."

Percy found the roots of the twentieth century's sentimental nihilism in science's bastard son, "scientism," by which he meant the pathological attempt to objectify humanity as simply one more organism trapped in its environment. He concluded:

[T]he modern objective consciousness will go to any length to prove that it is not unique in the Cosmos, and by this very effort establishes its own uniqueness. Name another entity in the Cosmos which tries to prove it is not unique.

The offense of mankind's uniqueness in the universe bemused Percy, and it became a predominant theme not only in his fiction but also in his engaging excursions into the philosophy of language. How mankind and language are each informed by the other, how neither man nor language can be understood apart from the other—these primary questions provoked Percy to challenge the "official version" of how humans acquire language skills promulgated by linguists, scientists, and philosophers such as Noam Chomsky, B. F. Skinner, and Jacques Derrida.

In Percy's hands, fiction and linguistics both became a subtle brand of apologetics, an inquiry into the nature of man, God, and the Cosmos that yielded an exhilarating (although indirect) defense of the Christian faith.

From his improbable base in Covington, Louisiana, Percy conducted anthropological safaris into the human psyche. His credentials as a navigator were impeccable, possessing as he did the single most important trait such a guide can have: He recognized a clue when he saw one. Each fact about human communication, its successes and its failures, pointed Percy to a transcendent order of meaning, a transcendence that could be explained only by reference to an Eternal Logos who made creatures in His own image and thus made them capable of responding to Him with language.

A traditionalist who lamented the twentieth century's loss of the perception of sin and its need for grace, Percy created protagonists who search for the source of their alienation and melancholy in the most prosperous country on earth. The typical Percy protagonist is a roughly middle-aged man, comfortable financially but plagued by a vague sense of disorientation and depression. This cerebral main character communicates his sense of disorientation through paradox and oxymoron. His story is always one of "coming to oneself," of suddenly discovering the extraordinary in the ordinary, of the transcendent in the mundane. To Percy, man is neither, "a beast nor an angel but a wayfaring creature somewhere between." His ultimate challenge is to seize his own destiny and act on his own or some other's behalf against the status quo.

As a narrator, Percy often came to readers in the guise of the island "castaway" desperately awaiting news from home. The "message in the bottle" (the title of his profound nonfiction study of language) found by Percy was language itself. Humankind is wallowing, Percy posited, in a spiritual malaise, a post-pagan, post-Christian identity crisis. Men and women, intended by their Creator to become full persons, settle for existence as ghostly personas—bifurcated creatures propped up by a pseudoscience all too ready to ratify humankind's soulless state.

Percy saw himself as a castaway with news even more newsworthy than a few tidbits from home. The "authorized version" of humankind's story is, according to Percy, a myth, yet a true myth, one that actually happened: a story of wickedness in high places, of a fall from grace, of a scandalous redemption achieved by a dying God. Percy's diagnosis of mankind's malaise at the end of the modern age will thus be his lasting legacy. Set in the then-future 1990's, his last novel, *The Thanatos Syndrome*, represents Percy's "final warning" to an age that seems to regard a death wish as the epitome of mature adulthood. Homeless, nostalgic, twentieth century man faces extinction, Percy believed, from a new gnosticism manifested in various permutations as deconstructionism, radical feminism, and overt racialism. This latest gnostic faith drives man further inside his own head and tribe, creating a cerebrating creature who nevertheless participates in the real, public cosmos only as a brute consumer. There is no "outside," no transcendent reference point that might give him direction or purpose.

Percy knew that the apologist must be careful, however; what he has to say must be heard as news and not mere gossip. His compatriots must connect the message in the bottle with the longings deep within their own hearts:

> What if the news the newsbearer bears is the very news the castaway had been waiting for, news of where he came from and who he is and what he must do, and what if the

newsbearer brought with him the means by which the castaway may do what he must do? Well then, the castaway will, by the grace of God, believe him.

THE MOVIEGOER

First published: 1961
Type of work: Novel

The story of a young man alienated from modern life who finds more meaning in the quest for God than in its resolution.

The Moviegoer won the 1962 National Book Award for Fiction for Percy at the age of forty-five and launched his career as a novelist. As a novel of ideas, *The Moviegoer* consistently raises the largest questions of human life. Is there a God? If so, what is mankind's relationship to Him and to the quest of knowledge of Him? As became Percy's trademark handling of plot, much of the action of *The Moviegoer* takes place within the mind of the protagonist, Binx Bolling, who, nearing his thirtieth birthday, retreats to a mentalist existence, "sunk in the everydayness of life," unequipped to live life to the fullest and baffled by its ambiguities and contradictions.

A successful broker in New Orleans and a war veteran, Binx nevertheless has few friends. Although he has had a number of affairs with his secretaries, he knows neither what friendship or love truly is nor how to find a purpose for living. Binx is stuck in the mundaneness of life, which saps his strength for caring and believing in others. Immersed in the obdurate ordinariness of his social life, family, and job, he is a "wayfarer" who feels homeless and abandoned.

Binx thus embarks on a quest for meaning that evolves into a veiled search for God. As a seeker he is discouraged, since "as everyone knows, the polls report that 98% of Americans believe in God and the remaining 2% are atheists and agnostics—which leaves not a single percentage point for a seeker." He wants to be "onto something," to feel authenticated as a human being, since "to become aware of the possibility of the search is to be onto something." In launching a search that takes him away from the consumerism and aestheticism of his environment, Bolling rebels against the mundanities of life: family heritage, job status, material good. Binx seeks a different kind of authentication and becomes obsessed with motion pictures. "The movies are onto the search," he says, but they always end in the same everydayness which brings him despair: The hero "takes up with the local librarian" and "settles down with a vengeance."

Ultimately his cinematic excursions bring him no closer to a solution, but when he is drawn into the life of Kate Cutrer, the stepdaughter of his great-aunt Emily, he finds both the courage and the determination to confront life as it is. When Kate's fiancé is killed in an automobile accident, she lapses into despair, secretly drinking heavily and contemplating suicide. After she jilts a willing suitor, Emily Cutrer enlists Binx as an aide and confidant in helping Kate through her emotional trauma.

During the Mardi Gras season, Binx is sent on a business trip; impulsively, Kate requests that he let her join him. In the aftermath of their trip and the growing empathy with which Binx perceives Kate's malady, he discovers his own humanity and worth. In his compassion and risk-taking on Kate's behalf, he has transcended the ordinariness in which he was trapped and has conquered his malaise.

In the novel's climax, Binx is lectured severely by his aunt for his failure to meet the standards of Southern gentlemanliness. Paradoxically, this liberates Binx: He and Kate marry, free of the façade of gentility in which they were both bred. In the epilogue, Binx reveals that his aunt has learned to understand and forgive him for what he is; "the Bolling family had gone to seed and . . . I was not one of her heroes but a very ordinary fellow."

In bringing Kate through her crisis, Binx resolves his own and discovers both humanity and purposefulness. Binx and Kate together discover that being is made meaningful through mutual trust and authentic, individual commitment. Consequently, Percy's characterization in *The Moviegoer* underscores the fact that in the modern South—indeed, in the world at large—this is the very kind of commitment that family, tradition, job, and the usual mundane social concerns can never engender or replenish. If anyone is to become a "person," he or she must step out of the security of established roles and stations and take the awful risk of individuality.

The same culture that detaches Binx from himself also permits his eventual return as a "reborn" southerner and human being, equipped both to critique and to coexist peacefully with his heritage. This can only occur, however, if Binx will act rather than merely contemplate the possibilities. In reaching out to Kate he finds the impulse he needs to free himself from the past and face the future with integrity and hope.

THE LAST GENTLEMAN

First published: 1966
Type of work: Novel

A young man relocated to New York from his native South finds release from his empty pondering of the meaning of existence by befriending a dying young man.

The Last Gentleman is Percy's most ambitious and overtly philosophical novel, one whose "ideas" take precedence over character, plot, or theme. It is as if Percy's long years of cogitation about language, man, and the cosmos and the alienation evident in American culture suddenly coalesced and compelled him to write a series of interesting, though convoluted, monologues to be placed in the mouths of the brooding searchers populating his narrative. Here the reader finds a compendium of Percy's personal indictments against crass "Christian America," modelled on the work of his existentialist mentor, Søren Kierkegaard, in nineteenth century Denmark.

The protagonist in his second novel, Will Barrett, has spent five years in psycho-analysis; he is a native Southerner serving as a "humidification engineer" at Macy's department store in New York City. An introspective, educated man vaguely aware of his own despair, Barrett is "dislocated in the universe." Percy's opening description of Barrett succinctly circumscribes his character: "He had to know everything before he could do anything."

Paralyzed by his commitment to abstract knowledge before making decisions, Barrett lives in a world pervaded by ordinariness. He despairs of clear answers to his nagging questions about the purpose of life—both for himself and others—but he shares some dim hopes that his quest will eventually bear fruit. One day, as he contemplates his station in life at Central Park, he opts to become, as Binx Bolling had in *The Moviegoer*, an observer and not merely the observed. He spots a beautiful young woman, Kitty Vaught, through his newly purchased telescope and sets out to meet her. Smitten, Barrett traces her to a New York hospital, where he discovers that she and the Vaught family are comforting her younger brother, Jamie, who is dying.

In an improbable sequence of events, Will Barrett's Southern charm and gentlemanly pose win over each of the Vaught family members, and he is invited to accompany them back home to Atlanta, mostly as companion and confidant to Jamie as he lives out his remaining days. Barrett agrees, interested as he is in staying as close to Kitty Vaught as possible. During his stay, Kitty's sister, Valentine, who has joined a Catholic order that takes care of indigent black children, enters Barrett's life and coerces him to seek Jamie's conversion, believing that he alone can ensure that Jamie enters eternity as a "saved" person. Soon thereafter, Sutter Vaught, Rita's estranged husband, arrives on the scene. Barrett finds in him a curious but appealing sense of daring and courage; he seems to be someone who has lived life and not merely hypothesized about it. Sutter and Jamie disappear, and it becomes Barrett's duty to track them down and return Jamie home—a task made all the more alarming and tenuous when Barrett discovers in Sutter's New Mexico apartment, along with some helpful maps, a stenographic notebook recording Sutter's jaded outlook on life and community in the United States.

Barrett familiarizes himself with the notebook during his subsequent trek, as Percy interweaves excerpts from Sutter's painful explorations with Barrett's unfolding search for the two brothers. Percy pushes the reader to diagnose the debilitating malady from which both Sutter and Barrett suffer: an utter sense of homelessness in the world that seems to make errant materialism or suicide the only alternatives for the thoughtful individual. Barrett quickly sees that while he shares Sutter's disaffection with the new paganism and its philosophical implications, "in fact my problem is how to live from one ordinary minute to the next on a Wednesday afternoon."

When Barrett catches up with Sutter, Jamie has been placed in a hospital, dying of a pulmonary edema, and Sutter is working at a Santa Fe guest ranch. Barrett brings calm to both Jamie and Sutter, and their independent friendships deepen. Barrett also discovers a passage in Sutter's notebook that indicates a previous suicide attempt and begins to recognize signs that he may try it again. Determined to forestall Sutter's suicide and to fulfill his commitment to bringing Jamie to faith, Barrett steels in himself the fortitude to act apart from exhaustive knowledge of the way the world works or what the consequences of his actions will be.

Before his death, Jamie is led to offer halting words of faith in the presence of Barrett and the hospital chaplain. Moments later, Barrett chases after the departing Sutter, hoping to assure him of his worth in the world, confident that he can and will convince him of that fact.

LOVE IN THE RUINS

First published: 1971
Type of work: Novel

A comic anti-utopian novel that satirizes liberal civil religion and oversexed American culture through the exploits of dissident psychologist Dr. Tom More.

Offered as a tongue-in-cheek, pre-holocaust tale, *Love in the Ruins* is subtitled *The Adventures of a Bad Catholic at a Time Near the End of the World*. Its protagonist and narrator, Dr. Tom More, named for the famous sixteenth century saint who authored *Utopia* (1516). More is a rueful psychologist who has developed an instrument for research which he calls the "lapsometer." The lapsometer is a device that measures certain psychic forces in the brain and thereby makes it possible to determine the source of man's irrationality, which for Percy is characterized by one of two extremes.

In Percy's view, the two most evident maladies of modern life are angelism, the tendency to abstract oneself from the ordinary circumstances of life and attempt to live above them in aloof intellectualism, and bestialism, the tendency to live as a brute consumer with an unrestrained, animal-like preoccupation with sex without procreation. This protracted indictment of modern culture surfaces frequently in Percy's later fiction, most prominently in *Lancelot* and in *The Thanatos Syndrome*.

The narrative is bracketed into five main sections, followed by an epilogue that delineates what has happened in the five years subsequent to the July 4 climax. It is an apocalyptic time in which the social institutions that are supposed to provide stability and continuity have broken down or become ridiculous parodies of themselves. The halls of academe, the medical profession, civil government, and a host of venerable religious institutions, particularly the Catholic church, are all satirized as ineffectual and compromised, each having sold out to the spirit of modernism and therefore being contemptible to Percy. Racial tensions have erupted into violent confrontations as the very fabric of American society is about to unravel. Under the accumulated weight of centuries of guilt and alienation, "ordinary folk" find their self-image slowly disintegrating, their sex lives impotent, and their digestion failing; they seek help from two main sources, proctologists and psychologists.

The reader discovers Dr. More in the midst of a personal and professional crisis made all the more difficult by heightened racial tensions across the country but particularly in his region of the South. He looks out over an interstate cloverleaf and describes the four quadrants of his city. One quarter is occupied by conservative Christian businessmen; another is the federal complex, where government funding has produced a hospital where More works, a NASA facility, a Geriatrics Center, and the Love Clinic; a third quarter encompasses Paradise Estates, the suburb where More lives in his deceased wife's house; and the fourth is the Honey Island swamp, where assorted antisocial derelicts, castoffs, and the ferocious Bantus, a group of militant black guerrillas seeking social justice, reside. As he speaks, More is awaiting the end of civilization, surrounded, nevertheless, by three attractive women— two erstwhile girlfriends and his loyal nurse, Ellen.

Dr. More's financial and professional situation is precarious, and he makes a dubious, Faustian bargain with the diabolical Art Immelmann, who promises to market his invention and help More earn favor with foundations to fund further research. More soon realizes that Immelmann is not to be trusted—he alters More's device so that it not only detects but also remediates the psychic imbalances, then distributes lapsometers to ill-trained students who misuse the lapsometers with sometimes hilarious consequences.

A racial uprising of "Bantus," planned for July 4, provides the comic backdrop for the novel's ambiguous ending. Praying to his sainted ancestor, Sir Thomas More, Tom More succeeds in thwarting Immelmann's evil plans. The social upheaval proceeds apace, however, and in his epilogue, More intimates that blacks have displaced whites as the ruling class but have acquired the same social pathologies that had plagued black-white relations in the first place. More, on the other hand, has settled peacefully into the "slave quarters" of a large apartment complex down by the bayou. Here he is safely ensconced in a new middle-class life, having married his faithful nurse, Ellen, content to live out his natural life in a new, though obviously imperfect, Eden.

Tom More serves Percy's satire of modern sensibilities toward spirituality and social decorum in two ways. First, as a "bad Catholic," More exhibits a healthy skepticism toward what Percy believed was an unwelcome shift away from tradition and authority in the American Catholic church; More holds no quarter for liberal scavenging of Christian doctrine. Second, More is heroic in standing against the excesses and, in fact, the megalomania of the medical profession. Percy mercilessly skewers his own compatriots in the practice of psychology for their preoccupation with relatively trivial or peripheral matters while ignoring the major sources of human foibles and sin. Percy revived the character of Dr. More seventeen years later for an even more devastating sequel, *The Thanatos Syndrome*, in which the disintegration of morality in the modern world is laid at the feet of the medical profession in its advocacy of abortion, euthanasia, and genetic engineering.

THE SECOND COMING

First published: 1980
Type of work: Novel

A middle-aged man, contemplating suicide, finds redemption when he asks for and receives a sign that God exists.

Twenty-five years later, Will Barrett of *The Last Gentleman* returns in this sequel as a wealthy middle-aged man, recently widowed, suffering both from inexplicable blackouts in which he loses consciousness and from his faltering sense of a calling in life. Also resurrected are Sutter Vaught, the depressed coroner of the previous work, whom Will counseled out of suicide, and his sister, Kitty, whom Will once courted. The three are brought together again in a most unusual circumstance as Will encounters Kitty's purportedly schizophrenic daughter, Allison, during a "scientific experiment" to determine if God exists.

Worn down by the affluence and religiosity—particularly his own daughter's rigid fundamentalism—that surrounds him in Southern suburbia in Linwood, North Carolina, Will Barrett is convinced that the only question left for him to answer about humankind is whether life has any transcendent meaning—that is, whether God exists. His late wife heavily invested herself and her family fortune in "do-gooding"; Will spends his days, when well, playing golf and more golf and obsessively recovering the lurid details of his relationship with his father, who himself committed suicide.

In his emptiness, he makes a vow of ending his life if he cannot ascertain there is a God who exists—and cares; he vouchsafes his "experiment's" details and its consequences in a letter to Sutter Vaught. His plan is implausible yet inspired: He will hide in a nearby cave and fast until God gives him a sign of his existence. If God calls, he will emerge wiser and more secure in his footing for the future; if God remains silent, he will embrace the heritage bequeathed him by his father. Ironically, all that Will receives is an excruciating toothache whose pain sends him stumbling toward the exit.

On his way out he plunges into an uncharted shaft directly into an abandoned greenhouse in which Allison, Kitty Vaught's daughter, is hiding, having escaped from a mental institution. She, like Will, is searching for stability and hope in an ambiguous world. Subjected to electroshock treatments after exhibiting extreme withdrawal and forgetfulness, Allie is determined to prove she can live without psychologists or her meddling parents. As she nurses Will back to health, Will has found God, and she has found a spiritual benefactor and protector of her own who understands her alienation and inner heart.

As the narrative ends, the resourceful couple outwit their various pursuers, rescuing other social outcasts along the way, and they plan a marriage. Both Will and Allie are "reborn," but in an unconventional fashion—a fashion utterly spiritual but apart from and oblivious to the normal routes exemplified by the thoroughly religious town in which they have found each other. Once again, Percy offers a strong rebuke to the easy belief of conservative Christianity, with its pat answers to deep questions, and also to the secular abandonment of spiritual values that, if understood, might enrich and give substance to the pursuits of the good life.

Summary

Walker Percy once commented that his major novelistic concern was to depict "what it means to be a man living in the world who must die." In his work, the modern South—the last authentic refuge of American religious faith—is the typical setting for protagonists beset by alienation and the conflicting demands of community and tradition in a hostile modernity. Only a recognition of a transcendent order may provide the basis for recovery of self and a unified vision of the world.

At the center of this recovery, Percy places the mystery of mankind's origin and the clues provided by language in solving it—specifically, man's ability to make symbol and metaphor. What separates Percy from other, more pretentious, writers of philosophical fiction is his keen sense of everydayness, the vivid capturing of the details of modern life.

Bibliography

Allen, William Rodney. *Walker Percy: A Southern Wayfarer.* Jackson: University Press of Mississippi, 1986.

Bigger, Charles. "Logos and Epiphany: Walker Percy's Theology of Language." *The Southern Review* 13 (1977): 196-206.

Brooks, Cleanth. "Walker Percy and Southern Gnosticism." *The Southern Review* 13 (1977): 677-687.

Broughton, Panthea Reid, ed. *The Art of Walker Percy: Strategems for Being.* Baton Rouge: Louisiana State University Press, 1979.

Coles, Robert. *Walker Percy: An American Search.* Boston: Little, Brown, 1978.

Crowley, J. Donald, and Sue Mitchell Crowley. *Critical Essays on Walker Percy.* Boston: G. K. Hall, 1989.

Lawson, Lewis, and Victor A. Kramer, eds. *Conversations with Walker Percy.* Jackson: University Press of Mississippi, 1985.

Lusher, Martin. *The Sovereign Wayfarer: Walker Percy's Diagnosis of the Malaise.* Baton Rouge: Louisiana State University Press, 1972.

Poteat, Patricia L. *Walker Percy and the Old Modern Age.* Baton Rouge: Louisiana State University Press, 1985.

Taylor, Jerome. *In Search of Self: Life and Death and Walker Percy.* Cambridge, Mass.: Cowley, 1986.

Bruce L. Edwards

JAYNE ANNE PHILLIPS

Born: Buckhannon, West Virginia
July 19, 1952

Principal Literary Achievement

Phillips, recognized as one of the most gifted writers of her generation, portrays the changes occurring in contemporary family relationships as reflections of a changing society.

Biography

Jayne Anne Phillips was born in Buckhannon, West Virginia, a pleasant middle-class town, on July 19, 1952, the middle child, between brothers, of Russell R. Phillips, a contractor, and Martha Jane Thornhill, a teacher. Phillips attended West Virginia University, where she earned a B.A. degree, and was graduated in 1974 magna cum laude. Four years later, she earned a master of fine arts degree from the University of Iowa's renowned writer's program. Phillips taught briefly at Humboldt State University and then held the Fanny Howe Chair of Letters at Brandeis University and the post of adjunct associate professor of English at Boston University. In 1985, she married Mark Brian Stockman, a physician.

Phillips began writing poetry in high school. Her childhood ended abruptly in the early 1970's, when her parents were divorced and she moved away from her hometown to begin college nearby. Her poetry was published while she still attended the University of West Virginia as an undergraduate. Only after graduation did she begin writing fiction, creating highly compressed stories in which her poetic discipline shone through. Phillips has continued in this vein, using carefully chosen words and images to their potential. She has tended to write, not from an outline as novelists often do, but line by line, as do poets.

In 1978, Phillips made the most of an opportunity when she gave Delacorte editor Seymour Lawrence a copy of *Sweethearts* (1976), one of her early chapbooks. Lawrence, within weeks, wrote Phillips a postcard with the career-launching message, "Bring your stories to Boston." This contact led to Phillips' first trade publication, *Black Tickets* (1979), which met with widespread praise and critical acclaim. In this collection of twenty-seven works, ranging in length from single-paragraph vignettes to well-developed short stories, Phillips displayed her talent at giving char-

acters from all walks of life, including the unsavory, an empathetic voice, while managing to avoid any traces of sentimentality.

Phillips gathered much of her sharp insight into the underworld in 1972, when she and a girlfriend hitchhiked from Cape Cod, Massachusetts, to California, and back again. The writer once remarked in an interview how during that odyssey she "learned what it meant to be afraid," as the twenty-year-old girls narrowly escaped physical violence several times.

In the novel *Machine Dreams* (1984), her second major publication, Phillips continued to create empathetic characters and again received largely favorable criticism. The film rights to her novel were purchased by actress Jessica Lange.

Phillips has won numerous awards for both her trade publications and chapbook stories. In 1977, 1979, and 1983, she was awarded the Pushcart Prize for four short stories. The Coordinating Council of Literary Magazines gave Phillips the Fels Award in fiction in 1978; she received National Endowment for the Arts fellowships in 1978 and 1985, and in 1979 she was awarded the St. Lawrence Award for fiction. A milestone was reached in her career in 1980 when she received the Sue Kaufman Prize for First Fiction from the American Academy and Institute of Arts and Letters, followed in that same year by the O. Henry Award. In 1981, Phillips won a Bunting Institute fellowship from Radcliffe College. Upon publication of her first novel, *Machine Dreams*, in 1984, Phillips won a National Book Critics Circle Award nomination, an American Library Association Notable Book citation, and *The New York Times* Best Books of 1984 citation.

Analysis

The long list of awards with which Phillips has been honored indicates how favorable the critics have been from the onset of her career. *Black Tickets* was released with advance praise from nine writers emblazoned on the back cover, a prophesy of what was to come, even from well-known critics, such as popular contemporary novelist John Irving. Irving noted that Phillips is "especially effective with sex and drugs."

Black Tickets, Phillips' first trade publication, contains three distinct subgenres: brief (as short as a single paragraph) literary exercises, more developed interior monologues of desperate or deranged individuals, and fully developed short stories about ordinary people struggling with family relationships. Irving, along with the majority of Phillips' critics, believed that, although her shocking shorter pieces and interior monologues were evidence of Phillips' extraordinary talent, her best work was done in the longer stories that explored the nature of the modern American family.

Phillips' preoccupation with generations of families and changing gender roles emerged as major themes in her first novel, *Machine Dreams*. This work displayed Phillips' talent at giving a range of characters unique and believable voices, which matured appropriately as the characters lost their youthful innocence and their world changed around them—inexplicably, yet permanently. During another interview, Phillips explained that her source for such honest, first-person prose, "has to do with ear, with listening in a particular way to how people talk and being able to expand on fragments of heard talk, staying with the sound and then enlarging it."

Because her main subject matter has been either social outcasts or the decay of American societal values, Phillips could not have avoided planting political messages within her fiction. Phillips' concern with the differences between the 1960's and the successive decades remains evident in her work. She has contrasted the community-oriented 1960's with the 1970's, when young people no longer rallied around unifying causes such as civil rights and lacked national heroes such as Martin Luther King, Jr. During an interview, she capsulized her perspective on changes between two decades in this example: "Kids dropping acid [in the 1970's] did it to obliterate themselves, not to have a religious experience." In a technologically advanced, mechanized world, Phillips has witnessed a decline in the richness of life. With more mechanization having pervaded Americans' lives during the 1980's, Phillips does not predict improvement over time. In the same interview, she continued: "In the '70's there was still enough security so that people felt they could be floaters. Now things are too shaky for that."

Her ominous perspective on modern times accounts for the shocking images of sexual deviation and drug abuse that she portrays in much of her short fiction. "Gemcrack," for example, is about a mass murderer, and even the title of "Lechery" indicates its unsavoriness. This focus on the most negative aspects of contemporary society contrasts sharply with Phillips' loving portrayal of a nostalgic past in *Machine Dreams*, complete with drive-in hamburger joints and the post-World War II American love affair with luxurious automobiles.

Phillips has been classed as a regional writer after the fashion of distinguished Southern storytellers Flannery O'Connor and Eudora Welty, whom she has claimed as two of her influences. While Phillips has objected to the term "regional," claiming that she, as well as her role models, have far more universal appeal than the classification "regional writer" would indicate, she has accepted the high praise of being grouped with these masters of fiction.

HOME

First published: 1975
Type of work: Short story

A young woman's return home makes her divorced mother confront her daughter's and her own sexuality.

Phillips' only story in the *Black Tickets* collection with any degree of humor, "Home" was considered by many critics to be the best work in the book. In reference to "Home," John Irving noted that Phillips "shows us the good instinct to tell stories in which something that matters takes place."

What matters to Irving, then, is telling the story of the ordinary American family. "Home" has all the typical elements of one of three distinct story types appearing in *Black Tickets*. It is of conventional short story length, and the plot depicts the tragedies that occur in ordinary family relationships. There is the typical protagonist in her middle twenties, a divorced parent, and strained conversation revealing unresolved conflict. These elements reveal Phillips' interest in the psychological connections and gaps found in generations of families.

With this well-crafted first-person narrative, Phillips brings her reader into an average American living room where an ordinary, uncelebrated homecoming takes place. The mother watches the evening news and worries about Walter Cronkite getting cancer while she warns her neglectful daughter that she "will be sorry when she is gone." Guilt plays a vital role in this mother-daughter relationship. The narrator's divorced mother reminisces about how devoted she was to the care of her own invalid mother, expressing, but never actually admitting, her hurt at being neglected by her own daughter. Unfulfilled needs for affection and for sex, nonexistent in her life for years, are interwoven inseparably with this guilt.

The conflict occurs when the narrator invites a former lover to visit. The mother overhears their lovemaking, which brings forth a cornucopia of negative emotions— embarrassment, guilt, shame, possibly even jealousy—to the surface. Confronting her daughter, she reveals the complexity of her mixed-up emotions: "I don't know what to do about anything."

Phillips' tendency to politicize is found even in this short story. The narrator's lover and mother both have visible scars, his from a botched napalm attack and hers from a bungled breast surgery. These healing physical scars foil the festering wounds lying below the surface. They are the result of divorce, or of the Vietnam War, hidden wounds hinting at the general deterioration of family life in the post-1960's era. Phillips' exploration of her generation's rootlessness and the difficulty of going "home" reflects modern times with the visual and aural acuity typically found in her work.

LECHERY

First published: 1975
Type of work: Short story

A teenaged prostitute who entices virginal young boys offers a glimpse into her life.

"Lechery" lends the reader insight into the gritty "urban underbelly" that Phillips encountered as she hitchhiked across the United States in the early 1970's. Several works in *Black Tickets* fall into this genre of disturbing stories in which the cruel side of life is examined, where people are denied unconditional love and beauty.

Combining an acute ear and eye for the most sordid details with her creative imagination, Phillips wrote a fully believable and horrifying narrative. She employed the first-person voice to enable the reader to identify with the wretched narrator, thus instilling the fear that this grotesque could have been the reader under similar circumstances.

In this and in similar stories, Phillips has given a voice to the inarticulate. In this narrative, told by a fourteen-year-old prostitute who molests little boys, the narrator recounts how, two years before, she was purchased by two sexually perverse drug addicts for thirty dollars. The simple, powerful prose overflows with sensually shocking images of the narrator's early life in the orphanage with her friend Natalie and of her current life as a peddler of pornography, a sexual toy for deranged adult drug addicts, and a seductress of virginal, preadolescent schoolboys. "I get them before they get pimples, I get them those first few times the eyes flutter and get strange," the narrator tells the reader without a hint of shame or embarrassment.

The narrator lacks any reason to feel guilt or shame because of her life-style. She opens with the following justification: "Though I have no money I must give myself what I need." Because it is for her own survival that she lives as she does, one of her final comments, "I'm pure, driven snow," is understandable, and even a relief to the reader, who has been pulled into her desperate world so quickly and has, by Phillips' design, identified with the narrator so strongly.

MACHINE DREAMS

First published: 1984
Type of work: Novel

A forty-year portrait of the Hampson family explores changes in the fabric of American society from the pre-World War II era to the years of the Vietnam War.

Phillips' first novel, *Machine Dreams*, focused on one very ordinary West Virginia family, the Hampsons. Phillips chose to write her first novel about the less shocking of her preoccupations in *Black Tickets*: generations of families and the changing roles of men and women. Written from many perspectives, the novel combines first-person narrative (each family member is given a chance to speak) and third-person narrative and includes two chapters of letters sent home from soldiers at war.

The letters are an effective tool that Phillips uses to reveal her interest in generations. First, one reads Mitch Hampson's letters written from boot camp, then from various stations in the Pacific during World War II, where he operates heavy machinery to bulldoze airstrips and sometimes to bury corpses. Later, one reads a modernized version of those same letters, this time written by Billy, Mitch's son. These letters are written from boot camp, then from South Vietnam, where he is a helicopter machine gunner.

The lives of the female generations also reflect, mirrorlike, upon one another. Jean Hampson, who, emotionally and financially, holds her family together until the children are grown, inherited her mother's strength, which she then passes on to Danner, her daughter. "I always assumed I'd have my own daughter," Jean tells Danner in the opening chapter. "I picked out your name when I was twelve, and saved it. In a funny way, you were already real. I never felt that way about your brother." The mother-daughter bond, regardless of the generation gap, is strong indeed.

Although both play a role, generation gaps have less impact than do gender gaps in the Hampson family. Billy inherits his father's fascination with machines as well as his selective telling of events from the war zone to female family members. "Of course you will not say anything about this to the family," writes Mitch to a male friend in the early 1940's. Billy follows in his father's footsteps as, from Vietnam, he writes pleasantries to his mother. He breaks out of his father's mold, however, when he depicts the brutal truth in letters to his sister. This departure from machismo also testifies to the strength of the siblings' relationship, made stronger by their parents' unhappy marriage.

While Phillips tells the story of the Hampsons' decline, she also tells the story of changing American life-styles and values from the Depression to the early 1970's. Jean contrasts her early life with Danner's as she explains that "Life wasn't like it is now. . . . [A]ll this I hear about drugs. We had the Depression and then the war; we didn't have to go looking for something to happen."

Phillips intended *Machine Dreams* to carry a political undercurrent, one of the novel's only facets that met with criticism in several reviews. Yet Phillips believes that all good writing is political, whether intentionally so or not. She imbued her novel with the nostalgia—parking dates, a dance at the community swimming pool, a summer waitressing job carrying heavy trays, heaving petting in the front seat of a car—that makes the Hampsons a family that is representative of middle America. Even if readers' own families do not resemble the Hampsons in the least, the family of that era as represented in television and motion pictures makes it possible for everyone to identify with the shattered dreams of the Hampson family.

Summary

A poet become short story writer become novelist, Jayne Anne Phillips has combined the disciplines of all three fields to create compact prose filled with imagery and with sometimes familiar, sometimes strange, yet always distinctive voices. Her stories of family life smell of Americana, while her tales of the deprived and depraved reek of the America that is ignored.

Phillips offers the reader an honest look at how contemporary issues have negatively affected the core of American society, the family. Her stories, while not cheerful, explore sensitive issues in an age of mechanization.

Bibliography

Baker, James N. "Being Led by a Whisper." *Newsweek*, October 22, 1979, 117-118.

Burke, Jeffrey. "Ineffable Pleasures." *Harper's Magazine* 259 (September, 1979): 99-100.

Irving, John. "Stories with Voiceprints." Review of *Black Tickets*, by Jayne Anne Phillips. *The New York Times Book Review*, September 30, 1979, pp. 13, 28.

"Jayne Anne Phillips." In *Dictionary of Literary Biography Yearbook, 1980*, edited by Karen L. Rood. Detroit: Gale Research, 1981.

Kakutani, Michiko. "Books of the Times." *The New York Times*, June 12, 1984, p. C17.

Phillips, Robert. "Recurring Battle Scars." *Commonweal* III (October, 1984): 567-568.

Prescott, Peter S. "A Debut to Celebrate." *Newsweek*, October 22, 1979, 117.

Straub, Deborah A., ed. *Contemporary Authors*. New rev., vol. 24. Detroit: Gale Research, 1988.

Tyler, Anne. "The Wounds of War." *The New York Times Book Review*, July 1, 1984, p. 3.

Yardley, Jonathan. "Jayne Anne Phillips: West Virginia Breakdown." *The Washington Post*, June 24, 1984, p. 3.

Leslie Pearl

SYLVIA PLATH

Born: Boston, Massachusetts
October 27, 1932
Died: London, England
February 11, 1963

Principal Literary Achievement

A leader in the "confessional school of poetry" that reigned in the 1960's and 1970's, Plath erased the barriers between poetry and one's most private life.

Biography

Sylvia Plath was born in Boston, Massachusetts, to Otto and Aurelia Plath on October 27, 1932. Her father, whose distorted and terrifying image dominates so much of her work, was a Polish German who taught at Boston University and whose beekeeping provided another central symbol for his daughter's poetry. Her mother, of Austrian descent, was an educated woman who later taught at the college level. Warren Plath, Sylvia's only sibling, was born on April 27, 1935. For most of Plath's early childhood the family lived in Winthrop, a seaside town near Boston, and as a child Sylvia spent much of her time exploring, collecting shells, and examining marine life. In her thinly veiled autobiographical novel, *The Bell Jar* (1963), she was to have her heroine, Esther Greenwood, reminisce about the happiness she had felt "running along the hot white beaches with my father the summer before he died," a feeling Esther could capture later only in almost uncontrollable headlong plunges.

The major event in Sylvia Plath's life was the death of her father, which occurred as a result of pulmonary embolism following an injury complicated by diabetes. His death occurred in November, 1940, when she was eight. The picture she paints of him throughout her work is not usually the idyllic memory of *The Bell Jar*, however, but a bitter assault. He becomes a Nazi, a demon, a devil—even a demon lover calling her to the grave. After her father's death, Plath distinguished herself as a student and a precociously talented writer. She won numerous school and local prizes and managed to publish her first short story, "And Summer Will Not Come Again," in the August, 1950, issue of *Seventeen*, just as she was entering college.

Plath went to Smith College on a double scholarship, one from the Wellesley Smith Club and the other a private fund endowed by Olive Higgins Prouty, the author of *Stella Dallas* (1922), who was later to help pay for Plath's medical treatment and was uncharitably caricatured in *The Bell Jar*. In August, 1951, her short story

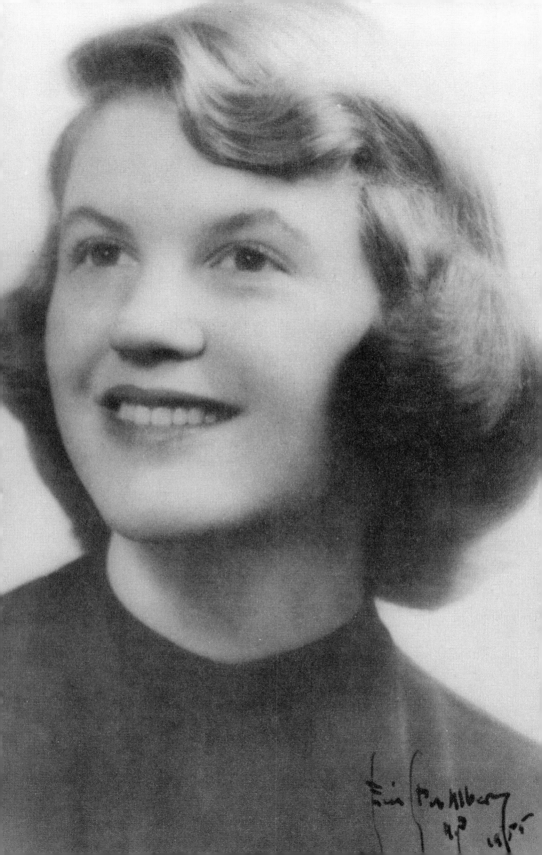

"Sunday at the Mintons" won *Mademoiselle*'s fiction contest; Plath also won great recognition at Smith for her poetry and her scholarship. In 1952, she won a guest editorship in *Mademoiselle*'s College Board Contest, giving her the experience in New York that she later recorded in *The Bell Jar*, and she had poems accepted by *Mademoiselle* and *Harper's*. From the outside, things seemed to be going perfectly.

Pressures were building up, however, and to Plath the few disappointments (such as not being received into a writing class she wanted) outweighed her many achievements. She sank into a serious depression and, after ineffective psychiatric treatment, attempted suicide in the summer of 1953 by hiding herself away in a womb-like hole in her cellar and taking an overdose of sleeping pills. This confusion of birth and death is a major theme in her novel and poems. Discovered and hospitalized, Plath was given electroshock treatments and psychotherapy and was discharged as cured. She returned to Smith for a triumphant final year, a year studded with prizes and publications and crowned by a scholarship to the University of Cambridge.

At Cambridge, Sylvia met the English poet Ted Hughes, a man whose decisiveness and authoritarianism reminded her of her father; she married him in London on June 16, 1956. The couple lived in Cambridge until the spring of 1957, when they moved to Boston and Plath became an instructor at Smith. Plath really wanted to be a writer and not an academic, however; she quit her post to spend her time revising and resubmitting her much-rejected poetry book, and then in December 1959 moved back to England with Hughes. Their first child, Freda, was born there in April, 1960; after a miscarriage and various medical problems, Plath became pregnant again. To her great satisfaction, her book of poetry, *The Colossus and Other Poems* (1960), was finally accepted by William Heinemann Limited for publication. In addition, she received a Eugene F. Faxton Fellowship to complete the novel she had begun about her nervous breakdown; the family was then living in Croton, Devon, a rural town outside London. By the time her son Nicholas was born in January of 1962, Plath was well at work on *The Bell Jar*.

Her marriage was going poorly, however, and she and her husband decided to separate in the fall of 1962. She moved back to London with the children and was overjoyed to find free an apartment in what had once been W. B. Yeats's house. Always a believer in signs and portents, she felt that this was surely an indication of coming good fortune. Although *The Bell Jar* was published in January of 1963, however, the reviews were not what she had wished, and the physical conditions of Yeats's house were not conducive to optimism. The apartment was cold and draughty, pipes froze, and Plath could not get a telephone installed. Ironically, at this time when she was despairing and often ill, she was driven to write almost furiously—she scribbled intense, desperate poems each morning before the children woke up. "The blood jet is poetry," she said in one of these poems, "There's no stopping it." She did find a way to stop the blood jet. On February 11, 1963, she placed towels on the floor to prevent seepage into the other room where the children were sleeping, and she turned on the gas. She died at thirty, leaving her most acutely painful autobiographical poems to be published posthumously in *Ariel* (1965), *Winter Trees* (1971), and *Crossing the Water* (1971).

Analysis

Sylvia Plath's poetry has a two-level audience—some readers are drawn to her work for its sensationalism, its willingness to share details of nervous breakdowns, sexual embarrassments, attempts at suicide. This aspect of her work has resulted in many imitators. On another level, her poems and stories, by showing the reactions of a raw-nerved, hyperaware individual to an indifferent if not hostile environment, provide a sensitive interpretation of universal vulnerabilities. Plath's strongest poems invoke archetypal figures and stories in a way that re-energizes early childhood images of the evil parent, the human sacrifice, and all forms of death-bringers.

The subject of Plath's poetry is Plath. Her feelings for her loved and hated father, her suicide attempts, her anger at the world and her existential loneliness are described in sharp detail. The poems rage or speak up faintly from a well of despair. Occasionally they scream a furious triumph over the forces that oppress her. These outcries are direct and unmediated by art, as the final lines of the devastating poem "Daddy" illustrate:

> There's a stake in your fat black heart
> And the villagers never liked you.
> They are dancing and stamping on you.
> They always *knew* it was you.
> Daddy, daddy, you bastard, I'm through.

Many of the poems express the need for purification—for a death followed by a rebirth. "Lady Lazarus" touches on her suicide attempt at twenty and looks toward her third, successful attempt at thirty; including a near-drowning at ten, the poem ritualizes suicide as an act of purification. The poem is cited by those who argue that Plath did not intend her third attempt to be successful, but wanted to be found just in time and revived, as she had been before. "Dying," she says, "Is an art, like everything else./ I do it exceptionally well." It could be said that Plath's basic subject is the art of dying.

Stylistically, the poems changed as her emotional intensity increased. Her first poems were carefully structured, delicately rhymed pieces, but she soon learned to do violence to form to produce tough, forceful poems that were spare and cutting. Her early poems were characterized by sharply detailed nature imagery, with verbs carrying much of the burden of description.

"Point Shirley," essentially an elegy for her grandmother, begins

> From Water-Tower Hill to the brick prison
> The shingle booms, bickering under
> The sea's collapse.
> Snowcakes break and welter.

Later on, after the grandmother's absence is noted, the poet returns to the natural scene with more verb-dominated detail:

> The waves'
> Spewed relics clicker masses in the wind,
>
> Grey waves the stub-necked eiders ride.

The rhymes are almost-rhymes (collapse/ leaps/ chips; against/ danced/ lanced). The off-rhymes and the alternating long and short lines suggest the rhythm of the sea, a movement that provides a subtle counterpoint to the argument of the poem.

The later poems are more direct, more personal, and far less pictorial. Nature images are pressed casually into the service of an emotional immediacy:

> I am incapable of more knowledge.
> What is this, this face
> So murderous in its strangle of branches?

The last poems are dominated by images of wounds and mutilations, surgical operations, Holocaust victims, illness. The final poems become incandescent in their suffering; Jew and Nazi become a metaphor for the relationship between Plath and her dead father and in fact the whole male, oppressive society. The natural world that was at first Plath's delight and absorption now becomes permeated with human pain, as in "Poppies in October":

> Even the sun-clouds this morning cannot manage such skirts,
> Nor the woman in the ambulance
> Whose red heart blooms through her coat so astoundingly.

All barriers between the metaphoric and the real, the interior and exterior world blur as Plath approaches her final act of self-deliverance.

Plath's autobiographical novel, *The Bell Jar*, shows the same confrontation between the hypersensitive female persona, Esther Greenwood, and a hostile world. Written in England during the period after the birth of her children, the novel describes the events that led up to her breakdown in 1953. Particularly vivid in her novel is the growing feeling of detachment from herself that she must have shared with her protagonist: Esther pictures herself as "a hole in the ground," "a small black dot," a vacancy. When she looks at herself in mirrors, she does not recognize herself, but sees the image as someone else.

Like the poetry, *The Bell Jar* is dominated by death and the oppressive male world that pulls Esther deathward. Esther's deterioration is chronicled from her New York experience, which Plath experienced when she won the *Mademoiselle* contest, back to Boston, where she sank deeper and deeper into depression, through her institutionalization and treatment, up to her release from the asylum as cured. The style reflects the content, as scenes become shorter and more disconnected to reflect Esther's progressive loss of contact with reality. The poems' preoccupation with purification and their confounding of life with death are also present in the novel. These recurrent, even obsessive themes are perhaps most directly described when Esther tells what happened when she tried to commit suicide, as Sylvia Plath herself had done at twenty, by climbing into a hole in the cellar:

> Cobwebs touched my face with the softness of moths. Wrapping my black coat around me like my own sweet shadow, I unscrewed the bottle of pills and started taking them. . . .
>
> The silence drew off, baring the pebbles and shells and all the tatty wreckage of my life. Then, at the rim of vision, it gathered itself, and in one sweeping tide, rushed me to sleep.

THE BELL JAR

First published: 1963
Type of work: Novel

An individualistic and egalitarian-minded young woman struggles with the suffocating conformism of the 1950's.

In *The Bell Jar*, the veil of fiction over the story of Plath's own life is so thin that her mother fought its publication in the United States, writing to Harper & Row that "practically every character represents someone—often in caricature—whom Sylvia loved; each person had given freely of time, thought, affection, and, in one case, financial help during those agonizing six months of breakdown in 1953." Nevertheless, the story has the appeal of the novel, and it uses the conventions of fiction in the structuring of the experience it narrates.

The heroine, Esther Greenwood, is looking back (like Holden Caulfield, J. D. Salinger's even more famous misfit) on the events leading up to her mental collapse. As in Salinger's *The Catcher in the Rye* (1951), readers will be split as to what is to blame for the breakdown—the self or the world. Through Esther's eyes are recorded the events of the early 1950's: McCarthyism, "I Like Ike," the electrocution of the Rosenbergs, the relative tameness of 1950's New York City. To the eyes of Esther, come to New York as the winner of a magazine contest to be guest editor of *Ladies' Day*, the real world is exclusively male and has no place for her. Women writers create fluffy fashion articles. Women English majors should learn shorthand. The only other option readily available, wifehood, is little more than death-in-life, a self-obliteration as certain as the fate of the rug her boyfriend's mother made out of pretty scraps, then put on the floor to become "soiled and dull and indistinguishable from any mat you would buy for a dollar in the five and ten."

The richness of detail re-creates the 1950's in their patriotism and naïveté. The standard female responses to the time period are represented in Esther's fellow contest winners, such as the innocent optimist Betsey, and Hilda, the right-wing zealot with a flair for housewifely economies. At least partly because Esther believes that there is no use for her talents, which are not in one of the standard female lines, she goes into a decline. Her inability to accept any accepted woman's role is demonstrated symbolically in a wonderful scene in which she throws her new clothes one by one out the hotel window, so that "flutteringly, like a loved one's ashes, the grey scraps were ferried off, to settle here, there, exactly where I would never know, in the dark heart of New York."

Back at her home in Boston, the depression deepens, and flashbacks into her experience with her boyfriend and her college years give more insight into the nature of her alienation. She is unable to accept that there is a double standard for sexual behavior—that her boyfriend Buddy is expected to be sexually experienced and she is not. In all the relationships she either sees or participates in, the woman appears to be a puppet or plaything for the man. Yet she does not want to give up her sexuality for her art, either. Unable to choose between mutually exclusive options, she is paralyzed. Trying to write a novel about someone trying to write a novel, she creates one paragraph. She investigates far-fetched career and education possibilities and gives up. She never changes her clothes. She is in a state of clinical depression, just as Plath herself was after her trip to New York for *Mademoiselle.* Her thoughts turn to suicide.

As the protagonist becomes more and more fragmented, the novel begins to mirror her inner world, its scenes becoming shorter and transitions being suppressed so that scenes are juxtaposed as they are in Esther's mind. The jumps in time and space are a key to Esther's inner world, a world in which birth is death, death is birth, and the ultimate loss of self is both the greatest fear and greatest desire. The association of death with freedom occurs again and again. Headlong speed, careening wildly down a hill on skis, is the only thing that makes Esther happy. The chance of getting out of herself, away from the prison of self that is represented by the bell jar of the title, comes with this speed; the mad flight is followed by a crash and pain—a small death.

More and more obsessed with death, Esther collects news clipping about suicides and reacts to only that part of any conversation that could possibly be related to suicide. An important element of the whole novel, the humor of the self-deprecating narrator is ever-present in the descriptions of the events leading up to the major suicide attempt, such as a discussion at a beach picnic in which Esther tries to get her blind date to tell her how to get at a gun:

> I rolled onto my back again and made my voice casual. "If you were going to kill yourself, how would you do it?"
> Cal seemed pleased. "I've often thought of that. I'd blow my brains out with a gun."
> I was disappointed. It was just like a man to do it with a gun. . . .
> "What kind of gun?"
> "My father's shotgun. He keeps it loaded. . . ."
> "Does your father happen to live near Boston?" I asked idly.

After the conversation, Esther does swim out and try (most ineffectively) to drown herself. The scene is followed by the flashback to an attempt to hang herself that morning—an attempt that left her "walking about with the silk cord hanging from my neck like a yellow cat's tail and finding no place to fasten it."

The true attempt, however, is described as a serious, almost mystical event: This death is a return to the womblike hole in the cellar where, after taking the pills she is swept away into darkness, purified of "the pebbles and shells and all the tatty wreckage" of her life. She is then reborn: "The chisel struck again, and the light leapt into my head, and through the thick, warm, furry dark, a voice cried, "Mother!"

The rest of the novel explores her treatment at the state hospital and at the private hospital that her novelist patroness sends her to, and it is perhaps less believable: Esther Greenwood recovers from the illness, takes charge of her life, and becomes a successful wife and mother. Her recovery is signaled by various events: She learns to admit her dislike of her mother and her mother's role; she loses her virginity, therefore making her equal to Buddy; she feels that the bell jar that had been stifling her has lifted. The final scene is the reconciliation ritual with the world. She is about to be interviewed by the doctors and dismissed from the hospital as cured. Many readers, however, will find her as lost and alienated as she was at the beginning, and will be disinclined to accept the optimistic prognosis.

The Bell Jar is a flawed novel, but it is striking in its appeal. It relies heavily on ritual, even on magic, in its obsession with exorcism, purification, and the death/rebirth cycle. It is also a Salingeresque tale of a young woman who does not accept things as they are and will not compromise. The events and realities of the 1950's are seen in sharp, grotesque detail through the curved glass of Esther's bell jar.

BLACK ROOK IN RAINY WEATHER

First published: 1960
Type of work: Poem

Unexpected, startling beauty is the gift of self-renewal that may be called miraculous.

An early work that is one of the few life-affirming Plath poems is "Black Rook in Rainy Weather," a description of a bird in a tree that uses terms of the heavenly ("angels," "radiance," and "miracles") to describe things of this earth. One of the most frequently anthologized early poems, it demonstrates the gift of the visual. Like many of the poems in *The Colossus*, it is formally controlled. It uses a unique stanza form of five-line stanzas with repeating rhymes of ABCDE throughout the poem; off-rhymes are common. (For example, the A-rhymes are "there," "fire," "desire," "chair," "honor," "flare," "fear," and "occur" from the beginning to the end of the poem.) This pattern helps to convey the impression that this is a diminished world with haphazard arrangements.

Seeing a "wet black rook/ Arranging and rearranging its feathers in the rain," the observer reflects that she no longer looks for intention in nature. She no longer believes that there is some kind of "design" in the world, that natural phenomena bear God's signature. She admits to wanting some kind of communication with the Other: "I desire,/ Occasionally, some backtalk/ From the mute sky." Yet she is willing to accept the physical delight of the occasional natural revelation in its place, the "minor light" that may transform an ordinary object into a vision: "As if a celestial burning took/ Possession of the most obtuse objects now and then."

It is these unexpected transformations, these "hallowing[s]" of the daily, that redeem time "by bestowing largesse, honor,/ One might say love." The rook with its shining feathers may be reminiscent of Gerard Manley Hopkins' windhover, whose beauty expresses God's grandeur, but the rook's transcendence is less clearly attributed. Still, it is a redemption for the watcher, who hopes to be relieved from boredom and despair by beauty.

The poem concludes that despite the dullness of the ordinary, miracles do occur "If you care to call those spasmodic/ Tricks of radiance miracles." The observer realizes that it is her part to be observant, to endure "the long wait for the angel,/ For that rare, random descent." Even this poem is not overly optimistic: The scene is rainy, the weather "desultory," and the season one "of fatigue." The miracles of transformation can be neither predicted nor controlled. Nevertheless, they do occur, and they redeem time from emptiness, filling it with purpose, even "love." Even with this limited affirmation, the poem becomes one of Plath's more positive statements.

THE DISQUIETING MUSES

First published: 1960
Type of work: Poem

The poet is graced not by the traditional figures of inspiration but by the bizarre distorted visitors of a surrealist painting.

Written in 1957, when most of Plath's work was still in formal verse, "The Disquieting Muses" is an unnerving explanation of alienation and otherness. The title, as Plath herself explained, refers to a painting by the artist Georgio de Chirico—a painting of three faceless dressmaker's dummies with elongated heads who cast eerie shadows in a strange half-light. "The dummies suggest a twentieth century version of other sinister trios of women—the Three Fates, the witches in Macbeth, de Quincey's sisters of madness," she commented. The equation suggests that the poet associates women, distortions, inspiration, magic, and poetry.

The poem is written in eight-line stanzas containing roughly four stresses per line and some rhyme, notably rhyme of the fifth and seventh line in each stanza. The poem is addressed to "Mother," who tried to teach her daughter a limited and accepted art, telling her stories of witches who "always/ Got baked into gingerbread" and praising her piano and ballet exercises. This mother, too, tried to teach her children how to keep irrational forces at bay, chanting at the hurricane winds that threatened to blow in the windows. The power of unreason is too strong, however; the art it engenders too compelling.

Like Plath's other parent poems, this one blames the parent at least in part for the situation of the poet. Mother failed to invite some "illbred aunt" or "unsightly cousin" to the christening, thus provoking the anger of the uninvited. The daughter is thus set apart, unable to continue the mother-daughter tradition of benign, trivial art. She could not dance with the other schoolgirls in the "twinkle-dress" but "heavy-footed, stood aside/ In the shadow cast by my dismal-headed/ Godmothers, and you cried and cried."

The conclusion of the poem indicates that the girl is still surrounded by her other-worldly company, the distorted muses, who are witches, fates, visitors from the world of madness. She indicates that she has learned not to betray her difference: "[N]o frown of mine/ Will betray the company I keep." The surrealist painting is reminiscent of Salvador Dali's deathscapes, although not so explicit as they in its message. The poem suggests that to be an artist is to look at eternities and infinities, and that this gift—in the speaker's case, caused in part by her mother's oversight— is a curse rather than a blessing.

STINGS

First published: 1965
Type of work: Poem

The bees sting a bystander in the transfer of a hive; this shakeup in the bee world facilitates the renewal of the queenship, a renewal in which the speaker participates.

One of a series of poems based on her father's (and subsequently her own) knowledge of beekeeping, "Stings" uses the behavior of bees within their hive as an allegory for her own perennial obsession of death and renewal. A free-verse poem, "Stings" describes the transfer of the bees to the woman who is their new owner. During this transfer, the bees sting a third person, a scapegoat figure; the stinging of the scapegoat enables the hive to renew itself and replace or awaken its sleeping queen.

In this hive there are drudges, "unmiraculous women" who are only interested in things of the household/hive, and there is a sleeping queen. The speaker refuses to identify with the drudges: "I am no drudge/ Though for years I have eaten dust/ And dried plates with my dense hair." She identifies with the queen, old and worn out, or more accurately with the queenship: The queen dies and is replaced by another queen, but the queenship is immortal, going through generation after generation.

When the bystander is stung, he takes away the pain and exorcises the male at once. The bees that stung him—they are presumably a part of her too—"thought death was worth it"; their sacrifice was needed to exorcise the male. The rebirth, or recovery, follows: "I/ Have a self to recover, a queen." Now that the scapegoat is gone, the queenship, glorious, can revive, with power and dominance and nothing of the drudge:

> More terrible than she ever was, red
> Scar in the sky, red comet
> Over the engine that killed her—
> The mausoleum, the wax house.

This poem, written a year before "Daddy," expresses much of the same theme, but here the theme is presented through the metaphor of the hive. The hive expends part of itself to expel the male and free the queen. The queen, liberated by the removal of the male, is triumphantly empowered.

DADDY

First published: 1965
Type of work: Poem

The dead father who has suffocated his daughter for thirty years of her life is exorcised.

"Daddy" has an ironically affectionate title, for this poem is a violent, discordant attack on the dead parent. One of the poems Plath wrote in the feverishly active last six months of her life, "Daddy" is a reworking of the evil-father theme so prominent in her poems. Because her father died when he still had mythic power to the child, the woman must deflate and exorcise the father figure somehow. She must go through a symbolic killing of the powerful ghost in order to be free.

In contrast to the subtle rhythms of her earlier work, this poem's movement is direct and obvious. It uses harsh, insistent rhyme to hammer its message home. Its banging, jangling rhythms unnerve the reader and lodge in the mind. It relies on one repeated rhyme, an "oo" sound that becomes a cry of pain. Read aloud, the poem sounds like a chant, a ritual chant of exorcism and purification. In this poem and some others, Plath seems to be using words for their apotropaic value—as charms to ward off evil.

A series of metaphors presents the relationship between father and daughter in graphically negative terms. Progressively throughout the poem, he is a "black shoe" in which she has "lived like a foot" for thirty years; he is a Nazi and she a Jew; he is a devil and she his victim; he is a vampire who drinks her blood. The vampire and the victim are perhaps the most telling images, for she sees him as a dead man draining her living blood, calling from the grave for her to join him. When she believes that she has broken his thrall, she announces victoriously, "The black telephone's off at the root,/ the voices just can't worm through," mingling images of telephone and grave.

The poem telescopes the events of Plath's life in her recurrent pattern of contamination and purification. The father was unreachable when alive; she could not talk to him: "The tongue stuck in my jaw," the speaker says. "It stuck in a barb wire snare./ Ich, ich, ich, ich." The repetition of the German word for "I" expresses that she could not articulate herself and establish her individuality, and it reinforces the German-Jew image while sounding like something flapping, painfully ensnared. "I was ten when they buried you," she says (inaccurately—Plath was eight when her father died). "At twenty I tried to die/ And get back, back, back to you," she continues. Unable to find and escape him simultaneously that way, she tried a kind of voodoo: She married a man like her father and separated from him, thus "killing" both the husband and the father. The end of the poem is a triumphant assertion of rejection and freedom: "Daddy, daddy, you bastard, I'm through."

Like the ending of *The Bell Jar*, this triumph seems to be contradicted by Plath's suicide four months later. Perhaps more accurate in reflecting her state of mind is the ambivalence in an earlier stanza:

> No God but a swastika
> So black no sky could squeak through.
> Every woman adores a Fascist,
> The boot in the face, the brute
> Brute heart of a brute like you.

MEDUSA

First published: 1965
Type of work: Poem

The monstrous, distorted mother-figure is rejected so that the self may find freedom.

As "Daddy" exorcises the powerful father, the companion poem "Medusa," written four days later, casts off the engulfing mother in order to free the emergent self. Medusa is a genus of jellyfish, and Judith Kroll has pointed out that Plath's mother's name, Aurelia, is a synonym for medusa. In this poem the scene suggests a delayed birth, a watery womb-world where the jellyfish's tentacles continue to enwind and stifle the speaker despite her desire for separation. Picturing herself as a ship chased by the medusa, she asks, "Did I escape, I wonder?" The medusa is compelling: "My mind winds to you/ Old barnacled umbilicus, Atlantic cable."

If the father is cold and distant in "Daddy," but sharply outlined and precise, in "Medusa" the mother is a blob without definition. She is "Fat and red, a placenta/ Paralysing the kicking lovers." She complains of suffocation and renounces the mother as she has the father in her desire to be herself. With the epithet "Blubbery Mary," the image slides from sea to church: "I shall take no bite of your body,/ Bottle in which I live,/ Ghastly Vatican."

The mother-medusa is swollen and grotesque; she presents a model of martyrdom and negativity whose attraction must be denied if the speaker is to be potent as an individual. Thus the poem concludes with a demand for the medusa's withdrawal:

> Green as eunuchs, your wishes
> Hiss at my sins.
> Off, off, eely tentacle!
>
> There is nothing between us.

For Plath, reaching selfhood does not involve the introjection of the parent figures but necessitates their rejection. This is the message of both "Daddy" and "Medusa."

EDGE

First published: 1965
Type of work: Poem

Perfection, for the woman who has accomplished her fate, is death.

"Edge" is dated February 5, 1963; a week after it was written, the poet was dead. It is possible to consider the poem a suicide note. The often-anthologized poem is not only a statement that the writer will commit suicide, however; it also contains subtle suggestions about the relationship between art and life and death.

"Edge" is a free-verse poem that maintains a formal appearance through its use of twenty paired lines. "The woman is perfected," begins its description of the dead woman. The reader is reminded of the "perfection" in the early poem "Medallion," in which the snake is translated by death into art: "The yardman's/ Flung brick perfected his laugh." The dead woman of "Edge," too, is a sort of artifact; endowed with the paraphernalia of tragedy, she has transcended life and become something else:

> The illusion of a Greek necessity
>
> Flows in the scrolls of her toga,
> Her bare
>
> Feet seem to be saying:
> We have come so far, it is over.

The dead children are there with her: "Each dead child coiled, a white serpent." Death is the work of art she has made of her life.

Yet the poem represents a splitting of consciousness. The moon, her muse, seems to be a symbol of mind that is detached from the individual self, and the moon "has nothing to be sad about." The poem seems to see the individual life as realized through death and turned into art through death. Yet the moon, symbol of inspiration (and of the female mind), continues to shine.

Nevertheless, although the poem may suggest some kind of immortality or transcendence through its personified moon, the image that remains with the reader from this final poem is of a deathlike stillness.

Summary

Sylvia Plath's art is a desperate dance between order and chaos, control and abandon. In its emphasis on death and rebirth, pollution and purification, it touches strings common to many readers. Her images are memorable for their violence and eerie appropriateness. Her exact, verb-dominated descriptions of the natural world and her use of the formal devices of poetry to communicate personal pain mark her work as unique. None of her many followers in the so-called confessional school of poetry so popular throughout the 1960's and 1970's achieved her intensity.

Bibliography

Aird, Eileen. *Sylvia Plath*. New York: Harper & Row, 1973.

Annas, Pamela. *A Disturbance in Mirrors: The Poetry of Sylvia Plath*. New York: Greenwood Press, 1988.

Kroll, Judith. *Chapters in Mythology: The Poetry of Sylvia Plath*. New York: Harper & Row, 1976.

Melander, Ingrid. *The Poetry of Sylvia Plath: A Study of Themes*. Stockholm: Almqvist & Wicksell, 1972.

Newman, Charles, ed. *The Art of Sylvia Plath*. Bloomington: Indiana University Press, 1970.

Tabor, Stephen. *Sylvia Plath: An Analytical Bibliography*. Westport, Conn.: Meckler, 1987.

Wagner, Linda, ed. *Sylvia Plath: The Critical Heritage*. New York: Routledge, 1988.

Janet McCann

EDGAR ALLAN POE

Born: Boston, Massachusetts
January 19, 1809
Died: Baltimore, Maryland
October 7, 1849

Principal Literary Achievement

Although best known as the author of Gothic tales, Poe's most important achievement was to provide a theoretical basis for short fiction and a critical foundation for American literature.

Biography

Edgar Allan Poe was born on January 19, 1809, in Boston, Massachusetts. His parents, David Poe, Jr., and Elizabeth Arnold Poe, were struggling actors who died while Poe was still a small child. The young Edgar was taken in by a wealthy Scottish tobacco exporter, John Allan, from whom he took his middle name. For most of his early life, Poe lived in Richmond, Virginia, with the exception of a five-year period between 1815 and 1820 when the Allan family lived in England. Back in America, Poe attended an academy until 1826, when he entered the University of Virginia. He withdrew less than a year later because of various debts, many of them from gambling, which his foster father refused to help him pay. After quarreling with Allan about these debts, Poe left for Boston in the spring of 1827, where he enlisted in the Army under the name Edgar A. Perry.

In the summer of 1827, Poe's first book, *Tamerlane and Other Poems*, signed anonymously, "A Bostonian," appeared, but neither the reading public nor the critics paid much attention to it. In January, 1829, he was promoted to the rank of sergeant major and was honorably discharged at his own request three months later. Near the end of 1829, Poe's second book, *Al Aaraaf, Tamerlane, and Minor Poems*, was published and was well received by the critics. Shortly thereafter, Poe entered West Point Academy.

After less than a year, however, either because he tired of the academy or because John Allan refused to pay his bills any longer, Poe got himself discharged from West Point by purposely neglecting his military duties. He then went to New York where, with the help of some money raised by his West Point friends, he published *Poems by Edgar A. Poe* in 1831. After moving to Baltimore, where he lived at the home of his aunt, Mrs. Clemm, and his cousin Virginia, Poe entered five short stories in a

Edgar A. Poe.

contest sponsored by the *Philadelphia Saturday Courier*. Although he did not win the prize, the newspaper published all five of the pieces. In June, 1833, he entered another contest sponsored by the *Baltimore Saturday Visiter* and this time won the prize of fifty dollars for his story, "MS. Found in a Bottle."

During the next two years, Poe continued to write stories and to try to get them published. Even with the help of a new and influential friend, John Pendleton Kennedy, a lawyer and writer, he was mostly unsuccessful. Poe's hopes for financial security became even more desperate in 1834 when John Allan died, leaving him out of his will. Kennedy finally succeeded in getting the *Southern Literary Messenger* to publish several of Poe's stories and to offer Poe the job of editor, a position that he kept from 1835 to 1837. During this time, Poe published stories and poems in the *Southern Literary Messenger*; however, it was with his extensive publication of criticism that he began to make his mark in American letters.

In 1836, Poe married his cousin, Virginia Clemm, a decision that, because of her young age and her relationship to Poe, has made him the subject of much adverse criticism and psychological speculation. In 1837, after disagreements with the owner of the *Southern Literary Messenger*, Poe moved to New York to look for editorial work. Here he completed the writing of *The Narrative of Arthur Gordon Pym* (1838), his only long fiction, a novella-length metaphysical adventure. Unable to find work in New York, Poe moved to Philadelphia and published his first important story, a Platonic romance entitled "Ligeia." In 1839, he joined the editorial staff of *Burton's Gentlemen's Magazine*, in which he published two of his greatest stories, "The Fall of the House of Usher" and "William Wilson."

In 1840, Poe left the magazine and tried, unsuccessfully, to establish his own literary magazine. He did, however, publish a collection of his stories, *Tales of the Grotesque and Arabesque* (1840). He became an editor of *Graham's Magazine*, where he published "The Murders in the Rue Morgue," in which he created the detective Auguste Dupin, the forerunner of Sherlock Holmes and numerous other private detectives in literature and film. In 1842, Poe left *Graham's Magazine* to try once again to establish his own literary magazine, but not before publishing two important pieces of criticism concerning other nineteenth century American writers: a long review of Henry Wadsworth Longfellow, in which he established his definition of poetry as being the "rhythmical creation of Beauty," and a review of Nathaniel Hawthorne, in which he proposed his definition of the short tale as being the creation of a unified effect. Between 1842 and 1844, after Poe moved to New York to join the editorial staff of the *New York Mirror*, he published many of his most important stories, such as "The Masque of the Red Death," "The Pit and the Pendulum," "The Black Cat," and two more ratiocinative stories, "The Mystery of Marie Roget" and "The Gold Bug." It was with the publication of his most famous poem, "The Raven," in 1845, that he finally achieved popular success.

Poe left the *New York Mirror* to join a weekly periodical, the *Broadway Journal*, in February, 1845, where he continued a literary war against the poet Longfellow, begun in a review written earlier for the *New York Mirror*. The series of accusations, attacks, and counterattacks that ensued damaged Poe's reputation as a critic at the very point in his career when he had established his critical genius. Poe's collection of stories, *Tales,* was published in July, 1845, to good reviews. Soon after, Poe became the sole editor of the *Broadway Journal.* In November, 1845, he published his collection *The Raven and Other Poems.*

The year 1846 marked the beginning of Poe's decline. In January, the *Broadway Journal* ceased publication, and soon after Poe was involved in both a personal scandal with two female literary "groupies" and a bitter battle with the literary establishment. Moreover, Poe's wife was quite ill, a fact that necessitated Poe's moving his family some thirteen miles outside the city to a rural cottage at Fordham. When Virginia Poe died on January 30, 1847, Poe collapsed. Although he never fully recovered from this series of assaults on his already nervous condition, in the following year he published what he considered to be the capstone of his career, *Eureka,* subtitled, *A Prose Poem,* which he presented as an examination of the origin of all things.

In the summer of 1849, Poe left for Richmond, Virginia, in the hope once more of starting a literary magazine. On September 24, he delivered a lecture on "The Poetic Principle" at Richmond in what was to be his last public appearance. From this time until he was found semiconscious on the streets of Baltimore, Maryland, little is known of his activities. He never recovered and died on Sunday morning, October 7, in Washington College Hospital.

Analysis

Edgar Allan Poe is best known as the author of numerous spine-tingling stories of horror and suspense. Poe should also be remembered, however, as the author who helped to establish and develop America's one real contribution to the world of literature—the short story form. Poe was the first writer to recognize that the short story was a different kind of fiction than the novel and the first to insist that, for a story to have a powerful effect on the reader, every single detail in the story should contribute to that effect. His stories and criticism have been models and guides for writers in this characteristically American genre up to the present time. No one who is interested in the short story form can afford to ignore his ideas or his fiction.

Poe was influential in making American literature more philosophical and metaphysical than it had been heretofore, especially in terms of the dark romanticism of Germany rather than the sometimes sentimentalized romanticism of New England Transcendentalists. Poe also helped to make periodical publishing more important in American literary culture. American writing in the mid-nineteenth century was often discouraged by the easy accessibility of English novels. Lack of copyright laws made the works of the great English writers cheaply available; thus, American writers could not compete in this genre. Periodical publishing, and the short story as the favored genre of this medium, was America's way of fighting back. Poe was an important figure in this battle to make America a literary force in world culture.

Although much of Poe's early criticism is routine review work, he began in his reviews to consider the basic nature of poetry and short fiction and to develop theoretical analyses of these two genres, drawing upon both the German criticism of A. W. Schlegel and the English criticism of Samuel Taylor Coleridge. Poe's most important contribution to criticism is his discussion of the particular generic characteristics of short fiction in his famous review of Nathaniel Hawthorne's *Twice-Told Tales* (1837). Poe makes such a convincing case for the organic unity of short fiction, argues so strongly for its dependence on a unified effect, and so clearly shows how it is more closely aligned to the poem than to the novel, that his ideas on the short tale have influenced short story writers and literary critics ever since.

In his theories of the short story, Poe argues that, whereas in long works one may be pleased with particular passages, in short pieces, the pleasure results from the perception of the oneness, the uniqueness, and the overall unity of the piece. Poe emphasizes that by "plot" he means pattern and design, not simply the temporal progression of events. It is pattern that makes the separate elements of the work meaningful, not mere realistic cause and effect. Moreover, Poe insists that only when the reader has an awareness of the "end" of the work—that is, its overall purpose—will seemingly trivial elements of the story become meaningful in its total pattern.

Poe is too often judged as being simply the author of some horror stories that many people remember vividly from their adolescent days but that few adult readers take very seriously. Moreover, Poe is often judged on the basis of errors and misunderstandings about his personality. He has been called an alcoholic, a drug addict, a hack, and a sex pervert. As a result of these errors, myths, and oversimplifications, serious readers are often reluctant to look closely at his work. There is little doubt that Edgar Allan Poe, however, both in his criticism and in his dark, metaphysically mysterious stories, helped create a literature that made American writing a serious cultural force.

THE FALL OF THE HOUSE OF USHER

First published: 1839
Type of work: Short story

A young nobleman, haunted by a family curse, buries his twin sister alive after she falls into a cataleptic trance.

"The Fall of the House of Usher" is Poe's best-known and most admired story, and rightfully so: It expertly combines in a powerful and economical way all of his most obsessive themes, and it brilliantly reflects his aesthetic theory that all the elements of a literary work must contribute to the single unified effect or pattern of the work itself. The central mystery on which the thematic structure of the story depends is the nature of Roderick Usher's illness. Although its symptoms consist of an extreme sensitivity to all sensory stimuli and a powerful unmotivated fear, nowhere does Poe suggest its cause except to hint at some dark family curse or hereditary illness.

The actual subject of the story, as is the case with most of Poe's work, is the nature of the idealized artwork and the precarious situation of the artist. Roderick, with his paintings, his musical compositions, and his poetry, is, above all, an artist. Yet it is the particular nature of his art that is inextricably tied up with his illness. Roderick has no contact with the external world that might serve as the subject matter of his art. Not only does he never leave the house, he also cannot tolerate light, sound, touch, odor, or taste. In effect, having shut down all of his senses, he has no source for his art but his own subjectivity. The narrator says that if anyone has ever painted pure idea, then Roderick is that person. As a result, Roderick has nothing metaphorically to feed upon but himself.

The house in which Roderick lives is itself like an artwork—an edifice that exists by dint of its unique structure. When the narrator first sees it, he observes that it is the combination of elements that constitutes its mystery and that a different arrangement of its particulars would be sufficient to modify its capacity for sorrowful impression. Moreover, Usher feels that it is the form and substance of his family mansion that affects his morale. He believes that, as a result of the arrangement of the stones, the house has taken on life. All these factors suggest Poe's own aesthetic theory, that the "life" of any artwork results not from its imitation of external reality, but rather from its structure or pattern.

The only hold Roderick has on the external world at all is his twin sister, who is less a real person in the story than the last manifestation of Roderick's own physical nature. By burying her, he splits himself off from actual life. Physical life is not so easily suppressed, however, and Madeline returns from her underground tomb to unite her dying body with Roderick's idealized spirit. As the story nears its horrifying climax, art and reality become even more intertwined, for as the narrator reads to Roderick from a Gothic romance, sounds referred to in the story are echoed in actuality as the entombed Madeline breaks out of her vault and stalks up the steps to confront her twin brother. Madeline, Roderick, and the house all fall into the dark tarn, the abyss of nothingness, and become as if they had never been. In Poe's aesthetic universe, the price the artist must pay for cutting himself off from the external world is annihilation.

THE MURDERS IN THE RUE MORGUE

First published: 1841
Type of work: Short story

Dupin, the great amateur detective created by Poe in this story, solves his first and most unusual case.

Experimenting with many different fictional forms, such as the Gothic tale, science fiction, occult fantasies, and satire, Poe gained great recognition in the early 1840's for his creation of a genre that has grown in popularity ever since: the so-called tale of ratiocination or detective story, which features an amateur sleuth who, by superior deductive abilities, outsmarts criminals and outclasses the police. Such stories as "The Murders in the Rue Morgue" and "The Mystery of Marie Roget" created a small sensation in America when they were first published. "The Purloined Letter," the third and final story in the Dupin series, has been the subject of much critical analysis as a model of ironic and tightly structured plot.

"The Murders in the Rue Morgue" is the most popular of the three because it combines horrifying, inexplicable events with astonishing feats of deductive reasoning. The narrator, the forerunner of Dr. Watson of the Sherlock Holmes stories, meets Auguste Dupin in this story and very early recognizes that he has a double personality, a bi-part soul, for he is both wildly imaginative and coldly analytical. The reader's first encounter with Dupin's deductive ability takes place when he seems to read his companion's mind by responding to something that the narrator has only been thinking. Dupin, as he explains the elaborate method whereby he followed the narrator's thought processes by noticing small details and associating them, is the first of a long history of fictional detectives who take great pleasure in recounting the means by which they solved a hidden mystery.

The heart of the story, as it was to become the heart of practically every traditional detective story since, is not the action of the crime but rather Dupin's extended explanation of how he solved it. The points about the murder that baffle the police are precisely those that enable Dupin to master the case: the contradiction of several neighbors who describe hearing a voice in several different foreign languages and the fact that there seems no possible means of entering or exiting the room where the murders took place. Dupin accounts for the first contradiction by deducing that the criminal must have been an animal; the second he explains by following a mode of reasoning based on a process of elimination to determine that apparent impossibilities are in reality possible after all. When Dupin reveals that an escaped orangutan did the killing, the Paris Prefect of Police complains that Dupin should mind his own business. Dupin is content to have outwitted the prefect in his own realm; descendants of Dupin have been outwitting police inspectors ever since.

THE TELL-TALE HEART

First published: 1843
Type of work: Short story

A young man kills the old man he lives with because of the old man's eye and then feels compelled to confess.

Poe is often thought to be the author of stories about mad persons and murders, but attention is seldom given to the psychological nature of the madness in his stories. "The Tell-Tale Heart," one of Poe's best-known stories about murderous madness, is also one of his most psychologically complex works. The story is told in the first-person by the killer himself, who has obviously been locked up in a prison or in an insane asylum for his crime. He begins by arguing that he is not mad and that the calm way he committed the crime and can now tell about it testify to his sanity.

The central problem of the story is the narrator's motivation for killing the old man. He begins by assuring his listeners (and readers) that he loved the old man, that he did not want his gold, and that the old man had not abused him or insulted him. There was neither object nor passion for his crime; instead, it was the old man's eye. He says that when the eye fell on him, his blood ran cold and that he made up his mind to kill the old man and rid himself of the eye forever. Because the narrator provides no explanation for his extreme aversion to the eye, the reader must try to understand the motivation for the crime, and thus for the story itself, in the only way possible—by paying careful attention to the details of the story and trying to determine what thematic relationship they have to one another.

To understand a Poe story, one must accept Poe's central dictum that every element in the work must contribute to its central effect. The determination of those elements that have most relevance to the central effect of the story, and are thus true clues rather than mere irrelevant details, is the principle that governs the communication of all information—the principle of redundancy or repetition. Because the narrator who tells the story is a man obsessed, those things that obsess him are repeated throughout the story.

In addition to the motif or theme of the eye, which lies at the center of his obsession and thus is repeated throughout, another central theme of the story is the narrator's identification with the old man. As he plots his crime by nightly placing his head inside the old man's bedroom door, he says the old man sits up in his bed listening, just as he himself has done night after night. Moreover, he says that the old man's groan is a sound he knows well, for many a night at midnight he has felt it rise up within himself. "I knew what the old man felt," he says, "and pitied him." If the reader ties these two ideas together and listens to the sound of "eye" rather than sees it, it is possible to understand the narrator's desire to rid himself of the "eye" as his desire to rid himself of "I"—that is, his own self or ego. Such a displacement of the image of an "eye" for that which it sounds like—the "I"—is not an uncommon "mistake" for the dreamlike nature of the narrator's madness.

In order to understand why the narrator might wish to destroy himself by destroying the old man—which he does indeed succeed in doing by the end of the story—one can turn back to the motifs of time and the tell-tale heart, which also dominate the story. Throughout the story, the narrator notes that the beat of the old man's heart is like the ticking of a watch. Moreover, he says, he and the old man have both listened to the "death watches" (a kind of beetle that makes a ticking sound) in the wall at night. Finally, there is the theme of the tell-tale heart itself—a heart that tells a tale. Although in the surface plot of the story, the narrator thinks that it is the old man's heart that "tells a tale" on him when the police come to check on a scream that has been reported to them, it is clear that it is his own heart he hears beating. On the psychological level of the story, however, the tale that the heart tells that so obsesses the narrator is the tale that every heart tells. That tale links the beating of the heart to the ticking of a clock, for every beat is a moment of time that brings one closer to death. Once the narrator becomes obsessed with this inevitability, he becomes obsessed with the only way one can defeat the tale of time—that is, by destroying the self, or "I," that is susceptible to time and thus death. Because the narrator cannot very well escape the time-bound death of self by killing the self, he must displace his desire to destroy the "I" by projecting it onto the "eye" of the old man with whom he identifies. Thus by destroying the "eye" he does, although indirectly, succeed in destroying the "I."

"The Tell-Tale Heart," like many of Poe's other tales, seems at first to be a simple story of madness; however, as Poe well knew, there is no such thing as "meaningless madness" in the short story. The madness of the narrator in this story is similar to the madness of other Poe characters who long to escape the curse of time and mortality but find they can do so only by a corresponding loss of the self—a goal they both seek with eagerness and try to avoid with terror.

THE CASK OF AMONTILLADO

First published: 1846
Type of work: Short story

In this sardonic revenge story, Poe undermines the plot with irony.

"The Cask of Amontillado" is one of the clearest examples of Poe's theory of the unity of the short story, for every detail in the story contributes to the overall ironic effect. The plot is relatively simple. Montresor seeks revenge on Fortunato for some unspecified insult by luring him down into his family vaults to inspect some wine he has purchased. Montresor's plot, however, to maneuver Fortunato to where he can wall him up alive, is anything but straightforward. In fact, from the very beginning, every action and bit of dialogue is characterized as being just the opposite of what is explicitly stated.

The action takes place during carnival season, a sort of Mardi Gras when everyone is in masquerade and thus appearing as something they are not. Montresor makes sure that his servants will not be at home to hinder his plot by giving them explicit orders not to leave, and he makes sure that Fortunato will follow him into the wine cellar by playing on his pride and by urging him not to go. Every time Montresor urges Fortunato to turn back for his health's sake, he succeeds in drawing him further into the snares of his revenge plot. Moreover, the fact that Montresor knows how his plot is going to end makes it possible for him to play little ironic tricks on Fortunato. For example, when Fortunato says he will not die of a cough, Montresor knowingly replies, "True, true." When Fortunato drinks a toast to the dead lying in the catacombs around them, Montresor ironically drinks to Fortunato's long life. When Fortunato makes a gesture indicating that he is a member of the secret society of Masons, Montresor claims that he is also and proves it by revealing a trowel, the sign of his plot to wall up Fortunato.

The irony of the story cuts much deeper than this, however. At the beginning, Montresor makes much of the fact that there are two criteria for a successful revenge—that the avenger must punish without being punished in return and that he must make himself known as an avenger to the one who has done him the wrong. Nowhere in the story, however, does Montresor tell Fortunato that he is walling him up to fulfill his need for revenge; in fact, Fortunato seems to have no idea why he is being punished at all. Furthermore, the very fact that Montresor is telling the story of his crime some fifty years after it was committed to one who, he says, "so well know[s] the nature of my soul," suggests that Montresor is now himself dying and confessing his crime to a priest, his final confessor.

That Montresor's crime against Fortunato has had its hold on him for the past fifty years is supported by another detail in the story, the Montresor coat of arms—a huge human foot crushing a serpent, whose fangs are embedded in the heel; the accompanying motto translates as: No one harms me with impunity. If the foot is a metonymic representation of Montresor crushing the metaphoric serpent Fortunato for his bite, then it is clear that, even though Montresor gets his revenge, the serpent continues to hold on.

The ultimate irony of the story then, is that, although Montresor has tried to fulfill his two criteria for a successful revenge, Fortunato has fulfilled them better than he has. Moreover, although Montresor now tells the story as a final confession to save his soul, the gleeful tone with which he tells it—a tone that suggests he is enjoying the telling of it in the present as much as he enjoyed committing the act in the past—means that it is not a good confession. Thus, although the story ends with the Latin phrase "rest in peace," even after fifty years Montresor will not be able to rest in peace, for his gleeful confession of his story damns him to hell for all eternity.

Although "The Cask of Amontillado" seems on the surface a relatively simple revenge story, it is in fact a highly complex story riddled with ironic reversals. Every detail in the story contributes to this central effect, and it is the overall design of the story that communicates its meaning—not some simple moral embedded within it or tacked on to the end.

THE RAVEN

First published: 1845
Type of work: Poem

A young student is visited by a raven that can only utter one ominous word.

"The Raven" is unquestionably Poe's most famous poem. After its publication, it became so well known that its refrain "nevermore" became a catchphrase repeated by people on the street. Poe, who told one friend that he thought the poem was the greatest poem ever written, was delighted one night at the theater when an actor interpolated the word into his speech and almost everyone in the audience seemed to recognize the allusion. The work remains Poe's best-known poem today partly because, in his "The Philosophy of Composition," Poe describes what he claims was the method by which the poem was composed. Whether or not that description is an accurate account of how Poe wrote the poem, it is surely a description of how Poe wished the poem to be read. Thus, Poe himself was the first, and is perhaps still the best, critic and interpreter of his own poem.

As Poe makes clear in "The Philosophy of Composition," he wished to create an effect of beauty associated with melancholy in the poem; he decided that the refrain "nevermore," uttered to a young man whose mistress has recently died, was perfectly calculated to achieve that effect. According to Poe, the basic situation, the central character, and the plot of the poem were all created as a pretext or excuse for setting up the "nevermore" refrain, to be repeated with a variation of meaning and impact each time.

The plot is a simple one: A young student is reading one stormy night in his chamber, half-dreaming about his beloved deceased mistress. He hears a tapping at his window and opens it to admit a raven, obviously someone's pet that has escaped its master, seeking shelter from the storm. The raven can speak only one word, "nevermore." When the student, amused by this incident, asks the raven questions, its reply of "nevermore" strikes a melancholic echo in his heart. Although he knows that the raven can only speak this one word, he is compelled by what Poe calls the universal human need for self-torture to ask the bird questions to which the response "nevermore" will cause his suffering to be even more intense. When this self-torture reaches its most extreme level, Poe says, the poem then naturally ends.

The sorrow of the young student and the stormy midnight hour contribute to the overall effect of the poem, but the most important feature is the sound of the refrain—a sound that is established even before the raven appears by the dead mistress' name "Lenore." The echo of the word "Lenore" by "nevermore" is further emphasized in stanza 5, when the student peers into the darkness and whispers "Lenore?" only to have the word echoed back, "Merely this and nothing more." Once the lost Lenore is projected as the source of the student's sorrow, the appearance of the raven as a sort of objectification of this sorrow seems poetically justified. When he asks the raven its name and hears the ominous word, "nevermore," the student marvels at the bird's ability to utter the word but realizes that the word has no inherent meaning or relevance. The relevance of the bird's answer depends solely on the nature of the questions or remarks the student puts to it. For example, when he says that the bird will leave tomorrow, like all his "hopes have flown before," he is startled by the seemingly relevant reply, "nevermore."

The student begins to wonder what the ominous bird "means" by repeating "nevermore." When he cries that perhaps his god has sent him respite from his sorrow and memory of Lenore, the bird's response of "nevermore" makes him call the bird "prophet" and compels him to ask it if, after death, he will clasp the sainted maiden whom the angels call Lenore; to this question he knows he will receive the reply, "nevermore." Obsessively pushing his need for self-torture to its ultimate extreme, the young man calls for the bird to take its beak from its heart and its form from his door, once again knowing what response he will receive. Although the poem is often dismissed as a cold-blooded contrivance, it is actually a carefully designed embodiment of the human need to torture the self and to find meaning in meaninglessness.

ULALUME

First published: 1847
Type of work: Poem

A young man visits the tomb of his deceased lover on the anniversary of her death.

"Ulalume" is a striking example of what Aldous Huxley characterized as the "vulgarity" of Poe's poetry when he was trying too hard to make his work poetical. It is also an example of what made critic Yvor Winters, in the most severe attack ever launched against Poe, call him an "explicit obscurantist." Winters' distaste for the poem begins with its use of unidentified places such as Weir, Auber, and ghoul-haunted woodlands, which he says are introduced merely to evoke emotion at small cost. He also claims that the violent emotion suggested by the references to Mount Yaanek and the Boreal Pole in the second stanza are not adequately motivated or accounted for. Finally, Winters argues that the subject of grief in the poem is used as a general excuse for obscure and only vaguely related emotion.

Such criticism, however, ignores Poe's critical theory that a poem should be the "rhythmical creation of Beauty" derived from those techniques that communicate the melancholy feeling of the loss of a loved one. "Ulalume" shares many characteristics with "The Raven," for the basic situation is the same. Instead of a repetition of a refrain as in "The Raven," however, the important repetition here is a dramatic one: the speaker's return to the place where he buried Ulalume exactly one year before—a return he seems to make in a dreamlike and hallucinatory trance.

The subtitle of the poem, "A ballad," justifies the rhythmic repetition of references to "crispéd and sere" leaves; the leaves serve as an objectification of the treacherous and sere memories that haunt the speaker and bring him unwittingly down by the dim lake of Auber, in the ghoul-haunted woodland of Weir. The narrator roams here with Psyche, his Soul, with whom he carries on an interior dialogue. When the narrator and his Soul see the planet Venus, the goddess of love, the narrator is enthusiastic about her, but the Soul says she distrusts the star and wishes to flee. The narrator pacifies Psyche and soothes her, however, and they travel on until stopped by the door of a tomb. When the narrator asks his Soul what is written on the tomb, Psyche replies, " 'Tis the vault of thy lost Ulalume!" At this point the narrator remembers that it was last October at this same time that he brought the body of Ulalume to the tomb. In the last stanzas of the poem, the narrator asks whether the spirits of the dead have thrown up the "sinfully scintillant planet" in front of them to hide the secret that lies in the wood.

Although "Ulalume" is indeed lush in rhythm, rhyme, and sonorous words, its actual subject—the thematic motivation for the repetitions and rhythms that hold the poem together—is Poe's notion that the ideal of love (as objectified by the goddess of love, Venus) can only momentarily obscure the fact that the physical beauty that arouses love ultimately leads to the dark secret of the ghoul-haunted woodlands—the ultimate secret of death itself. Thus, although what is most obvious about the poem is its dark music, its theme of the transitory nature of physical beauty is what makes it a typical Poe poem.

THE PHILOSOPHY OF COMPOSITION

First published: 1846
Type of work: Essay

Poe explains his theory of aesthetic unity and describes how he wrote "The Raven."

From the beginning of his career as a poet, short story writer, and critic and reviewer, Poe was developing a body of critical doctrine about the nature of literature. Basically, the doctrine assumes that, whereas the lowest forms of literary art are realistic works and works created to illustrate a didactic moral lesson, the highest form of literary art is the aesthetic creation of beauty. Bits and pieces of this theory can be found developing from Poe's earliest reviews and prefaces; however, the theory comes together in a unified fashion in Poe's most extended and famous theoretical statement, "The Philosophy of Composition."

Poe begins his discussion by asserting that literary works should start with the conclusion or denouement and then work back to the motivation or causes that lead to the "end." Only in this way, Poe insists, can the writer give his plot an indispensable air of consequence by making both the incidents and the tone contribute to the development of the overall intention. Poe says he always begins with an "effect," preferably a novel and a vivid one; then he determines what combination of incidents and tone will best aid him in the construction of that effect.

Poe then launches into an extended discussion of "The Raven," his best-known poem, to illustrate this procedure. The first consideration in the writing of the poem, Poe asserts, was the issue of the length and scope of the work. Poe always argued that a long poem was a contradiction in terms—a long poem is actually a succession of brief ones. His first criteria for the length of a work is that it can be read at a single sitting. If the work is too long to be read at a single sitting, it loses the important effect derivable from unity of impression. Thus, Poe arbitrarily decided to limit his poem to about one hundred lines; "The Raven" is actually 108 lines.

Second, Poe decided on the "impression" or "effect" that he wished to convey.

Because for Poe the sole province of all poetry is beauty, he decided that his poem should focus on this universally appreciable effect. Once making that decision, he had to decide on the "tone" of the poem. Because beauty always excites tears in the sensitive person, he concluded that his tone should be one of sadness and melancholy. Having made these decisions about the effect he wished to achieve, Poe then made decisions about what techniques would best bring about these effects. His first decision about method was to make use of the refrain, for it is universally appreciated in poetry and its impression depends on repetition and a monotone of sound. Although the sound would remain the same, however, the thought conveyed by the sound should constantly vary. Deciding that the best refrain would be a single word, Poe claims that the first word that came to his mind to suggest the melancholy tone he had chosen was the word "nevermore."

After he made those decisions, Poe says he then decided on a "pretext" for the use of this word in such a manner. This is an important point, for Poe does not begin with the plot, theme, or the so-called personal dilemma of his primary character. Rather, the character and the plot—what one often thinks are the most important elements—are really only a pretext or an excuse for using the techniques that will create the effect that he wants. Realizing that the monotonous repetition of the word "nevermore" would belie any reasoning person, Poe decided to have an unreasoning creature utter the word; the raven, a bird of ill omen, was the natural choice. Next, Poe decided on the subject of the poem. After admitting that the most melancholy subject is death, Poe then, in one of his famous pronouncements, asserts that the most melancholy subject occurs when death is associated with beauty: "the death, then, of a beautiful woman is, unquestionably, the most poetical topic in the world."

Readers and critics have often criticized Poe for this essay, arguing that it makes the creation of a poem sound cold-blooded and rational, rather than the stroke of inspiration some would prefer to think. Poe's central theoretical assumption, however, is that poetry is the careful creation of beauty and should create pleasure in the reader. Above all, Poe is a formalist for whom the technique and pattern of a poem, not its so-called theme or human interest, is its sole reason for being.

Summary

Because of critical bias against the short story in general and the Gothic horror story in particular, the works of Edgar Allan Poe have not often received the serious attention they deserve. Once one sees that all Poe's fiction, poetry, and criticism revolve around his central aesthetic ideas about the self-contained pattern of the artwork, however, it becomes clear that Poe is America's single most important nineteenth century precursor to what is now often called postmodernism. Reality, for Poe, is constantly created in an aesthetic process. If it is the task of the artist to reflect true reality, then the artist must be concerned with the fiction-making process itself. Art is not a reflector of reality; reality is a function of art.

Bibliography

Broussard, Louis. *The Measure of Poe*. Norman: University of Oklahoma Press, 1969.

Buranelli, Vincent. *Edgar Allan Poe*. 2d ed. Boston: Twayne, 1977.

Carlson, Eric W., ed. *Critical Essays on Edgar Allan Poe*. Boston: G. K. Hall, 1987.

Davidson, E. H. *Poe: A Critical Study*. Cambridge, Mass.: The Belknap Press of Harvard University Press, 1964.

Hoffman, Daniel. *Poe Poe Poe Poe Poe Poe Poe*. Garden City, N.Y.: Doubleday, 1972.

Krutch, Joseph. *Edgar Allan Poe: A Study in Genius*. New York: Russell & Russell, 1965.

Quinn, A. H. *Edgar Allan Poe: A Critical Biography*. Carbondale: Southern Illinois University Press, 1957.

Regan, Robert, ed. *Poe: A Collection of Critical Essays*. Englewood Cliffs, N.J.: Prentice-Hall, 1967.

Thompson, G. R. *Poe's Fiction: Romantic Irony in the Gothic Tales*. Madison: University of Wisconsin Press, 1973.

Charles E. May

KATHERINE ANNE PORTER

Born: Indian Creek, Texas
May 15, 1890
Died: Silver Spring, Maryland
September 18, 1980

Principal Literary Achievement

Porter's fiction is of the highest quality; her mastery of the art of short fiction is unquestioned, and it is noted for being distinct, concise, subtle, and elegant.

Biography

The details of Katherine Anne Porter's life are obscured by her own account of them. Through imagination, wish-fulfillment, and embellishment, she created a personal history in conversations and interviews that reflected her great storytelling ability but not the facts. She was reared in an impoverished environment that she longed to escape. Once free, she was constantly on the move, creating a stir wherever she went, dominating her surroundings, pursuing an active social artist's life, procrastinating her writing, yet constantly plagued by frail health, as she frequently extended herself to exhaustion.

She was born in a log cabin in the frontier settlement of Indian Creek, Texas, on May 15, 1890, the daughter of Harrison Boone Porter and Mary Alice Jones Porter. They were both educated but did not have much money. Named Callie Russell at birth, she was the fourth of five children (the third child, Johnnie, died of influenza shortly before Callie was born). Callie's mother died at the age of twenty-three, less than a year after her fifth child was born, and Callie was only two. The family then moved to Kyle, Texas, to live with Harrison's strong-willed mother, Catherine Anne Porter (called Aunt Cat). They lived in poverty; Harrison Porter never recovered from Alice's death, growing increasingly despondent and not providing for his family's needs. Callie resented this neglect and had a difficult relationship with her father, which later manifested itself in a long series of failed marriages and love affairs. Aunt Cat was the dominant force in Callie's upbringing, and from her, Callie got not only a name but also her independent and forceful spirit and her ability for and love of storytelling. Porter's childhood ended at age eleven with her grandmother's death.

Porter's education reflected the family's circumstances. She was schooled at home, and in the local school houses. Porter's father borrowed enough money, however, to give Callie one year at a private school, exposing her to the classics, music, theater, the arts, and manners. A beautiful young girl, Porter escaped her family's circumstances, at the age of sixteen, by marrying John Henry Koontz, in a double ceremony with her older sister, Gay. This first marriage lasted nine years.

Katherine Anne Porter made her debut as a writer on September 15, 1917, with the *Fort Worth Critic*, filling in for a friend she met in a sanatorium while recovering from a bout with tuberculosis. She wrote light reviews of local theater and reported on social events. She then moved to Denver, Colorado, and got a job with the *Rocky Mountain News*, eventually running the entire theater section; then to Greenwich Village, where she held several jobs, wrapped herself in a circle of writer friends, and published a number of stories in 1920. Writing work took her on her first visit of many to Mexico City, and two years later, back in New York, she published what she designated as her first story in *Century* magazine: "María Concepción." This publication marks the launching of her "artistic" career. The next eight years included stints in Mexico, New England, New York, and Bermuda, another marriage and several love affairs, but not many stories. In 1930, her first book appeared: *Flowering Judas and Other Stories*, a collection of eleven stories.

A Guggenheim Fellowship gave her the means to sail to Europe in August, 1931, aboard the SS *Werra*—a trip that provided the basis for her one novel *Ship of Fools*. She lived in Berlin, Paris, and Basle, and returned to her favorite Paris, marrying her on-again, off-again companion of the previous three years, Eugene Dove Pressly, on March 18, 1932. Three years later, they returned to the United States (again Porter lived in several locations) and were officially divorced on April 9, 1938. Porter then married Albert Erskine in New Orleans ten days later, with Robert Penn Warren and his wife as witnesses. The marriage was a disaster from the start, and they were divorced in 1942 after a two-year separation, and the same year Porter's father died. During the 1930's and 1940's, Porter published some of her best-known fiction, including the stories in *Pale Horse, Pale Rider: Three Short Novels* (1930) and *The Leaning Tower and Other Stories* (1944); she also regularly wrote literary reviews and essays for journals.

Although her personal life caused her much grief and despair, and frequently interfered with her writing, Porter became a critically acclaimed, honored, and nationally recognized short-story writer. Looking for steady income, Porter accepted her first teaching position at Stanford University, in 1948. She received the first of many honorary doctorates from the University of North Carolina that academic year as well. From 1949 to 1963, Porter was a lecturer and teacher at writers' conferences at hundreds of locations in the United States and in Europe, she also held faculty positions at several universities. She changed publishers twice, fell in and out of love, maintained a busy social schedule, traveled frequently, occasionally focused on her fiction, but mostly procrastinated writing.

In 1961, Porter finally forced herself into seclusion in Pigeon Cove, Massachusetts, and after twenty-two years of sporadic work, finished *Ship of Fools* one month before her seventy-first birthday. Published in 1962, it was immediately a great success, securing for Porter enduring literary acclaim and financial security. Although in demand now more than ever for social functions and speaking engagements, Porter began to settle in the Washington, D.C., area, where she felt most comfortable. She was greatly flattered and took great interest in the film version of her novel. In 1965, *The Collected Stories of Katherine Anne Porter* was published, winning for her the Pulitzer Prize and the National Book Award, among other recognitions.

Outliving most of her friends, lovers, and enemies, Porter remained active and independent until she started having strokes in 1977; she was unable to regain her health, dying on September 18, 1980, at the age of ninety.

Analysis

Compared to many other successful and renowned writers, Porter published a rather small amount of writing. She did not start writing until she was almost thirty and after that she was often easily distracted from it. Her fiction comprises twenty-three short stories, four short novels, and one long novel.

Porter's fiction is related to her own first-hand experiences, thus avoiding generalizations in favor of close observation, deeply felt emotions, and careful craft. Although the work is not obviously autobiographical, it is clearly based on places and people she knew. Three distinct groups constitute Porter's fiction: working-class or middle-class families, situations and persons in Mexico or Germany (including a ship voyage between the two countries), and various relationships explored against a background of the South and the Southwest.

Porter lacks what could be called "vulgar appeal," but her meticulous devotion to clear, plain writing and her conviction that human life has meaning, even in the chaos of world catastrophe, made her a writer whose themes—love, marriage, other relationships, and alien cultures—appeal to readers who value serious subjects treated seriously and language that is precise and pure. In a foreword to *Flowering Judas*, Porter wrote about her craft and asserted her faith in "the voice of the individual artist" and in the unchanging survival of the arts, which, she said, are indestructible because "they represent the substance of faith and the only reality." It is this conviction and this spirit that informs in some way everything Porter wrote.

With her own credo in mind, Porter's fiction can be seen to have a meaning that is related to her views of human nature and her ideas about the human spirit. For example, *Ship of Fools*, her only novel and her most ambitious work, explores the ways that humans reveal themselves—in all their meanness, self-centeredness, vanity, lust, and greed. In the foreword mentioned above, Porter indicated the connection between her fiction and her effort to "grasp the meaning" of threatened world catastrophe and to "understand the logic of this majestic and terrible failure of the life of man in the Western world." Her attempts to deal with this large question are found primarily in *Ship of Fools*, but her faith in the larger human spirit of love, generosity, and tenderness is present only by implication as she exposes without pity that side of human nature which is least admirable, least lovable.

In her shorter fiction as well, Porter presents the same ambiguity. For example, *Noon Wine*, "Theft," and "Magic" are only three stories that portray human nature at its worst—weak, dishonest, and cruel. By contrast, seven stories set in the South and drawn from her childhood (including "The Old Order," "The Source," "The Last Leaf," and "The Grave") are tender, gently humorous, and poignant evocations of people and situations. These stories and others portray a view of humanity that is in strong contrast to the harsher realities of *Ship of Fools*.

A notable quality of the fiction that depicts people in friendly, loving, close relationships, such as *Old Mortality, Pale Horse, Pale Rider*, and "The Fig Tree," is that of timelessness. These works are not dated in the way that *Ship of Fools* is. Thus Porter seems to be asserting the faith that is mentioned in the foreword to *Flowering Judas*, though the title story itself seems to belie it.

It is these contradictory elements that make Porter's work ambiguous, not easy to summarize or categorize. Within individual works, Porter uses counterpoint to underline the ironies of life. In "Holiday," for example, she contrasts the busy, matter-of-fact lives of the Müllers with the lonely, strenuous life of the crippled mute who is a member of the family yet totally ignored by them. Another counterpoint is that of the narrator, a young woman who may well be Miranda, though she is not named. (Several of Porter's stories have as their main character a girl or young woman named Miranda or someone like her; she is a kind of stand-in for the author.)

Porter's relatively small body of work encompasses a notable variety of characters, situations, and settings. In itself, that is not a remarkable achievement, but when one also notes the skill with which Porter selects her details, the concentration of effect, the way that the impact of the story is sometimes felt only after one has finished reading it and put it aside, and perhaps most especially, the transcendent beauty of the style, one understands why Porter's work is so admired by critics, academicians, other writers, and ordinary readers.

SHIP OF FOOLS

First published: 1962
Type of work: Novel

On a ship traveling in 1931 from Veracruz, Mexico, to Bremerhaven, Germany, more than thirty passengers of various nationalities reveal themselves as they interact with one another.

Katherine Anne Porter derived the title of her only novel, *Ship of Fools*, from a fifteenth century moral allegory by Sebastian Brant. In her brief introduction, Porter states that she had read a German translation of the work while she still vividly recalled her impressions of her first trip to Europe in 1931. The thirty-odd important characters include men and women of various ages and classes from the United

States, Germany, Switzerland, Spain, Cuba, Mexico, and Sweden. The novel opens as the passengers embark on August 22, 1931, from Veracruz, Mexico. (Part 1 is entitled "Embarkation"; the middle section, "High Sea"; and the third and final section, "The Harbors.") The novel ends on September 17, 1931, when the ship, having stopped at several ports to allow all the passengers except the Germans and three Americans to disembark, finally reaches the last port, Bremerhaven, Germany.

The ancient and familiar image of the world as a ship on its journey to eternity provides the framework of the novel. Temporarily isolated from their normal, ordinary lives, the travelers include people of all kinds and conditions as well as the ship's officers at one end of the ship's social scale and 876 passengers in steerage at the other end. Thus Porter can examine a large number of her many characters in highly concentrated and revealing detail—their personalities, their principal relationships of varying duration and quality, and, by implication, her own attitudes toward the people she has collected and brought together in association with one another for a brief time.

There is no one protagonist, but two characters are notable for their singularity: Dr. Schumann, the ship's physician, and La Condesa (the countess), a fallen noblewoman being deported for revolutionary activities from Cuba to exile in Tenerife. Addicted to drugs and adored by a group of six noisy Cuban medical students, La Condesa becomes a patient of Dr. Schumann, who falls despairingly and futilely in love with her. The physician is also suffering from a weak heart and a sense of alienation and depression.

Two American women are especially distinguishable from the crowd because of the apparent sympathy felt for them by the author, a feeling that she does not show for the other characters. The latter are pitilessly exposed in all their unlikable natures and habits, such as the elderly couple who lavish inordinate amounts of attention on their white bulldog, the alcoholic hypochondriac, the lecherous publisher of a ladies' garment trade magazine, the abusive mother of a sickly little boy, two psychopathic children, and the company of singers and dancers who prey upon the ostensibly respectable passengers.

Instead of a plot in the usual sense, the novel consists of a series of anecdotes or scenes in which the characters appear in groups, usually as a family or a couple, with a few solitary figures. Porter's skill as a writer of stories is evident; the novel is a collection of scenes that reveal the weaknesses if not vices of a large number of repellent people who can only be characterized, because of the way Porter portrays them, as hateful, destructive, and evil.

Porter presents a portrait of humanity that is characterized by a large assortment of follies and sins, unrelieved, for the most part, by any redeeming qualities. The general situation of the book is that of Western civilization heading toward Fascism and on the brink of another world war. Lacking a narrative structure that builds on developing action, conflict, and resolution, the novel instead depends for its interest on the author's apparent theme of Western man's failure. This theme must be inferred from the unattractive, even despicable characters, not from any direct or clear statement by the author, who tells her tales, as usual, with dramatic intensity, vivid characterization, and plain, direct language.

When *Ship of Fools* appeared, the large majority of critics were enthusiastic if not ecstatic in their praise, but a small percentage found the book dull, repetitive, indiscriminate, and harsh—redeemed by neither humor nor compassion. As the immediate responses to the book were followed by more considered and objective evaluations, it seemed clear that Porter's reputation as a distinguished woman of American letters would rest on her short fiction, not her novel.

NOON WINE

First published: 1937
Type of work: Short novel

An encounter between a poor, shiftless farmer and a stranger seeking a hired man ends in murder.

Noon Wine is the second of a trilogy of short novels, as Katherine Anne Porter preferred to call them (instead of novelettes or novellas, as many critics and commentators have insisted on designating those pieces of her fiction that are longer than a short story but shorter than a conventional novel). *Noon Wine* appeared in book form with *Pale Horse, Pale Rider*, from which the book took its title, and *Old Mortality*. In an essay, " 'Noon Wine': The Sources," published in her *Collected Essays* in 1970, Porter explained how she shaped a work of fiction out of her memories of disparate incidents, persons, and impressions.

The setting of this short novel is a small farm in south Texas; it begins in 1896 and moves swiftly to 1905. As befits the concentrated form of a short novel, there are only three major characters in *Noon Wine*: Royal Earl Thompson, a proud and slothful man; Ellie, his weak-eyed, ailing wife; and Olaf Helton, a taciturn Swede from North Dakota, who appears one day in search of a job as a hired hand and who through untiring industry transforms the farm from a run-down subsistence-level operation into a profitable concern. Helton does not endear himself to the family, however, which includes two small boys, Arthur and Herbert, whose growth over the next nine years marks the passage of time. One day there arrives the last person to take a prominent part in the story, Homer T. Hatch, to whom Thompson takes an immediate dislike even before he has reason to do so. Hatch is seeking Helton, who escaped years ago from a lunatic asylum to which he had been committed after killing his brother for losing one of his harmonicas, the only possessions he seems to have or care about. Hatch admits that he earns handsome rewards for rounding up escaped lunatics and convicts. In a confused burst of actions by Thompson, Hatch, and Helton, the farmer kills the stranger, believing that he was attacking the hired man. In court, Thompson is exonerated, but he still feels a need to justify his act, and he and his wife go from farm to farm as he tries to explain himself and to understand what happened. Finally, when his two sons turn on him, he realizes that he cannot continue. He writes a short note, and the story ends as he figures out how to work his shotgun with his big toe, the barrel of the gun under his chin.

The story takes its title from a drinking song that the hired man played endlessly on one of his harmonicas. As Hatch explained to Thompson when they heard Helton's tune, it is about feeling so good in the morning that all the wine intended for the midday break is drunk before noon. It is typical of Porter to choose such a passing reference for her title; the reader may comment on the significance of such a title, but Porter does not. Thus she maintains her impersonal, detached position and forces the reader to confront the story itself without hindrance or help from the author except in the matter of a tightly constructed, unembellished tale with an impact that has its source in the tale itself.

FLOWERING JUDAS

First published: 1930
Type of work: Short story

A young woman works so diligently and selflessly to help Mexican revolutionaries and children that she seems untouched in her secret inner self.

Laura, the principal character in "Flowering Judas," is a young woman who spends her days teaching English to Mexican Indian children, attending union meetings, and visiting political prisoners, for whom she runs errands and brings messages. Despite all this activity, Laura appears emotionally uninvolved, doing her work, listening to the children and the prisoners, and particularly, listening courteously to the wretched singing almost nightly of Braggioni, a revolutionary leader. Egotistical and cruel, Braggioni appears unaware of Laura's unspoken revulsion and anger at him.

Laura does feel betrayed by the discrepancy between the way she lives and what she feels life should be. She also feels fear—of Braggioni, who symbolizes her disillusionment, of danger, of death. She is caught between her commitment to her present life and her rejection of her life before she came to Mexico.

Laura has been courted by a young captain in Zapata's army, but she rejects him, making her horse shy when the soldier tries to take her in his arms. Another young man has serenaded her as he stood under the blossoms of the Judas tree in her patio, but again she is only disturbed by him; she feels nothing more for him than she does for her pupils, who she realizes are strangers to her. Wearing a nunlike dress with a lace-edged collar, Laura strives to attain stoicism, drawing strength from a single word which epitomizes her aloofness and fear: no. Using that word as a talisman, she can practice denial, fearlessness, detachment.

Eugenio, the third young man in Laura's life, is not a suitor; he is a prisoner to whom she brought the narcotics he had requested. When she tells Braggioni that Eugenio has taken all the tablets at once and has gone into a stupor, Braggioni is unmoved, calling him a fool. He then departs, and Laura senses that he will not return for a while. She realizes that she is free and that she should run, but she does not leave. She goes to bed; in her sleep, Eugenio appears and takes her to "a new country," which he calls death. He makes her eat of the flowers of the Judas tree, calling her a murderer and cannibal. The sound of her voice crying "No!" awakens her, and she is afraid to go back to sleep.

The theme of betrayal is first suggested by the title of the story, the red blossoms of the Judas tree being a well-known symbol of the betrayal of Christ by one of his disciples. Laura feels that she has been betrayed by the separation between her past life and her present one. She does not seem to realize fully that she has also betrayed herself by closing herself off from commitment and love. This is an ambiguous story which, like so many of Porter's stories, places the burden of interpretation upon the reader. Porter offers only subtle hints and clues to what she might mean.

THE GRAVE

First published: 1935
Type of work: Short story

Two children hunt rabbits and explore the emptied graves in their family cemetery.

"The Grave" is the final story in a collection entitled "The Old Order," which was included in *The Leaning Tower and Other Stories.* The seven stories in the collection are commonly called "the Miranda stories," as the principal character in each one is a girl named Miranda, who also appears in *Old Mortality* and *Pale Horse, Pale Rider.* It is generally thought that Miranda is the author herself at different points in her life.

In "The Grave," Miranda is nine and her brother, Paul, twelve. While hunting rabbits, they come upon the family cemetery, which has been emptied because the land has been sold. The children explore the pits where the graves had been and discover two small objects: a gold ring and a tiny silver dove. Miranda persuades Paul to give her the ring he has found, and Paul is pleased with the dove, which he guesses was once the screw head for a coffin. Feeling like trespassers, they then continue to look for small game, and Paul shoots a rabbit. Skinning it, he discovers that the rabbit was pregnant and carefully slits the womb, exposing the tiny creatures within. At first Miranda is filled with wonder (not by chance is she named Miranda), but then she becomes agitated without understanding what it is that disturbs her. Paul cautions her not to tell a living soul what they have seen.

Miranda never does tell their secret, which sinks into her mind, where it lies buried for nearly twenty years. One day, wandering in the market of a foreign city, the episode returns to her consciousness as she looks with horror at a tray of candy in the shapes of small animals and birds. The heat of the day and the market smells remind her of the day that she and her brother found their treasures.

The theme of death and birth is expressed in several ways. The family graves and the body of the dead rabbit are related; perhaps most important, however, is the image of Miranda's mind as a burial place. For many years, she has not thought of her brother's face as a child, but it is that sudden recollection of him smiling, pleased, sober, as he turned "the silver dove over and over in his hands" that wipes out the horror and disgust at the sight of the candied creatures and the long-forgotten feeling of agitation at the sight of the unborn rabbits.

Summary

The critic Edmund Wilson called Katherine Anne Porter's stories "baffling" and "elusive." These are apt descriptive terms, for Porter's stories and her single novel do not yield their meaning easily. Yet the experiences narrated are intense, the characters are undeniably human and real, and their feelings are clear and strong. The human spirit is presented in all its variety, and this spirit is not easily described. In her own words as well as in the comments of many critics, it is just this spirit that Porter's works are all about, however difficult it is to identify and define.

Bibliography

Givner, Joan. *Katherine Anne Porter: A Life.* New York: Simon and Schuster, 1982, 1991.

_____, ed. *Katherine Anne Porter: Conversations.* Jackson: University of Mississippi Press, 1987.

Hartley, Lodwick, and George Core, eds. *Katherine Anne Porter: A Critical Symposium.* Athens: University of Georgia Press, 1969.

Hilt, Kathryn. *Katherine Anne Porter.* New York: Garland, 1990.

Liberman, Myron M. *Katherine Anne Porter's Fiction.* Detroit: Wayne State University Press, 1971.

Nance, William L. *Katherine Anne Porter and the Art of Rejection.* Chapel Hill: University of North Carolina Press, 1964.

Waldrip, Louise, and Shirley Ann Bauer. *A Bibliography of the Criticism of the Works of Katherine Anne Porter.* Metuchen, N.J.: Scarecrow Press, 1969.

_____. *A Bibliography of the Works of Katherine Anne Porter.* Metuchen, N.J.: Scarecrow Press, 1969.

Warren, Robert Penn, ed. *Katherine Anne Porter: A Collection of Critical Essays.* Englewood Cliffs, N.J.: Prentice-Hall, 1979.

Natalie Harper

CHARLES PORTIS

Born: El Dorado, Arkansas
December 28, 1933

Principal Literary Achievement

Portis carries on the proud tradition of the Southwestern humorists, while writing novels that are highly humorous without being frivolous.

Biography

Charles McColl Portis was born in El Dorado, Arkansas, on December 28, 1933, the son of Samuel Palmer and Alice Waddell Portis. His father was a school superintendent, and his mother was a woman of strong literary inclinations. He grew up and went through public schools in Hamburg, Arkansas, located in the southwestern corner of the state. There the Old South plantation culture of neighboring Mississippi gradually gives way to the frontier culture which characterizes most of Arkansas. Portis was graduated from high school in 1951. In 1952, he left Arkansas for the first time to join the United States Marine Corps. He served during the latter part of the Korean War and was discharged in 1955, having attained the rank of sergeant.

Portis returned to his home state and entered the University of Arkansas, where he studied journalism. He received the B.A. in 1958. Upon graduation, he pursued a career in journalism. He had worked for the *Northwest Arkansas Times* and during 1958 was a reporter for the *Commercial Appeal* of Memphis, Tennessee. The next year, he moved to Little Rock, Arkansas, as a reporter on the *Arkansas Gazette*. In 1960, he left Arkansas again, this time to take a reporting job with the *New York Herald Tribune*. He remained there until 1964, eventually becoming the newspaper's London correspondent. In that year, he quit his job and began a career as a full-time writer. He returned to Little Rock, Arkansas, where he still resides.

Portis' four-year sojourn at the *New York Herald Tribune* was very successful. He became a feature writer as well as a reporter, and his feature stories were so effective that at least one of them appeared in a college composition text as a model for student writing. His job as London correspondent was one of the most attractive the newspaper had to offer. Also, he came into close contact with Tom Wolfe and other architects of the "new journalism." His desire to devote all of his time to fiction, however, was so strong that he resigned abruptly from the newspaper and returned to Arkansas.

He moved into a fishing shack and began to write. His long article "The New

1665

Sound from Nashville," appeared in *The Saturday Evening Post* for February 12, 1966. (It is an interesting coincidence that the career of another regional humorist was launched a few years later when Garrison Keillor also published a long article on Nashville's country music scene in *The New Yorker.*) This was the first piece by Portis to reach a national audience, and more important, it led to the serialization of his first two novels. "Traveling Light" appeared in two numbers of *The Saturday Evening Post*, those for June 18 and July 2, 1966. A considerably altered version of that short novel was published in the same year under the title *Norwood*. A condensed version of *True Grit* appeared in *The Saturday Evening Post* on May 18, June 1, and June 15, 1968. The full text appeared in book form that same year.

True Grit was both a critical success and a best-seller. It was subsequently adapted for the screen in 1969; the veteran film star John Wayne played the role of Deputy Marshal Rooster Cogburn. Wayne was such a success in the part that he won an Academy Award and went on to reprise the role in *Rooster Cogburn* (1975). The latter film simply borrowed the character from Portis' novel (Portis was not involved in the preparation of either screenplay). In 1970, *Norwood* also became a film, with two of the principal players from *True Grit* acting the leading roles. Again, Portis took no hand in writing the screen version.

So commercially successful were his first ventures into fiction—especially *True Grit* and its irascible Rooster Cogburn—that Portis was able to spend eleven years on the preparation of his next novel. *The Dog of the South* was published in 1979. It was brought out by a different publishing house and did not prove nearly as successful as its predecessors, although it has won a coterie of devoted admirers. His fourth novel, *Masters of Atlantis*, appeared in 1985.

Analysis

Charles Portis is a regional writer whose works occupy an honored place in the line of descent from the "Old Southwestern" humorists of the 1840's and 1850's. He has been compared to Mark Twain and, even though any humorist emerging from the South or West is likely to be compared to Twain, in Portis' case the comparison is appropriate. Like the best of the regional writers (Twain, William Faulkner, Eudora Welty, Flannery O'Connor, and Larry McMurtry, for example), his work has a much broader than regional appeal, as the commercial success of his first two novels attests. Still, his home state of Arkansas is always his center of consciousness.

Portis takes the cliché of the Arkansas Traveler and stands it on its head. In the old folktale/song, the Traveler is an outsider, and the lazy Arkansawyer is content to sit and fiddle at his cabin door. Portis takes his Arkansas protagonists and sets them on the move, launching them into a bewildering, and sometimes dangerous, world. Norwood Pratt (technically a Texan but living only a few miles beyond the border city of Texarkana) sets off to collect a debt owed him. Ray Midge of Little Rock, Arkansas, is trailing his runaway wife and his stolen car. Mattie Ross, the most determined traveler of them all, is pursuing her father's killer. Portis' motif of the odyssey is well grounded in his home state's recent past. In the Dust Bowl days of the 1930's, many of the so-called Arkies went west, especially to California, seeking better economic opportunities. Many returned to Arkansas after having accumulated a little capital. Many others continued to regard their emigration, even after it had stretched into a period of many years, as temporary. Among Arkansas natives, it became proverbial that the wandering Arky would eventually return. Portis, who himself gave up an excellent job in Eastern journalism to come home and write, always brings his peripatetic protagonists full circle, back to Arkansas. Rooster Cogburn, a central character in *True Grit*, roams for the last twenty years of his life, but, significantly, he returns to die and be buried in Arkansas.

Arkansas, along with Texas and Louisiana, is westernmost among the states of the Old Confederacy. Throughout most of the nineteenth century, the western border of Arkansas was the frontier where the West began. The frontier quality of Arkansas is treated explicitly in Portis' "western," *True Grit*, but it is also treated implicitly elsewhere. Norwood Pratt and Ray Midge might seem unlikely frontiersmen at first glance, but they share several of the frontiersman's traits. They are disposed to leave a settled life and see where the road will lead them. Neither is much attached to material possessions. Norwood is supposedly seeking repayment of a debt, but as soon as he gets his money he lends it right out again. Midge trails his stolen car through several countries, but when he finds that it has been destroyed he shrugs off the loss. The objects of these searches were merely calls to exploration and adventure. Both Norwood and Midge are uncomplicated and inner-directed. Both hold to a simple moral code that grows out of life experiences rather than religious or philosophical theory.

There is a kindliness and an affirmative quality in Portis' novels that sets them apart from most comic fiction of the period. Norwood takes a pregnant girl, abandoned by another man, as his wife. Midge takes his errant wife back, only to have her desert him yet again. The first impulse of Norwood and Midge is to care for anyone who needs caring for. The fourteen-year-old Mattie Ross and the grizzled bounty hunter Cogburn develop a chaste love that is totally convincing, never cloying or contrived. The eccentrics who abound in Portis' novels are not the southern Gothic horrors encountered elsewhere; they are objects of gentle mockery. Although *True Grit* is a novel containing fine scenes of comedy and action, it is essentially a story of courage, honor, and fidelity.

Portis is not an experimenter in fiction. His narratives, though often loose, are constructed along traditional lines. He writes with precision and economy. His pacing is effective, even when his plots turn episodic and erratic. His finest achievement is his dialogue and his flawless representation of idiomatic language. He is a master of the dialects of Arkansas, Texas, and the Southwest. In fact, his dialogue rings so true when read aloud that huge chunks of it were used verbatim in the film version of *True Grit*.

Although he has so far elicited little interest from the scholarly community, Charles Portis is a major comic writer. Indeed, the chief complaint that critics have made about his work is that he has chosen to publish so little of it over the years.

NORWOOD

First published: 1966
Type of work: Novel

The title character undertakes a comic quest, encountering eccentrics and zany situations every step of the way.

Norwood contains the autobiographical elements so often found in a first novel. Norwood Pratt served in the Marine Corps, as did his creator. Norwood lives in Ralph, a little town in the northeastern corner of Texas, only a few miles from the Arkansas line. The protagonist travels to New York City, then returns home, completely unaltered by the many adventures he has had during his odyssey. The novel is set in the late 1950's.

There are many suggestions of Voltaire's *Candide* (1759) in the story line. Norwood is a lovable, optimistic innocent. He works at a gas station for which unpretentious would be the most charitable characterization. Like Candide with his Pangloss, Norwood lives in the same house as a mentor. His brother-in-law lives on disability checks from the Veterans Administration and spends his many hours of leisure spouting crack-brained philosophy. Norwood is a simple young man, both intellectually and in the sense that he is unaffected in the extreme. His ambitions are modest. He loves country music, and his life's dream is to sing on the Louisiana Hayride in Shreveport—he does not even aspire to the Grand Ole Opry.

Norwood's motivation for leaving Ralph is modest as well. A buddy from Marine Corps days still owes him seventy dollars. He believes his friend to be living in New York City, and he heads east to collect his money. At this point, the novel becomes picaresque. As he meanders around the country on a Trailways bus, he has a series of encounters with grotesque characters. Foremost among them are Edmund B. Ratner, a "wonder hen," and Rita Lee. Edmund B. Ratner is a midget with a philosophical turn of mind. When Norwood finally gets his money, he immediately lends it to the midget. The wonder hen is a version of the performing animal with amazing powers familiar from so many off-color jokes. Rita Lee is a hapless, jilted, and pregnant young woman, who will eventually become Norwood's bride.

The part of the novel which Portis fleshes out the least is the New York segment. His former colleagues on the *New York Herald Tribune* recall that throughout his tenure there he remained the droll Southerner, unchanged by the New York environment. Norwood is similarly unscathed by his big-city adventures. Ironically, the trail of the elusive seventy dollars leads finally to Old Carthage in southwestern Arkansas, only a few miles up the highway from Norwood's hometown. There both Norwood and his creator seem most comfortable.

It is the tone of the novel which causes the analogy with *Candide* to break down. Whereas Voltaire's satire is sharp and often bitter, Portis makes good-natured fun of virtually everyone and everything in the novel. The mood is genial. Portis seems to have no particular satirical target. Everyone's character traits verge upon the ridiculous, he suggests—they are merely more pronounced and exaggerated in the novel's eccentrics. This lack of focus has been criticized, but it does give the novel that buoyant comic tone which lifts it lightly over the rough spots in the episodic plot.

The author's journalistic background can be seen in the crisp, straightforward prose and the sharply delineated characters and scenes. The real strength of *Norwood*, however, lies in its dialogue, in the authenticity of the characters' vernacular speech, and—especially—in the portrayal of Southern dialect.

TRUE GRIT

First published: 1968
Type of work: Novel

Two characters who appear to be opposites but are really kindred spirits undertake an exciting and hazardous mission.

True Grit is a first-person narrative which exploits the tradition of the "innocent eye"—a story seen through the eyes of an unsophisticated adolescent—a tradition going back at least to *The Adventures of Huckleberry Finn* (1884). The narrator-protagonist, Mattie Ross, is fourteen, the same age Huck was supposed to be when he experienced his adventures on the mighty Mississippi. Mattie's narration, however, strikes a very different tone from Huck's for two reasons. First, Mattie is looking back over a period of fifty years on the events she recounts. Second, Mattie was much the same at fourteen as she is in her sixties—the kind of girl who is an adult from birth.

The setting is Arkansas and the Indian Territory in the late 1870's. Mattie lives on a farm in Yell County, Arkansas, located near Dardanelle, an Old South settlement on the banks of the Arkansas River. Mattie's father, Frank Ross, travels on business to Fort Smith—where the West begins—and there he is shot down and robbed by Tom Chaney, one of his farmhands. Chaney flees into the Indian Territory and joins a band of outlaws led by Lucky Ned Pepper. Mattie leaves her mother, sister, and brother at home and travels to Fort Smith, ostensibly to claim her father's effects but in reality to bring Tom Chaney to justice. Portis utilizes his Presbyterian background and the cultural geography of his home state to their fullest effect. Mattie is a girl of the Old South. She is self-confident and self-righteous in her flinty Protestantism, prim, proper, absolutely single-minded, and totally lacking in patience for the follies of her fellow man. She is also cool-headed, dogged, and courageous. She habitually speaks in the elevated prose of genteel Victorian literature. To her, Dardanelle and Yell County represent civilization, and she repeatedly threatens the frontier barbarians of Fort Smith with her family lawyer, J. Noble Daggett.

These are the days of Judge Isaac Parker, the notorious "hanging judge," and

Mattie witnesses the public hanging of three outlaws on her first day in Fort Smith. To bring in Chaney, Mattie turns to Reuben J. "Rooster" Cogburn, U.S. deputy marshal for the Western District of Arkansas. Cogburn is approaching middle age, has lost an eye, is growing fat, and drinks too much. Mattie is looking for someone with grit, however, and Cogburn has killed twenty-three men in the past four years; he appears to possess the desired commodity. Rooster is unwilling to accept the commission without some payment in advance, and Mattie's machinations in getting the needed money produce a series of wonderful comic scenes. A horse trader named Stonehill had sold Frank Ross four cow ponies just before the farmer was killed. Mattie insists that Stonehill buy the ponies back, in addition to paying for her father's horse, stolen by Chaney. Stonehill begins by haughtily declaring that he does not conduct business with children but eventually crumples beneath Mattie's onslaught. After he has bought back the ponies, he is even forced to sell the best one of them to Mattie at a price greatly advantageous to her (this is Little Blackie, who will play a crucial role in the climactic scenes of the novel). Mattie leaves Stonehill huddled and shivering beneath a blanket, as much the victim of her indomitable will as of his recurring malaria.

The pursuit of Chaney is complicated by the appearance of a Texas Ranger named LaBoeuf. He announces that Chaney is really Theron Chelmsford, who murdered a state senator in Waco, Texas. La Boeuf is on detached service, working for the senator's family, and plans to take Chaney back to Texas. Naturally, Mattie wants Chaney to hang in Arkansas for the murder of her father. When Mattie, Rooster, and LaBoeuf finally cross the Arkansas River into the Indian Territory, they form an uneasy alliance. Portis skillfully plays upon the rivalries existing among the states of his native region and incorporates the resulting raillery into the novel. To Mattie the Arkansas girl, the Indian Territory (one day to become the state of Oklahoma) is the end of the world, a savage and lawless robbers' roost. Both she and Rooster are irritated by the young Texan, whom they take to be representative of his state. LaBoeuf is flashy, conceited, and condescending. Yet, in the moment of crisis, all three—the priggish Mattie, the brash LaBoeuf, and the drunken Rooster—will prove their mettle, for they share the one crucial quality, true grit.

Pepper's gang is finally run to ground. Mattie shoots and wounds Chaney (whom Rooster later kills) with her father's service revolver. Rooster single-handedly destroys half the gang in an exciting shoot-out on horseback, and LaBoeuf kills Lucky Ned Pepper with a magnificent 600-yard rifle shot. In the course of this action, Mattie falls into a pit of rattlesnakes, where she breaks her left arm and is eventually bitten. Rooster makes manifest his growing affection for the girl; he pulls her from the pit and races the many miles back toward Fort Smith and medical attention. Rooster's horse, Bo, has been shot from under him, so he takes Mattie's Little Blackie. The pony gallantly carries the big man and the girl at full gallop until he falls dead. Rooster then carries Mattie on his back as far as the Poteau River, where he commandeers a wagon and a team of mules at gunpoint. As a result of the wild ride, Mattie survives, although she loses the injured arm just above the elbow.

In the final pages, Mattie summarizes Rooster's fading career. As the frontier has disappeared, men like Rooster Cogburn have become increasingly anomalous. By the turn of the century, he is traveling with Cole Younger and Frank James in a Wild West show. Rooster dies suddenly while the show is at Jonesboro, Arkansas. Mattie has Rooster's body exhumed from the Confederate cemetery in Memphis and re-buried in the Ross family plot at Dardanelle. She knows that her neighbors consider this the act of an old maid going funny in the head, but Mattie is still Mattie and will be ruled by no judgment other than her own. The crisp prose and the nineteenth century flavor of the dialogue make Mattie's narrative seem plausible from the first page to the last.

THE DOG OF THE SOUTH

First published: 1979
Type of work: Novel

An Arkansan sets out on a quest, this time for a stolen car and a stolen wife.

By the time Portis' third novel, *The Dog of the South*, was published, his central fictional motif, the quest, was well established. *The Dog of the South* is slightly longer than the first two novels and is more whimsical even than *Norwood*. This novel, like *True Grit*, is a first-person narrative told by the protagonist. As the story begins, Ray Midge, a twenty-six-year-old resident of Little Rock, Arkansas, has just made a startling discovery. His wife, Norma, has run away with her loathsome first husband, Guy Dupree, a would-be radical. Even more distressing is the discovery that the pair has fled in his new Ford Torino. In its place, they have left Dupree's compact, a 1963 Buick Special with 74,000 miles on the odometer and slack in the steering wheel.

Like Norwood, Ray Midge is innocent, placid, long-suffering, and optimistic. He holds no grudges and wishes no one ill, but he does want that Ford Torino back. Norma and Dupree have also taken Midge's American Express and Texaco cards. As the bills start coming in, Midge is able to follow their paper trail. Norwood's quest for his seventy dollars led him north and east; Midge's leads south and west. He follows the lovers to Texas, from there into Mexico, and finally to a remote planta-tion in Honduras. The trip is the best part of the novel, as it allows Midge to meet the sorts of misfits and oddballs that Portis writes so well.

Dr. Reo Symes travels with Midge. He is a "defrocked" old M.D. from Texas who is constantly pursuing the American Dream in his own fashion, through a series of harebrained get-rich-quick schemes. He drives a broken-down bus, the Dog of the South. Dr. Symes emulates the super salesmanship of John Selmer Dix, M.A., whom he knows through the latter's self-help books. The Doc considers Dix the world's greatest author. His most enduring dream, or delusion, of a great financial coup cen-ters upon Jean's Island. The "island" is a Mississippi sandbar the Doc hopes to inherit from his mother. While he waits for it to come into his possession, he lays innumerable absurd and grandiose plans for its development. With the publication of *True Grit*, much critical commentary placed Portis in the tradition of Mark Twain, and as Ray Midge travels southward with the scheming Doc, the reader is reminded of Huckleberry Finn's journey in the company of the two confidence men, the King and the Duke. Some critics consider Dr. Symes Portis' finest comic creation.

Midge encounters a number of other slightly loony characters as well: Norma, who wishes to be known as Staci or Pam; Symes's mother and another perky old lady, who operate an ineffectual nondenominational mission in Central America; Dupree's chow, who wears plastic bags on his paws; a pugnacious artist whose specialty is overpriced rabbits. Midge faces a number of obstacles—the first husband, jail, a hurricane—but none of them is truly threatening in Portis' comic world. It is a formless and haphazard world, which the structure of the novel mimics.

Midge wants to recover his Ford because he feels that his cuckolding will thus be lessened somehow. When he finally catches up with Dupree, he learns that the car has been ruined and sold for junk. Instead, he gets Norma back and takes her home. At the end of the novel, she runs off again. In an objective sense, the quest has been fruitless; now the car and the wife are gone for good. Yet Midge accepts these vicissitudes with relative equanimity. After all, in the Portis novels (even *True Grit*), it is the quest rather than the outcome which is important.

MASTERS OF ATLANTIS

First published: 1985
Type of work: Novel

A good-natured spoof of the cult phenomenon in twentieth century America.

Masters of Atlantis is perhaps Portis' most curious novel. It deals humorously with a fictional cult not unlike many which have flowered and then wilted in twentieth century America. The story begins in 1917. Lamar Jimmerson—an American soldier and, like so many of Portis' characters, an innocent—is in France with the American Expeditionary Force. For two hundred dollars, a gypsy sells Jimmerson a handwritten Greek manuscript. It is a copy of a book written in legendary Atlantis many thousands of years ago. When the destruction of the city was imminent, the book was sealed in an ivory casket and committed to the waves. This book is the *Codex Pappus*. After floating at sea for nine hundred years, it washed ashore in Egypt and was found by Hermes Trismegistus. After nine years of diligently studying the book, Hermes is able to read the text. Only after another nine years is he fully able to understand it, thus becoming the first modern Master of the Gnomon Society.

Jimmerson vainly searches on Malta for Pletho Pappus, the Master of Gnomonry, and the Gnomon Temple; however, he does find his first convert, Sidney Hen, a young Englishman. Jimmerson marries Hen's crippled sister Fanny and returns to the United States. He has fifty copies of an English translation of the *Codex* printed and sets out to win more converts. Gnomonry languishes during the prosperous and high-spirited 1920's (Jimmerson wonders if he will ever get the fifty copies off his hands), but it begins to flourish during the bleaker days of the 1930's. On April 10, 1936, the Gnomon Temple is dedicated in Burnette, Indiana—characterized as Gary's most fashionable suburb.

Through twenty-four chapters, the novel traces the rise and fall of Gnomonry. It chronicles the mystical careers of Jimmerson, Hen, and the other Masters of Atlantis. During the sixty years of the pseudo-religion's existence, the Gnomon leaders must face the competition of Rosicrucians, alchemists, and charlatans and loonies of every stripe. The Masters must watch the decline of their sect from the glory days of the limestone temple in Indiana to the final housing of the sacred artifacts in a polystyrene mobile home in Texas. Portis has traced another odyssey—this time it is the journey of a harmlessly and charmingly insane idea rather than an individual.

Masters of Atlantis is certainly a satire on the tendency of many Americans to take up—briefly—the latest guru to claim a knowledge of the secrets of the universe. Since the *Codex Pappus* is a jumble of non sequiturs (aphorisms, riddles, and puzzles, which combine to mean nothing or anything), the novel is also a satire on the popular books of psychic enlightenment that expound the appealing thesis that there is more to be learned from feelings and intuitions than from a rigorous study of the traditional arts and sciences. In fact, in the novel, the *Codex Pappus* spawns a hilarious brood of just such books. *Masters of Atlantis* is a gentle satire, however; Portis has Gnomonry come into being in the period of H. L. Mencken's virulent attacks upon what he considered the invincible arrogance of Southern fundamentalists and Sinclair Lewis's exposé of fraudulent evangelists in *Elmer Gantry* (1927). There is no such sense of outrage in Portis' novel.

It has been noted that Portis is sometimes compared to Mark Twain, but he is assuredly not like Twain in his equanimity, geniality, and tolerance. Even in his earliest books, Twain was often angered almost to the point of madness by the perfidy and stupidity of humankind. Portis is, in this respect, much closer to the great Renaissance poet Geoffrey Chaucer. He finds humanity infinitely fascinating, curious, and entertaining—and most entertaining of all when combining extravagance with wrongheadedness.

Summary

Without any exaggeration of his abilities, Charles Portis can be compared to several literary masters. Like Mark Twain, he has perfected the fictional representation of the dialect of the Upper South and the Mississippi River Valley. Like Charles Dickens, he delights in the eccentric and the absurd and depicts them wonderfully well. Like Geoffrey Chaucer, he portrays his fellow humans, no matter how outrageous their behavior, with sympathy and tolerance. His books are more than funny, but, if they were only funny, they would still be valuable.

Bibliography

Blackburn, Sara. *"True Grit."* *The Nation* 207 (August 5, 1968): 92.

Clemons, Walter. *"The Dog of the South."* *Newsweek* 94 (July 9, 1979): 12.

Disch, Thomas M. "Cultcrazy." *The Nation* 241 (November 30, 1985): 593-594.

Garfield, Brian. *"True Grit."* *Saturday Review* 51 (June 29, 1968): 25.

King, L. L. *"The Dog of the South."* *The New York Times Book Review*, July 29, 1979, p. 12.

"Masters of Atlantis." *The New Yorker* 61 (November 25, 1985): 163.

Shuman, R. Baird. "Portis' *True Grit*: Adventure or *Entwicklungsroman*?" *English Journal* 59 (March, 1970): 367-370.

Wolfe, Tom. *The New Journalism*. New York: Harper & Row, 1973.

Patrick Adcock

CHAIM POTOK

Born: New York, New York
February 17, 1929

Principal Literary Achievement
In his insightful and sympathetic portrayals of Orthodox and ultra-Orthodox Jewish communities, Potok has given dramatic form to the confrontation between religious tradition and modern secularism.

Biography
Chaim Tzvi Potok was born in the Bronx, New York, in 1929, the son of Benjamin Max Potok (a businessman and Belzer Hasid) and Mollie (Friedman) Potok, a descendant of a Hasidic family. Though Potok was reared in Jewish Orthodoxy and was sent to Orthodox parochial schools, by the age of ten he was showing an interest in drawing and painting, something frowned upon by both his father and his teachers. For the Orthodox Jew, art is at best a waste of time and at worst a violation of the Commandment forbidding graven images. Potok was told that it was better to study the Hebrew Bible and the commentaries on it (the Talmud) than to engage in such "foolishness." Writing, however, had a more ambiguous place among the Orthodox, and by 1945 Potok's reading of Evelyn Waugh's *Brideshead Revisited* (1945) had convinced him to become an author.

Potok's father was a Polish émigré whose stories of the suffering of the Jews in the Eastern European pogroms taught the young Potok that Orthodoxy must be preserved in the face of a world bent on destroying it and the Jews, and that one day the suffering of his people would play a part in the world's redemption. Much later, Chaim Potok would stand at the Hiroshima memorial in Japan, contemplating the atomic destruction unleashed upon the world and his own place in such a world. As he told an interviewer in 1981, all of his novels would flow from that moment in Japan.

Potok's Orthodox childhood brought him into contact with the ultra-Orthodox, the Hasids ("pious ones"). Within the wide range of Judaism, from Liberal and Reform to Conservative, Orthodox, and Hasidic, the Hasids are the most rigorously fundamentalistic. Originating in Poland in the eighteenth century as a reaction against an over-intellectualized faith controlled by the rabbis, Hasidism at first emphasized the mystical elements of Judaism though it, too, came to stress the study and interpretation of the Talmud. Central to the Hasidic movement was the *tzaddik* ("righ-

teous one"), a powerful leader who, it was believed, embodied the essence of the Jewish community and whose word was law. Various Hasidic sects followed different *tzaddiks*, each sect claiming to be the true faith. What was common to all was their separation from the world and even from other Jewish groups, their tightly knit communities, and the immense persecution they suffered. Potok's novels express an ambivalence regarding the Hasids and thus reveal a tension within his own life. The movement had enabled Judaism to survive despite the European pogroms and had stood in the way of assimilationist tendencies that would have diluted and eventually purged the faith of its uniqueness; yet in its unyielding demand for obedience to "the rebbe" and its suspicion of modern scientific and literary studies, Hasidism, he felt, was in danger of making Judaism irrelevant in the twentieth century. For Potok, the world of the Hasidim was narrow and confining, as was his own Orthodoxy. In 1950, after taking his graduate degree in English literature from Yeshiva University, he began his studies for the Conservative rabbinate.

Ordained as a Conservative rabbi in 1954, Potok became national director for the Conservative youth organization, the Leaders Training Fellowship, and in 1955, as a chaplain in the United States Army, he served in Korea. His overseas experience proved to be formative for his writing career. In *Wanderings: Chaim Potok's History of the Jews* (1978), his nonfiction account of Jewish history, Potok explains:

> My early decades had prepared me for everything—except the two encounters I in fact experienced: a meeting with a vast complex of cultures perfectly at ease without Jews and Judaism, and a confrontration with the beautiful and the horrible in the world of oriental human beings. . . . Jewish history began in a world of pagans; my own Judaism was transformed in another such world.

Though his first novel, about his Korean experiences, was repeatedly rejected, a second novel, *The Chosen* (1967), became a popular success. In the intervening years, Potok had married a psychiatric social worker, Adena Mosevitzky (their daughter Rena was born in 1962, Naama in 1965, and son Akiva in 1968), and had become managing editor of the New York-based *Conservative Judaism*. In 1965, Potok received his doctorate in philosophy from the University of Pennsylvania and became associate editor of the Jewish Publication Society of America. A year later, he was named editor-in-chief and appointed to the society's Bible Translation Committee. *The Promise*, a sequel to the *The Chosen*, followed in 1969; *My Name Is Asher Lev* was published in 1972 (its sequel, *The Gift of Asher Lev*, appeared in 1990). Then followed *In the Beginning* in 1975, *The Book of Lights* in 1981 (which gave literary form to Potok's Korean chaplaincy), and *Davita's Harp* in 1985.

After living for some four years in Jerusalem in the mid-1970's, the family settled in Pennsylvania, where Potok taught the philosophy of literature at the University of Pennsylvania.

Analysis

In his first attempt at dramatizing his experiences as a chaplain during the Korean

War, Chaim Potok had planned a series of flashbacks to the protagonist's Jewish boyhood which would show the stark contrast between the ingrown world of the ultra-Orthodox Hasidim and the secular, non-Jewish world confronted by the chaplain. A crisis of faith would find the chaplain rejecting strict Jewish fundamentalism but adhering to the Commandments in a stance of openness toward the science and literary methodology produced by other cultures.

That original unpublished novel became instead a series of books thematically linked, each exploring some aspect of the nature of a strict orthodox religious community in its confrontation with the world of secular learning and values. Rather than speak from an assimilationist or modernist position, as do the creations of Jewish-American writers Saul Bellow and Philip Roth, Potok's characters must choose between two versions of the same living faith: the world of the Hasidim, closed yet immensely resilient in the face of suffering, and the world of Jewish Orthodoxy, reverent to the Commandments but open to the insights of modern science, psychology, and literary criticism, and whose adherents are thus tempted to forsake the One True God.

In his published novels, Potok returns again and again to the *Bildungsroman*, the "novel of education," to show the intellectual and spiritual development of his main characters and how they wrestle with the main questions set by each book. In *The Chosen* and *The Promise*, for example, Danny Saunders, genius son of a Hasidic rabbi, must reconcile his strict upbringing in Talmud studies with his growing appreciation of Freudian psychology. *In the Beginning* traces the intellectual growth of young David Lurie, who decides to confront anti-Semitism and show the relevance of Judaism to the modern world by using the tools of textual analysis developed in Germany. *Davita's Harp* considers the place of women in Jewish Orthodoxy, and *My Name Is Asher Lev* and *The Gift of Asher Lev* take up the plight of the artist whose work wounds those dearest to him.

Potok pits good against good. His sympathies for the Hasidic community and the importance of Jewish practice mean that his characters cannot simply abandon their childhood nest without a deep struggle to keep what is of value and to add from the outside world what is also of value. It is a male-dominated society (Potok's usual first-person narrator is almost always a young man, always a genius), and fathers and sons form the core of most of the novels. Some fathers, such as David Malter in *The Chosen*, are veritable saints in their compassion and understanding; others, like Asher Lev's father Aryeh, cannot understand their son's preoccupation with the world.

Potok's stories develop in diary-like fashion, full of everyday experiences told in simple diction. It is a conscious style, one patterned after that of American writers Stephen Crane and Ernest Hemingway, the short, simple declarative sentences achieving a kind of "flattening" effect as incident follows incident. The simple style belies the careful construction of each novel, and Potok has acknowledged the influence of Irish writer James Joyce, especially Joyce's *Ulysses* (1922), which is a modernist parallel of the ancient Homeric epic. In *The Promise*, Potok has Rachel Gordon write a paper on the "Ithaca" section of the Joyce novel, in which the artistic young Stephen Dedalus is contrasted with the earthbound Leopold Bloom. Potok's references to Joyce are far from subtle, and the point is driven home that Rachel, in love with literature and reared by secular Jewish parents, must come to terms with her love for Danny Saunders, reared by a Hasidic rebbe, and whose passion is psychology.

In the Beginning is patterned after the biblical book of *Genesis*, with David Lurie's many illnesses paralleling the rise and fall of the Jewish people (Lurie as a child is literally dropped by his mother in an accident that shapes the rest of his life). *The Book of Lights*, with its references to the mystical Jewish Kabbalah, is divided into ten chapters corresponding to the ten emanations of God. Protagonist Gershon Loran's Kabbalah teacher is named Jakob Keter; "keter" is the name for the primary emanation.

Each novel unfolds chronologically against the background of world events. *In the Beginning* takes the reader from the Depression of the late 1920's into the World War II era, *Davita's Harp* from the 1930's through the Spanish Civil War (1936-1939) and into World War II, and *The Chosen* and *The Promise* from 1944 to the mid-1950's. *The Book of Lights* takes its story to the late 1950's, and the two Asher Lev books encompass the 1940's through the 1980's.

Throughout the novels, a radio station or newspaper headline reminds readers that the story of the central characters mirrors the struggles in the wider world: anti-Semitism in the United States during the Depression, the attraction of Communism to partisans in the Spanish Civil War, the confrontation of Jewish Orthodoxy with alien cultures, the Hasidic and Orthodox conflict over whether Israel should be formed as a political state, and the question of the Holocaust and how the Master of the Universe could have allowed it. In each novel, Potok has reworked his own experiences to provide something of a tentative solution to the problems he has set for himself.

Controlling images shape his works. The baseball game in *The Chosen* is symbolic of the competition between Hasidic and Orthodox Jewish communities; the funeral of his uncle in *The Gift of Asher Lev* speaks of the sacrifice Asher must make for the sake of his art and his Hasidic community; the vision of the pups being born in the rundown Brooklyn neighborhood in *The Book of Lights* represents the fertile, mystical Jewish experience which, Potok believes, can enrich the intellectually sterile study of Jewish law.

Potok has found such mysticism novelistically useful in crafting his stories. From *In the Beginning* onward, dreams, visions, and mystical visitations haunt most of his main characters, and the ability of the artistic imagination to fashion some resolution to the novel's questions reflects Potok's own position that Jewish fundamentalism can be enriched by its painters and writers, were they allowed the freedom to work out their gift within the community.

THE CHOSEN

First published: 1967
Type of work: Novel

THE PROMISE

First published: 1969
Type of work: Novel

Jewish cultures conflict in the lives of two brilliant young men who must unite in their efforts to help a young friend.

The Chosen met with popular success upon publication, despite the fact that it concerns itself with a small and narrow Hasidic Jewish community in the Williamsburg section of Brooklyn. Yet the story of Danny Saunders, son of the imperious and strictly Orthodox Reb Saunders, and Reuvan Malter, son of a teacher at a Jewish yeshiva (parochial school), has universal implications: Can the culture of one's early years be transcended without being denied? Danny has been chosen by his father to be the next leader of the Hasidic sect, but Danny feels trapped. His father, in an effort to impart a compassionate soul to his genius son, has reared him in silence; all the while, however, Danny has been exploring secular psychology at the library under the guidance of David Malter, Reuvan's father. After the two boys clash at a baseball game, their friendship gradually develops, though when David Malter becomes active in the project of building a new Jewish homeland in Palestine after the revelations from the German concentration camps, Reb Saunders imposes silence between Danny and Reuvan. The rebbe is saddened by the news of the Holocaust, but he believes that a new state of Israel can only be built by the Messiah, not by human politics.

Following the creation of Israel as a state in 1948, the ban is lifted between Danny and Reuvan; the two must now explain to Reb Saunders that Danny will not wear the rebbe's mantle but will instead study psychology. In a climactic conversation, Reb Saunders explains to Danny (through Reuvan) that the silence he had experienced will allow him to hear the cries of the world. The rebbe himself cries and finally speaks directly to his son, this time as a father, not as a teacher. Reb Saunders accepts Danny's decision; Levi, Danny's younger brother, will become the leader of the Hasids.

Danny's own freedom is mirrored in the news reports of the Israeli war of liberation. Ironically, Reuvan, reared by his father to be a keeper of the Commandments yet open to the world's learning, becomes a rabbi after studying at an Orthodox seminary. Danny, who has removed his distinctive Hasidic adornments of earlocks and beard, is graduated from Columbia University.

The Promise continues the story of the two men, now in their twenties, and intertwines their lives with those of Professor Abraham Gordon and his family. Gordon has earned the disdain of Orthodox Jews for his unorthodox questioning of Jewish verities, such as the literal truth of the Hebrew Bible. When Gordon's fourteen-year-old son Michael explodes in a violent denunciation of Orthodoxy for its excommunication of his father, Michael is taken to a psychological treatment center to be helped by Danny Saunders.

Reuvan's father David has also published a book, one criticizing the reliability of certain texts of the Talmud, and that has earned him the wrath of Reuvan's teacher Rev Kalman. The Holocaust survivor fears modernism will make deadly inroads into Orthodoxy. Reuvan can thus understand Michael's feelings, though David Malter has taught his own son about the value of Hasidic Orthodoxy in preserving Judaism in the midst of terrible suffering.

Michael refuses to talk until Danny isolates him with silence. Broken at last, Michael voices hatred for his father, whose condemnation Michael himself is forced to share. Once having expressed his true feelings, Michael can begin to heal. Meanwhile, Gordon's daughter Rachel, at first Reuvan's date, falls in love with Danny and the two are soon married, a union of the deeply religious psychologist with the cosmopolitan secularist.

The Chosen and *The Promise* share in their cores a profound love of learning, and if both Reuvan and Danny are a little too perfect, they engagingly express the ideas of silence and its power, the varying forms of love of fathers for sons, and the journey of two young men seeking to reconcile their faith with the wider world of knowledge. David Malter had told his son Reuvan in *The Chosen* that a person must make his own meaning; both Reuvan and Danny chose meaning that encompassed the past as well as the present, though each in his own way. Such choices, the novel suggests, are the stuff of heroism.

MY NAME IS ASHER LEV

First published: 1972
Type of work: Novel

THE GIFT OF ASHER LEV

First published: 1990
Type of work: Novel

A gifted artist faces self-imposed exile in order to pursue his work; in middle age, he finds that the price he must pay for his creativity includes his only son.

A perennial theme in Potok's work is that of the place of the artist (painter or writer) within the Hasidic community. In *My Name Is Asher Lev*, the controversy is over representational art. Asher is born in Crown Heights in Brooklyn in 1943, and as he grows it is evident that he has a gift for drawing and painting. Asher's father is frequently away on trips for the rebbe as the Ladover Hasid community (patterned perhaps on Lubavitch Hasidism) seeks to expand throughout Europe. While Aryeh Lev is arranging help for Jewish families emigrating to the United States, Asher and his mother spend long nights in loneliness. (Asher had refused to join his father in Europe.)

When his mother's brother is killed on a mission for the rebbe, Rivkeh Lev suffers a breakdown. Later, taking up her brother's uncompleted work, she surrounds herself with her Russian studies so as to forget the heartache. Images of work completed and uncompleted are present throughout the novel, and Asher finds as he develops his gift that he must complete his understanding of the world by painting not only what he sees with his eyes but also what his inner vision shows him. The pictures he paints often depict the reality of evil. At the end of the novel, Asher has revealed two crucifixion paintings to his parents. In both, the face of his mother stares from the cross, looking in abstract fashion at the ever-traveling husband on one side and at Asher the stranger on the other. Asher's parents are horrified, and the rebbe tells Asher that the artist has passed a boundary where even the rebbe is powerless to help.

Earlier, sensing Asher's talent, the rebbe had put him into the capable hands of painter Jacob Kahn, a nonobservant Jew, who introduces Asher to the work of Pablo Picasso, especially *Guernica* (1937), the painting of the horror of the German bombing of the Basque capital during the Spanish Civil War. Asher in time will leave for France, there to work with Kahn, who tells Asher that the young man's genius is the only justification for all the hurt his paintings will cause. Yet in his exile Asher will not cease to be a keeper of the Commandments (though the Commandment to obey one's parents must be reinterpreted); Potok is saying that the genuine artist must, perhaps inevitably, leave the Orthodox community, but not necessarily Orthodoxy.

Asher frequently dreams of his "mythic ancestor" (a Jew who served a nobleman only to have the nobleman visit evil upon the world) and realizes that just as the ancestor might travel the world to redress the wrongs done by the nobleman, so the artist, as he reshapes the images of a world of suffering, himself can bring a kind of balance to that world. It is a kind of completion.

The Gift of Asher Lev begins many years later; Asher is in his forties, married to Devorah, with a daughter, Rocheleh, eleven, and a son, Avrumel, five. The family has returned from France to the home of Asher's parents for the funeral of Asher's uncle Yitzchok. The old rebbe convinces Asher to stay past the week of mourning, and soon it becomes clear that the rebbe, who had once put a blessing on Asher's talent, is now blessing him for another of his gifts: his son. Asher's father will become the new rebbe someday soon, but to ensure continuity to the Ladover community, some successor must be guaranteed. Normally that would be Asher's position; but, as Danny Saunders did in *The Chosen*, Asher removes himself from consideration. It falls upon Avrumel, the father's grandson, to be next in the line of succession.

In the end, visited by visions of the dead (Picasso, Jacob Kahn), Asher returns to France, alone, to paint, promising a return trip to the United States to see his wife and their children. Death enfolds the story, with the funeral of uncle Yitzchok and the "loss" of Asher's son to the Ladover community framing the novel. Asher is convinced that his painting gift is from the Master of the Universe, yet he cannot understand why that same God would exact such a price for that gift. Avrumel himself will be reared in the Hasidic tradition, but, though not an artist, he will also know art. Potok seems to suggest that the child may one day bring a new appreciation of creative talents to the Ladover. As Asher lifts Avrumel over his head and hands him to Aryeh Lev, his father, Asher hears the voice of his mythic ancestor shouting something. In some way the artist has atoned for his gift, the gift that brings both blessings and curses upon the earth.

IN THE BEGINNING

First published: 1975
Type of work: Novel

In the Bronx, in New York City, a young boy struggles against anti-Semitism.

In the Beginning, Potok's fourth published book, marked a stylistic advance in his art. In its extensive use of flashbacks and impressionistic language, Potok is able to move forward and backward in time to create a concrete world suffused with the stuff of dreams, preparing the reader for the final vision of the climax. The novel is David Lurie's story; now a teacher, Lurie's reminiscences take him back to his sixth year. At the close of the novel, Lurie has become a graduate student at the University of Chicago.

The Luries, an Orthodox Jewish family, had emigrated from Poland and settled in the Bronx. David's father, Max, had founded the Am Kedoshim (Holy Nation) Society to bring fellow Jews to the United States and away from the bloody pogroms of their homeland. Max Lurie is full of rage at the Gentiles who would perpetrate such violence; David himself falls victim to anti-Semitism after he accidentally runs over the hand of a neighbor boy with his tricycle. Eddie Kulansky torments the sickly David, who struggles in his thoughts against the bullies of the world. David dreams of the Golem of Prague, similar to Frankenstein's monster, and imagines him putting to rest all those who would persecute the Jews.

Though often ill, David is (as are all Potok's narrators) a prodigy, making adults uncomfortable with his questions and picking up attitudes of anger against the Gentiles. With the failure of Max Lurie's real estate business during the Depression and the financial ruin of the Am Kedoshim Society, the family must face Max's own depression. Max's wife, Ruth, the widow of Max's brother David (Max married her according to the Law of Moses) is frail and superstitious. Ruth reads to her son in German, and the young David begins a study of the Torah, the Five Books of Moses, with businessman Shmuel Bader.

It is Bader and David's Hebrew Bible teacher, Rav Sharfman, who encourage the boy to use his intellect to argue against the traditional Jewish commentators. For David, the study of the Bible texts is infused with life. His father's watch repair business prospers, and the family is able to move to a larger apartment house, but Max Lurie is burdened by his older son's interest in the new science of textual criticism, developed in Germany. There is still much rage in him, for his brother David had died in a pogrom, and his son's study seems to be bringing the Jewish tradition into question. Max's younger son, Alex, has taken up the study of modern novels and Sigmund Freud. David tries to explain that his intention is to use the learning of the secular world as a weapon against that world.

A visionary reconciliation comes at the end of the novel, during David's visit, years later, to the site of the Bergen-Belsen concentration camp. David is joined by the spirit of his father, now dead, and by Max's brother David, who tells Max that there has been no betrayal, that Orthodoxy must be enriched by outside knowledge. Rage will not overcome anti-Semitism; only a deep penetration of pagan culture with the insights of Orthodoxy, tempered by modern science, can ever succeed. In this vision, Potok draws upon the principles of argumentation and consolidation in Orthodoxy itself. Orthodoxy is not one generation's interpretation, but the whole tradition of interpretation, wherein one rabbinical argument is countered with a second, reconciled by a third, and so on down through the centuries. David's explorations of new knowledge outside the tradition may well return to enrich the tradition itself and enable it to better penetrate the modern consciousness.

As in Potok's other *Bildungsromane*, the most fascinating scenes in the novel involve David's challenge of his instructors, and the ancient rabbinical commentators as well, on points of scripture. The conflict here is that of good against good; the ultra-Orthodox tradition is drawn with sympathy and care, for these are the people of Potok's past. Yet, as the author's own break with the Hasidim came, so David Lurie must strike out on his own, the burden of his people still in his heart. David will fight the anti-Semitic words with words of his own, not with guns, as his father had; he will make a new beginning.

DAVITA'S HARP

First published: 1985
Type of work: Novel

A young girl, spurned by the very Jewish community she hoped to embrace, finds that her time of innocence is over.

Ilana Davita Chandal, Potok's precocious narrator of *Davita's Harp*, is in sharp contrast to David Lurie of *In the Beginning*. Ilana Davita is Potok's first female protagonist, but she is also the first main character in Potok's novels to seek to join Orthodoxy from pagan society. She is rebuffed by that Orthodoxy, and in the end expresses the rage that David Lurie hoped to overcome by his mediation of secular learning and Orthodox tradition.

Ilana Davita's mother is a nonbelieving Jew, her father a nonbelieving Christian. Growing up in the New York area before World War II, Davita is accustomed to frequent moves. Her parents are involved in the Communist Party in its attempts to fight Fascism in Spain and in the United States. Davita's early life is full of stories; Aunt Sara, a devout Episcopalian, tells Davita tales from the Bible. Jakob Daw, an old family friend, aging and infirm after having been gassed in World War I, tells Davita the story of a little bird and its futile efforts to stop the beautiful and deceitful music that lulls the world into accepting the horrors of war.

Davita's father, a writer for *New Masses*, is killed at the bombing of Guernica during the Spanish Civil War. In *My Name Is Asher Lev*, the artist protagonist was introduced to Picasso's famous painting; now, in *Davita's Harp*, Potok provides a dramatic account of the event that inspired it. Soon both Davita's mother and Jakob Daw have rejected the Communists because that group had also committed atrocities. Spiritually homeless, Davita begins attending a Jewish high school, where she excels. Her mother marries an Orthodox Jew who had loved her years before, and though Jakob Daw dies in Europe, his last story remains in Davita's heart.

The little bird ceased its search for the music of the world, Jakob had told her, and instead made itself very small to fit inside Davita's harp to bask in the music of innocence. Hers is a small door harp with little balls that strike piano wires whenever the door is opened. Her time of innocence has ceased as well. Though the most brilliant student in her yeshiva, in 1942 Davita is passed over for the Akiva Prize because she is a woman; another student, Reuvan Malter (first introduced in *The Chosen*) refuses to accept the award after he learns the truth. Davita feels betrayed by her adopted community and her lack of opportunity to speak a few parting words on behalf of all those who suffered in the twentieth century.

Potok provides Davita with a vision of a meeting inside the harp, where Jakob Daw, Davita's father, and Aunt Sara appear. Davita says she does not understand a world that kills its own, its best. The harp sings in memorium to all the Davitas who would never be able to speak their own few words. Aunt Sara offers parting advice that Davita be angry with the world, but always respectful. Davita would go on to public school, but the betrayal would change her life. The conflict between Orthodoxy and feminism was a new exploration for Potok, but the theme of the artist making a reconciliation with the world through art is reaffirmed.

Summary

The novels of Chaim Potok represent both a personal quest and an artistic achievement. The quest is that of finding a viable faith which affirms ancient beliefs yet is open to the best thinking of modern times; the artistic achievement is in the working and reworking of personal experience into the stuff of human transformation, an invitation to readers to learn from their own past and draw on the strength of their community even as they move beyond or away from the tradition that nurtured them.

Potok's quiet tales of small Jewish sects in New York are poignant in their simplicity and powerful in their evocation of the mending that art can accomplish in one burdened by suffering, anger, and betrayal.

Bibliography

Abramson, Edward A. *Chaim Potok*. Boston: Twayne, 1986.

Forbes, Cheryl. "Judaism Under the Secular Umbrella." *Christianity Today* 22 (September 8, 1978): 14-21.

Kauvar, Elaine M. "An Interview with Chaim Potok." *Contemporary Literature* 28 (Fall, 1986): 290-317.

Potok, Chaim. "A Reply to a Semi-Sympathetic Critic." *Studies in American Jewish Literature* 2 (Spring, 1976): 30-34.

Studies in American Jewish Literature 4 (1985). Special Potok issue.

Dan Barnett

EZRA POUND

Born: Hailey, Idaho
October 10, 1885
Died: Venice, Italy
November 1, 1972

Principal Literary Achievement
One of the most innovative and accomplished of twentieth century writers, Pound determined the standards and direction of much of modern literature, especially poetry.

Biography

Ezra Loomis Pound, one of the most influential and controversial figures in modern literature, was born in the mining town of Hailey, Idaho, in 1885. When Pound was only eighteen months old the family moved to Philadelphia, Pennsylvania, where his father Homer became an official with the United States mint—an occupation that perhaps influenced Pound's later interest in economic and monetary matters. Pound made his first trip to Europe in 1898 with his great aunt; he would later live most of his adult life on the Continent, becoming a virtual exile from his native country. To some he would be more than that: a traitor.

In 1901, Pound began college at the University of Pennsylvania, then completed his undergraduate degree at Hamilton College, in Clinton, New York, in 1905. He received an M.A. in Romance languages from Hamilton the following year, then a fellowship to travel in Spain, Italy, and Provence (southern France), where he gathered material for a book on the troubadours—the poets of courtly love who flourished during the late middle ages. Returning to the United States, Pound was briefly an instructor in French and Spanish at Wabash College in Crawfordsville, Indiana; he was dismissed after he allowed a stranded young actress to share his room in a boardinghouse.

Having determined—at fifteen—to become a poet, Pound considered his dismissal a release, and he returned to Europe, writing and traveling, mainly in Italy. In 1908, he published his first books, a slim volume entitled *A Lume Spento* ("with candles extinguished") and *A Quinzaine for This Yule*. Both were heavily influenced by the troubadour poets and by the highly elaborate and artificial diction of late nineteenth century verse.

In 1908, Pound moved to London, where he remained until the end of World

War I, establishing himself as a flamboyant personality as well as an aspiring poet. He affected earrings, flowing capes, and a dramatic red beard; his antics were wild and outrageous. Partially he sought to mask his own social insecurities, but he also wished to draw attention to his commitment to art. He became known by the major writers of the time, including Ford Madox Ford, Wyndham Lewis, and William Butler Yeats, and he continued to publish poems, translations, reviews and essays.

Around 1912, Pound developed a poetic doctrine which he termed Imagism, which put emphasis upon clear, specific language and poems stripped of excess ornament and useless words: The particular image was to be the new focus of verse. Within two years Pound had moved in another direction, that of "vorticism," which was based on the concept of energy as symbolized by the vortex, a whirlpool or spiral form. Although Pound soon abandoned the formal aspects of these theories, their central tenets remained part of his poetry for the rest of his life.

A third enduring influence from this time was that of Chinese poetic and philosophical thought. Believing that Chinese poets had used their language to reach the very essence of meanings naturally inherent in words, Pound eagerly translated their writings, adapting them in his volume *Cathay* (1915). Later he would incorporate Chinese ideograms themselves, without translation, into *The Cantos* (1917 through 1970).

After World War I, Pound believed that London was exhausted as an intellectual center; he moved to Paris, first publishing *Hugh Selwyn Mauberley* (1920) as a scornful, satirical farewell. Established in France, he continued to write, but much of his energies were taken up with assisting fellow artists: Pound was unique among moderns in being an untiring champion of others. He secured grants and patrons for James Joyce, assisted T. S. Eliot in being able to leave his work at Lloyd's Bank (and then helped edit *The Waste Land*, 1922, into its final shape), and generally used every opportunity to advance the careers of any artist he believed talented and worth notice.

After only four years Pound moved from Paris to Rapallo, Italy, which was to be his home for most of his life. In 1914, he had married Dorothy Shakespear, but he had since met the musician Olga Rudge; in Rapallo, Pound established two separate households for himself and the women. On July 9, 1925, Pound and Olga Rudge had a daughter, Mary; on September 10 of that year Pound and Dorothy became the parents of a son, Omar Shakespear Pound. The dual arrangement would continue throughout Pound's life.

Pound had early conceived the notion of writing an epic poem based on history. The first parts were published in 1917, and in 1925 a substantial portion appeared with the title *A Draft of XVI Cantos*; it has become known simply as the *Cantos*. Pound continued to work on it for the rest of his life; it was never completed, only abandoned. The work is one of the most important of twentieth century literature; ironically, it is more influential than read, more discussed than known.

Disgusted by the senseless slaughter of World War I and insulted by the degradation of culture that followed, Pound was convinced that social and economic matters needed reform. Artists, he believed, had an obligation to lead in this effort. Unfortunately, his path led to unsound fiscal theories such as "social credit" and to the dangerous political doctrines of Fascism. Believing that Italian Fascist leader Benito Mussolini was an authentic heir to Confucian ideals of the enlightened ruler, and infected by the anti-Semitism of the times, Pound began to make broadcasts over Italian radio when World War II began; he continued these even after the United States entered the conflict. His talks were too rambling and bizarre to be effective propaganda, but they did get him indicted for treason, in absentia, in 1943. In 1945 U.S. troops arrested Pound in northern Italy.

Held as a prisoner for six months in the Army disciplinary center at Pisa, Pound was returned to the United States, but he was declared mentally unfit to stand trial in 1946. Committed to St. Elizabeth's Hospital in Washington, D.C., he remained there until 1958, receiving visitors, reading, and continuing to write and publish, including new sections of the *Cantos*. One of these, *The Pisan Cantos* (1948), won the Bolligen Prize for Poetry in 1949, causing an immense literary and political furor. Ironically, Pound's imprisonment was a period of great productivity, and he brought out a major work almost every year while in St. Elizabeth's.

Through an arrangement devised between such noted literary figures as Ernest Hemingway and Archibald MacLeish on one hand and the United States Government on the other, Pound's indictment for treason was dismissed in 1958 and he was freed to return to Italy. During the last years of his life Pound, once so voluble and self-confident, subsided into silence. His writing became less frequent, and his doubts about himself and his work seemed to increase. He despaired over completing the *Cantos*, and the great work trailed off into fragments as its author concluded, "I cannot make it cohere." In 1970, he published *The Cantos of Ezra Pound I-CXVII*: It is not the "finished" version, because Pound had come to realize there could be no such thing. After so many years, his life's work still remained a draft.

Refusing to speak and brooding over the past, Pound made his final visit to the United States in 1969. He had already attended the rites of many of his friends and companions from the earlier days; when he died in Venice on November 1, 1972, Ezra Pound was the last of a generation that had changed modern writing.

Analysis

Pound's influence on twentieth century literature was felt in three ways: through his life, his theories, and his poetic practice. It can be plausibly argued that the first two were of greater impact than the third, and while this may seem unusual for a writer, Pound's career made this result almost inevitable.

Pound decided when he was only fifteen that, by the time he was thirty, he would know more about poetry than any man living. Although this might seem at first the typical dream of a talented, ambitious adolescent, Pound obviously meant it, and his dedication to his art was so intense that he largely fulfilled his pledge. His knowledge of verse form, meter, rhythm, and poetic devices and traditions was unrivaled among his contemporaries. In pursuit of his goal, Pound became the image of the modern poet: He dressed the part, acted the role, and subordinated almost everything in his personal life to his poetry. Pound the character could be dismissed were it not for his interaction with other writers of his time. He was a generous friend, securing funds for men such as Joyce, tutoring aspiring poets such as Hilda Doolittle (whom he renamed H. D., by which she is now known to literary history), and assisting T. S. Eliot in editing *The Waste Land* into final form. Pound was concerned with promoting true talent wherever he discovered it, and it is likely that many modern classics would have been unwritten—or written less well—without Ezra Pound.

In his theories, Pound exerted a similar influence. He found English poetry to be verse that was largely content with outworn techniques, sentimental vision, and an inability to distinguish excellence from mediocrity. Although Pound despaired over his lack of influence, he actually succeeded remarkably well in establishing higher poetic standards and forcing modern poets to abide by them. Pound brought renewed attention to the key elements of poetry: precise word choice, attention to rhythm, and creation of poems that were organic wholes rather than vaguely pleasing collections of soothing sounds.

Some complained, and still complain, that this made modern poetry difficult, even incomprehensible. These objections do have a certain merit, because Pound articulated theories that led to poetry which made greater demands on the reader. If at times modern poetry cries out more for translation than simple reading, this is the legacy of Ezra Pound. Because it focuses more attention on the poem itself, however, and causes the reader to become a participant in the work of art, this is a legacy which has strengthened true poetry while giving the attentive reader more worthwhile pleasure.

Pound's own poetry, as contrasted to his theories, has not had a comparable effect, at least among the poetry-reading public. He is a difficult poet—although not intentionally so—and his work requires a level of knowledge and sensitivity which some readers cannot bring to the page and which others do not believe worth the effort. It is among fellow poets that Pound's verse has been most important. Although he founded no real school and established no specific tradition—other than a general "modernism" which was only partially his and is impossible to define narrowly—Pound created an atmosphere which expanded the horizons of modern poetry.

The *Cantos* have been called the great unread poem of this century; along with Joyce's *Finnegans Wake* (1939), they mark the outer boundaries of modern literature, perched on that edge where creativity and incomprehensibility come dangerously close. Pound may have been right when he concluded that he could not make the *Cantos* cohere. Still, in their individual sections they offer breathtaking vistas of language and thought, a collection of shining images that radically redefine what poetry can be and what it can do. Perhaps it was inevitable that Pound's practice should fall short of his own stringent standards, but by having the standards and attempting to fulfill them, Pound once again made poetry matter.

Yet it was a paradoxical, perhaps pyhrric victory, because Pound's poetry could never be truly popular poetry—certainly not in the sense that Walter Scott or Lord Byron once had the poetic equivalent of best-sellers. Without intending to do so, Pound's theories led to a poetry that could be understood only by a relatively limited, elite audience. To his credit, Pound recognized this and sought a solution. No ivory tower intellectual, but a socially committed writer, he wanted to include, rather than exclude, and he consistently advocated education, true education, as essential for a fully human society. In a sense, Pound wanted a society where anyone had the opportunity and the ability to read the *Cantos*. It was only a vision, perhaps, but a worthy one.

PORTRAIT D'UNE FEMME

First published: 1912
Type of work: Poem

Pound presents a satirical yet ambiguously affectionate depiction of a literary hostess.

The literal translation of Pound's title, "Portrait d'Une Femme," is "portrait of a lady," which has inevitable associations with the novel *The Portrait of a Lady* by Henry James, published in 1881. Pound greatly admired James's book, especially for its keen psychological insights, and in this poem he attempts to re-create the same sort of description, outlining the character of a person by detailing her surroundings.

The woman is a London literary hostess who rules over a conventional, if slightly boring, salon where writers and artists have come for "this score years," amusing the lady and themselves with clever but, it would seem, inconsequential conversation. Nothing really important is said here, possibly because it would be wasted: "Great minds have sought you—lacking someone else," Pound writes.

The woman is compared to the Sargasso Sea, that area in the North Atlantic where floating seaweed from the Gulf Stream gathers and where tradition says that wrecked ships, lost hulks, and vanished vessels are mired forever. In much the same way, the lady of the title has gathered cast-off ideas, second rate notions, and "fact that leads nowhere." In this respect the poem is in keeping with Pound's satirical verse on the English literary scene, a view which he expressed more forcibly and much more bitterly in *Hugh Selwyn Mauberley*. Thus, by extension, the woman in "Portrait d'Une Femme" becomes an embodiment of an entire culture, one which is incapable, or at least unwilling, to recognize and appreciate true originality in art. Perhaps it would be threatened by it; perhaps it is simply not interested.

On the other hand, there is a certain affection for the character, and Pound's poem sounds wistful, almost elegiac, when it recounts the meager hoard the woman has gathered after twenty years of association with artists and writers. While she is compared to the Sargasso Sea, a stagnant backwash of the vital ocean, she is not explicitly condemned. Perhaps, the poem implies, she, like the artists of the time, has been a victim of the culture.

The style of the poem is notable for Pound's use of blank verse, a poetic form that he seldom employed and seems to have thought the refuge of second-rate writers of his time. It has become a critical commonplace to remark on Pound's ear for the music of English poetry, while at the same time maintaining that he could not discipline himself to write in conventional forms. "Portrait d'Une Femme" shows that the first half of this commonplace is precisely right, the second half, decidedly wrong.

IN A STATION OF THE METRO

First published: 1913
Type of work: Poem

Pound uses a brief, vivid image to express a profound aesthetic experience that occurred in everyday life.

The short poem "In a Station of the Metro" is an example of Pound's artistic theory of Imagism, which he advocated for a brief while in his career and which had a lasting impact on his writing and modern poetry. During his time in London, just before World War I, Pound developed a theory of poetry, which he termed Imagism, that stripped away the rhetorical excesses and vagueness that he believed obscured so much of contemporary poetry. In their places he advocated precise, careful presentation of specific images accurately rendered. Although Pound would later move beyond this rather limited concept, he retained the essential parts of it, and many of the passages in the *Cantos* are basically Imagist in their style.

An Imagist poem, by the very definition of the term, was brief. Seldom has the concision been carried so far as Pound's 1913 verse, "In a Station of the Metro," which consists of only two lines. The poem appears to be a translation of some Japanese haiku, and while Pound was undoubtably influenced by that tradition, his poem was completely original.

He has left a description of how it was composed. One evening, while coming out of the London subway (the "metro" of the title) Pound was struck by the sight of a beautiful face, then another and yet another. Seeking to express this experience, he began writing a poem which ran to thirty-two lines. After much paring and revision, he finally achieved the image and effect he sought:

> The apparition of these faces in the crowd;
> petals on a wet, black bough.

Although at first reading the poem seems to be about very little (and even that little is mysterious), a second glance shows how well it fits into Pound's theory of imagism and just how Imagism works. To begin with, there is the single image, designed in this case to reproduce an experience not literally but emotionally and psychologically. Further, the image is presented in a specific literary form, the metaphor, recognized since ancient Greece as one of the most powerful devices of poetry; Aristotle, for example, termed the proper use of metaphor the supreme test of a writer. This use of metaphor is worth noting, because Pound is often considered a poet who rejected past conventions and techniques; actually, he delighted in the poetic devices and scorned only their inferior use.

In keeping with Imagist theory, the words in the poem are, with one significant exception, concrete and specific: "faces," "crowd," "petals," and "bough" are all common English nouns, strung together in conventional English syntax. The two adjectives, "wet" and "black," are hardly unusual, and are just the sort of precise words to modify a noun such as "bough." Moreover, the metaphor is logical: Beautiful faces seen against a rainy London evening are like flower petals on a dark, wet branch. Through a careful selection of relevant images, Pound has re-created for the reader the effect impressed upon him that night.

The one word that is not a concrete noun is "apparition," and its unusual nature is highlighted by its placement at the beginning of the poem. By using this word, suggestive of ghostly sightings or supernatural experiences, and linking it with a string of commonplace nouns and modifiers, Pound is again re-creating what happened and what he experienced: a seemingly ordinary climb up a flight of subway stairs that turned into a vision.

In only two lines and fourteen words, Pound managed to re-create an entire experience by careful use of a specific image. A brief poem has been made to carry more emotional and psychological weight than Pound's contemporaries would have thought possible; his poetic successors would find the techniques used here essential in writing the poetry of the rest of the twentieth century.

HOMAGE TO SEXTUS PROPERTIUS

First published: 1919
Type of work: Poems

A re-creation, rather than a translation, of the work of a Roman poet, in which Pound comments upon contemporary society.

When Pound published *Homage to Sextus Propertius* in 1919, a surprisingly large number of readers apparently thought that the work was intended to be a literal, or at least close, translation of classical Roman poetry. This misperception came despite the obvious clue in the title: Pound was paying tribute to Propertius and attempting to capture the spirit of his verse rather than the word-by-word meaning.

Still, a number of classical scholars attacked Pound for his many supposed mistakes and errors in translation. One of the more intemperate attacks, by William Hale of the University of Chicago, stated flatly: "If Mr. Pound were a professor of Latin, there would be nothing left for him but suicide." Dr. Hale missed the point sublimely; Pound was not a professor of Latin, but was a poet, paying homage to another poet.

Sextus Propertius was a Roman writer who lived during the first century B.C. He was a contemporary of poets better known today—Vergil, Ovid, and Horace—but during his time, Propertius was judged one of the finest elegiac poets in Latin. The elegy was a particular poetic genre, whose subject matter was most frequently lost love and whose tone was a mixture of wistfulness and sadness. Propertius gave the elegy a different twist, because his treatment of the form used language that was satirical, even bitter. He not only mocked the conventions of the traditional elegy but also used the form to mock the pretensions of imperial Rome. These qualities were the most congenial to Pound when he undertook his version of Propertius.

Pound wrote *Homage to Sextus Propertius* in 1917, when the slaughter of World War I was at its greatest; he had come to detest the war for its senseless destruction of life and culture, and his re-creation of another anti-imperial poet was an expression of that disgust. There was a connection, Pound noted, because the ancient Roman poems presented "certain emotions as vital to me in 1917, faced with the infinite and ineffable imbecility of the British Empire, as they were to Propertius some centuries earlier, when faced with the infinite and ineffable imbecility of the Roman Empire."

Pound constructs his poem by rearranging Propertius' verse into a twelve-part structure, sometimes combining different elegies, sometimes taking passages or even single lines from several different poems and linking them together. The twelve parts of the poem fall into two major categories: despair over the poet's love affair with Cynthia, who is certainly unkind to him and probably unfaithful as well; and his mocking commentary on the accepted poetry of the time (heroic verse celebrating the glories of empire) contrasted to his own intense, highly personal, and ultimately more honest writing. Even the poems that supposedly have Cynthia as their theme generally manage to include the comparison between epic verse and love poetry, clearly favoring the latter.

In adapting Propertius, Pound retained much of the original: The references to Roman history, mythology, and literature are frequent and require a reader able to catch the full range of allusions and their meanings. By contrast, however, even someone ignorant of Latin history and poetry should be able to respond to the poetic force and power that Pound retained from Propertius.

To achieve this, and to make Propertius once more a contemporary poet, Pound deliberately employed a number of anachronisms—terms or references which are outside Propertius' time. In one passage, for example, he calls the ancient Greek poet Hesiod a "respected Wordsworthian," and in another section he parodies the style of Yeats. In his most celebrated anachronism, Pound even brings in a twentieth-century kitchen appliance:

My cellar does not date from Numa Pompilius,
Nor bristle with wine jars,
Nor is it equipped with a frigidaire patent.

The impact of these jarring references is to heighten the satirical nature of the poems, and that seems to have been Pound's major intention. What he was doing with *Homage to Sextus Propertius* was not only re-creating a dead poet's work but also reanimating the dead poet himself. In a sense, Sextus Propertius, the actual poet, becomes "Sextus Propertius," a literary mask (or persona, to use one of Pound's favorite words) for the modern poet, Ezra Pound.

Pound was clearly fascinated by the concept of the persona. He used the Latin plural of the noun, *Personae*, twice as a title: in 1909, for a slender volume of his early verse, and again in 1926, for a much more extensive book, *Personae: The Collected Poems of Ezra Pound*. His masterwork, the *Cantos*, is a series of masks or personae through which Pound enters the personalities of figures from all times and places in human history. *Homage to Sextus Propertius* is more limited than that. In this work, Pound is concerned with linking an ancient Roman's vision of true, personal poetry with his own and with showing that poets, no matter how separated by time or language, share essential qualities. These qualities may be, perhaps must be, in conflict with the values of emperors or empires—but in the end it is Propertius, not Caesar, who will prevail.

HUGH SELWYN MAUBERLEY

First published: 1920
Type of work: Poems

A bitter, satirical farewell to English society and its corruption of the values of life and art.

In the poems of *Hugh Selwyn Mauberley*, Pound expressed the disgust and rejection of British society which had been building in him all during World War I. Increasingly at odds with a culture that had embraced sordid economic gain at the expense of art and lives—10 million people died in the war, and for nothing, in Pound's view—Pound used *Hugh Selwyn Mauberley* to pen a sharp, critical farewell to England and to his own poetic theories and practices. The book is thus a dual break: with his society and with his own poetic style.

The book is in two parts, and it comprises eighteen short poems. In the first part, Pound gives a general survey of contemporary England, attacking the low value it places on true art, especially poetry. There is much trenchant social criticism in these brief poems, and Pound makes direct attacks on a corrupted civilization whose marketplace ethics debase everything, especially human life and art. The second part of the book focuses on the career of a representative poet of the time, the fictitious Hugh Selwyn Mauberley, and his gradual descent into a sterile and isolated aestheticism, an artistic philosophy which Pound once shared, at least in part, but which he found artistically and morally untenable after the cataclysm of the war.

The work opens with one of Pound's best-known and most often anthologized poems, "E. P. Ode pour l'Election de son Sepulchre" ("E. P. ode for carving upon his tomb"). In this introductory poem, Pound, the E. P. of the title, gives an ironic, mocking farewell to his own artistic efforts in England: In an artistic sense, he is dead, and this brief work is his epitaph. The poem is satirical, but its satire is double, aimed at both Pound and his society. He was, Pound writes, "wrong from the start" in his attempts to bring a new renaissance into such indifferent, even hostile surroundings.

The rest of the poems in the first part show just how indifferent and hostile that culture was to poetry. In succeeding poems, Pound turns to the baleful effects of artistic philistinism, unjust economics, social indifference, and, inevitably following, a senseless war whose only real result was the death of millions—as Pound puts it: "Quick eyes gone under earth's lid." Although he mentions no names, Pound was undoubtably thinking especially of his friend, the brilliant young sculptor Henri Gaudier-Brzeska, killed in the trenches of France. Much of Pound's fury in *Hugh Selwyn Mauberley* is fueled by intense personal anger and anguish.

Having renounced his society, Pound next renounced much of the artistic credo he had embraced during his stay in England. The poem "Yeux Glauques" (gray eyes) is the occasion for this renunciation. It refers to a painting by the Pre-Raphaelist artist Edward Burne-Jones which was itself an attack upon the crass materialism and hypocrisy of English culture. Pound rejects both the culture and the artistic responses of the Pre-Raphaelites and the aesthetic movement, because both were ultimately inimical to true art: the first because it placed no value on such creations, the second because they neglected the duty of artists to improve their society. From this point on in his poetic career, Pound was increasingly outspoken about social and economic matters; though he may often have been wrong, he was seldom silent.

Part 1 of *Hugh Selwyn Mauberley* ends with a poem called "Envoi," based on the verse "Go, Lovely Rose," by the seventeenth century English writer Edmund Waller. By using Waller's poem, Pound is being subtly but severely ironic, for he believed Waller to have been one of the greatest of English lyric poets. In modern England, Pound is intimating, Waller would be rejected and unhonored—just as Pound is.

Part 2 gives the fictional case history of a modern English poet, Hugh Selwyn Mauberley, who is in many ways a mask, or persona, of Pound himself. Attempting to write true, rather than merely popular, poems, Mauberley is battered by life, ignored by the public, and tempted by the cynical advice of more successful writers. Mr. Nixon—perhaps based on well-known author Arnold Bennett—is one such character, a thorough materialist who has prostituted his talent for monetary reward and a "steam yacht." Other literary figures encountered by Mauberley are equally spurious as guides, having abandoned art for the momentary success of the marketplace world.

Yet Pound lets the reader understand that Mauberley's way is ultimately no more correct than Mr. Nixon's. The poem which ends the book, "Medallion," seems to be a typical piece by Mauberley, although critics have debated this point. At any rate the poem, while technically proficient, is limited. It employs many of the poetic devices that Pound advocated—close attention to detail, the creation of a sharp visual image, the juxtaposition of elements—but it employs them in a way that limits, rather than expands, the reader's comprehension. In a sense, "Medallion" bids farewell to an aspect of Pound's career, just as *Hugh Selwyn Mauberley* does: After this, he would write on a larger scale.

THE CANTOS

First published: 1917-1970
Type of work: Long poem

Pound's ambitious masterwork, a sprawling epic that attempts to include all human history and culture.

Pound began writing the *Cantos* in 1915, published the first ones in 1917, published his first collection in 1925, and continued on them for almost the rest of his long life. He finally abandoned them after fifty-three years of effort. The *Cantos* are his most notable work, crammed with allusions, learning, splendid poetry, musical notations, Chinese ideograms, bitter invective and insults, baffling transitions and private jokes, and characters from Pound's personal life as well as from world history. They form an immensely long work, and the *Cantos* have caused despair in ordinary readers and produced an entire Pound industry among literary scholars.

Although it is not immediately apparent, there is a loose but definite structure to the poem. Crucial concepts reappear throughout the work, embodied in specific actors who are either actual historical figures or characters from literature or mythology. These concepts can also be expressed by reference to images from the natural world or by artistic creations—specific examples of music, architecture, poetry—which Pound thought especially significant.

In this way, the nineteenth century American president Martin van Buren appears to underscore the idea of economic justice, while a single column in a cathedral, signed by its carver, represents the ideal of true art as opposed to mass-produced imitations. Because Pound presents these images in quick flashes without overt connections, the reader must rely on juxtaposition rather than narration to discover the meanings. Despite their expansive nature, and although they were composed over a period of half a century, the *Cantos* contain only a few major subjects: the importance of knowledge and art, the power of nature, the need for economic justice, and the necessity to order human society in accord with natural rhythms and cycles.

As befits a work that attempts to survey all human history, the *Cantos* contain many changes—metamorphoses, or shifts from one form to another. It was a concept pervasive in Greek mythology, and a continual fascination for Pound. These metamorphoses can be for good or evil; the first lead to harmony, while the second cause decay in society and culture. The chief villain for Pound was economic injustice, which inevitably changed societies for the worse. Usury, the lending of money at excessive rates of interest, was Pound's primary economic concern, and he railed against it powerfully in his famous "Usury Canto," XLV:

> With usura hath no man a house of good stone
> each block cut smooth and well fitting
> that design might cover their face,
> with usura
> hath no man a painted paradise on his church wall

This concern with economics appears throughout the poem, sometimes expressed openly, as here, sometimes inferred. The same is true of the other concepts which interested—some might say obsessed—Pound. They weave throughout the *Cantos*, changing form and shape, presenting themselves in many disguises, literally embodying the theme of metamorphoses.

As Pound worked on the *Cantos*, his emphasis on history gradually shifted. In the earlier sections he presented events largely from an outside point of view, sometimes commenting upon them directly, but generally using persons beyond his contemporary world. Cantos VIII through XI, for example, are known as the "Malatesta Cantos," since they concern the fifteenth century Italian soldier and ruler Sigismundo Malatesta, who becomes a figure of the enlightened ruler. In later cantos, Pound draws more on his own times and injects himself more personally into the poem (although he had never been completely absent, even from the very start). The major break comes with the section of the poem known as the "Pisan Cantos." These were written while Pound was imprisoned in the U.S. Army Disciplinary Center at Pisa, awaiting return to the United States for his treason trial. Allowed access to writing materials but denied books or notes, Pound was forced to rely solely on his memory; from this point on, memory itself becomes a key motif in the *Cantos*. Pound turned inward, examining his own life and actions, trying to strip away all that was dross and retain only the essentials. A note of uncertainty and self-doubt appears; as Pound worked on in his later years, this tone becomes stronger.

Pound did not doubt the underlying validity of his themes, merely his ability to express them adequately. Faced with the task of pulling together the work of half a century, he wondered if he could accomplish it. Toward the end he decided that he could not: "I cannot make it cohere," he announced in one of the last fragments. Pound overstated the case. True, he was unable to conclude the *Cantos* in a well-rounded finale. His ambition to compose a long poem equal to Homer's *Odyssey* (c. 800 B.C.) or Dante's *La divina commedia* (c. 1320; *The Divine Comedy*) proved beyond his reach. The fault, however, was not solely with Pound: His era lacked the underlying unity and intellectual harmony required for such an undertaking.

Because of the diversity and complexity of modern life, Pound's method was probably the only one he could have used. He himself termed it the "ideogrammic method," by which he meant the juxtaposition of significant details which would fuse together in the mind of the reader to express more than was openly stated. For this method to work, the reader must either have Pound's knowledge of all the details and allusions found in the *Cantos* or must accept moments of confusion to arrive at some sort of total understanding. It is only when readers try to track down every reference, understand each cryptic comment, that the *Cantos* become confused and incomprehensible; the proper method is to plunge on, trusting that the poem will, despite Pound's doubts, cohere.

After a contentious lifetime, Pound came to realize that he had made many mistakes. He admits this in the *Cantos*:

> Pull down thy vanity, it is not man
> Made courage, or made order, or made grace,
>   Pull down thy vanity, I say pull down.
> Learn of the green world what can be thy place
> In scaled invention or true artistry,
> Pull down thy vanity,

Yet, having admitted this, Pound also realized that his vision and goal of true art had been valid ones and that the *Cantos*, flawed though they are, cohere though they did not, were a worthy effort:

> To have gathered from the air a live tradition
> or from a fine old eye the unconquered flame
> This is not vanity.

Summary

Ezra Pound's impact on twentieth century literature and culture was twofold. First, he largely re-established the artist as a figure of important, and often provocative, influence in contemporary events. Calling artists "the antennae of the race," Pound implied that they not only anticipate society's direction but also influence its course. Second, he provided poetic techniques that are able to accept and incorporate all that is vital of past art into the art of the present and future. All artists can draw upon and use the same themes, images, and words, so long as they revitalize them; in Pound's words, as long as they "make it new."

Pound articulated and demonstrated literary theories; he also assisted other writers. In the end, he staked his own reputation upon an immensely long and wide-ranging work, the *Cantos*, which has become the supreme example of modernism in twentieth century literature.

Bibliography

Carpenter, Humphrey. *A Serious Character: The Life of Ezra Pound*. Boston: Houghton Mifflin, 1988.

Davie, Donald. *Ezra Pound*. New York: Penguin Books, 1976.

_____. *Ezra Pound: Poet as Sculptor*. New York: Oxford University Press, 1964.

Froula, Christine. *A Guide to Ezra Pound's "Selected Poems."* New York: New Directions, 1982.

Heymann, C. David. *Ezra Pound: The Last Rower*. New York: Viking Press, 1976.

Kenner, Hugh. *The Pound Era*. Berkeley: University of California Press, 1971.

Knapp, James F. *Ezra Pound*. Boston: Twayne, 1979.

Stock, Noel. *The Life of Ezra Pound*. New York: Pantheon Books, 1970.

Sullivan, J. P. *Ezra Pound and Sextus Propertius: A Study in Creative Translation*. Austin: University of Texas Press, 1979.

Michael Witkoski

J. F. POWERS

Born: Jacksonville, Illinois
July 8, 1917

Principal Literary Achievement

Known as a writer's writer, Powers has been acclaimed as one of the finest storytellers of his day, a talent revealed in his meticulously crafted and understated short stories and novels.

Biography

Born on July 8, 1917, in Jacksonville, Illinois, James Farl Powers was one of three children of James Ansbury and Zella Routzong Powers. His father was the dairy and poultry manager for Swift and Company, and his mother, an amateur painter. Powers grew up in a comfortable, middle-class environment in which he played the usual sports and read Tom Swift adventures, the Arthurian legends, Charles Dickens' *Oliver Twist* (1837-1839), and *Pinocchio*. What set him apart from his neighbors was that he and his family were Catholics in a predominantly Protestant town.

In 1931, his family moved to Quincy, Illinois. Spending four years at Quincy Academy, taught by the Franciscans, Powers was more skilled as a basketball player than as a student. Upon graduation in 1935, he went to live with his parents and took on various jobs during the next several years, including being the chauffeur for a wealthy investor in the South, an editor with Chicago Historical Records Survey, and a clerk at Brentano's bookstore. While working at Brentano's in 1942, he wrote his first short story, "He Don't Plant Cotton." He was dismissed from his job in the bookstore for refusing to buy war bonds. During the early war years in Chicago, Powers associated with various radical groups such as the Catholic Worker movement, political exiles from Europe, and jazz musicians from the South. During this time he became a pacifist and turned to his writing to develop his sense of the clash between spiritual ideas and American materialist values.

In 1945 he married Betty Wahl, and they set up house in Avon, Minnesota. In 1947, he was briefly a resident at Yaddo, a writer's conference, where he completed his collection of short stories *Prince of Darkness and Other Stories* (1947). While teaching classes at St. John's College, Minnesota, and Marquette University in Milwaukee, he began publishing his stories in such magazines as *Collier's*, *The New Yorker*, and *Partisan Review*.

In 1951, Powers moved with his family to Greystones, Ireland, where they lived

for two years. In 1952, they returned to the United States and took up residence in St. Cloud, Minnesota, for the next five years. In 1956, he published his second collection of short fiction, entitled *The Presence of Grace*. He and his family again lived in Ireland (in Dublin) for a year and then returned to St. Cloud in 1958, where they remained until 1963. It was during these last years at St. Cloud that Powers worked on his first novel, *Morte d'Urban*; when published in 1962, it was awarded the National Book Award.

Many of Powers' short stories continued over the years to appear in *The New Yorker*, a magazine well suited to his subtle, ironic style and to his satiric portrait gallery of fallible and quietly heroic priests. Although a few of his stories focus upon such social issues as the plight of blacks and Jews, most of Powers' tales, including his third collection of short fiction, *Look How the Fish Live* (1975), dwell upon the clergy. Powers' second novel, *Wheat That Springeth Green* (1988), reverts to the theme of *Morte d'Urban* as his new hero attempts to balance priestly spiritual values against the forces of American secular life. Not the same critical success as *Morte d'Urban*—some reviewers found the spiritual rebirth of the hero in the last chapter to be unconvincing—*Wheat That Springeth Green* nevertheless offers a perceptive insight into the character of the American priesthood and the need to rethink accepted middle-class American values.

Powers' five children are all grown; his wife, Betty Wahl, also a writer, died in 1988. He teaches writing at St. John's University in Collegeville, Minnesota, during one term and devotes the rest of his time to his writing. In 1989 he received an award from the Wetherfield Foundation in New York City.

Analysis

The focus of all Powers' major stories and two novels is upon the clash between the secular values of American society and the spiritual ideals of the Catholic church. Breaking away from the tradition of sentimental portraits of the religious life that characterized popular Catholic literature and film (Bing Crosby and Barry Fitzgerald as idealized priests, for example), Powers depicts his priests with a satiric and yet compassionate eye. How is a man to model his life after Jesus Christ and yet survive in an attractive materialistic society that demands success? In answering that question, Powers has created some of the most memorable characters in recent literature: Fathers Didymus, Urban, and Hackett.

Powers' failure to become a popular writer may be his singular focus upon the psychological and spiritual struggles of priests to discover themselves and the meaning of their vocations. This is not the stuff of popular literature, especially since his books are notably devoid of overt sex and violence. While it is true that he lacks the scope of Catholic writers such as Graham Greene, Evelyn Waugh, and François Mauriac, Powers' intense and perceptive analysis of the priestly mind has no equal. Despite the simple surface of his stories, Powers draws upon a rich tradition within and without his church to develop his characters. His works are filled with allusions to medieval Christianity, Arthurian legends, and arcane theological writings, and he skillfully blends the bountiful texture of Catholic tradition with the most mundane affairs of modern life. A Trappist monk watches the Minnesota Twins on television. A priest, loosely drawn after Sir Lancelot, constructs a golf course to increase the number of retreatants for his order.

Although Powers' fiction can be comic, it also confronts and examines serious issues, ranging from the mistreatment of blacks and Jews to his more familiar subject of the inner struggles of clerics to achieve a balance between physical and spiritual values. Powers' pacifism and critical attitude toward American superficiality underlies many of his stories. One does not need to be a Catholic to appreciate Powers' portrayal of young men, who happen to be priests, doing battle with the symbols of corporate America while sometimes falling prey to its seductive attractions. Powers, in short, is fascinated with a fallen humanity that has not abandoned its dreams and ideals. Despite all the irony and satire, his writings attest the obsessive desire all good people share to make their lives worthy of memory.

Powers is noted for his crisp dialogue and transparent narrative. There is not an abundance of action or painterly passages in his works. Rather, he establishes a believable setting—usually in small-town America—in which he develops his characters. Even when he is not writing from the first-person point of view, he stages his dialogue and narrative so as to reveal the mind and character of his hero. Careful not to moralize or judge his characters, Powers presents to the reader a series of characters who are neither villains nor saints but a complex amalgam of good and evil, innocence and experience. Through the use of irony, he provides a comic perspective from which to view his characters, careful always of maintaining a detached and frequently compassionate attitude toward them.

Finally, it is important to note Powers' uniquely American priests. Like the author, they are devoted to such national sports as football and baseball, enjoy such things as drinking (sometimes too much), golf, flashy automobiles, television, and entering into the competitive fray (like any good American businessman) to satisfy their ambitions for power, prestige, and the material symbols of success. This tradition of American materialism, however, frequently clashes with the European Catholic tradition of asceticism and the Puritan values of early America. J. F. Powers has no peer when it comes to capturing this cultural duality in the Catholic church poignantly.

MORTE d'URBAN

First published: 1962
Type of work: Novel

A go-getting priest attempts to revitalize the stagnant Order of St. Clement by applying the methods of corporate America.

In the epigraph to *Morte d'Urban*, a quotation from J. M. Barrie, Powers sets forth the central ironic theme of his novel: "The life of every man is a diary in which he means to write one story, and writes another." Father Urban (Harvey Roche), a clever, manipulative speaker and organizer, while dedicating his life to making the Church a prospering and efficient social institution, comes to discover in the eleventh hour that what really counts in the religious life is one's spiritual well-being.

Acknowledged by many critics as Powers' best book, *Morte d'Urban* was originally written from the point of view of its hero, Father Urban. Powers recast his novel, employing a third-person narrative while skillfully retaining Father Urban as the central intelligence of the story. This shift in point of view enabled Powers to develop the important ironic perspective that shapes the entire novel. Funny, ironic, satiric, and compassionate, Powers brings a Chaucerian tone to the modern novel.

A middle-aged member of the fictitious Order of St. Clement, Father Urban travels out of Chicago, raising money, preaching dynamic sermons to standing-room-only crowds of admiring listeners. His charm, energy, and go-getting spirit would have made him an outstanding success in business, but the Clementines are run by and constituted of priests who are largely conservative, fumbling, and doddering fellows. As far as religious orders go, the Clementines are losers: Their vocations are down, some of their houses have been taken over by more aggressive diocesan priests, and none of their members but Father Urban seems to understand their problem.

By wooing a wealthy benefactor named Billy Cosgrove, an egotistical son of Mammon, Father Urban manages to obtain new quarters for the Clementines. Instead of nurturing Father Urban's enterprising spirit, however, the provincial sends him, along with Father John (Jack), to the order's failing retreat center in the remote community of Duesterhaus (meaning "house of gloom"). Father Wilfrid, the rector, obsessed with the petty details of maintaining the retreat house and with asserting his dominance over Father Urban, sets Jack and Father Urban to the task of painting walls and varnishing floors (with the cheapest materials) in order to make the house more attractive to retreatants.

Having spent more than a month wasting his talents at St. Clement's Hill (so named by Father Urban), Father Urban is sent by Father Wilfrid to replace a vacationing pastor at St. Monica's Church. During the next month and a half, Father Urban manages to convince the cautious and ailing pastor, Father Phil Smith, to build a new church. When he later discovers that Father Smith has died during his vacation, Father Urban thinks that he may be chosen to be the new pastor. The bishop, however, offers him an Indian mission, which he rejects in favor of returning to St. Clement's Hill.

Father Urban persuades Billy Cosgrove to buy a tract of land adjoining St. Clement's Hill, have it developed as a golf course, and donate it to the order. Hearing that the Bishop is interested in taking over the Hill as the site for a new seminary, Father Urban invites the bishop to play a round of golf with him in the hope of convincing him of the Hill's productive future. During the course of the game, however, the bishop's ball strikes Father Urban in the head, sending him to the hospital. After he regains consciousness at the hospital, Father Urban learns that the bishop, feeling guilty for striking him in the head with his golf ball, has decided not to take over St. Clement's Hill.

Nevertheless, after being struck by the ball, Father Urban moves into a series of adventures that totally changes his life. He goes to live at the estate of the wealthy benefactor of St. Clement's, Mrs. Thwaites, in order to recuperate from his trauma. While there, he attempts to help out Mrs. Thwaites's servant, an Irish girl named Katie, who has lost most of her earnings playing dominoes with Mrs. Thwaites. Father Urban learns later that his intervention has proven fruitless. Later, Father Urban goes on a fishing trip with Billy Cosgrove and again rebels against the wealthy establishment by undermining Billy's attempt to drown a deer. As Billy struggles to drown the deer, Father Urban revs the engine of the boat, causing Billy to fall into the lake. Angered by his humiliation, Billy gets into the boat and drives away, leaving Father Urban to fend for himself. On his return to St. Clement's Hill, Father Urban is picked up by Sally Thwaites Hopwood, the married daughter of Mrs. Thwaites. She drives him to an island tower, where she attempts to seduce him by stripping nude for a swim. He resists the temptation, and, furious at his chastity, she drives away from the island in her boat, leaving Father Urban stranded.

Plagued by headaches and aging rapidly, Father Urban attempts to carry out his work at St. Clement's Hill. Beaten down by his recent trials, he no longer attempts to challenge the plans of Father Wilfrid. During a conference at the Hill, however, he receives the news that he has been appointed the new provincial of the Order of St. Clement. Ironically, he no longer possesses the energy and will to develop the order's material well-being. He gains a reputation as a pious priest who finds himself comfortable in his home at St. Clement's Hill. Has Father Urban become more spiritual and saintly, or has he simply been beaten down by the unexpected turns of the economic forces that he had formerly mastered? Like Lancelot, Father Urban has chosen earthly desires over heavenly bliss and thus failed to discover the Holy Grail. Having withstood the temptations of Mrs. Thwaites, Billy Cosgrove, and Sally Thwaites, however, he, like Lancelot, may have achieved his sanctity by becoming a true priest—one devoted to spiritual rather than material values.

As in so many of Powers' stories, he develops the tension between action and contemplation and suggests that only a balance between the two forces may bring about inner peace and salvation. "Should be two kinds of men in every busy parish," Father Smith says, "priest-priests and priest-promoters." Father Urban replies, "I'd say a man *has* to be both. At least a man can try. Sometimes that's the most a man can do." Up until the time he is hospitalized, however, Father Urban is almost exclusively the priest-promoter. He is a regular guy who is at his best when raising money, shaking hands with parishioners who have been dazzled by his sermons, and persuading wealthy businessmen to contribute to the Church. All these activities, to be sure, seem necessary if the Church is to compete in an America that prizes new construction, growth, numbers, and other visible signs of achievement. On the other hand, if the Church models itself after successful corporate America, how is it to model itself after Christ? The seemingly simple admonition of Christ to render unto

Caesar the things that are Caesar's and to God the things that are God's proves to be a very difficult and complex task, especially if one is an American who is hell-bent upon being a winner.

Father Urban's getting struck in the head by a golf ball proves to be the ironic turning point in his life (and in the novel). Hoping to bring into St. Clement's Hill a better class of retreatants by constructing an attractive golf course on the adjoining grounds, Father Urban—at the top of his game as a promoter—is physically stopped in his tracks by a golf ball, the very emblem of his new enterprise. As Powers himself has said, "the hit on the head is a real factor. It is not psychological. It's physical. Nothing else could have slowed up a man like Urban, but he is also a wiser and a better man. He has lost this aggressive 'be a winner' kind of thing, which in an American, I think is not a bad thing."

Although the last chapter of the novel is entitled "Dirge," Father Urban's "death" proves to be metaphorical. His former self has died, and he is resurrected from his previous life as a go-getter to accept the spiritual values of the Church. It no longer matters to him that the incompetent Father Wilfrid continues to run St. Clement's Hill, that the order has lost its building on the North Side of Chicago, and that its weekly radio program had been canceled in favor of news and music. Many of the younger Clementines cannot understand why their new provincial is allowing their order to slide back into its dilatory and unproductive ways. Father Urban thus finds himself in the position of the previous provincial when he (Father Urban) had rebelled against him for the very same reasons.

Morte d'Urban may, then, simply be read as a Catholic novel in which an aggressive, worldly wise priest discovers spiritual values after he is chastened by a physical disability, sexual temptation, and betrayal by his wealthy sponsors. The novel, however, has broader implications. It may also be read as the story of the hollow success of the American Dream. Although a priest, Father Urban has most of the characteristics of the successful American businessman: He is smooth, glib, manipulative, on the move, and desperate to be in the center of new development, new ideas, new growth. He believes in going first class or not at all. The nearly fatal blow to his head, however, makes it clear to him that the world will go on without him and that his previous bravado, based in part upon his childlike denial of mortality, has left him with an empty, worrisome world.

WHEAT THAT SPRINGETH GREEN

First published: 1988
Type of work: Novel

In developing his suburban parish and in working with his new curate, a middle-aged diocesan priest rediscovers his true vocation and turns to working with the poor.

Taking its title from a medieval French carol, *Wheat That Springeth Green*, like *Morte d'Urban*, develops the great Christian theme of the resurrection from the dead. The novel tells the story of Joe Hackett, a Midwestern Catholic diocesan priest. At age forty-four, he is pastor of a comfortable suburban church in Inglenook, Minnesota. Despite his successful building campaign, he is an unhappy man who begins drinking; he is headed for despair until his curate, Father Bill, arrives. A priest of the 1960's, immature and idealistic, Father Bill unwittingly elicits Joe's paternal and pastoral instincts. In his struggle to shape Father Bill into a solid, responsible priest, Joe regains his sense of vocation, abandons his suburban parish, and dedicates his life to working with the poor in a slum parish.

Although writing from a third-person point of view, Powers frequently interjects dialogue and comment within parentheses to reflect Joe's inner thoughts or to pick up talk that he hears going on around him. For example, when Joe is discussing his building plans with the archbishop, Powers projects within parentheses Joe's imagined interpretation of his remarks:

> So Joe, then living in a room in the school and quite prepared to go on living under such conditions if advised to build a new church but dearly wishing, as he'd told the Arch and his reverend consultors, to keep the best wine till last ("*Wine*, Archbishop? Did he say *wine*?" — "Means a new *church*, you dummy"), had got his rectory.

After briefly tracing some of Joe's tribulations and humiliations as a boy, Powers develops his character's growing spiritual idealism as a seminarian. Convinced that the only ambition worthy of the priest was holiness—getting to know God and growing more like Him—Joe begins to wear a hair shirt, like the saints of old, in order to subdue the flesh. He is determined to become a contemplative—otherwise, as he says, "our life . . . becomes one of sheer activity—the occupational disease of the diocesan clergy."

Joe's initiation into the practical world comes with his assignment as curate in Holy Faith Church, the pastor of which, Father Van Slaag, is the only known contemplative in the diocese. As he gradually learns, Father Slaag's detachment from worldly matters means that he, Joe, must take on most of the duties to keep the parish going. After five years at Holy Faith he openly admits, in what seems like an act of betrayal not only of Father Slaag but also of his own high spiritual standards, that Father Slaag is not doing his job.

Joe finally obtains his own parish in the upper-middle-class suburbs of Inglenook, Minnesota. Having put his priestly idealism (the hair shirt, the life of contemplation, Father Slaag) behind him, Joe quickly establishes one of the finest rectories, schools, and convents in the diocese. Joe has become a go-getter, much like Father Urban, and is proud of his accomplishments. In the process of developing his parish and educating his new curate, however, Joe becomes increasingly disillusioned about the values embodied in this upper-middle-class world. Although taking to drink as a means of escape, he continues to battle materialist corruption as embodied in one of his wealthy parishioners, who uses his wealth and influence with the archbishop to get his children into the parish school over Joe's objections. His growing radicalism can also be seen in his moral support of a young man in the parish who flees to Canada to avoid fighting in Vietnam.

Tempered with the wisdom that comes from experience, Joe's youthful idealism returns with renewed vigor. Believing that "the separation of Church and Dreck was a matter of life and death for the world, that the Church was the one force in the world with a chance to save it," Joe abandons his suburban parish for one in the slums, appropriately named Holy Cross.

THE FORKS

First published: 1947
Type of work: Short story

The opposition between a wordly pastor and his idealistic young curate leads to a series of comic confrontations.

In "The Forks," Powers depicts two very different kinds of priests. On the one hand is Monsignor, a snobbish man very much at home with the things of this world. He wears a Panama hat, uses Steeple cologne, and drives a long black car. Doomed to remain a monsignor now that all his intercessors are dead, he determines to live as comfortably as he can. He orders for himself the luxury of a medieval garden with a spouting whale jostling with Neptune in the waters of the fountain. He has no intellectual pretensions and maintains his mental calm by either ignoring or condemning innovations and controversy: "His mind was made up on everything, excessively so." In his eyes, Communism and organized labor are the chief dangers to society. The status quo has been kind to Monsignor, and he wants no interference with tradition now. His curate, Father Eudex, on the other hand, reads the radical *Catholic Worker*, neglects to shave under his armpits, contemplates buying a Model A in opposition to Monsignor's contention that a shabby car is unbefitting a priest, works in his undershirt with Monsignor's gardener, and sympathizes with labor unions.

In short, Powers has placed in one rectory an old, worldly traditionalist and a young, idealistic radical, and the drama that unfolds from their interaction is what the story is about. On the surface, Powers seems to be satirizing the worldly monsignor and lauding the saintly and socially conscious curate, but upon closer reading one discovers that Father Eudex, with his blinkered vision and unyielding idealism, is also the object of Powers' satire.

Assuming Christlike motives in his concern for social justice, Father Eudex (his name in Latin means "judge") actually appears to be driven by perversity. If Monsignor enjoys his prestigious automobile, Father Eudex rejoices in its humble counterpart, the Model A. When the Monsignor accepts a check from the Rival Tractor Company, Father Eudex, to show his support for labor, destroys his. The Monsignor condemns Communism; Father Eudex reads *The Catholic Worker*. The very title of the story suggests the opposition between the two priests. After dinner, Monsignor notices that his curate has failed to use all the silverware provided at his plate and declares that "Father Eudex did not know the forks." The implication is that the young man's idealism is naïve and a little foolhardy, that it has blinded him to the religious, social, and political exigencies of parish life. The ideal priest, one might assume, would be one who could balance the experience and wisdom of the monsignor with the idealism and energy of his curate.

Powers implies a judgment of Father Eudex not only through Eudex's own series of negative judgments of his superior but through an allusion to the parable of the talents. In order to solve its excess-profits problem, the Rival Tractor Company annually sent checks to local clergymen. Father Eudex is the only character in the story reluctant to accept the money, which he views as Rival's dishonest attempt to win away sympathy from its union workers who have have frequently struck the company. On the surface, Father Eudex seems to have acted nobly by destroying his check. In the parable of the talents, however, Father Eudex's biblical counterpart is described as foolishly burying his one talent and is declared wanting in his stewardship.

Paradox and irony keep the reader from being too harsh a judge of either character. Perverse, idealistic, naïve, Father Eudex is not a bad priest, nor is he a saintly one. Rather, like his superior, he is a flawed human being. Although the parable of the talents clearly implies a judgment upon Father Eudex, the Rival Tractor Company is not truly analogous to the just Master in the Bible; consequently, one's final judgment of Father Eudex is tempered with mercy and compassion.

LIONS, HARTS, LEAPING DOES

First published: 1943
Type of work: Short story

An aged, saintly Franciscan friar seeking spiritual perfection believes, shortly before his death, that he has failed God.

The setting for "Lions, Harts, Leaping Does" is a Franciscan monastery during a bleak, snowy winter. Father Didymus, an aged priest, is being read to by his friend, Brother Titus, a simple, holy, and rather forgetful old man. As this elegaic story opens, Titus reads from Bishop Bale's critical *Lives of the Popes*, which reminds Didymus of the foibles of even great church leaders. As the two friars go for a walk in the cold snow, Didymus meditates upon his own spiritual lapses. He is especially distressed with his decision not to visit his ninety-two-year-old brother Seraphin, also a priest, recently returned from Rome after twenty-five years. Didymus feels that by adhering to the letter of his vows as a cloistered priest in not visiting his brother he has exhibited spiritual pride and has hurt his brother. Upon returning from his walk, he receives a telegram informing him that his brother has died.

Later, during the Vespers ceremony, Didymus collapses and wakes to find himself confined to a wheelchair. Titus brings a caged canary to his room for companionship and continues to read to him. This time, however, he reads from the writings of the mystic saint and poet Saint John of the Cross. One of Saint John's paradoxical tenets is that one may be closest to God during the moments one believes oneself to be abandoned by Him. Powers clearly implies that Didymus, despite his religious scruples and his sense of failure, achieves a heightened sanctity through his present suffering.

Projecting his own sense of imprisonment unto the canary, Didymus releases the bird from its cage, and it flies out the window and disappears into the snowy trees, "the snowy arms of God." Didymus will die without discovering a sign of God's presence within himself. Knowing he still has to look outside himself for such a sign, he turns to Titus. "God still chose to manifest Himself most in sanctity," he thinks. Didymus' denial of a sign, however, is paradoxically the very sign he is seeking. Like the canary that vanishes among the dark, cold trees, the soul of Didymus blends into the bleak landscape that occupied so much of his attention during his last days. His soul has become "lost in the snowy arms of God"; his soul was saved without his ever being conscious of the spiritual climax.

"Lions, Harts, Leaping Does" was Powers' first clerical story. Unlike his subsequent fiction, this story eschews satire and comedy for a compassionate, sensitive, and theologically rich portrait of a priest's quest for sanctity. Temptation here is not of the usual, dramatic kind—sex, money, or ambition—but of a subtle, almost unrecognizable variety that stems from doing the right thing for the wrong reason—in this case, obeying the rules of the cloister out of pride. Didymus' suffering is quiet and internal, and Powers attempts to portray it by describing Didymus' dreams and by using such symbols as the caged canary.

Summary

J. F. Powers is one of the most accomplished Catholic authors of the twentieth century. Unlike James Joyce or Graham Greene, he lacks breadth and variety in his writing, but his perceptive, ironic, and compassionate probing of the clerical mind has no equal. Like Jane Austen, he works on a small scale, but within that framework he has proved himself a master chronicler of American Catholicism by exploring life in the rectory, parish, and diocese.

Some critics believe that his short stories are his true metier. His two novels, however, which have grown out of his short fiction, contain complex characters and exhibit an ample, Chaucerian humor that require a larger canvas to develop. The crisp dialogue that captures the comic human voices of the time can be heard in their eloquence in both the short fiction and the novels.

Bibliography

Evans, Fallon, ed. *J. F. Powers*. St. Louis: B. Herder, 1968.

Hagopian, John V. *J. F. Powers*. New York: Twayne, 1968.

Kelly, Richard. "Father Eudex, the Judge and the Judged: An Analysis of J. F. Powers' 'The Forks.'" *University Review* 35 (June, 1969): 316-318.

Lebowitz, Naomi. "The Stories of J. F. Powers: The Sign of Contradiction." *Kenyon Review* 20 (Summer, 1958): 494-99.

Merton, Thomas. "*Morte D'Urban*: Two Celebrations." *Worship* 36 (November, 1962); 645-650.

Sisk, John. "The Complex Moral Vision of J. F. Powers." *Critique* 2 (Fall, 1958): 41-58.

Richard Kelly

REYNOLDS PRICE

Born: Macon, North Carolina
February 1, 1933

Principal Literary Achievement

Focusing usually on a small area on the Virginia-North Carolina border, Price has insightfully transformed the people of that area into universal types.

Biography

Reynolds Price was born during the Great Depression in the small town of Macon on the North Carolina side of the Virginia-North Carolina border. His birth was difficult and almost killed both him and his mother, Elizabeth Rodwell Price. Price's father, William Solomon Price, a salesman with a taste for liquor, vowed that if his wife's life was spared, he would give up drinking. After a prolonged labor, the first of the Prices' two children was born. Will, whose twenty-seven-year marriage to Elizabeth was happy and passionate, struggled to keep his vow.

A second son, William, was not born until eight years later, so Reynolds was reared as an only child for nearly a decade, doted on by a gallery of aunts and uncles, most of whom crop up in one form or another in his writing. Money was tight, and the Prices moved from town to town. They lost their house when Will fell short of a fifty dollar mortgage payment that was due.

Reynolds, having few playmates and being brought up among adults with the penchant for story-telling common to people from small Southern towns, depended upon his imagination for company. Besides being good storytellers, Price's relatives were readers, so, following their examples, he developed an early enthusiasm for books. He was a good enough listener that he learned early the rhythms, cadences, vocabulary, and syntax of Southern speech, which he was later to reproduce easily and authentically in his writing.

The adolescent Price liked to sing. He experimented with painting, and he wrote poetry, as well as some plays. Reynolds grew close to his mother's sister, Ida Drake, who was forty-six when he was born (she was eighteen years older than Reynolds' mother). Price's early school experiences were good ones. Jane Alston (called Miss Jennie) and Crichton Thorne Davis, his seventh-grade and eighth-grade teachers at the John Graham School in Warrenton, were exceptional teachers who recognized the young Price's potential. The family moved to Raleigh when Reynolds was to enter high school. There Phyllis Peacock, head of the English department at

1715

Needham-Broughton Senior High School, a demanding taskmistress, taught Reynolds how to write.

Price entered Duke University as an English major in 1951, beginning an association that has continued throughout his professional life. When, at the invitation of Professor William Blackburn, Eudora Welty came to Duke University early in the 1950's to give a reading for undergraduates interested in creative writing and to comment on some of their work, Reynolds Price's submission rose above the rest.

A decade later, Price was back at Duke, having completed a residence at Merton College, University of Oxford, which he had attended as a Rhodes Scholar and from which he received a bachelor of letters degree in 1958. Now a promising assistant professor of English, he was pushing hard to finish his first novel.

Eudora Welty not only gave Price perceptive critiques of his early writing, she also had a hand in helping him to place *A Long and Happy Life*, which was published in 1962. It was through her interest and intervention that *Harper's* agreed to publish this first novel in its totality in its April, 1962, issue. The novel won for Price the William Faulkner Foundation Award for a first novel. Following a return to England in 1963, Price published a collection of short stories, *The Names and Faces of Heroes* (1963). His early story that Eudora Welty had praised during her visit to Duke a decade earlier, "Thomas Egerton," is included in this collection.

Price's second novel, *A Generous Man*, was published in 1966. Although it was not artistically up to *A Long and Happy Life*, it is, nevertheless, interesting for its frank phallic symbolism as represented by a python named Death that is suspected of having hydrophobia and has recently escaped from a traveling circus. The novel is funny if heavy-handed in its symbolism, which includes the bloodstained shirt of a retarded adolescent who has gone into the wilderness and had a fight with a fox.

Price's next novel, *Love and Work*, published in 1968, is an academic novel, but Price does not stray far from his Southern roots: Town in this book is more pervasive than gown. Even though the protagonist, Thomas Eborn, is a thirty-four-year-old college professor, he cannot legitimately be viewed as a completely autobiographical character. The book received mixed reviews. Some of what Price experimented with in *Love and Work*, the intermixing of autobiographical fact with fiction, continued in his next book, *Permanent Errors* (1970). In that year, Price received an award from the American Academy and National Institute of Arts and Letters.

As the 1970's began, Price had started work on a more ambitious novel than he had yet undertaken, *The Surface of Earth*, which was finally published in 1975 and was followed by its sequel, *The Source of Light*, in 1981. A collection of essays, *Things Themselves: Essays and Scenes* (1972), was his only other book in the early 1970's. The critics were divided in their reception of the two novels.

In 1977, *Early Dark*, a play based on *A Long and Happy Life*, was published. At about the same time, he published *A Palpable God: Thirty Stories Translated from the Bible with an Essay on the Origins and Life of Narrative* (1978), which brought him considerable critical praise. A collection of poetry, *Vital Provisions*, followed in 1982. *Mustian*, a collection that includes Price's first two novels and "A Chain of

Love," was released in 1983.

A turning point came in Price's creative life in 1984, when an operation for spinal cancer left him a paraplegic. To help control the pain he was suffering, Price underwent hypnosis, and this course of treatments resulted in unlocking for him much of his distant past, putting him in touch with information that helped him to produce a flood of books in the next few years.

Another volume of poetry, *The Laws of Ice*, appeared in 1986, as did the immensely popular *Kate Vaiden*. A collection of Price's essays, *A Common Room: Essays 1954-1987*, was published in 1987. In 1988, another novel, *Good Hearts*, came from his pen, and in the next year his extensive autobiography, *Clear Pictures: First Loves, First Guides*, appeared, followed in 1990 by another novel, *The Tongues of Angels*.

In 1988, Price was elected to membership in the American Academy and National Institute of Arts and Letters. During the 1980's, he taught at Duke University, where he was named James B. Duke Professor of English in 1977.

Analysis

Reynolds Price has consistently written of human affirmation, and his depiction of the South and his presentation of race relations in the South have been authentic and commendable. Superficially, one might compare Price to William Faulkner. Both write about the South, and both focus on a limited geographical region. Also, as Price's work continued, particularly in *The Surface of Earth* and *The Source of Light*, his style became increasingly complicated, and some critics thought that it had been directly influenced by Faulkner. Before leaping to such conclusions, however, one must remember that Reynolds Price is a John Milton scholar who regularly teaches a course on that seventeenth century English poet. Close examination is likely to reveal that Miltonic elements are more evident, particularly in Price's later work, than Faulknerian influences.

Price has acknowledged his debt to Milton as well as to Russian novelist Leo Tolstoy and the Bible. His association with Eudora Welty provided another significant influence, as has the work of Flannery O'Connor. Price, who is unusually open in discussing his own approach to writing, has admitted in *Things Themselves* the impact that Ernest Hemingway's writing has had upon him stylistically.

Price has never denied that his works are strongly autobiographical. He contends that although a writer's imagination is fundamental to any significant piece of fiction writing, writers cannot write from anything but their experience. He cautions, however, that art reshapes that experience so that few one-to-one correlations exist between writers' experience and their lives. Therefore, it is risky to draw conclusions about authors from characters that resemble them in their novels.

The two of Price's books that have the strongest correlations to his own life are *Love and Work* and *Permanent Errors*, but the protagonists in these books do not exist within the limited context of one person's life; rather, they function symbolically and metaphorically as types. *Kate Vaiden* also has strong elements that make Kate resemble Price's mother, of whom he admittedly was trying to reach deeper understandings when he wrote the book, but Kate clearly is not Elizabeth Rodwell.

The nexus Price uses to relate his stories to society on a universal level is the family, which he considers the quintessential element in human existence, the fundamental organism within which society functions. This emphasis on the family is a particular emphasis in Southern literature, although it pervades the writing of many other major writers as well. Certainly it was the central force in John Steinbeck's *The Grapes of Wrath* (1939) and later in his less successful *East of Eden* (1952). It is the driving force behind most of Faulkner's novels and certainly motivates the action in such Eugene O'Neill plays as *Desire Under the Elms* (1924), *Mourning Becomes Electra* (1931), *Long Day's Journey into Night* (1956), and *A Moon for the Misbegotten* (1947).

The first fictional family that Price examined closely was the Mustians, who are central to *A Long and Happy Life*, *A Generous Man*, "A Chain of Love," and to his play, *Early Dark*, based upon *A Long and Happy Life*. This examination was essentially of the Mustian characters living at the time of the story being told. In his examination of the Kendal-Mayfield family in *The Surface of Earth* and *The Source of Light*, however, Price undertakes something much more ambitious: He seeks to understand four generations of a family.

In his examination of both families, he is much concerned with questions of heredity, and his overall conclusion is that no matter how hard people try to be different from their progenitors, they inevitably are like them. He postulates this as an axiom that cannot be overturned in the course of human existence. Price is much concerned with the concept that the sins of the father are visited upon the children, and both *The Surface of Earth* and *The Source of Light* are concerned directly and overtly with the biblical question of Original Sin. Even though people are born with the burden of sin, Price implies, they have free will, and in its exercise lies some hope of salvation.

In *The Tongues of Angels*, the protagonist, Bridge Boatner, an adult, has spent the past thirty-four years living with the burden placed upon him in the summer before his senior year at the University of North Carolina in Chapel Hill. Then struggling to come to grips with the recent death of his father, Bridge became very close to one of the fourteen-year-old campers in his charge. The boy, Raphael Noren, was talented beyond any of the other boys at the camp. His accidental death has haunted Bridge, particularly because he fears that in some way he may have caused it. In this book, Bridge is trying to cope not only with Original Sin but also with a great guilt and emotional upheaval relating to Raphael's death.

The "permanent errors" of which Price speaks in his book by that title are the sins of the fathers. For Price, they persist, generation after generation. The determinism of heredity is inexorable for Price, as it was for O'Neill, Faulkner, and Steinbeck before him. In much of his work, Price deals with the tensions created by the paradoxes in the Christian mystique. He sees these paradoxes in the whole of Southern culture and finds them personified in family relationships.

A LONG AND HAPPY LIFE

First published: 1962
Type of work: Novel

A novel about small-town Southerners whose hope for a long and happy life is constantly overshadowed by the specter of death.

Few authors have the good fortune to have a whole issue of a major, high-circulation magazine devoted to the publication of their first novel at about the time the hard cover edition is released. Such was Reynolds Price's good fortune, however, when *Harper's* published *A Long and Happy Life* in its April, 1962, issue. The book went on to win a William Faulkner Foundation Award for a first novel, and the critical reception of this first book was singularly favorable.

A Long and Happy Life presents Rosacoke Mustian to the reading public, as well as her erstwhile boyfriend, Wesley Beavers, an eager beaver, who gets the innocent girl pregnant. Although he condescends to marry her, he then pretty much leaves her on her own. The book is alive with local color. In one of the early, most memorable scenes, Rosacoke needs to attend a funeral at a black church on a sizzling day in summer. Her friend Mildred Sutton has died in childbirth and is to be eulogized. Wesley Beavers drives his noisy motorcycle up to deliver Rosacoke to the funeral, but he does not go inside. Instead, he lingers outside and polishes his motorcycle, which is an extension of his being. Before the services are over, he leaves precipitously to get ready for the church picnic that he and Rosacoke are to attend that afternoon. As he screeches away from the church, he raises a trail of red dust behind him that one can almost taste, so vivid is Price's description.

The book is divided into three long chapters, each with appropriate subdivisions. The action takes place between July and Christmas, and each section marks a visit from Wesley, who three times comes the 130 miles from the naval base in Norfolk to see Rosacoke, his girlfriend. They have known each other for six years. Rosacoke is now twenty, Wesley twenty-two. Wesley is sexually experienced; Rosacoke is not.

Price supplies necessary details unobtrusively, partly through Rosacoke's interior monologues, partly through the letters she exchanges with Wesley, and partly through flashbacks, most of them part of her interior monologues. He also introduces his readers to an amusing, warm-hearted cast of small-town characters who are far removed from the world outside their own community.

At the church picnic, Wesley tries to seduce Rosacoke, but she resists his advances. It is not until his next visit in November that he succeeds in deflowering Rosacoke, for whom the sexual experience is especially threatening because the death of her friend Mildred is still in the forefront of her mind. Rosacoke realizes that her long and happy life could be cut short by a pregnancy if it were to be a difficult one.

Death is very much a part of the novel. Rosacoke's brother, Milo, suffers the loss of his first child, a baby meant to carry on the family name, but who, dying at birth, takes the name Horatio Mustian III to the grave with him. Mildred's baby, Sledge, has survived, and Rosacoke visits him, doing her duty and being calmed by her visits, although they constantly remind her of what could happen to her, because she soon knows that Wesley's child is growing within her.

Through a series of mischances, Rosacoke is forced to play the Virgin Mary in the annual Christmas pageant that her mother is directing at the Delight Baptist Church. The Christ child is an overgrown eight-month-old child, Frederick Gupton, who has been drugged with paregoric so that he will not disrupt the pageant. Rosacoke realizes what her lot will be with Wesley, but she comes to an acceptance of it—partly through her participation in the pageant.

Price chose his microcosm well and constructed it with an authenticity that gained the respect of most of the critics. His dialogue is easy and believable. His humor is irrepressible, as in the scene in which Uncle Simon misplaces his false teeth at the church picnic and in the scene in which the preacher who can walk on water sinks.

The isolation of his characters from the world, being drawn as they are into the social and religious web of their own community, encapsulates them and insulates them from outside influences. Some outside influences—although not very desirable ones—intrude upon the story by means of Wesley's periodic visits.

Within the limited confines in which he works, Price has been able to find universal significance in his characters and has been able to deal intricately with questions of life and death, with the dream of a long and happy life, and with the fact of quick death for infants and other relatively young people within the story.

A GENEROUS MAN

First published: 1966
Type of work: Novel

A story about a Southern posse's search for a hydrophobic python and about the meaning of life and death.

The story of the Mustians that Price initiated in *A Long and Happy Life* is also the focus in *A Generous Man*, his second novel. The cast of characters is not identical, but enough of them overlap that readers of the first novel will have a sense of identity with the main characters in the second.

The action of *A Generous Man* takes place nine years before the action of *A Long and Happy Life*. Wesley Beavers is not a part of the narrative because Rosacoke, now only eleven years old, has not yet met him. Milo, married and a father in *A Long and Happy Life*, is a fifteen-year-old boy in *A Generous Man*.

The book revolves around an unlikely event that imposes a light, sometimes hilarious tone upon a story that deals with matters of enduring importance with universal meaning. As the story opens, Milo Mustian, fifteen, has just lost his virginity to Lois Provo—a girl who, significantly, works with the snake show at the Warren County fair. Milo, waking the next morning, finds that the family dog, Phillip, is sick. In typical Southern fashion, the whole family must go with Phillip to the veterinarian, a drunkard who quickly misdiagnoses Phillip's ailment as rabies, although Rato later discovers it is only worms.

His dire diagnosis does not cause the doctor to confine or destroy the dog. Rather, he provides a muzzle, and Phillip goes off to the fair with the family. Rato, the retarded son, takes Phillip's muzzle off, and before long, the dog gets into a fight with the eighteen-foot python, Death, that Lois's father gave to her pregnant, unmarried mother as a parting gift before he deserted her years before.

Rato, the python named Death, and Phillip all disappear into the woods. Realizing that they might have a hydrophobic python on their hands, the townsmen form a posse to save the town from impending disaster—their real motive, however, is to bring a little excitement into their flat lives. The men in the posse quickly become drunk and comradely. Price's symbol, of course, is completely outrageous, his basic premise patently absurd. Yet that does not matter. It is clear that he is carefully constructing an allegory whose wit and good nature entice readers.

Sheriff Rooster Pomeroy leads the posse, leaving his wife, Kate, to her own devices. Kate seeks sexual fulfillment wherever she can find it; her husband is impotent. As the posse scours the woods, Milo, now one of its more intoxicated members, stumbles from the woods into the Pomeroy house, where the eager Kate whisks him into her bed. Their pillow talk includes Kate's reminiscence about her first sexual encounter with, of all people, Milo's cousin, the very cousin who had left Lois's mother pregnant and in possession of Death, the eighteen-foot python.

Milo is not to have complete satisfaction with Kate. The doorbell rings, and the terrified Milo is out the window, clutching his clothing in his hands. He goes back into the woods and finds the python. He wrestles with Death and is on the verge of defeat when Sheriff Pomeroy shoots and kills (defeats) Death, enabling Milo to escape. When Milo next meets Lois, he is eager for another tussle in bed, but Lois rejects him, accusing him of being uncaring and insensitive. Milo, having bungled their first encounter through his inexperience, asks for and receives another chance. He has now learned to give as well as to take; he is both generous and a man.

LOVE AND WORK

First published: 1968
Type of work: Novel

An academic novel in which the protagonist deals with the death of his parents and learns a lesson about sharing.

Thomas Eborn, *Love and Work*'s protagonist, is a writer and a professor. Although he is largely an autobiographical reflection of Price, one would be mistaken to presume that he is completely so. He is partially a fiction, so one cannot reach conclusions about Reynolds Price's own life and personality on the basis of what he tells about this character who is, admittedly, quite like him.

Many writers try to understand their own problems and personalities through writing about situations that have eaten away at them for years. *Love and Work* is obviously an example of a work by an author who is wrestling with his own past, a past in Price's case that became much clearer to him after hypnosis in 1984, a decade and a half after the appearance of this novel, released from his unconscious mind many details about his past.

Much that Price could not present clearly in *Love and Work*, because he did not yet have enough information to understand it, he was able to present in clearer perspective in his autobiography, *Clear Pictures: First Loves, First Guides*, that he published twenty-three years after *Love and Work*, having come to grips with a past that was lost to him until his hypnosis.

Thomas Eborn is a dutiful son, but his sense of duty sometimes precludes warmth and love. He believes that work frees a person. He becomes so devoted to work that he allows it to intrude upon his life, which becomes increasingly mechanistic and impersonal. In the final hours before his mother's unexpected death, she, perhaps having a premonition of what lies ahead, tries to reach out to Eborn, but he is busy with his work and will not talk with her on the telephone. It is interesting to compare this account with Price's account of his last telephone call from his own mother as he recounts it in *Clear Pictures*.

Much of *Love and Work* takes place after Eborn's mother has died. He is clearing out her house, disposing of the past. He comes upon papers that enable him to reconstruct his parents' relationship with each other and with society. In the course of this activity, Eborn realizes that his mother's death, which frees him of a pressing responsibility, really does not free him at all, because he imposes his own type of personal bondage upon himself.

Eborn maintains his own house, and its inner sanctum, his study, is surrounded by an invisible moat that makes it inviolable to everyone. He has tried to put all of his human relationships into pigeonholes, to file them away, to prevent them from intruding upon his work. In so doing, he has also kept himself from having any genuine human relationships, even within the closeness of his immediate family.

In this book, Price's sense of place is strong; place, however, becomes the constraint that stands in the way of one's having personal relationships.

KATE VAIDEN

First published: 1986
Type of work: Novel

Kate Vaiden reflects on the death and desperation in her past and emerges an admirable woman who has learned how to be strong.

Kate Vaiden is an unusual book in that it has its base in a sensationalism that is almost melodramatic, yet its author has the skill to elevate the narrative above the level of sheer sensationalism into the realm of serious literature that deals with and presents universal truths. Before she was eighteen, Kate Vaiden, now a fifty-seven-year-old woman looking back, had survived the murder of her mother by her father and his suicide, the accidental death of her favorite lover, the suicides of two of her lovers, the illegitimate birth of a son, and the wrench of giving him up. The basic story has the makings of a cheap, tawdry novel, but Price imbues it with dignity and shows nobility in its protagonist, Kate.

The telling of the narrative occurs in 1984, when Kate—like Price himself—was recuperating from cancer surgery. Her brush with death has made her determine to find the son she bore some forty years before; facing pressures with which she was quite unequipped to deal, she had abandoned him when he was four months old. Her story unfolds as a justification, an explanation that will possibly help her child, Lee, to understand, possibly even to love, his natural mother. The story is also a step in Price's quest to understand his own mother, a quest that is prevalent in *Love and Work* and that he deals with more overtly in *Clear Pictures*, his autobiography.

In the first scene of the novel, Kate has accompanied her mother, Frances, to the funeral of her cousin, Taswell Porter, who has been killed in a motorcycle accident. Dan, Kate's father, does not want Frances to go to the funeral, and he stays home in Greensboro in a rage. The day after the funeral, however, he goes to Macon, the rural community in Warren County where the funeral took place, and follows his wife to the gravesite, where she has gone with her cousin, Swift, to check the flowers on the grave. Later Frances' sister, Caroline, who had virtually reared Frances, comes to Kate with Swift, whom she forces to tell the eleven-year-old the news: Both of her parents are dead.

An oppressive burden of guilt is placed upon Kate. She muses that had she gone with her father to look for her mother, the killing might have been avoided. She inherits fully, as many Price protagonists do, the sins of the father.

Kate, even before her parents' deaths, was distrustful. Now that she is faced with the abandonment that their deaths imply, she is still more distrustful. People reach out to her with love. She returns their love in some measure, but never fully; she cannot trust enough to abandon her emotions to another person. Kate is not Price's own mother, Elizabeth, but certain correspondences—Elizabeth was an orphan reared by an older sister—suggest that in Kate, Price was certainly trying to understand some of his mother's personality traits and conflicts.

Left to be reared by Frances' sister, Kate at thirteen has a rewarding love relationship with Gaston Stegall, a sixteen-year-old, who eventually joins the Marines and is killed. Kate's adolescent happiness is snatched from her by death, just as her childhood happiness was destroyed by the death of her parents. She learns early that she cannot depend upon anyone, that, as the slogan in her penny-show garden proclaimed, people will leave you. If they do not leave voluntarily, death will take them away.

Kate's life is filled with sorrow and disappointment. She finally tracks down Douglas Lee, the father of her son, who had lived with her cousin Walter in Norfolk. Walter had rescued Douglas from an orphanage and had exploited him sexually. In retaliation, the young Douglas seduced Kate, resulting in her pregnancy. Now, after all these years, Kate reestablishes contact with Douglas, who works as a chauffeur in Raleigh. Before long, however, Douglas commits suicide.

Price does not provide the outcome of Kate's reunion with her son after so many years. That is left to the reader's imagination. Lee will hear the story that the reader has just read; what he makes of it, one can only surmise.

Summary

Reynolds Price is more than merely the regional author that many people consider him. He is regional in the sense that William Faulkner was regional, but his concerns are also as broad as Faulkner's were. Fate plays a strong role in Price's work, and this fate is connected to heredity. Free will enables people to make choices, but in exercising their free will, Price's characters often make the same choices their parents made in exercising their free will; therefore, the results are almost identical. Hereditary determinism is stronger in Price than in almost any other contemporary American author.

Bibliography

Drake, Robert, ed. *The Writer and His Tradition*. Knoxville: University of Tennessee Press, 1969.

Hoffman, Frederick J. *The Art of Southern Fiction*. Carbondale: Southern Illinois University Press, 1967.

Price, Reynolds. "A Conversation with Reynolds Price." Interview by Wallace Kaufman. *Shenandoah* 17 (Spring, 1966): 3-25.

Rooke, Constance. *Reynolds Price*. Boston: Twayne, 1983.

Woiwode, Larry. "Pursuits of the Flesh, Adventures of the Spirit." *Washington Post Book World*, April 26, 1981, p. 5.

Wright, Stuart, and James L. West III. *Reynolds Price: A Bibliography, 1949-1984*. Charlottesville: University Press of Virginia, 1986.

R. Baird Shuman

THOMAS PYNCHON

Born: Glen Cove, New York
May 8, 1937

Principal Literary Achievement

Pynchon is recognized as one of the leading practitioners of metafiction, the dominant avant-garde style in novels of the 1960's and 1970's.

Biography

Thomas Ruggles Pynchon, Jr., descendant of an early New England Puritan family, was born and reared in a middle-class Long Island suburb. His first known literary works were satiric essays published in the literary magazine of Oyster Bay High School, from which he was graduated in 1953. He enrolled at Cornell University in that year, majoring in engineering physics. His college career was interrupted by a two-year hitch in the U.S. Navy; he returned to Cornell and was graduated in 1959. While at Cornell, he took writing courses from the novelist Vladimir Nabokov, who was evidently impressed by the younger man's abilities but who had little direct influence on Pynchon's style or themes. Pynchon may have been married briefly during the 1950's, but careful investigations have produced no concrete evidence of this.

In 1959, he published two stories, one in the Cornell literary magazine, the other in *Epoch 9*; he published four more stories in 1960 and 1961. Most of these stories were eventually collected in *Slow Learner: Early Stories* (1984). Also in 1959 he began work on his first novel, *V.*, while living in New York's Greenwich Village; during 1960 and 1961 he worked as a technical writer for the Boeing Company in Seattle, Washington.

Virtually nothing is known about Pynchon's life after 1961. *V.* was published in 1963 and received the William Faulkner Foundation Award for the best first novel of that year. Pynchon's second novel, *The Crying of Lot 49*, appeared in 1966. He published *Gravity's Rainbow* in 1973; it has attracted what amounts to a cult of readers and massive critical attention.

Pynchon has chosen to live in obscurity, and his family and friends have cooperated in his wish to live outside the glare of publicity. In the years since 1961, he has supposedly spent most of his time in Calfornia and Mexico (his novels tend to confirm this speculation), but he has given no interviews and made no public appearances; no photographs of Pynchon since he was graduated from high school are known to exist. Apart from a few endorsements of other writers' fictions, the intro-

By the author of GRAVITY'S RAINBOW
and winner of the National Book Award

Thomas Pynchon

The Crying of Lot 49

"A bizarre, saturnalian
plunge into the underground
doomsday machine"
"A streamlined doomsday machine"
—THE NEW YORK TIMES

T5320 • $1.50 • A BANTAM BOOK

V.

A NOVEL BY THOMAS PYNCHON

duction to his own collection *Slow Learner*, an introduction to a friend's book, and two book reviews, he published nothing between the appearance of *Gravity's Rainbow* and *Vineland* (1989). He took no part in the controversy over the 1974 Pulitzer Prize in Fiction; the prize committee voted to present the award to *Gravity's Rainbow*, but the decision was overruled by the board which governs the Pulitzer awards. In 1975, Pynchon declined to accept the Howells Medal (named for William Dean Howells, nineteenth century American editor and novelist) from the American Academy of Arts and Letters. In 1988, he was awarded a fellowship by the MacArthur Foundation; there is no record that he declined this award.

Analysis

Thomas Pynchon is among the best known of the writers who came to prominence in the 1960's and 1970's with a new kind of fiction. At first this movement was called "black humor," since the novels and stories written by such authors as Pynchon, John Barth, Joseph Heller, Bruce Jay Friedman, and Gilbert Sorrentino, among others, tended to present events that were grim and terrifying but to deal with them in a wildly humorous manner. This style was also called "fabulation," a term coined by the critic Robert Scholes to reflect the idea that these writers rejected realism and deliberately called attention to the fabulous nature of their stories and novels. More recently, most critics have taken to using the term "metafiction" to describe the works of these writers. The term is intended to suggest that these writers have gone beyond conventional fiction and are creating works that make no pretense of representing reality.

Pynchon occupies a special place among this group of writers. All of them attempt to create distinctive styles, since style is an essential element in a fiction which does not try to represent human reality, but Pynchon commands a wider and wilder variety of styles than any of his contemporaries. He moves readily from wise-cracking informality to obscenity to elegiac prose to fast-paced narrative. He employs humor ranging from high-comedy word play to pie-throwing and outrageous puns. From the beginning, he gives his characters names which are significant or simply silly (Jessica Swanlake, Benny Profane, Herbert Stencil, Mucho Maas, Stanley Kotecks, Dr. Hilarius the psychiatrist).

More important, Pynchon's novels, especially *Gravity's Rainbow*, generally acknowledged to be his masterpiece, deserve to be called "encyclopedic," a critical term used to describe huge novels which contain vast amounts of information about the writer's culture. In Pynchon's work, this means that the reader is presented with obscure lore about films, technical data from physics and mathematics, folklore from a number of cultures, new readings of historical events, informed references to popular and classical music, and various other types of knowledge. No other contemporary writer commands such a wide range of information.

Pynchon's stories and novels, at least until the publication of *Vineland*, have been dominated by two themes. The first is the concept of entropy (the second law of thermodynamics), which states that particles in any closed system tend to become increasingly agitated and their movements increasingly random as the system decays until they reach a stage ("heat death") in which no energy is exchanged, no further motion is possible, and the system dies. Pynchon owes to Henry Adams, the nineteenth century American novelist, historian, and autobiographer, the idea of applying this principle from physics to human organizations, especially to political entities. One of Pynchon's first stories is entitled "Entropy" and tries to spell out how the idea can be used in fiction.

The other dominant concept in Pynchon's fiction is paranoia, the psychological condition which has been popularly called a persecution complex: the idea that the individual is the target of the unmotivated hatred of almost everyone and everything. As the fourth of Pynchon's "Proverbs for Paranoids" states in *Gravity's Rainbow*, "*You* hide. They seek." For Pynchon's characters, the idea that they live in a world in which everything is connected and everything is hostile to them is basic; a few of these characters, however, find themselves even more terrified by anti-paranoia— the idea that nothing is connected, that everything is totally random.

The paranoid concern is certainly present in Pynchon's first novel, *V.*, where hints of an all-encompassing plot disturb the lives of most of the characters, but it becomes more dominant in *The Crying of Lot 49*, whose central figure keeps stumbling across indications of an ancient conspiracy whose manifestations include mass murders which are sometimes fictitious, sometimes apparently real. Pynchon's preoccupation with paranoia reaches a climax in *Gravity's Rainbow*, which includes the five Proverbs for Paranoids, a song entitled "Paranoia," and discussions of the phenomenon by the narrator and by the characters. The problem is less noticeable in *Vineland*, Pynchon's fourth novel, but it clearly affects a number of the characters.

The concerns with entropy and paranoia are developed, in all his novels, through plots that detail quests. The important characters in all these books are in search of something. Although in *Gravity's Rainbow* Pynchon relates his characters' questing to the ancient quest for the Holy Grail, these fictional searches are often for vaguely defined goals, and in Pynchon's hands the quests almost always fail or end ambiguously.

Benny Profane, the nearest thing to a protagonist in *V.*, is looking for something he cannot define, something which would give a meaning to life, but many of the other characters are involved in a search for the mysterious woman known by several names, all beginning with the letter "V." This woman, or one of her manifestations, appears at places and times where violence is imminent. The violence may or may not occur, but the mysterious woman—becoming less and less human—may be the cause of it, or she may be attracted to it. The truth of this is never made clear, but the characters are no less determined in their quest for V.

Oedipa Maas, the central figure in *The Crying of Lot 49*, is on a more clearly defined quest. She finds that she has been made the executor of the will of a former lover, a tycoon whose estate she must try to discover and define. Oedipa falls into a nightmarish California world, stretching from Silicon Valley to San Francisco, where she encounters hints of a secret organization called Tristero and what seems to be a subversive postal system called WASTE. She pursues her quest through encounters with human wreckage and scientific puzzles, never knowing with any certainty whether the tycoon is really dead or whether she is deliberately being led through a maze which has no solution.

The object of the quest involving almost every character in *Gravity's Rainbow* is an advanced German rocket, fired in the final days of World War II. In more or less elaborate ways, each of the characters searches for evidence of the rocket. For the British, American, and Russian officials, the search is for technology which will be useful in trying to gain a military advantage in the postwar world. For the survivors of an African tribe which has been living in Germany, locating the rocket would provide a means to regain their tribal unity and character. For Tyrone Slothrop, the American lieutenant who is the central character in the novel's early sections, the search is a compulsion forced on him by the manipulation of his subconscious mind. For other characters, the search for the rocket is an end in itself, something that gives form and meaning to otherwise pointless lives.

In *Vineland*, the quest is diffuse. Zoyd Wheeler is hiding out, looking for security, while his daughter Prairie searches for her mother, Frenesi Gates, who left husband and daughter years before, fatally attracted to Brock Vond, a menacing federal prosecutor. Prairie, whose search is the nearest thing in this novel to a genuine quest, is also trying to find the truth about her mother and the reasons for her departure. Frenesi seems to have disappeared; Vond is also looking for Frenesi and, incidentally, for Prairie. Other characters have their own searches; as in other Pynchon works, many of these have no real goal but serve to provide a shape for otherwise formless lives.

ENTROPY

First published: 1960
Type of work: Short story

Dwellers in two separate apartments provide a lesson in the workings of entropy.

"Entropy" was the second professional story published by Pynchon, and this comic but grim tale established one of the dominant themes of his entire body of work. The setting is an apartment building in Washington, D.C., on a rainy day early in 1957. In a third-floor apartment, Meatball Mulligan and a strange group of friends and interlopers are in the fortieth hour of a break-the-lease party. Some of Mulligan's friends are listening to rock music played on a huge speaker bolted to a metal wastebasket; when the music ends they carry on a hip discussion of the jazz music of the time, centering on Gerry Mulligan's piano-less quartet. The Duke di Angelis quartet, as they call themselves, carry on an experiment, playing music without any instruments and without any sounds, a kind of telepathic nonmusic. Women guests are passed out in various places in the apartment, including the bathroom sink.

As the party continues, more people arrive. One man comes because he and his wife have had a fight about communication theory and she has left him. A group of coeds from Georgetown University arrives to join the party. So does a group of five sailors, who have been told that Mulligan's apartment is a brothel. They refuse to leave, latch onto the unattached women, and continue the party. At one point a fight almost breaks out between the sailors and the musical group, but Mulligan decides to intervene and calm people down. At the end of the story, the party is continuing.

On the floor above, a man named Callisto and his girlfriend, Aubade, live in a closed environment. Over seven years, Callisto has created a sealed space, complete with vegetation and birds, cut off from the world outside. The temperature inside and outside is holding steady at 37 degrees. Callisto is holding a sick bird, trying to make it well with the warmth of his body, but in the end the bird dies. They have reached the moment of stasis predicted by the theory of entropy: There is no longer any heat exchange. Aubade breaks the window and they wait together for all life to end.

The story intends to illustrate Pynchon's understanding of the theory of entropy as it might be applied to human beings and their activities. He acknowledges that the idea came from Henry Adams, who first applied the physical law to society, but Pynchon sets up the contrasting apartments as a means to demonstrate the differences between open and closed systems. Callisto's system is totally closed, and in a relatively short time loses all motion based on the exchange of heat; when everything is the same temperature, nothing moves. The bird's death prefigures the death of the entire system.

Mulligan's apartment, on the other hand, is for the time being an open system. People come and go. The Duke di Angelis quartet can play its silent music, and the sailors can get drunk and flirt with the women. Choice is still possible, so Mulligan can choose to defuse the fight rather than allow the party to degenerate into total chaos. The laws of thermodynamics apply here as well as in Callisto's apartment, however; the party verges on chaos because, as a system heats up, motion within it becomes increasingly random and violent. The system in this apartment will continue to function as long as fresh energy can enter from outside, but once external stimuli cease to arrive, this system, too, will reach a point of stasis.

THE SECRET INTEGRATION

First published: 1964
Type of work: Short story

Three boys and an imaginary playmate try to subvert the world of their prejudiced parents.

"The Secret Integration" is the longest and most interesting of Pynchon's early stories. Set in Mingeboro, a small town in the Berkshire Hills of Western Massachusetts, it concerns a group of teenaged boys who have hatched a plot to disrupt the adult community and eventually to assume control of the town themselves. At the time of the story they are preparing their second annual trial run, pretending to attack the school and considering what other steps they might take.

The four boys most deeply involved are Grover Snodd, a kind of genius, an inventor whose inventions rarely work, but who has convinced his parents and the school board to let him leave the local school to study at the nearby college; Tim Santora, a typical teenager; Étienne Cherdlu, a compulsive joker (his name is a pun on the old printers' fill-in line, etaoin shrdlu); and Carl Barrington, son of a black family that has just moved into a new housing development. The mothers of Grover and Tim make anonymous obscene phone calls to the Barringtons' home, trying to force them to leave town.

The story depends on misdirection. The four boys seem to be cast in the mold of Booth Tarkington's Penrod and Sam or Mark Twain's Tom Sawyer—mischievous but good-hearted, involved in boys' games that cannot harm anyone. (Tarkington was a twentieth century novelist who wrote about boys' games in a small Indiana town; Twain was a nineteenth century American novelist, some of whose works dealt with boys' adventures.) It seems to be merely a joke that one of their other friends, Hogan Slothrop, son of the town doctor, has been an alcoholic at age eight and a member of Alcoholics Anonymous since age nine. The boys even have a secret hideout where they do most of their planning, a basement room in an abandoned mansion. The mansion seems to be haunted, and it has to be approached in a leaky boat—classic conditions from adventure tales for boys.

Their plot has been going on for three years and seems to be running out of steam as they leave their hide-out, but then the story seems to lurch into a long digression on events that had occurred previously. It concerns Hogan Slothrop, who a year earlier was supposed to infiltrate a PTA meeting and set off a smoke bomb but was called by the local A.A. to go to the local hotel and sit with a fellow alcoholic who is under stress. Tim accompanies Hogan, and Grover and Étienne soon appear at the hotel as well. They try to help the black musician, Carl McAfee, who has somehow wandered into Mingeboro, broke and miserable. They are let in on McAfee's life and his misery. They try unsuccessfully to help a man who is beyond any help they can provide. Eventually they witness his removal by the local police.

After this episode, the boys' lives return to normal; they even have a successful adventure, using small children and a kind of stage set to terrify the crew and passengers of a railroad train one night. Then, the following summer, the Barringtons move into the new development, and they find Carl and make him their friend. As the climax of the story makes clear, however, Carl is a fantasy, made up by the three other boys to compensate for their parents' prejudice and hatred. When the boys visit the new development and find definite evidence that their parents have been involved in dumping garbage on the Barringtons' lawn, they try to clean up the mess, only to be sent away by Mrs. Barrington. Carl then departs; they send him away, because they cannot bear to give up their need for their parents and the comforts of their homes. They are becoming adults.

V.

First published: 1963
Type of work: Novel

Characters either wander aimlessly in postwar America or search for a woman who may provide a clue to the violent nature of the modern world.

Thomas Pynchon's first extended work of fiction focuses on two disparate plots. At the center of the first of these is Benny Profane, a self-styled "schlemiel," a veteran of the Navy who spends his time going up and down the East Coast (in the novel his movement is called "yo-yoing") between New York City and the naval base at Norfolk, Virginia. Profane's life has no real purpose, and he has no deep attachments to anyone; his parents are never mentioned, and his girlfriends come and go. He takes only jobs that are by their nature temporary. At one point he is a night watchman in a crazy kind of computer laboratory; at another he is part of a crew that roams New York's sewers at night, shooting the alligators which have been flushed down when they grew too big to be pets. His friends are a group who call themselves "The Whole Sick Crew"; like him, they have no sustaining purpose in life.

The other continuing thread running through *V.* has to do with a mysterious woman who began appearing around the time of a crisis in East Africa before World War I, known in history as the Fashoda affair, which seemed likely to bring about an armed conflict between Great Britain and France. The woman has many names (Veronica, Victoria, Vera), all beginning with the letter V. She appears in other places, as well, first in German Southwest Africa at a time of native rebellion, living among a besieged group of Europeans in a fortified farmhouse. She is present when a group of South Americans in Italy is planning a revolution in their homeland, and still later she is the lover of a young ballerina in Paris between the two world wars. Finally she appears on the Mediterranean island of Malta during World War II, at a time when the island is subject to intense bombing by the Italian and German air forces.

V. metamorphoses from a seemingly innocent English girl with a fascination for violence into a cosmopolite whose ethnic origins are obscure and who seems to feed on violence done to herself as well as to others. In the German redoubt she is German herself, but in her later manifestations her origins and her real nature are unclear; one mad priest in New York even believes that she manifests herself as a rat living in the sewers beneath the city. Over the years she becomes less and less human as mechanical devices are substituted for parts of her body. By the 1940's she is almost entirely a machine.

The connection between Benny Profane and The Whole Sick Crew on the one hand and V. on the other hand is an Englishman who associates with them named Herbert Stencil. Stencil's father, a British agent, had known and been fascinated by V. since the Fashoda affair. There is also a link through a young woman, Paola

Maijstral, who is a friend of Benny and a member of the Whole Sick Crew. Paola is Maltese by birth; her parents had married during the war and had endured the air raids together. Paola's father, Fausto Maijstral, has written a diary (it occupies a long chapter of *V.*) which provides important information about the character V. Paola finally convinces Benny to visit Malta in the 1960's.

In general terms, the different plot lines represent the two different themes of *V.* Benny and the Whole Sick Crew represent the forces of entropy; their activities become increasingly frenzied and random as the novel progresses and as the system of which they are a part becomes more closed. The searchers for V. are subject to strong forces of paranoia, believing that there is a gigantic plot they can uncover if only they can find the key. The mysterious land called Vheissu, a kind of fantasy British colony of which no one knows anything real, reinforces their belief. At the same time, it is evident that the characters in Benny's world are subject to paranoid fears; moreover, the world of the spies and agents is also a closed system, increasingly frenetic and destructive, likely to either explode or end in an inertial balance.

Despite all the humor and wild improbability it involves, *V.* is finally a grim book. Benny Profane is loved by several women but is unable to return their love in a meaningful way. When last seen, he is standing on the shore in Valletta, the capital of Malta, in total darkness, no happier and no wiser than he was in the beginning. The epilogue to the book shows that the older Stencil, having located V. on Malta in 1919, disappeared when a waterspout suddenly appeared on a calm day and destroyed the boat on which he was leaving the island.

V. is not, however, a hopeless book. The very vividness of its writing, the inventiveness of many of its characters in the face of potential disaster, and the humaneness some of them exhibit show that some of these strange creatures, at least, are capable of a sort of redemption. Pynchon in *V.*, as in other stories and novels, suggests that art, in its many forms, can provide potential alternatives to chaos or to entropy. He puts in the mind of a black jazz musician named McClintock Sphere the palliative words: "The only way clear of the cool/crazy flipflop was obviously slow, frustrating and hard work. Love with your mouth shut, help without breaking your ass or publicizing it: keep cool, but care."

THE CRYING OF LOT 49

First published: 1966
Type of work: Novel

A California housewife embarks on a quest for the real nature of a secret organization called Tristero and its underground postal system called WASTE.

The Crying of Lot 49 is Thomas Pynchon's briefest book and the one with the least complicated plot, although it contains plenty of twists and turns. Oedipa Maas, a bored California housewife, is informed that she is the executor of the estate of

Pierce Inverarity, a former lover. Oedipa is plunged into an increasingly complicated and increasingly sinister search for the estate, which becomes a search for meaning.

Oedipa uncovers what seems to be a vast underground conspiracy with ancient origins. Its present manifestation is an illegal communications system whose origins go back to the Middle Ages, when the private European postal service operated by Thurn and Taxis (this is historically accurate, as is so much in Pynchon's work) gained a monopoly on mail delivery in Europe. In the novel, a rival group calling itself Tristero began a bitter and violent attempt to take business away from Thurn and Taxis. Remnants of the subversive group found their way to the new world and tried to subvert the U.S. Postal Service. Their system is called WASTE, which may mean that the alternative system is a waste of time and effort (some of their mail drops are garbage cans), but which may be an acronym and slogan: "We Await Silent Tristero's Empire."

Oedipa first finds the system operating among employees at a Silicon Valley electronics company called Yoyodyne, located in a town called San Narciso, which, seen from a hill, looks like a printed computer circuit. She follows clues to a housing development in the area, where she is told a story about an American detachment in World War II that was wiped out by Nazis on the shores of an Italian lake. Later she attends a play, "The Courier's Tragedy," supposedly written by a contemporary of William Shakespeare, in which a similar massacre took place at the same spot as the climax of an Elizabethan tragedy of revenge. There are suggestions that Tristero was somehow responsible for both events, but Oedipa is unable to track down the original version of the play. The man who staged and acted in it mysteriously dies.

Oedipa's search continues through encounters with strange people, including a crazy psychiatrist; a scientist who is trying to prove the existence of a puzzle in physics called Maxwell's Demon, named for the famous British physicist Clark Maxwell; her increasingly deranged husband Mucho; and a conference of deaf persons who dance in perfect rhythm to music they cannot hear. At the end of the novel she is waiting for the opening of a stamp auction (the title, *The Crying of Lot 49*, refers to the opening of bidding for one item or group of items at an auction) which may reveal the meaning of Tristero, if indeed it has a meaning.

All of this sounds somewhat grim, but like Pynchon's other works, *The Crying of Lot 49* is lightened by the style, by high and low comedy, and by Pynchon's verbal gymnastics. The characters' names include Mike Fallopian, Stanley Koteks, Randolph Driblette, Bloody Chiclitz, and Arnold Snarb, among many others. There is a rock group calling themselves the Paranoids, who imitate the Beatles in every possible way. There is a law firm called Warpe, Wistfull, Kubitschek and McMingus. The canned music in Oedipa's local supermarket plays a nonexistent Vivaldi Kazoo Concerto, performed by the Fort Wayne Settecento Ensemble (also nonexistent). "The Courier's Tragedy," summarized at considerable length, is an accurate parody of the Elizabethan tragedy of revenge, exemplified by Thomas Kyd's *The Spanish Tragedy* or by Shakespeare's *Titus Andronicus*.

More clearly than *V.*, *The Crying of Lot 49* focuses on questions of behavioral psychology and free will. It is never clear to Oedipa whether Pierce Inverarity has really died; she becomes uncomfortably aware that if he has not, all of her investigations may be part of a complicated game in which Inverarity maneuvers her every move. If she is little more than a robot, the possibility exists that American culture has eliminated most possibilities for diversity. If Tristero exists (and even this is never certain), it may be only a feeble final protest against a society that is as carefully organized as a computer chip. It is also possible that Oedipa is hallucinating the whole thing. Yet there is the chance that a genuine resistance to an overly controlled society is really functioning. *The Crying of Lot 49* raises these issues but leaves them unresolved.

GRAVITY'S RAINBOW

First published: 1973
Type of work: Novel

A huge cast of characters searches through post-World War II Europe for a super rocket invented by the Nazis.

The questions of free will and determinism in a universe which may be subject to entropy are most sharply defined by Pynchon in his longest and most complete novel, *Gravity's Rainbow*. Set in the closing days of World War II and the months immediately following the end of the war, this novel takes the themes and techniques of the two earlier novels to higher levels. *Gravity's Rainbow*—in part because many regard it as a masterpiece and in part because it is so complex, involves so many strands of action, and poses so many unanswered questions—has been the subject of more critical attention than any novel in English since James Joyce's *Ulysses* (1922).

The central symbol of *Gravity's Rainbow* is a new type of rocket developed by the Germans at the end of World War II, designated the A-4. The first rocket designed to carry a human being into space, it is a triumph of technology. It suggests the possibility that man may have found a way to transcend his earthly origins, but it is much more likely that it carries beyond previous limits—beyond any limits—man's ability to destroy himself. Technology, in Pynchon's view, has a capacity for destruction that threatens to overwhelm its capacity for construction. At the beginning of the novel, a screaming in the sky seems to indicate that a rocket is on the way; at the very end, the reader sits in a theater with a descending rocket poised just overhead.

The action of *Gravity's Rainbow* centers on attempts to trace the A-4 rocket and its components, especially an advanced form of plastic called Imipolex-G. The British, the Americans, and the Russians, nominal allies in the war against Adolf Hitler's Germany, are rivals in trying to find the rocket and its makers in order to gain an advantage in the postwar world. One part of the British effort is managed by a behavioral scientist named Ned Pointsman.

Pointsman is the spokesman in the novel for the Pavlovian idea (named for the

Russian psychologist, Ivan Pavlov) that man, like every other animal, acts in response to stimuli. Pointsman believes that if the correct stimuli are applied, anyone can be trained to undertake any action his controller directs. He makes use of the fact that an American lieutenant named Tyrone Slothrop (he is, incidentally, the younger brother of Hogan Slothrop in "The Secret Integration") was the subject of an early experiment in conditioning a young baby. The experimenter, a mysterious figure named Lazslo Jamf, who also invented Imipolex G, supposedly removed "Baby Tyrone's" early conditioning, although remnants of it apparently remain.

Using a variety of behavioral methods, Pointsman sets Slothrop on the track of the A-4 rocket, and for much of the first half of *Gravity's Rainbow* Slothrop is the center of the action. He moves from London to the Riviera to Switzerland; when the war ends he moves into the "Zone," an area geographically similar to the British, American, French, and Russian zones of occupied Germany, but much larger, symbolically encompassing all the postwar world. Slothrop encounters a variety of adventures, some frightening, some hilarious.

Other characters are involved in their own quests for the rocket. The Hereros, remnants of a tribe transplanted to Germany years before from what was (before World War I) German Southwest Africa, have assisted in work on the rocket and now search for left-over parts to construct a rocket for themselves. Their leader, Enzian, is convinced that the rocket will provide a new center for the tribe, without which it will wither away. Enzian's path crosses Slothrop's from time to time. So does that of the chief American searcher, Major Marvy, a gross and vicious scout not only for the American armed forces but for American industrial interests as well. All of them, at one time or another, encounter the Soviet agent, Tchitcherine, who happens to be Enzian's half-brother.

There are dozens of other characters and other plots involved in the novel. Countering Pointsman is a British officer named Roger Mexico, a mathematician who rejects Pointsman's determinism and argues that traditional Western ideas of cause and effect are too limited; in his view, new scientific ideas about chance and indeterminacy are more important. Mexico's affair with a member of the British WAAF (Women's Auxiliary Air Force) named Jessica Swanlake is the nearest thing the novel contains to a love story. It ends when the war is over and Jessica chooses a more conventional man. A British secret agent called Pirate Prentice is also involved, along with one of his spies, a Dutch woman named Katje Borgesius.

While these characters (and many others) are engaged in their quests, the novel also recounts the story of the German characters who built and launched the rocket. Chief among these is the sinister Captain Weissman (also known as Blicero), who was responsible for assembling the men with the special skills needed to create and build the rocket. Once the rocket was launched, he evidently died. He has been Enzian's lover. One of his aides is a scientist named Franz Pokler, who is forced to keep working on the project because his wife, a radical, and his daughter are being held in a prison camp; if he fails to cooperate, they will presumably be killed.

Entropy is less important in *Gravity's Rainbow* than in Pynchon's earlier work; it still operates, but it seems to be less an immediate threat than the nuclear weapons which could destroy the known world in a few minutes. Paranoia, however, is more important than ever. The novel includes many episodes in which characters' suspicions that they are involved in some gigantic plot are supported by all the available evidence. The most perceptive characters have frequent intimations that there is a group called only "They," which is international in scope and which intends to gain control over everything: people, resources, and ideas. At one point, for example, Enzian experiences a revelation that all the destruction caused by bombing and shelling in World War II has been specifically planned to wipe out the old industrial establishment in order to make way for a new and more efficient physical plant.

There are small rays of hope. Art provides an alternative to the regimentation of modern society. Rebellion is still possible; when Slothrop disappears, his friends and supporters form a group called the "Counterforce" to oppose "They." The Counterforce inevitably becomes bureaucratic and public relations oriented, but members are capable of individual acts of defiance which can provide hope. The style of the novel, varied and spectacular, is itself the strongest denial of the grayness and blandness that result from the control of society by those who use technology for their own ends. At the end of the novel, however, destruction seems to be inevitable.

VINELAND

First published: 1989
Type of work: Novel

In 1984, a teenage girl searches the past and present-day California for information about her mother, who disappeared around 1970.

Vineland is Pynchon's most accessible novel, the one in which he makes his most direct statements about politics and repression in the United States, and the one in which the "good guys" and "bad guys" are most clearly distinguished. It is also, paradoxically, the one in which he makes use of the most indirect narrative methods.

There has always been an element of indirection in Pynchon's fiction, a technique related to sleight-of-hand in which the author seems to be pointing in one direction, only to shift to something unforeseen. There have also been elements of surprise in the depiction of many of Pynchon's characters. In *Vineland*, however, indirection becomes a basic technique. For example, an important chapter which will lead Prairie Wheeler, the central figure, to essential information about her mother begins with an extended depiction of a mobster, Ralph Wayvone, Sr.

At the outset, *Vineland* centers on a former hippie named Zoyd Wheeler. He lives in Northern California with his daughter, Prairie, a teenager who works in a "New Age" pizza parlor. Zoyd has a small business and receives a government allotment for engaging in one crazy act a year, usually leaping through a plate-glass window in a local restaurant. He is harried by drug enforcement agents and, early in the novel, by a federal prosecutor who is trying to find Zoyd's ex-wife, Frenesi. It seems clear that Zoyd will be the central character in the novel.

The fact is, however, that Zoyd virtually disappears from the action for a long period once Prairie leaves with her boyfriend and his punk band, Billy Barf and the Vomitones. The real quest in the novel is Prairie's search for her mother, Frenesi Gates, and for the truth about Frenesi. Her father and grandmother, Frenesi's radical mother, have always told her that Frenesi offended the establishment and was forced to go underground. Through a series of improbable coincidences (another common element in Pynchon's fiction), she meets DL Chastain, a woman martial arts expert who was a close friend of Frenesi when both were involved with radical politics during the Vietnam War era. DL takes Prairie to a women's colony, the Sisterhood of Kunoichi Attentives, where women learn Ninja, and where she finds records that begin to reveal the truth about Frenesi.

What Prairie learns, over a period of time, is that her mother had been part of a radical film collective which had, at the height of the protests against the Vietnam War in the late 1960's, been filming a student uprising on a college campus in Southern California. Her friends did not realize that Frenesi had been seduced by Brock Vond, the federal prosecutor and the blackest of all Pynchon's villains. Just as the troops and police were about to move in to break up the students' rebellion, Frenesi betrayed her friends by acting as the agent for the murder of a professor, the leader of the student movement (and incidentally one of Frenesi's lovers). When the troops moved in, Frenesi was taken to a detention center, from which DL Chastain rescued her. She then married Zoyd and gave birth to Prairie before Brock reclaimed her. Since then she has lived as a protected government informer, with a fellow informer named Flash and their son, Justin.

As the novel nears its end, the characters gather in Vineland, a fictional town and county in Northern California. Zoyd, Frenesi, Prairie, DL, her partner Takeshi, and some others attend a reunion of the large extended family of Sasha, Frenesi's mother. Brock Vond is on hand as the leader of what is supposed to be a huge government operation aimed at the marijuana crop, but which is in fact intended to be more generally repressive; on a personal level, it is his opportunity to kidnap Frenesi and Prairie, whom he believes is his daughter. Hector Zuniga, a drug enforcement agent, is trying to arrange a motion picture based on Frenesi's life.

It is clear in *Vineland* that Pynchon's sympathies are with anyone and anything that represents resistance to what he regards as an increasingly repressive government. The use of drugs such as marijuana, LSD, and even cocaine is seen as part of such resistance; any harm they might do is harm only to the user, while a character such as Vond, in his lust for power, harms everyone he touches. Government installations built in recent years to house potential resisters in a time of national emergency are used by Pynchon to suggest the lengths to which the government is prepared to go in stamping out resistance to its policies. Raids on marijuana growers are seen as exertions of power aimed at controlling everyone.

Despite the power wielded by Vond and his agents, the ending of *Vineland* is more hopeful than that of any of Pynchon's other novels. At the very moment when Vond is about to abduct Prairie, her sharpness and a sudden cutting off of his funding by Reagan-era reductions in government spending frustrate him; he is then carted off and destroyed. Prairie, although she has felt the power and attraction which seduced and nearly destroyed her mother, is safe. In the final lines, her dog, Desmond, who had disappeared when Zoyd's house was occupied by government agents, reappears. At least for a time, she has escaped from danger.

Vineland includes elements of fantasy, most important among them the creatures called "Thanatoids," who are spirits of the unquiet dead, and there are plenty of coincidences and improbabilities. For the most part, however, this novel attempts to depict what Pynchon sees as the important realities in the world of the 1980's and 1990's. Paranoia is clearly present, but the emphasis on entropy has largely disappeared, replaced by concern about the effect on individual freedoms of these recent developments. Pynchon finds these frightening, but not yet clearly triumphant.

Summary

Thomas Pynchon's stories and novels depict a wild modern world in which motion pictures, rock music, and drugs provide an outlaw alternative to an increasingly repressive society. His characters inhabit a landscape of their own which nevertheless bears eerie resemblances to everyday life. Pynchon uses a wide range of styles, employing slang, obscenity, vivid narrative, and poetic prose to convey his sense of the hazards and possibilities of the second half of the twentieth century, in which the forces of repression have all the power but in which creative art and occasional joy are still possible.

Bibliography

Clerc, Charles, ed. *Approaches to Gravity's Rainbow.* Columbus: Ohio State University Press, 1983.

Cowart, David. *Thomas Pynchon: The Art of Allusion.* Carbondale: Southern Illinois University Press, 1980.

Hite, Molly. *Ideas of Order in the Novels of Thomas Pynchon.* Columbus: Ohio State University Press, 1983.

Levine, George, and David Leverenz, eds. *Mindful Pleasures: Essays on Thomas Pynchon.* Boston: Little, Brown, 1976.

Mead, Clifford. *Thomas Pynchon: A Bibliography of Primary and Secondary Materials.* Elmwood Park, Ill.: Dalkey Archive Press, 1989.

Schaub, Thomas H. *Pynchon: The Voice of Ambiguity.* Urbana: University of Illinois Press, 1981.

Seed, David. *The Fictional Labyrinths of Thomas Pynchon.* Iowa City: University of Iowa Press, 1988.

Tanner, Tony. *Thomas Pynchon.* London: Methuen, 1982.

John M. Muste

Born: Chattanooga, Tennessee
February 22, 1938

Principal Literary Achievement

One of the leading African-American satirists of the century, Reed integrates African aesthetics and religion into American popular culture in what he calls "Neo-HooDoo" fiction and poetry.

Biography

Ishmael Scott Reed was born in Chattanooga, Tennessee, on February 22, 1938, the son of Henry Lenoir and Thelma Coleman. A year later, his mother married Bennie Stephen Reed, and the infant Ishmael assumed his stepfather's name.

When World War II began, Reed's mother moved north to find work in factories depopulated by the draft, and young Ishmael came with her. They settled in Buffalo, New York, where Reed would spend the next twenty years. Reed's first encouragement in his writing came from his mother: When he was a boy, she asked him to write a poem for the birthday of one of her coworkers. He remembers writing another poem for Christmas, 1952, but did not return to poetry until after college. He spent his first two years of secondary school at Buffalo Technical High School but finished at East High, from which he was graduated in 1956.

Finding employment as a clerk in the Buffalo public library system, Reed attended night classes at the State University of New York at Buffalo. In an English class at the university, he received further encouragement for his writing. Feeling alienated from the university's predominantly white, middle-class student body, however, Reed withdrew in 1960 and moved to a government housing project. In September of 1960 he married Priscilla Rose.

Reed began writing professionally at this time for a Buffalo-based African-American newspaper, *Empire State Weekly*. Through the paper, and a weekly community affairs show he cohosted on a Buffalo radio station, Reed became increasingly involved in civil rights activism. He also became active in Buffalo's growing theater groups; learning roles in contemporary classics such as Edward Albee's *The Death of Bessie Smith* (1960) and Lorraine Hansberry's *A Raisin in the Sun* (1959) helped Reed to develop his ear for dialogue.

In 1962, the birth of his daughter Timothy Brett Reed (for whom he wrote the poem "instructions to a princess") was, he says "the only friendly event." Sepa-

rated from his wife, he left Buffalo to seek better literary opportunities in New York City, and he found them. He became a member of the Umbra Workshop, a seminal black writers' group on the Lower East Side, whose magazine, *Umbra*, published his poetry.

On the trip from Buffalo to New York, Reed had lost all of his early poems, but he immediately began writing more. "The Ghost in Birmingham," published in 1963, shows the influence, Reed admits, of the white poets he read in college. "The Jackal-Headed Cowboy," written only a year later, shows some of the amalgamation of African myths and American popular culture that would result in his later "Neo-HooDoo" novels.

In 1965, Reed founded a newspaper for the black community in Newark, New Jersey, called *Advance*, which gave first publication to many young writers, black and white. A landmark underground newspaper, *The East Village Other*, was influenced by *Advance* and was named by Reed, who was involved in its creation. In the same year, Reed and three other black writers organized the American Festival of Negro Art, and Reed began writing his first novel, *The Free-Lance Pallbearers* (1967). The immediate critical success of this novel assured Reed's reputation, and, riding the crest of this success, he moved to Berkeley, California, to teach at the University of California.

Another purpose for the move was to get a feel for the American West for his second novel, *Yellow Back Radio Broke-Down* (1969). This book, a "Neo-HooDoo western," was another public and critical success. By the end of the 1960's, Reed enjoyed wide recognition. One acknowledgment of his position as an authority on American dialects came in the first edition of the *American Heritage Dictionary* (1969), which employed Reed on its "usage panel" as a contributor of informed opinions on contemporary American usage. The banner year 1969 also saw the second American Festival of Negro Art.

Now established as a major African-American writer, Reed used his experience as an editor to help other minority writers get their works published. His anthology, *19 Necromancers from Now* (1970), brought together the works of many new black writers and included his own piece, "Cab Calloway Stands in for the Moon," which featured the first appearance of his detective character Papa La Bas. A year later, he and *Umbra* editor Steve Cannon founded Yardbird Publishing Company, dedicated to publishing writers of all ethnic backgrounds who could not get into print elsewhere.

In 1970, Reed was divorced from his first wife and married modern dancer and choreographer Carla Blank. Reed's early poems were published as a *Catechism of D Neoamerican Hoodoo Church* (1970) in London and later as *Conjure: Selected Poems, 1963-1970* (1972) in the United States. Two Neo-HooDoo detective novels followed, *Mumbo Jumbo* (1972) and *The Last Days of Louisiana Red* (1974), both featuring Papa La Bas. Reed's next novels, *Flight to Canada* (1976) and *The Terrible Twos* (1982), no longer emphasized the Neo-HooDoo aesthetic but continued to mix dream-fantasy with contemporary reality and to combine historical periods. Reed continued to teach at the University of California, Berkeley, despite being denied tenure in 1977. The story of his tenure battle is told in an essay in *Shrovetide in Old New Orleans* (1978). He has held visiting professorships at the University of Washington (1969), his alma mater at Buffalo (1975), Yale University (1979), and Dartmouth College (1980).

Reed has continued to write poetry, fiction, and essays and to help other writers into print. He brought together his first quarter-century of poetry in *New and Collected Poems* (1988). His work has influenced contemporary writers and established him as one of the foremost satirists of the late twentieth century.

Analysis

An understanding of Ishmael Reed's fiction must begin with his concept of "Neo-HooDoo." The term "hoo doo," sometimes spelled and pronounced "voodoo," is derived from the East African religion of *vodun*. In his fiction and poetry, Reed traces the influence of this religion, brought to America by the slave trade, in American popular culture. Reed's Neo-HooDoo seeks to capture the spirit of this African religion and integrate it with the concerns of contemporary America.

Reed's first expression of his theory was "Neo-HooDoo Manifesto," published in the *Los Angeles Free Press* September 18-24, 1970, and reprinted several times. "Neo-HooDoo is a 'Lost American Church' updated," the manifesto begins. Reed describes the integration of African and Western culture in Neo-HooDoo:

> Africa is the home of the loa (Spirits) of Neo-HooDoo although we are building our own American "pantheon." Thousands of "Spirits" (Ka) who would laugh at Jeho-vah's fury concerning "false idols" (translated everybody else's religion) or "fetishes." Moses, Jeho-vah's messenger and zombie swiped the secrets of VooDoo from old Jethro but nevertheless ended up with a curse.

Western culture's "swiping" of African culture through Judaism during the Egyptian exile is a common theme in Reed's fiction, which is an important vehicle for popularizing the discoveries of anthropologists in this area.

Reed's fiction is sharp-edged satire, and the gift for it seems to have found him early. In his junior year at East High, he was sent to the principal for writing a lampoon about his teacher called "A Strange Profession." In his first college English class, he wrote a satire called "Something Pure," in which Christ returns to earth as an advertising agent. The focus of his satires is wide: All the follies of American culture, right or left, black or white, are ridiculed in his fiction. Just as important as the cultural criticism in his books is the formal criticism: His novels parody various forms of writing. His first novel, *The Free-Lance Pallbearers*, parodies African-American "confessional" novels; critic Henry Louis Gates identifies Ralph Ellison and James Baldwin as particular targets, although the content is drawn mostly from Reed's own experience. His second novel, *Yellow Back Radio Broke-Down*, parodies the Western, pulp fiction, and old radio adventures. *Mumbo Jumbo* and *The Last Days of Louisiana Red* lampoon the detective story and *Flight to Canada*, the slave narrative.

Time in Reed's fiction is fluid; while set in another time (the Jefferson era in *Yellow Back Radio Broke-Down*, the 1920's in *Mumbo Jumbo*, the Civil War in *Flight to Canada*, and the near future in *The Terrible Twos* and the 1989 novel *The Terrible Threes*), his novels refer to all points in American history, especially the second half of the twentieth century. In a 1974 interview in *Black World*, he called this process "necromancy": "I wanted to write about a time like the present or to use the past to prophesy about the future—a process our ancestors called necromancy."

Necromancy is an important word for Reed. He titled his first anthology of black poets *19 Necromancers from Now* and called the reader's attention to the word's etymology in the preface. It means "black magic," and writing is magic for Reed. "A man's story is his gris-gris," he says in the first chapter of *Flight to Canada*, using another black magic term. In Haitian voodoo, a gris-gris is a sacred object, a charm that gives a magician power as long as it is kept. Creole voodoo terms are never used to obscure or decorate Reed's fiction. They are always precisely the right words, and the meaning can usually be found in context.

If writing is magic, it is also a way to strike back, to define one's self against oppressors. In the opening of his 1974 interview in *Black World*, Reed quotes Muhammad Ali's dictum, "writing is fighting," and he made that phrase the title of his book about boxing literature. Reed does not limit his sparring to his critical essays: It shows up in his fiction as well. His novels usually have at least one scene of confrontation between two literary points of view.

In *Yellow Back Radio Broke-Down*, the scene is Bo Shmo's meeting with Loop Garoo in the desert, where Shmo tries to get Loop to conform to Marxist realist ideas of what the African-American novel should be. The scene is repeated in *Mumbo Jumbo*, in which the Marxist realist is Abdul Sufi Hamid and Reed's point-of-view character is Papa La Bas. In *The Last Days of Louisiana Red*, the conflict is embedded in the character of Chorus, who objects to her disappearance in modern literature. Reed's appearance in a Buffalo production of Jean Anouilh's *Antigone* (1944) in 1960 may have led to his interest in the Antigone myth in which Chorus appears in his novel.

In *Flight to Canada*, Raven Quickskill has literary arguments with his lover Qua Qua and presents post-Civil War literature as a continuation of the struggle: "What the American Arthurians couldn't win on the battlefield will now be fought out on the poetry field." In *Reckless Eyeballing*, Ian Ball objects not only to feminist attacks on his writing but also to the critiques of fellow black playwright Jack Brashford.

The feminist critique reflects attacks on Reed's own works, as do the other literary arguments in his fiction. Reed has been labeled sexist by feminist critics for his portrayal of women and for what is perceived as his ratification of black "macho" stereotypes. In a 1981 essay in *Playgirl*, Reed reiterated a thesis that the black male was victimized by feminist gains in the 1970's and that popular images of middle-aged males, black or white, are invariably villainous. The thesis is central to *Reckless Eyeballing*, where it is developed more fully. The biggest irony of Ishmael Reed's

status in American letters is that this radical black writer seems to have more enemies on the left (Marxist and feminist) than on the right.

YELLOW BACK RADIO BROKE-DOWN

First published: 1969
Type of work: Novel

The Loop Garoo Kid, a HooDoo cowboy, fights the powers of evil in their
current manifestation: a powerful Old West rancher.

In a self-interview in the journal *Black World*, Reed explained the title of *Yellow
Back Radio Broke-Down* word by word. "Yellow back" refers to the pulp-novel
fiction that created the myth of the Old West at the end of the nineteenth century;
"radio" continued it. "Broke-Down" means stripped to its essence. The novel, then,
is a dissection of the popular-culture images of the Old West and an indictment of
the way they portrayed minorities.

Reed's first HooDoo hero, the Loop Garoo Kid, is not only the black cowboy who
runs the circus at the opening of the novel; clues to a larger identity begin to ac-
cumulate as the novel progresses, and Loop is revealed as an eternal, the trickster
figure from African myth, mistakenly identified by Western rationalists as the power
of evil. Loop Garoo (whose name means "werewolf" in Haitian Creole) is the
eternal good guy of Western fantasy.

The bad guy is Drag Gibson, a powerful rancher who jealously protects his way of
life by trying to kill Loop and his circus people. He is hired by the people of Yellow
Back Radio to return their town to them; it has been taken over by their children—
an allegory of what seemed to be happening to the United States when the novel was
written in 1969. Drag's men attack and defeat the circus train, and Loop is stranded
in the desert. He is picked up, however, by Chief Showcase, "the only surviving
injun," in a high-technology helicopter, one of the many examples of anachronism in
the novel. Showcase, as another exploited minority, identifies with Loop and offers
clandestine aid. Loop returns to haunt Drag's men on the desert.

When Loop continues on the loose, the secretary of defense, General Theda Doom-
pussy Blackwell, is called in. With Congressman Pete the Peek providing military
appropriations, Blackwell hires the scientists Harold Rateater and Dr. Coult to develop weapons to subdue Loop. Here the satire is aimed at the military development
of the Vietnam War era, contemporary with the novel.

In the final section of the novel, Pope Innocent arrives from Europe, giving an
idea of the cosmic scope the conflict is about to assume. The Pope, representing
Western orthodoxy and authority, is upset that his American minions, the likes of
Blackwell and Gibson, have been unable to subdue Loop Garoo. He has not always
been Loop's foe, however: His discussion with Drag reveals that Loop had originally
been a member of the divine family of the Christian mythos. Put off by Jehovah's

demand of exclusive worship, Loop left him. Jehovah, however, now dominated by the feminine principle represented by Mary, needs Loop's help. Only Loop could keep the feminine force under control: He knew her as his lover, Black Diane (the Greek Artemis). One of her followers appears as Mustache Sal, another former lover of Loop, now Drag's wife.

Yellow Back Radio Broke-Down may be enjoyed on a number of levels. A parody of Western thrillers, it is as exciting and quick-paced as any of the horse operas it parodies. One index of its success as a story is a laudatory review in *Western Roundup*, a rodeo magazine written by and for modern-day cowboys. On another level, the novel functions, as does all Reed's fiction, as a critique of American culture. Because the Western as a genre illustrates the errors of American culture—looking on the resources of the American West, including the human resources of its aboriginal people, as sources of wealth to be exploited—Reed uses the genre to exorcise those errors.

On a third level, the novel attacks critical presuppositions about what constitutes African-American fiction. Instead of limiting himself to the black urban experience, Reed takes the popular forms of the majority culture and skews them to his own comic vision. The reaction of the literary establishment, black and white, to Reed's choice of form is embedded in the novel itself. The Marxist "neo-realists" who have claimed black fiction for their own political uses show up as a posse seeking to hang Loop Garoo. They are led by a spokesperson, Bo Shmo, who delivers a hilarious parody of the leading arguments of Reed's literary enemies. Loop's reply to Bo is such a succinct summary of Reed's poetics that it is often quoted: "What if I write circuses? No one says a novel has to be one thing. It can be anything it wants to be, a vaudeville show, the six o'clock news, the mumblings of wild men saddled by demons."

Reed has certainly let his novels be anything they want to be, and they are never the same thing twice. *Yellow Back Radio Broke-Down* delivers his now-familiar Neo-HooDoo picture of the United States, and it is appropriate that his first use of the HooDoo aesthetic was in a Western.

MUMBO JUMBO

First published: 1972
Type of work: Novel

HooDoo detective Papa La Bas seeks the origins of the disease "Jes Grew" while pursued by agents of the mysterious Wallflower Order.

Reed's characteristic use of fluid time, effective in other novels, is particularly apt in *Mumbo Jumbo*. The Harlem Renaissance, the setting of the novel, has striking parallels to the African-American experience of the late 1960's and early 1970's. The fact that the 1920's were called "the jazz age" indicates how much black culture was affecting the white majority. *Mumbo Jumbo* traces that influence; the rhythms, the dances, sometimes the words of ragtime and jazz songs came from rituals of the African *vodun* religion, transplanted to America by the slave trade. Reed documents those connections by footnotes and a "Partial Bibliography" at the end of the novel.

The novel is not a documentary, however. The quick-spreading influence of African culture in America is represented as an epidemic, "Jes Grew" (a phrase from Harriet Beecher Stowe's *Uncle Tom's Cabin*, 1852, referring to the character Topsy, whose origins were unknown). The Wallflower Order, a secret society dedicated to maintaining the power of white Western rationalism, seeks to stop the disease. Unlike other plagues, however, instead of harming the hosts, Jes Grew makes them feel better. Thus, the Wallflower Order shows itself to be an enemy of pleasure.

Yet Jes Grew has powerful friends as well as powerful enemies. Papa La Bas, the HooDoo detective in Harlem, tracks down Jes Grew in order to find it a sacred text and to protect it from the Wallflower Order. The Wallflowers, under the leadership of Hinckle von Vampton (after they kidnap him), seek to contain Jes Grew by sponsoring black poets, thereby limiting and defining what black literature is. To some extent, that happened in the Harlem Renassiance of the 1920's, though the motives may not have been so overt. Von Vampton is modeled after Carl Van Vechten, among others, who brought the Harlem poets into prominence in white literary circles.

La Bas is joined by T Malice and Black Herman, who, though of a younger generation, share Papa's views about black culture. One of their circle who does not is Abdul Sufi Hamid, the Muslim who wants to coopt the entire Harlem culture into the leftist politics he sees as the only means to black liberation. Von Vampton's young black protégé, Woodrow Wilson Jefferson (W. W.), is a fan of Abdul who also wants Jes Grew stamped out. W. W. is hired as "The Negro Viewpoint": by trying to define African-American art, limiting it to one point of view, von Vampton feels he can control it.

A subplot in *Mumbo Jumbo* involves the Mútafikah, a multiracial group dedicated to returning non-Western art objects that came to New York after World War I. To the Mútafikah, these were stolen under cover of the war, and they represent an irony: The majority culture that denies any value to non-Western art objects steals them and puts them into museums (or "Centers for Art Detention," as Reed calls them, lampooning the Western "curator" mentality).

Fighting the Mútafikah directly is Biff Musclewhite, a parody of the white strong-arm hero. Former Police Commissioner of New York, now charged with guarding the Center for Art Detention (C.A.D.), he is kidnapped by three Mútafikah in the process of raiding the C.A.D. (a telling acronym). Representing three races—the African Berbelang, the Asian Yellow Jack, and the Nordic Thor—they are in solidarity against the suppression of non-Western culture, though Thor is of Western origin himself. In fact, that proves his undoing. Left alone with the bound Biff Musclewhite, Thor succumbs to his accusations of being a traitor to the white race and lets Musclewhite go.

All threads of the plot come together when von Vampton, seeking writers for his periodical *The Benign Monster,* discovers the dead body of Abdul. The corpse clutches a rejection slip, which gives La Bas a clue: Apparently Abdul had found the text Jes Grew was seeking and tried to publish it as his own. All the pieces are put together in a parody of the final explanation scene of detective fiction.

La Bas's explanation is the longest chapter in the book and takes in thousands of years of history. The battle between Jes Grew and the Wallflowers turns out to be a recent outgrowth of an eternal struggle between followers of the Egyptian gods Osiris and Aton. The Wallflowers are Atonists, worshippers of the cruel god who forbade them to follow any other. Moses introduced his worship to the Israelites, and thence to the West, when he lived in Egypt, transferring Aton's qualities to Jahweh. The chapter acts as a fitting punch line to Reed's most popular satire.

FLIGHT TO CANADA

First published: 1976
Type of work: Novel

The money from his published poem about escape allows a slave to escape a Virginia plantation and flee to Canada during the American Civil War.

Although *Flight to Canada* is Reed's Civil War novel, all ages of American history are squeezed into this satire. As in all Reed's novels, time is fluid. It opens with Reed's poem "Flight to Canada," followed by a present-day reflection on the ways in which Josiah Henson's escaped slave narrative and Harriet Beecher Stowe's more celebrated version of it helped create the history of the war.

Thus, the time-consciousness of this novel is always double, referring to the events, real and fictitious, of the 1860's and the 1970's simultaneously. Deliberate anachronisms are commonplace; when Abraham Lincoln first meets the Virginia aristocrat Arthur Swille, Swille is talking on the telephone. The play at Ford's Theater at which Lincoln is assassinated is carried on public television.

There is a tinge of autobiography in the novel's protagonist, Raven Quickskill. Quickskill is a poet, and it is his writing that helps him to escape slavery on a Virginia plantation. The Civil War ends before Quickskill actually leaves, but his master, Arthur Swille, pursues him anyway.

Swille is a seductive villain. A powerful international businessman and financier, he deals with both sides in the war, and treats President Lincoln, Jefferson Davis, and Generals Lee and Grant like toadies. The scenes with Lincoln produce some of Reed's most enjoyable satire. Reed's Lincoln is a bit of a hick, and his assistance to the slaves is shown to be political expediency. Nevertheless, Reed makes him likable: He defends his wife against cruel attacks by Swille, and though he takes Swille's money, he does not trust him. Lincoln's assassination is presented as Swille's revenge for freeing the slaves.

Flight to Canada gains additional meaning when read against *Uncle Tom's Cabin.*

Reed's Uncle Tom (there are references to him and the "Legree plantation") is Uncle Robin, an old compliant black slave who has so capitulated to the machinery of slavery that he keeps Swille's records. Robin's fawning is only apparent, however; by juggling the books, he is able to cover for escaped slaves, and he always destroys the invoices so that Swille will have no proof of "ownership." His final bit of forgery tops them all: He doctors Swille's will so that Robin inherits the plantation.

As in his other novels, the supporting characters carry much of the satire. Raven's lover, Princess Qua Qua Tralaralara, is a Native American dancer and tightrope walker; he wins her away from Yankee Jack, whom Raven exposes as a pirate who killed Qua Qua's father. Mammy Barracuda, as her name suggests, is the secretly ruthless plantation mammy; Reed suggests that is is her conversion to Christianity that makes her so nasty. Swallowing whole the value system of her oppressors, she turns oppressor herself, of such poor creatures as the slave girl Bangalang (a version of Stowe's "Topsy") and even her master's wife, beating her until she becomes the model of a Southern belle. Cato the Graffado, Swille's white servant, is so self-abasing that he is indistinguishable from the slaves, who laugh at him.

While much of the book is social satire, a major theme is the power of literature itself to emancipate. Reed, like Raven, has freed himself with his words, despite the ridicule of white and black enemies and misunderstanding friends. For a black artist, however, there is a further barrier: the dominant white culture that suppresses black art by ridicule, theft, and denial. Part of what Reed has achieved in *Flight to Canada* is returning the story of the escaped slave to its rightful owners, the former slaves themselves. Josiah Henson's autobiography foundered in obscurity; Harriet Beecher Stowe made it famous, but by whitewashing it into sensationalism aimed at a white audience. *Flight to Canada* corrects Stowe's distortion, not by re-creating the clinical facts, but by skewing it in another direction, giving us the slave's-eye view through one hundred years of history.

RECKLESS EYEBALLING

First published: 1986
Type of work: Novel

A black Southern male playwright fights whites, Northerners, and feminists to get his new play produced.

As in *Flight to Canada*, the title of *Reckless Eyeballing* is the name of a work within the novel, written by the main character. Ian Ball, a Southern black playwright, has been "sex-listed"—that is, blacklisted as sexist—by the feminist critics who control New York theater. In an attempt to redeem himself, he has written a play called *Reckless Eyeballing*, which caters to feminist views.

Ian Ball bears some resemblance to Reed, who dabbled in playwriting in the 1980's, though he is clearly not Reed's point-of-view character. In a carefully controlled ironic narration, Reed makes it clear that Ball has sold out his real beliefs in order to be popular, yet neither Ball nor the narrator ever says so explicitly. In fact, Ball himself is guilty of "reckless eyeballing"—that is, looking at women lasciviously, "undressing them with his eyes." Even while he argues with the feminists who oppose him, he is thinking about them sexually. Further, his very name is "I. Ball."

Like Reed's other novels, *Reckless Eyeballing* coalesces several simultaneous plots. While Ball is trying to get his play produced, Detective Lawrence O'Reedy, a parody of Clint Eastwood's Dirty Harry Callahan (whom Reed mentions several times in the novel), is chasing the "Flower Phantom," who accosts feminists who have denigrated black men, shaves their hair, and leaves them with a chrysanthemum. In a third plot, Jim Minsk, the powerful director who stands up to the feminist bullies Tremonisha Smarts (playwright and director) and Becky French (producer), is murdered in an anti-Semite conspiracy that is never explained.

Jim's murder puts Ian at the mercy of his enemies, Tremonisha, who takes over as director, and Becky, who moves the play to a smaller, less prestigious "workshop" theater. During the course of their collaboration, however, Ian has his consciousness raised, and Tremonisha begins to see some truth in his point of view, which she had previously discarded as sexist. Ian beings to think of women as more than sex objects, and Tremonisha begins to realize that men are not monsters.

If Reed had left the plot there, it would not be much more than a trendy situation comedy. The last chapter, however, provides an ironic subtext to the whole novel. In an interior monologue, Ian's mother Martha recalls a hex placed on him at birth, making him "a two-head, of two minds, the one not knowing what the other was up to." This revelation is foreshadowed in Ball's reaction to the "Flower Phantom" in chapter 11: "Ian's head told him that this man was a lunatic who should be put away for a long time, but his gut was cheering the man on. His head was Dr. Jekyll, but his gut was Mr. Hyde." In the final paragraph of the novel, it is revealed than Ian, unknown to himself, is actually the Flower Phantom.

A fourth interwoven plot counterbalances the main story of Ball's struggle to mount his play. The lush theater originally scheduled to house his play is now running *Eva's Honeymoon*, a feminist romp presenting Eva Braun, Adolf Hitler's lover, as a victim. Mysterious scenes in the novel with an old lady who mumbles about leaving Hitler in a bunker forty years earlier make the reader realize that the play is in fact written and subsidized by Eva Braun herself, still alive and hiding in New York.

Stylistically, *Reckless Eyeballing* is more conservative than any of Reed's novels before it. The only remotely HooDoo character is Ian's mother, a Caribbean peasant with "second sight," a fortune teller very powerful in the politics of New Oyo, Ian's island birthplace. Yet none of the scenes are given a surreal or otherworldly point of view, with the possible exception of O'Reedy's hallucinations of the ghosts of innocent minorities he killed while on duty. There is no use of unusual spelling and punctuation to reproduce dialect, as in Reed's previous novels. The novel is uncharacteristically realistic.

Reckless Eyeballing is an accurate portrait of every conceivable type of hatred in contemporary America—racism, sexism, anti-Semitism, regionalism, classism, and infighting among factions of every group. Yet the attitude that Reed himself projects in the novel is not hatred but ridicule. By exposing every type of extremism—racial, gender-related, cultural—Reed has made many enemies, but he has also helped American readers see their demons and, it is hoped, exorcise them.

Summary

Ishmael Reed is an innovative black satirist. His Neo-HooDoo style, a mixture of African religion and art with American popular culture, created fiction that is popular, yet educates the reader about the African roots of American culture. Defining the African-American artist as a "necromancer," or magician, Reed sees his art as a form of conjuring, calling up the spirits of his African ancestors to comment on the past, present, and future of America. Reed's heroes are underdogs fighting oppression in many forms, usually by turning the system upside down.

Bibliography

Beauford, Fred. "A Conversation with Ishmael Reed." *Black Creation* 4 (1973): 12-15.

Bryant, Jerry H. "Old Gods and New Demons: Ishmael Reed and His Fiction." *The Review of Contemporary Fiction* 4 (1984): 195-202.

Gates, Henry Louis. "Ishmael Reed." In *Afro-American Writers After 1955*, edited by Thadious M. Davis and Trudier Harris. Detroit: Gale Research, 1984.

O'Brien, John. "Ishmael Reed." In *The New Fiction*, edited by Joe David Bellamy. Urbana: University of Illinois Press, 1974.

Schmitz, Neil. "Neo-HooDoo: The Experimental Fiction of Ishmael Reed." *Twentieth Century Literature* 20 (April, 1974): 126-140.

John R. Holmes

ADRIENNE RICH

Born: Baltimore, Maryland
May 16, 1929

Principal Literary Achievement

A major American poet, Rich voices the concerns of a generation of American women and is widely known for her feminist poetry and essays.

Biography

Adrienne Cecile Rich was born in Baltimore, Maryland, on May 16, 1929, the elder of two daughters. Her father, Dr. Arnold Rich, was a medical professor at Johns Hopkins University, and her mother, Helen Jones, was trained as a concert pianist but abandoned this career to devote herself to her domestic responsibilities and to teach. While growing up, Rich was steeped in the tradition of English poets such as Alfred, Lord Tennyson and John Keats, the favorites of her father, who was extremely well-educated in the humanities, especially for someone whose career lay primarily in the sciences. The relationship with her father dominated both her upbringing and her subsequent poetic career.

While in her senior year at Radcliffe College (1951), Rich won the Yale Younger Poets Award. This resulted in the publication of her first collection of poems, *A Change of World* (1951), with an introduction by the noted English poet W. H. Auden (who had judged the award), who praised her poems for their modesty and discretion. Rich has thus enjoyed poetic success and recognition from an early age, although she has had to struggle to find her own authentic poetic voice.

After graduation, she was awarded a Guggenheim Fellowship, which enabled her to travel in Europe. In 1953, she married Alfred Haskell Conrad, a Harvard economist six years her senior. They lived in Cambridge, Massachusetts, where their first son, David, was born in 1955. Rich also published her second book of poetry, *The Diamond Cutters*, the same year (1955). This collection, which contained a number of travel poems based on her experiences in Europe, displayed the same formalism as *A Change of World*. Two more sons followed: Paul (1957) and Jacob (1959). During this time, Rich was able to devote little energy to writing because those years were taken up with fulfilling the socially prescribed roles of wife and mother. (Rich describes the problems of this period of her life in "When We Dead Awaken" in *On Lies, Secrets, and Silence: Selected Prose 1966-1978*, a collection of essays published in 1979.) Rich found those roles at odds with her own aspirations, and this

1753

tension would become a productive force in later work.

After eight years, Rich broke her silence with *Snapshots of a Daughter-in-Law* (1963), a more personal work, in which Rich began to explore her identity as a woman, marking a significant new direction in her work. The book received much criticism for its focus on women, however, and therefore, in *Necessities of Life* (1966), Rich retreated to more "universal" and traditional themes, such as death.

In 1966, Rich moved to New York City, where she became involved in the Civil Rights movement, the anti-war movement, and the women's movement. She was also active in the literary field, teaching and giving lectures and poetry readings. Rich's father died in early 1968 after a long illness, and in *Leaflets* (1969), Rich confronted both the personal changes taking place in her own life and the problems of American society as a whole as she grappled with the need to break with the past. Rich had excelled early as a technical virtuoso in her poetry, but now she abandoned that formal expertise and experimented with fragmentation, pushing at the limits of coherence, to express new poetic ideas. This experimentation resulted in *The Will to Change* in 1971.

This period of experimentation was interrupted by a personal loss. Rich's marriage had deteriorated during the 1960's, and after the couple separated in 1970, Alfred Conrad committed suicide. Rich has seldom referred to this event publicly (one important exception is "From a Survivor" in *Diving into the Wreck*, 1973), consistently refusing to use the event as "a theme for poetry or tragic musings." The impact of the loss therefore remains difficult to trace in her work, but it clearly precipitated many changes. It forced Rich to explore a new way of writing and allowed a different side of her identity to emerge in the early 1970's. In 1973, Rich published *Diving into the Wreck*, one of her most important collections. Rich was again criticized for the personal and even militant tone of her poetry, but *Diving into the Wreck* nevertheless was a winner of a National Book Award in 1974. As a token of her new-found sense of shared identity with other women, Rich accepted the award on behalf of Audre Lorde and Alice Walker, who had also been nominated. Rich's poetic career thus far was summarized in *Poems: Selected and New, 1950-1974* (1975), a retrospective containing a selection from her previously published works, as well as a number of new poems.

In the 1970's, Rich also began the process of coming out as a lesbian. This involved not only taking a personal stand but also developing the theme of sexuality to explore broader political issues, connections that become increasingly evident in her work. An example is *Twenty-One Love Poems* (1976), which was reprinted as part of the important collection *The Dream of a Common Language* (1978), a work that contributed significantly to Rich's poetic reputation. In this collection, Rich continued her formal experimentation while developing the theme of women's love and commitment as a source of power. Rich also began publishing her most important prose works in the 1970's. These include *Of Woman Born: Motherhood as Experience and Institution* (1976) and *On Lies, Secrets, and Silence.*

In *A Wild Patience Has Taken Me This Far* (1981), Rich reached an acceptance of anger and shifted her focus to a reverence for everyday life, in which she was able to perceive the connections with all forms of life. This reconciliation with the present allowed Rich to take up the unfinished business of her own past. In *Sources* (1983), Rich undertook an investigation of her repressed roots as a Southern Jew, her source of power. Rich's mother was not Jewish, but her father—that great influence upon her—was, and yet through internalized anti-Semitism, he was proud of his ability to become assimilated into non-Jewish society, leaving a complex legacy for Rich to unravel.

In 1984, Rich left the East Coast for California. A second retrospective of her work appeared in 1984, entitled *The Fact of a Doorframe*, and *Sources* was reprinted as part of *Your Native Land, Your Life* in 1986. Rich extended her investigation of the continued relevance of the past in *Time's Power* (1989). She also continued to publish her collected prose writings: *Blood, Bread, and Poetry* (1986), a collection of essays and speeches, testifies to the importance of her role as spokesperson for the women's movement and contains important essays (for example, on the role of memory) that inform the reading of her poetry.

Analysis

In the ghazal (a verse form borrowed from Middle Eastern poetry) "7/14/68: ii," published in *Leaflets*, Rich rhetorically asks: "Did you think I was talking about my life?/ I was trying to drive a tradition up against the wall." This couplet summarizes Rich's poetic career: Autobiography is used to examine universal issues in order to effect change. *Snapshots of a Daughter-in-Law* was the first volume in which this important aspect of Rich's work was apparent. Starting with this collection, Rich began to write more personal and experimental poetry in which meaning was not subordinate to form. Rich assumed a somewhat more personal voice, addressing more directly the issues she faced as a woman and allowing herself more formal innovations. Although Rich did not yet allow herself to speak directly (the daughter-in-law of the snapshots, an important autobiographical sequence, is referred to as "she," not "I"), these were Rich's first feminist poems and drew their inspiration from the work of Simone de Beauvoir and Mary Wollstonecraft. Rich's mature work is intensely biographical, not merely for the sake of pure honesty and personal expression, but because by describing her own struggles, she wishes to stimulate what she has called "the will to change" and thereby bring about political transformation in others.

The "will to change" is created by the rigorous examination of one's own inner self as well as by "diving into the wreck" of past tradition. As Rich states in "Tear Gas" (in *Poems: Selected and New*), "the will to change begins in the body not in the mind," thereby linking biography to larger issues. In pursuing this rigorous self-examination, one is carried by a kind of visionary anger best described as "a wild patience," which provides the energy to create the dreamed-of community that speaks "a common language." In this way, then, Rich is interested in the real world and is concerned with the way poetry can affect daily life. She is not a poet interested only in form or the purely abstract or self-referential aspects of writing.

That the personal is political was a slogan of the 1960's and 1970's, and Rich's poetry examines and exemplifies that connection. As she states in "The Blue Ghazals: 5/4/69" (in *The Will to Change*): "*The moment when a feeling enters the body/ is political. This touch is political.*" The feeling, the touch, could be caused by pain (the context of this poem suggests torture) or by love (as in "Twenty-One Love Poems"), but what matters to Rich is that such personal interactions are conditioned by larger, political structures. As Rich states in "The Phenomenology of Anger" (in *Diving into the Wreck*), "every act of becoming conscious// is an unnatural act." Thus, for Rich, the lesbian theme in her poetry is not only a personal statement but becomes a metaphor for all the "unnatural acts" of becoming conscious of oppression and making a choice to resist.

Rich finds the energy to change in anger, an important and powerful emotion in her work, although alienating to some readers. She explores this theme explicitly in "The Phenomenology of Anger," in which she allows herself to explore her fantasies of murder, which result in "a changed man." She describes anger as a kind of "wild patience" and, in "Natural Resources" (in *The Dream of a Common Language*), as "impatience—my own—/ the passion to make and make again/ where such unmaking reigns/ the refusal to be a victim." It is thanks to such fuel that she has been able to sustain her poetic explorations, and she speaks positively of the potential of "visionary anger" as a force that others, too, can draw upon. In *A Wild Patience Has Taken Me This Far*, she even describes her anger as an "angel," a striking and suggestive image for the role it has come to assume in her work.

Rich finds her insights increasingly hard to express, however, as she becomes aware of the ways in which language reflects the assumptions and values of dominant culture. In *The Will to Change*, she is aware of the limitations of what she calls "the oppressor's language" and later allows herself to "dream of a common language," the title of one of her most important collections. She explores, too, the visionary potential of poetry as she imagines a world in which women are not divided against one another but where their shared community is a source of transformative power. The idealism of this vision is tempered, however, by the recognition that, in the real world, language can be distorted and taken out of context ("North American Time").

Having once defined her vision, Rich realizes that it requires continual effort to maintain it. This daily struggle incorporates the past, which is far more than a mere "husk" (as Rich suggests in *A Wild Patience Has Taken Me This Far*), and leads Rich to the personal interrogations of her own past, best represented by *Sources*. The recognition that ideals such as freedom depend on the prosaic, everyday act of remembering also leads Rich to be more attentive to the ordinary routines of her own daily life. Her descriptions of New England landscapes are the occasion for striking and beautiful imagery, such as the description of beet roots in "Culture and Anarchy" (from *A Wild Patience Has Taken Me This Far*). This element of her work places her firmly in the tradition of poets she admired and was influenced by, such as Robert Frost.

The attempts to break with poetic tradition and forge something entirely new (yet that will incorporate the past) result in what Rich calls "a whole new poetry beginning here" ("Transcendental Ètude" in *The Dream of a Common Language*). It is this originality, which transforms the most intensely personal material into statements that reflect a wider truth, that has compelled respect and admiration for Rich's work. Although Rich has been criticized for her anger, unremitting seriousness, and occasional self-righteousness, her work has been favorably compared to that of major poets such as Anne Bradstreet, Emily Dickinson, Robert Frost, Robert Lowell, Sylvia Plath, and Anne Sexton.

AUNT JENNIFER'S TIGERS

First published: 1951
Type of work: Poem

Aunt Jennifer creates a work of art that lasts beyond her death.

"Aunt Jennifer's Tigers," which appeared in Rich's first collection of poems, is typical of her early work, illustrating the modest poetic ambitions for which she was praised by Auden. Technically, the work displays flawless craftsmanship, with a carefully regulated meter and rhyming couplets. Only later did Rich recognize how formalism functioned like—in her words—"asbestos gloves," enabling her to grasp potentially dangerous materials without putting herself at risk, as in this poem.

The formalism of "Aunt Jennifer's Tigers" hides the more disturbing aspects of the poem and subordinates the theme of Aunt Jennifer's "ordeals" in marriage to the more "poetic" theme of the transcendence of art. The first verse of the poem describes the fearless tigers Aunt Jennifer has created in needlepoint. Their freedom and dignity is contrasted in the second verse to the restrictions of marriage, symbolized by the wedding band that weighs down Aunt Jennifer's fingers as she sews. The themes are resolved in the final, third, verse: Even death will not free Aunt Jennifer from her "ordeals," but the tigers she has created will continue to appear "proud and unafraid."

While the poem is technically brilliant, the themes that art endures beyond human life and that suffering may be redeemed through art are hardly original. Rich, however, uses an inventive image to recast these conventional themes in a new way and even hints, in the image of Aunt Jennifer weighed down by an oppressive marriage, at the feminism that would inform her later work. Yet the poem remains quite impersonal; the reader sees Aunt Jennifer but is scarcely aware of the voice of the poem's narrator. For the reader, it is as though the picture were framed by an invisible hand, in contrast to Rich's later work, where the reader cannot help being aware of the poet's personal presence.

THE BURNING OF PAPER
INSTEAD OF CHILDREN

First published: 1971
Type of work: Poem

A comparison between the burning of books and physical human sufferings, and an observation of the inadequacy of language to convey pain.

"The Burning of Paper Instead of Children" is a good example of Rich's developing experimental style. Between 1968 and 1970, Rich had confronted in her poetry the inability of the language she had inherited to express the pain both of her own life and of society as it underwent turbulent social change. The results of this experimentation can be seen in *Leaflets*, but are also evident in this collection, *The Will to Change*. Whereas in Rich's early work, exemplified by "Aunt Jennifer's Tigers," the poem encapsulates a certain experience, in this experimental vein, the poem itself is the experience. As Rich allows the unconscious to speak through her poetry, the poem contributes to the creation of new experiences for both poet and reader, as this poem illustrates. The poem consists of five interrelated sections, which vary in form from fragmented free verse to prose poetry.

The starting point for the poem is autobiographical—a neighbor calls to complain about the poet's son burning a textbook—and here the poet does not hesitate to use the first person ("I"), illustrating both the role of personal memory as the key to political connections and also Rich's assumption of a personal presence in her work. The poet juxtaposes this incident with a picture of Joan of Arc being burned at the stake, a memory from childhood, the privileged childhood in which she had access to books and education, but that failed to teach about the reality of suffering. This memory also serves as the occasion for Rich to explore the difficult relationship of "love and fear" to her father, a relationship she now begins to perceive as oppressive. The relationship with her father is another recurrent theme in Rich's work, and some critics have gone so far as to suggest that it is the dominant theme.

In the second section, the poet records her frustration that language is necessary, yet inadequate, to communicate. The third section lists different forms of suffering and concludes with the observation that, in order to overcome suffering, the language must be repaired. Rich thereby links the themes of the first two sections and illustrates the connection, for her, between language and politics. Once Rich broke away from the formalism that conveniently shielded her from the power of raw language, she became increasingly preoccupied with this subject.

The fourth section again explores frustration in a personal relationship and the uselessness of written texts to describe and understand experience (suggesting that burning books is a reasonable response). The final section further explores the problems described above in a stream-of-consciousness list that strives to capture the poet's own feeling of burning with impotence to solve the different yet related problems that range from poverty in America to the burning of children by napalm in Vietnam.

The experimental form of the poem forces the reader to confront a complexity that resists easy summary, in marked contrast to Rich's earlier work, where the "theme" of the poem was often easily extracted. Rich has abandoned conventional form and attempted to put into language thoughts that were not previously considered poetic, to push at the limits of what is considered "poetry." Along with the exploration of form, Rich allows a more personal voice to be heard in the poem, blending autobiographical scenes and reminiscences with only minimal clues for the reader as to their context and significance. Rich does not even pretend to maintain traditional poetic language and integrates black dialect into the poem as a means of illustrating the inadequacy of standard English to capture some forms of experience. This incorporation of different voices also symbolizes the connections Rich perceives between different struggles for change and justice.

ORIGINS AND HISTORY OF CONSCIOUSNESS

First published: 1978
Type of work: Poem

The poet tries to explain the connection between the true nature of poetry and life.

"Origins and History of Consciousness," as the title suggests, is an account of the poet's gradual awareness of what poetry means to her and how it is connected to personal issues in her life. Appearing in *The Dream of a Common Language*, one of Rich's most critically acclaimed works, it represents an important summary of themes and concerns at the center of her work.

The first section consists of what appears to be a relatively straightforward description of a room, but it rapidly becomes clear that this description incorporates many layers of symbolism. The blank walls, for example, represent the erasure of women writers from history, an absence of tradition that the woman poet must confront. The search for origins, and foremothers, that the poet undertakes also recalls the archaeological explorations of *Diving into the Wreck*. The social change movements of the 1960's and 1970's had helped to create an atmosphere in which questioning the past and the need for change—both personal and political—were widely accepted.

Rich's work echoed these concerns and gave poetic expression to ideas that many were struggling to articulate, both in *Diving into the Wreck* and in *The Dream of a Common Language*. In this latter collection, Rich understood that sexuality is only one of the ways women express a commitment to each other (these ideas were later developed in her influential essay "Compulsory Heterosexuality and Lesbian Existence," first published in 1980). The theme of a community of women began to figure more prominently in her work, along with peace, feminism, and antiracism. The three sections of the book, focusing on power, love, and the need to confront the immediate context, explore the dream, or ideal, of a community based on values of nurturance and care and mirror the concerns of the burgeoning women's movement.

In "Origins and History of Consciousness, from the first part, entitled "Power," the poet acknowledges that for her, the "true nature of poetry" is "the drive/ to connect/ The dream of a common language." In the second section, the poet contrasts the simplicity of falling in love to the difficulty of integrating this private life into the public world of the surrounding city, an example of how Rich uses personal situations such as sexual orientation to draw larger connections. She continually emphasizes that various aspects of life cannot be kept separate but overflow into one another, just as the lines of her poem run on into one another.

In the third and final section, the poet names the problem as one of trust. Using an image of lowering herself on a rope, an image reminiscent of her earlier work "Diving into the Wreck," the poet describes how she gradually began exploring the problem. Having gained an understanding of the situation (having explored its "origins and history"), however, the poet ends by stressing the need for public acknowledgment of those connections in order to reconcile the splits and forge a more holistic vision of life.

The poem uses experimental forms such as incomplete sentences and fragmented phrases to capture the difficulty of formulating the message. The descriptions of the room at the beginning of the poem retain a certain even structure; the punctuation, though minimal, lends coherence. As the poet delves further into her inner consciousness, however, the poem becomes more fragmented. The lines are more varied in length, greater use is made of italics and dashes (the characteristic punctuation of Emily Dickinson, who figures so frequently in Rich's work), and imagery is accumulated without an attempt to impose order, as a means of conveying the dreamlike state of the poet. Rich uses both striking poetic imagery and prosaic language inspired by her surroundings in New York City to blend a dreamlike poetic vision with the everyday reality, a fusion that represents in the poem the integration she seeks in life.

NORTH AMERICAN TIME

First published: 1986
Type of work: Poem

A meditation on the power and responsibility of words.

While continuing to explore themes (such as the power of language) taken up in other poems, "North American Time" places these concerns in the context not of new discoveries, but of continued struggle. As in *A Wild Patience Has Taken Me This Far*, Rich rejects the Romantic emphasis on certain peaks of perception and instead focuses on the dailiness of the struggle to change the world through quiet strength and resistance. In *Your Native Land, Your Life*, Rich continues to explore the ways that daily experience, especially the natural and indigenous scenes of her "native land," provides the raw material of art that becomes the artist's life. The phrase that gives the title to the collection occurs in a poem entitled "Emily Carr," about the Canadian artist who painted the totem poles of the Northwest Coast Indians, and encapsulates the importance of art rooted both in landscape and in traditions, especially those of minorities. Rich also continues to incorporate the past, on a personal level by analyzing the powerful relationship with her father and the role of her background, and on a general level by attending to the indigenous history of the United States and its connections to the rest of the world.

The collection echoes the tripartite structure of *The Dream of a Common Language*, with sections entitled "Sources," "North American Time," and "Contradictions: Tracking Poems." The poem "North American Time" is part of the second section. In this poem in nine parts, Rich takes stock of her accomplishments as a poet and discusses the connection of poetry to history. She begins to wonder about these matters in the first verse, when she fears that her poetry has become circumscribed and predictable. As she explains in subsequent verses, the issue is not only one of personal importance but has wider ramifications because, once words become part of the world, they take on a life of their own; they escape the speaker's control and can be used in a way the speaker never intended. Attempts to deny political responsibility are futile, Rich maintains, and she goes on to sketch connections between "North American Time" and other world events, figures, and places that are routinely denied or ignored because of ethnocentrism. This attention to lost or muted voices becomes an increasingly important theme in Rich's work, as her sensitivity to the supression of women's culture makes her aware also of the erasure of Native American Indian, black, and other minority experiences.

Rich views herself as a kind of messenger, a prophet or seer, called upon to engage the reader with these issues, and uses this image, which she admits is rather grandiose, as an incentive to continue writing and speaking out. She concludes by characteristically incorporating the words of another woman writer, the Puerto Rican poet Julia de Burgos, and, as she watches the moon rise over New York City, an image that portends change, she shifts from introspection to action—that is, speech.

The attention to the lives of other women (artists, writers, explorers, and scientists) is one of Rich's enduring concerns. In this poem, Rich both quotes Julia de Burgos and refers to other women whose names have been erased from the "almanac" of North American time. In this collection, as in her previous work, such allusions are pervasive and telling. Such "re-visions" (a central concern of literature, as Rich explained in *On Lies, Secrets, and Silence*), are an inspiration to Rich, a celebration of the buried traditions of women's writings she has excavated elsewhere, and a benchmark for women's experience.

Summary

Taken in its entirety, Adrienne Rich's work may be viewed as what Albert Gelpi has called "a poetics of change," a systematic attempt to explore and understand change through poetry. Rich gradually developed a poetic voice that is both personal and universal.

Her consummate works of poetry, *The Will to Change*, *Diving into the Wreck*, and *The Dream of a Common Language*, along with some of her prose works, are frequently quoted because they seem to express the essence of a new woman's consciousness; many of her phrases name important experiences in new ways. Rich's use of poetry to link abstract metaphysical questions to concrete daily life has revitalized poetry and made it seem relevant in new ways.

Bibliography

Altieri, Charles. *Self and Sensibility in Contemporary American Poetry*. Cambridge, England. Cambridge University Press, 1984.

Bennett, Paula. *My Life a Loaded Gun: Female Creativity and Feminist Poetics*. Boston: Beacon Press, 1986.

Cooper, Jane Roberta, ed. *Reading Adrienne Rich: Reviews and Re-visions, 1951-1981*. Ann Arbor: University of Michigan Press, 1984.

Gelpi, Barbara Charlesworth, and Albert Gelpi, eds. *Adrienne Rich's Poetry*. New York: W. W. Norton, 1975.

Kalstone, David. *Five Temperaments: Elizabeth Bishop, Robert Lowell, James Merrill, Adrienne Rich, and John Ashbery*. New York: Oxford University Press, 1977.

Keyes, Claire. *The Aesthetics of Power: The Poetry of Adrienne Rich*. Athens: University of Georgia Press, 1986.

Martin, Wendy. *An American Triptych: Anne Bradstreet, Emily Dickinson, Adrienne Rich*. Chapel Hill: University of North Carolina Press, 1984.

Ostriker, Alice. *Writing Like a Woman*. Ann Arbor: University of Michigan Press, 1983.

Stimpson, Catharine. "Adrienne Rich and Lesbian/Feminist Poetry." *Parnassus: Poetry in Review* 12, no. 2; 13, no. 1 (1985): 249-268.

Melanie Hawthorne

CONRAD RICHTER

Born: Pine Grove, Pennsylvania
October 13, 1890
Died: Pottsville, Pennsylvania
October 30, 1968

Principal Literary Achievement

Best known for his fiction about pioneer life in Pennsylvania, Ohio, and the Southwest, Richter contributed significantly to the development of the realistic historical novel of American westward expansion.

Biography

Conrad Richter was born on October 13, 1890, in Pine Grove, Pennsylvania, the first of three sons of John Absalom and Charlotte Henry Richter. His ancestors were tradesmen, soldiers, blacksmiths, farmers, and ministers. As a boy accompanying his clergyman father on pastoral calls among the farm settlements and coal-mining regions of Pennsylvania, Richter carefully observed the manners and behavior of the people, developing a keen ear for their idiomatic language. He took note of their strength of character and sturdy fortitude in the face of hardships, values derived from their pioneer forebears.

Richter's family expected him to follow in his father's footsteps and become a clergyman. Accepting the assumptions of science with as much faith as his grandfather and father had accepted the assumptions of Christianity, however, he found himself doubting Christian beliefs. At the age of thirteen he declined a scholarship that would have taken him through preparatory school, college, and seminary on condition that he become a Lutheran minister.

Graduated from high school at the age of fifteen, Richter continued to educate himself, reading widely and working at various jobs as a teamster, mechanic, farm laborer, coal breaker, timberman, and bank clerk. Inspired by a series of articles about newspaper writers, he decided to become a journalist, reporting for and editing small-town newspapers and eventually working for *The Pittsburgh Dispatch*. Moving to Ohio in 1910, he wrote for the *Johnstown Leader*. In 1913 he began to write short stories, and a year later *Forum* published his "Brothers of No Kin," a widely acclaimed work of fiction that Edward J. O'Brien selected for *The Best Short Stories of 1915*.

Disappointed by the low payment he received for his first serious fiction, Richter

decided to concentrate his main energies on journalism and business, devoting his spare time to writing the kind of stories that brought a fair price. He married Harvena Achenbach of Pine Grove in 1915 and started a small publishing company and a juvenile periodical, *Junior Magazine Book*. Turning his hand to juvenile fiction, he wrote children's stories for his own periodical and other magazines. A daughter, Harvena, was born on March 13, 1917, and five years later Richter moved his family to a farm in Clark's Valley, Pennsylvania, where he continued his publishing work and the writing of fiction. In 1924, he had collected enough of his previously published stories to make up a volume entitled *Brothers of No Kin and Other Stories*.

While establishing himself as a journalist, publisher, and writer of fiction, Richter sought a scientific and factual explanation of the eternal enigmas. His desire to seek answers to questions about human nature and destiny led to his interest in widely discussed notions of evolution, psychology, and related aspects of physical and biological science. In 1926 he published a book-length essay, *Human Vibration: The Mechanics of Life and Mind*; this was followed by *Principles in Bio-Physics* (1927). Both books are serious if amateurish attempts to understand first causes, human vitality, the relationship of mind and body, and creative evolution. Their limited reception convinced Richter that he would do better to dramatize his ideas through fiction.

Because of his wife's failing health, Richter sold his business and moved his family to Albuquerque, New Mexico, in 1928. His philosophical ideas and growing discontent with the modern drift toward an industrial, urban civilization kindled his interest in the frontier, and Richter decided in 1933 to become a writer of serious fiction, devoting himself to painstaking research in diaries, journals, and old newspaper accounts of frontier life in the Southwest. The short stories that grew out of this research were collected in *Early Americana and Other Stories* (1936), marking the beginning of a distinguished career as a writer of fiction using American backgrounds. His first novel, *The Sea of Grass* (1937), was well received and was later made into a first-rate film.

In the decade from 1940 to 1950, Richter published six novels, including his major work, the Ohio trilogy—*The Trees* (1940), *The Fields* (1946), and *The Town* (1950)—and became widely recognized as an important historical novelist. The Society of Libraries of New York University awarded him the gold medal for literature for *The Sea of Grass* and *The Trees*. In 1944 he received an honorary doctoral degree from Susquehanna University, and three years later the Ohioana Library Medal Award for Literature. Although the historical trilogy was clearly at the center of Richter's attention during these years, he published another novel about the early Southwest, *Tacey Cromwell* (1942), and two less successful novels, *The Free Man* (1943) and *Always Young and Fair* (1947). At the end of the decade, he moved his family back to Pine Grove, the town of his birth. The following year (1951), he was awarded the Pulitzer Prize for Fiction for *The Town*.

In the last fifteen years of his life Richter continued to publish impressive novels of American backgrounds and to gain recognition for his achievement. He explored complex racial relationships in *The Light in the Forest* (1953) and *A Country of Strangers* (1966), companion novels about the forcible repatriation of whites from Indian captivity. His third book-length essay, *The Mountain on the Desert* (1955), revealed his continuing interest in the psychological and mystical ideas that had always informed his fiction. After publishing his last Southwestern novel, *The Lady* (1957), Richter received an honorary doctoral degree from the University of New Mexico (1958). In 1960, he won the National Book Award for *The Waters of Kronos*, the first novel of a projected autobiographical trilogy, which was followed by *A Simple Honorable Man* (1962). Although Richter did not complete this trilogy, he published three more novels, *The Grandfathers* (1964), *Over the Blue Mountain* (1967), and *The Aristocrat* (1968). The Ohio trilogy was republished as *The Awakening Land* (1966) and later dramatized on television. Richter died of heart disease in Pottsville, Pennsylvania, on October 30, 1968. *The Rawhide Knot and Other Stories*, a collection of his short stories, was published posthumously in 1978.

Analysis

Conrad Richter's literary reputation rests chiefly on his achievement in writing the historical novel. In his fictional recovery of the past, he avoided the weaknesses and limitations inherent in the genre of historical fiction. He shunned the costume romance, with its emphasis on action, exciting narratives of adventure and love, and sensational events. He had no interest in the novel of recognizable events or personages or in the fictionalized biography of important men and women. At the same time, he eschewed the period novel, which is more concerned with background details than with the whole of life.

Richter knew that his strength as a writer lay in his ability to keep in touch with the living muscle and tissue of actual experience, to keep the destiny of common people central to his vision. He believed that the greatest influence on historical events was the broader stuff of reality lived by the majority of men and women who led quiet, obscure lives, but who found life itself endlessly resourceful and inexhaustible. To recapture the spirit and flavor of an age as revealed in the everyday relations of people, Richter steeped himself in the documents of social history— diaries, journals, letters, newspapers, and oral histories.

The desire to give fictional form to the experience of American westering derived in large part from Richter's homespun theories of human behavior and destiny. Although his speculative theories, which he named "psycho-energies," are too complex and esoteric to consider in detail, it is important to see their relationship to his major themes. According to Michael, the rug-weaving philosopher in Richter's *The Mountain on the Desert*, the distinguishing feature of life is limited energy, and the basic primal motive is energy hunger. Creative growth, which requires the body and mind to expend energy, is the purpose of being. This growth is always accompanied by pain or discomfort; to remove all occasions of disharmony or suffering, however, results in the stifling of creative growth. Moreover, human attempts to avoid hardship and suffering are inevitably thwarted by a mystical force that Richter calls fate or destiny. Natural adversity will assure creative growth, but people can cooperate with this cosmic plan by practicing self-discipline and embracing a life-style that values hardihood.

Richter's fiction invariably reflects his belief that the universe uses hardship and discipline to assure human progress. The implications he draws from this life pattern account for most recurring themes in his fiction: adversity and hardship as a means of growth, the development of higher intelligence wrought by experience, the intuition of a cosmic destiny ordering human affairs, the stoic conception of *amor fati* (love of the order of God), and the superiority of the primitive and natural over the civilized and artificial.

All Richter's narratives are implicitly concerned with the relationship of the past to the present. His knowledge of the American past provided him with a well-defined historical image of a change in the human condition attended by cultural loss. This accounts for the persistent lyrical and elegiac tone of his fiction; there is undeniable nostalgia, but Richter stops short of sentimentality by revealing the human weaknesses and failings as well as the courage and strength that emerge under the pressure of harsh reality. In *The Sea of Grass*, for example, he tells the story of a people and land ravaged by years of conflict and change as the cattleman resists the homesteader in the battle for the ranges of Texas and New Mexico. The focus of the story, however, is not on sensational events (violence is normally muted and offstage) but on certain distinguishing traits in the major characters brought out by the conflict— Colonel Brewton's practical intelligence, hardness, and self-discipline, in contrast to the shrewd opportunist Chamberlin, who relies on political influence and the collective will to impose an agricultural economy on a fragile range environment suited only to stock raising.

The Ohio trilogy similarly offers an interpretation and judgment of the cultural loss that accompanied the change from a harsh frontier to a settled civilization. Richter's sense of the continuity of past and present enabled him to weave into a meaningful whole the epic strands of the archetypal American experience: the nomadic penetration into primeval wilderness in *The Trees*; the clearing and cultivation of the land in *The Fields*; and in *The Town*, the growth of community from the soil and the inevitable emergence of an industrial civilization and mode of life that threaten to erode something vital in the human spirit. The narrative is objectified in the experiences of a pioneer family through four generations. The heroine, Sayward Luckett Wheeler, one of Richter's most memorable characters, is strong, elemental, and determined to survive. The surface narrative of Sayward's life is effectively connected with a background meaning: the cosmic role of hardship and adversity as a means of growth. The theme of cosmic order and individual destiny thus gives unity to the three novels by providing a principle for selecting those details and episodes that enable Richter to coordinate structure and meaning.

As useful as Richter's theories are in understanding the design of his work, however, it is his artistic transmutation of historical materials into realistic narratives that gives his novels enduring appeal. From the beginning, Richter's aim was to give the sensation of living in the past by recreating the details and authenticities of early life in a style suggestive of the times. Richter defines a story as the record of human achievement; he thus reveals his meanings in terms of characterization. He conveys habits of mind, indigenous patterns of speech, characteristic actions—all embedded in authentic folk traditions—in a simple, colloquial style, rich in feeling and precise in the rendering of effect. The form of his fiction, rooted in the novella, is essentially episodic, concentrating on central situations that reveal character. Striking an artistic balance in blending fact and fiction, he effectively integrates character, setting, and action. The overall effect is of careful artistry, classical condensation, and emotional restraint.

THE LIGHT IN THE FOREST

First published: 1953
Type of work: Novel

When a white boy reared by Indians is repatriated to his family, he cannot readjust to civilization or reconcile the claims of blood and loyalty.

In *The Light in the Forest*, Richter presents the Indians' point of view toward the settlement of the wilderness, putting an unusual twist on the traditional captivity tale: He tells the story of a white boy who resents being returned to his natural parents. John Butler was only four years old when Delaware Indians captured him during a raid on his father's farm in western Pennsylvania. Adopted by a tribal chief and renamed True Son, he lived for more than a decade in the Ohio wilderness until Colonel Bouquet's treaty with the Delaware Indians called for the repatriation of all white captives. On True Son's reluctant journey to the Paxton settlement, he sees an ancient sycamore at the forks of the Muskingum that symbolizes his predicament. A dead limb points toward the white settlement, while a live branch points back toward his beloved Indian culture. The conflict in the story turns on these two claims to his loyalty.

Stubbornly insisting on his Indian identity, True Son refuses all efforts to reinstate him into the life of family and community. His invalid mother seems ineffectual, and his father preoccupied with business ledgers and property. Only his little brother, Gordon, provides comfort and companionship. True Son reserves his greatest hostility for his uncle, Wilse Owens, an Indian-hater and one of the Paxton Boys, who had massacred Indian women and children in an earlier reprisal against the Conestoga.

True Son's smoldering resentment at his "captivity" in the white settlement reaches a crisis when Half Arrow, his adopted Indian cousin, visits one night to show True Son the body of Little Crane, slain when he tried to visit his repatriated white wife. True Son confronts his uncle, accusing him of the murder. In the ensuing struggle, Half Arrow wounds Owens and the two boys flee after failing to get

Owens' scalp as a trophy.

True Son's reunion with his Indian family is joyful but short-lived. Joining Cuyloga, his Indian father, and a group of braves in a war party to avenge Little Crane's death, True Son is appalled to see one of the warriors massacre and scalp little children. The warriors compel him to serve as a decoy to lure white settlers into an ambush and thereby prove his loyalty, but he cannot repudiate his blood ties to the whites and he warns the intended victims. This betrayal causes Cuyloga to reject his adopted son, declaring him an enemy and banishing him from the tribe. Adrift between two cultures, True Son cries in despair, "Then who is my father?"

The details, anecdotes, and incidents Richter derived from his historical sources enabled him to provide an authentic sensation of life on the Pennsylvania-Ohio frontier without the distortions of sensationalism or sentimentality. Although objective in his portrayal of both the Delaware Indians and the white settlers, Richter carefully controls the narrative point of view, rendering most of the experience through True Son's consciousness. This allows Richter to convey the poetic imagery and idioms of Indian thought and language as True Son expresses delight in the wild, joyous freedom of the natural world and disgust at the whites' thoughtless destruction of the forest, their building of fences, walls, and roofs to shut out nature, and their relentless accumulation of material wealth. One of Richter's aims in writing the novel was "to point out that in the pride of our American liberties, we're apt to forget that already we've lost a good many to civilization."

True Son's predicament not only objectifies the theme of the organic unity of man and nature inevitably giving way to the restrictions of civilization in the historical process of westering, it also dramatizes the archetypal experience of youth who must give up an idyllic and secure child's world and take on the responsibilities of adulthood, with its painful moral choices. His discovery that hateful racial prejudice exists in both Indian and white culture and his costly moral choice at the climax of the story reflect his spiritual maturation and intuitive understanding of the need for brotherhood. The novel's conclusion is a concession to harsh reality: True Son must accommodate his alienation and work out his own identity without the guidance of an earthly father or the comfort of a sustaining cultural community.

Summary

One of the values of literature is that it gives form to life so that it may be analyzed and understood—a particularly formidable task when that life must be reconstructed from the past. Richter's fictional recovery of the past and celebration of traditional values will strike some as old-fashioned, especially those who equate progress with comfort and values with expediency. Yet no American writer has more successfully re-created in fiction that early American quality of strength and hardihood. Richter truly enables his readers to understand, feel, and sense what it was like to live in earlier times.

Bibliography

Barnes, Robert J. *Conrad Richter.* Austin, Tex.: Steck-Vaughn, 1968.

Carpenter, Frederic I. "Conrad Richter's Pioneers: Reality and Myth." *College English* 12 (1950): 77-84.

Edwards, Clifford D. *Conrad Richter's Ohio Trilogy.* The Hague, The Netherlands: Mouton, 1970.

Flanagan, John T. "Conrad Richter: Romancer of the Southwest." *Southwest Review* 43 (1958): 189-196.

Gaston, Edwin W., Jr. *Conrad Richter.* Rev. ed. Boston: G. K. Hall, 1989.

Kohler, Dayton. "Conrad Richter's Early Americana." *College English* 7 (1947): 221-228.

Clifford Edwards

THEODORE ROETHKE

Born: Saginaw, Michigan
May 25, 1908
Died: Bainbridge Island, Washington
August 1, 1963

Principal Literary Achievement
Roethke became one of the leading personal, confessional, and nature poets of the twentieth century, reaffirming the principles of the Romantic movement for the modern period.

Biography

The circumstances of Theodore Roethke's birth and childhood were very important for his development as a poet. Roethke was born in 1908 in Saginaw, Michigan, to a family of gardeners and florists. His father and uncle built and maintained a huge greenhouse complex which was considered one of the best in the country and which was used primarily to grow roses, orchids, and other ornamental plants. Roethke grew up in the midst of this fecundity, and in later years he returned to it in memory and spirit as the source of inspiration and power in his poetry.

Although Roethke's father loved his son and that love was returned, there was conflict between them. Otto Roethke was an outdoorsman and wanted his son to be a man's man and a lawyer; young Ted was clumsy at sports and outdoor activities and preferred books and the life of the mind and imagination. The Roethke brothers sold the greenhouse in 1922, and the next year, when Theodore was only fourteen, his father died, dealing his son a wound and a sense of unfulfillment that the poet was able to relieve only near the end of his life. Subconsciously, Roethke felt that his father had betrayed and abandoned him by dying; consciously, he believed that he had a debt to his father which he had to repay.

After Roethke was graduated from high school in Saginaw, he attended the University of Michigan, receiving a bachelor of arts degree in 1929. He then attended graduate school at Harvard University but did not take a degree, returning to the University of Michigan for a master of arts diploma in 1936. Although Roethke had always been interested in literature (he subscribed to *The Dial* when he was in the seventh grade), at Harvard he began to write poetry seriously and was encouraged to publish. From that time on, it was clear to him that it was his destiny to be a poet, and he devoted as much of his time as possible to studying the poets of the past,

writing notes and lines, and trying to improve his craft. He published in journals and magazines throughout the 1930's and produced his first volume of poems, *Open House*, in 1940.

Meanwhile, Roethke earned a living through a series of teaching jobs, which was the way he was to sustain himself for the rest of his life. His first appointment was at what was then Michigan State College in 1935, and there began another feature of Roethke's life which was both disturbing and, finally, transforming. Roethke lost his job at Michigan State after only one semester because of a mental breakdown which required hospitalization. The nature and cause of Roethke's illness were never determined; he was diagnosed with familiar catch-all designations—paranoid schizophrenic and manic depressive—and several times again he became unable to deal with everyday reality and had to be institutionalized. Whether his mental problems were based on something in his upbringing (perhaps his strained relationship with his father) or were congenital is problematical. Whatever the reason, Roethke was quite insecure, demanding the constant approval of those around him and finding it difficult even to maintain a public personality. This affliction caused great pain and humiliation for Roethke and much sorrow and discomfort for his friends. He was refused service in World War II because of his condition, and when courting his future wife, he did not tell her of his mental problems. Later in life Roethke began to see his illness as a gateway to new imaginative and spiritual realms, and he allied himself proudly with other "mad" poets such as Christopher Smart and William Blake.

In spite of his inner turmoil, Roethke's life as a poet and academician continued to grow. In 1936 he obtained a position at Pennsylvania State University, where he also coached the tennis team, and remained there until 1943, when he moved to Bennington College. There he had the good fortune to meet a brilliant group of faculty members, including literary critic and semanticist Kenneth Burke, who admired Roethke's poetry and urged him to continue to develop his own style and outlook. The result of this stimulation from Burke and others, along with Roethke's own hard work, was the breakthrough volume *The Lost Son and Other Poems* (1948), in which Roethke produced the emotionally strongest poems he had yet written in a manner which was his alone. He was now a significant poet with a message and voice of his own.

After his appointment at Bennington ended in 1946, he returned to Pennsylvania State for one semester in 1947 and then moved to the University of Washington the same year. He remained in Seattle, except for occasional trips abroad (such as when he won two Guggenheim fellowships and a Ford Foundation fellowship), for the rest of his life. Poems and collections continued to come, and with them increasing critical recognition. *Praise to the End!* appeared in 1951; *The Waking: Poems 1933-1953*, for which he won the Pulitzer Prize, in 1953, and *Words for the Wind*, a collection of previous work and new material for which he won both the Bollingen Prize and the National Book Award, in 1958. Roethke also wrote two books for children, *I Am! Says the Lamb* (1961) and *Party at the Zoo* (1963). While on a visit to New York in 1952, he happened to meet one of his former students at Bennington, Beatrice O'Connell, and the two were married early in 1953. She was both an inspiration and a helpmate to him for the rest of his life.

In 1962, Roethke was awarded the title Poet in Residence at the University of Washington, but his physical health had begun to decline. On August 1, 1963, while he was swimming, he was stricken with a massive heart attack and died. The volume of poems he had been preparing, *The Far Field*, was published posthumously in 1964; it, too, won the National Book Award. Some critics have said that many of the poems in that book suggest that their author knew that his days were short. *The Collected Poems of Theodore Roethke*, containing most of his published work, appeared in 1966. Roethke's reputation has continued to grow since his death, and he is recognized as one of the major American poets of the twentieth century, influencing not only a younger group of poets who were his students, such as James Wright and David Wagoner, but also previously established writers such as Robert Lowell and Sylvia Plath.

Analysis

Since Theodore Roethke used the world of nature as his primary source of inspiration and imagery, one can easily use an organic metaphor to describe the nature and growth of his poetry. Roethke believed, like the Romantics, that ultimate meaning grew from the encounter of the sensitive individual with nature in an attempt to determine personally the relationship between man and all existence. In his first volume, *Open House* (1941), the seeds of Roethke's poetic thought have taken hold and are beginning to poke above the soil. They burst into full flower in the next volume, *The Lost Son and Other Poems*, and in the succeeding volumes, *Praise to the End!*, *The Waking*, and *Words for the Wind*, the reader discovers not only blossoms and fruit but also the root system and nutrients (the subconscious mind) from which the poems spring. Finally, in the last volume, *The Far Field*, the poet's mind and his creation are seen not only close up but also in panorama as they assume their place in the entire biosphere—that is, the world wider than the life of one individual.

Open House, in spite of its expansive title, contains poems which are rather guarded in their expression. This was Roethke's first collection, and rather than hosting a party he is really knocking at the door, asking to be admitted to the company of poets. Roethke shows that he can manage traditional forms such as the sonnet and the Spenserian stanza, so that the emphasis is more on pleasing the assumed academic audience rather than saying what he himself wants to say in a manner that is unmistakably his. Nevertheless, a great artist finds his themes early, and the reader familiar with Roethke's career can easily recognize the preoccupations of his later work appearing like tendrils in a garden in early spring. In the first and title poem, Roethke states that he will tell all his secrets and withhold nothing from the reader, but the poem remains on a general level and the secrets are not named. The last two lines, however, produce a shudder: "Rage warps my clearest cry/ To witless agony." Roethke's mental illness had already asserted itself, and here the poet recognizes that this "secret" will be both a barrier to communication and a source of emotion for the rest of his life.

In "The Premonition," Roethke remembers trying to keep up with the wide strides of his father as they walked through the fields and the older man's dipping his hand into a stream so that his reflection was shattered. The poem suggests simultaneously the importance of nature in Roethke's life and poetry, Roethke's difficult relationship with his father, and Otto Roethke's death, which was to trouble the poet until late in his career. In "The Signals," Roethke maintains, "Sometimes the blood is privileged to guess/ The things the eye or hand cannot possess," indicating that he relies on intuition and nonrational knowledge more than most poets. In "For an Amorous Lady," he compares his lover to the snake, which enjoys giving as well as receiving caresses, in a poem which combines sensuality and humor in the manner of his best later love poems.

Roethke abandoned his attempt to please an audience of older, accepted poets in the poems collected in his next book, *The Lost Son and Other Poems*. This volume contains the "greenhouse poems" which, all of his critics agree, mark the beginning of his career as an independent craftsman and which some think are his best work. In this series, Roethke returns in his imagination to the world of his childhood, finding there not only pleasant memories, such as in "Big Wind," which describes how everyone worked to save the roses in the greenhouse during a bitterly cold and stormy night, but also scenes of horror and fright. "Root Cellar" tells of how the discarded bulbs, manure, and other greenhouse trash continued to put out roots and stems, stinking up the area but refusing to die: "Nothing would give up life:/ Even the dirt kept breathing a small breath." In "Weed Puller," young Roethke is himself plunged into this dirty womb; as a child, he was small enough to get under the benches where the roses and other flowers grew to cut and pull away the roots and undergrowth that were not wanted. "Tugging all day at perverse life," young Roethke considered this work an "indignity," and describes it in such terms that it is almost revolting: "Me down in that fetor of weeds,/ Crawling on all fours,/ Alive, in a slippery grave." The word "fetor" suggests "fetus," combining both birth and death images. Although the emphasis in this poem is on the horror and fright of the young boy thrust into the grimy scene, later Roethke would use the union of life and death as a central theme of his poetry. Life both feeds upon death and arises from death; it is impossible to separate the two, which are part of the same process.

In this volume, Roethke sees nature not only as overwhelmingly powerful but also as a comforting friend. Here he comes closest to his Romantic predecessors, such as William Wordsworth and Samuel Coleridge, but there is a difference. While Wordsworth drew comfort from the quiet splendor of the English lake country and Coleridge admired the grandeur of the vale of Chamouni, in "The Minimal," Roethke examines the barely visible insects on a leaf, little beetles and lice, and finally comments on bacteria, which can only be seen with a microscope; each has its role to play in the cycle of life. Roethke is the poet of small nature: toads, slugs, sparrows, and minnows are the heroes of his poems and the inspirers of his life with their reminder that the nameless and the small are no less important than the large and famous, that—as another of Roethke's Romantic poetic models, William Blake, said—"Everything that lives is Holy."

Another theme with which Roethke grapples appears in the title poem of the volume, "The Lost Son." In this long, multipart, and multistyle poem, Roethke attempts to come to terms with his grief and guilt over the loss of his father and with his own mental illness. He dips into his unconscious to find a way out of his depression and confusion and regresses to childhood, using the meter and subject of nursery rhymes and childish taunts to gain some understanding of the roots of his problem. At the end of the poem, he has not attained understanding but at least finds solace.

The psychological investigation continues through the major poems in Roethke's next collection, *Praise to the End!*, the title of which is a quotation from Wordsworth. This volume contains more poems in the manner of "The Lost Son," poems in which Roethke dives into the subconscious, a psychic adventure expressed in the form of extremely short lines reminiscent of the thoughts and sensations of a child. These poems include the title poem, the remarkable "Where Knock Is Open Wide," "I Need, I Need," "Sensibility! O La!," and "Unfold! Unfold!" In some of these poems Roethke may be trying to hit a high note that no one else can hear, for many critics think that they plumb the subconscious so deeply that their meaning becomes lost in obscurity or in purely personal reference. To others, these poems present Roethke as most himself and provide a deep well from which interpretations and insights may be continually drawn.

In *The Waking*, Roethke continues the long confessional and personal poems but also begins to write poems of a more traditional form and content in which he acknowledges his kinship with and debt to other poets, chief among them William Butler Yeats (mentioned in "Four for Sir John Davies") and T. S. Eliot. From Yeats, Roethke borrowed the metaphor of the dance as a symbol for the totality and interaction of all life, as well as certain stylistic approaches to poetry: "I take this cadence from a man named Yeats;/ I take it, and I give it back again." (Roethke later said that it was not really the meter but the manner of writing poetry that he took from Yeats.) From Eliot, he took the bitter, almost conversational line reflecting the staleness and disappointment of modern life (as seen in "Old Lady's Winter Words"). The two earlier poets had also reacted to modern life by finding comfort in religion, and in this area Roethke shied away from Eliot's Anglo-Catholicism and favored the mysticism of Yeats.

In his earlier collections, Roethke had firmly established his own style and approach; now he could move back to the world of traditional poetry and not feel as if he were intruding. This new nimbleness produced poems which both pleased more traditional readers with their mastery of familiar and difficult poetic forms and satisfied Roethke's own audience with their presentation of his own particular themes, such as the villanelle which provides the title of the book, "The Waking:" "I wake to sleep, and take my waking slow./ I learn by going where I have to go." This volume contains Roethke's most famous and frequently anthologized poem, "Elegy for Jane," a tribute to one of his students who died young.

Words for the Wind collected much of the previous work and also added some beautiful love poems which Roethke wrote after his marriage, such as "I Knew A Woman." The collection also contains another tribute to Yeats, "The Dying Man," and another multipart poem in which Roethke considers death by separating himself from the event by adopting the persona of his mother, "Meditations of An Old Woman." In his last book, the posthumous *The Far Field*, Roethke presents both his most powerful expression of the mystic union with all life that sometimes resulted from his struggles with insanity, "In a Dark Time," and a more conventional poem (in the manner of "Meditations of An Old Woman"), "North American Sequence," in which he describes his whole life as a journey across the northern United States from east to west, ending with a vision of a rose growing from the rocks on the Pacific Coast, a flower which reminds him of his own childhood and life with his father, whose life and death he can now accept as his own death approaches.

CUTTINGS (LATER)

First published: 1948
Type of work: Poem

The poet identifies with vegetable life reasserting itself in the face of death.

This poem, one of the most frequently reprinted of the "greenhouse" series, shows Roethke's close attention to the plant world and his identification with it; his sense of unity with the rest of life transcends the ordinary and becomes a spiritual experience, while at the same time remaining grounded in everyday reality. The highly emotional poem is also written using a style and themes that could only be Roethke's.

As in "Root Cellar," the discarded cuttings from the greenhouse refuse to die, putting forth new shoots and roots although they are only the mutilated parts of other plants. When Roethke compares the "struggling" plants to tortured saints trying to return to their religious battles, the spiritual connection between the human and vegetable world is established, and it is made more definite in the second verse paragraph, in which the poet himself identifies with the chopped up, but still living, plants. He implies that his growth also comes as a result of a long struggle, for it has come "at last." The last two lines introduce a familiar motif, fish, with which Roethke was fascinated for a number of reasons (one of which was their ability to thrive in a mysterious other world which humans can only visit) and a familiar theme, birth ("sheath-wet") combined with fear ("I quail"). Birth, the inevitable result of the struggle for life, must happen, but it is terrifying for the new creature to be thrust into the living world.

THE LOST SON

First published: 1948
Type of work: Poem

A son, grieving for his father, returns to the world of his childhood in an attempt to comprehend and assuage his loss.

"The Lost Son" has five parts: "The Flight," "The Pit," "The Gibber," "The Return," and " 'It was Beginning Winter,' " each of which describes a stage in the grief of the poetic persona (in this case, surely Roethke himself). The poet works through the various stages of his feelings of sorrow and desolation to reach a conclusion which is not really a relief of his feelings but a hope for future solace.

Part 1, "The Flight," begins with a reference to a cemetery ("Woodlawn"), and it is from this place and the fact of death that the flight occurs. From other references later in the poem, one can deduce that the death which has so shocked the poet is that of his father. Although the poet hopes to find some comfort in the little creatures of nature and specifically asks them to help him, he receives no such comfort: "Nothing nibbled my line,/ Not even the minnows came." He feels alone and isolated and specifically asks for help, praying not to God but to the creatures of nature to tell him something and give him some sign. They only answer him in riddles ("The moon said, back of an eel") and in negatives: "You will find no comfort here,/ In the kingdom of bang and blab." As if in response to this comment, the section ends with a riddle posed by the poet himself which describes a strange creature, part land animal and part amphibian. Critics have suggested that the creature is an unborn child, and this answer compels the poet to delve deeper into his unconscious mind back even further than childhood, to find the relief for his fear and depression.

Accordingly, the next section, "The Pit," which is the shortest, describes a literal hole in the ground filled with roots, moss, and little animals such as moles, but this section also contains a warning that the unconscious may be a dangerous place, a trap wherein waits the death that must finally take us all: "Beware Mother Mildew." Thus, in trying to understand the death of his father, the poet finds an even more terrifying truth; the death which has touched another will also come for him.

"The Gibber" is an aptly named segment of apparently disconnected lines and elements through which the poet appears to be wandering without plan merely in the hope of finding some help. His old friends in nature are not only not helpful but actively hostile: "The cows and briars/ Said to me: Die." The poet also examines his own life in society and finds it empty of spiritual and emotional value: "I run, I run to the whistle of money."

The poet begins to find his way back to order and stability in "The Return," which is a memory of his childhood and his life with his father. He sees and describes the life of the greenhouse, describing in particular the morning coming, the steam knocking its way through the radiator pipes, and frost slowly melting from the panes of glass, suggesting the return of order, meaning, clarity, and peace: "Ordnung! ordnung!/ Papa is coming!"

The last section, "'It Was Beginning Winter,'" reveals that although a kind of peace has been reached, there is still no understanding; after such emotional turmoil, however, mere rest is a great comfort. The poet first describes a quiet winter scene, then tries to evaluate it without success. The lines "Was it light within light?/ Stillness becoming alive,/ Yet still?" suggest that the speaker is searching for a unity which would resolve opposites by containing and transcending them; significantly, this analysis is not an answer but another question. The poem ends with a kind of emotional blessing, its origin unclear:

> A lively understandable spirit
> Once entertained you.
> It will come again.
> Be still.
> Wait.

This section, with each line becoming shorter and simpler than the previous one until the last, which is only one syllable, reminds the poet (and the reader) that life is a cycle and that—even if there are no final answers to one's problems—happiness and joy will come again. One needs the intelligence and the courage not to act, but to wait.

IN A DARK TIME

Type of work: Poem
First published: 1960

The poet confronts his own fear and triumphs over it in a mystic vision.

Several of the elements of Roethke's mind, personality, and poetic skill combine to assert themselves in "In a Dark Time," one of his most personal and most powerful works. The poem begins with a violent description of a psychic breakdown, a comment on Roethke's own mental illness, and ends by invoking the vocabulary of religious mysticism. Underlying the whole poem is the startling and questionable assumption that such a collapse may be necessary in order for a person to reach truth and achieve integration of the personality and unity with the rest of nature. Whether this theory is true for everyone, Roethke certainly thought it true for himself; the end of the poem is stated in the first line, for in Roethke's view, it is only "in a [psychically] dark time" that "the [inner] eye begins to see."

The natural imagery in the poem does not refer to the neat, ordered, and humanly understandable world of the greenhouse, where growth takes place in regular, ordered patterns. Roethke knew that the greenhouse was an artificial place sustained by rational activity; the world outside was a far different place, teeming with wild and threatening life and unexplained and unexplainable creatures and events. In this poem there are no beautiful roses, but instead "beasts of the hill," "serpents of the den," and "a ragged moon." The natural world is not a comforting place, but instead is an index of madness, as outer reality reflects the inner turmoil of the poet. The last natural image in the poem, the fly which buzzes at the window sill, seeing the world it desires but unable to reach it, frequently appears in his writing as a symbol of insanity.

Roethke's presentation of this condition is clinically accurate; it is common, for example, for the psychotic person to think that everything is obviously related to everything else ("a steady storm of correspondences") but also to think that knowledge of these relationships is useless or uncommunicable: "The edge is what I have." At the same time that thoughts and ideas may occur with unusual clarity, sense impressions may mirror the lack of a frame of reference for these ideas or may defy common sense: "I meet my shadow in the deepening shade," "all natural shapes blazing unnatural light." Another such discordant image, "in broad day the midnight come again," may be a description of a sudden dislocation of the senses, but it may also describe how the sufferer is plunged without warning into meaningless confusion. The poetic images shift back and forth from the physical to the mental, both indicating the welter within the mind of the poet and perplexing the reader and thus forcing him or her to join and endure the poet's wild ride.

In the last stanza, there is a resolution of these contradictions but not a peaceful resolution. After touching bottom, plumbing the depths of disaster, the poet is finally free of his fear, presumably because he has experienced what he was afraid of and survived, and therefore need fear no longer, but that is only a presumption. Roethke does not offer a logical explanation for the change, nor did he feel that one was necessary, for he thought that human life was based on much more than cogitation; as he had written in "The Waking," "We think by feeling. What is there to know?" Whatever the reason, the poet finds himself united with God, but still in the midst of a maelstrom: "free in the tearing wind."

The most pregnant lines in the poem are "What's madness but nobility of soul/ at odds with circumstance?," Roethke's answer to those who would dismiss his more difficult poetry as mere babble. The "insane" person may very well be the one who can see life more clearly than others precisely because he or she has not abandoned his or her moral or personal vision for a utilitarian view commanded by "the whistle of money." That is a large and perhaps unfair claim, but at the end of the poem, Roethke is clearly a twentieth century Romantic, for unlike his fellow "mad" poet and mentor, William Blake, Roethke did not insist that the vision of mystic union with God should be true for all people; he merely described it happening to himself, recognizing the twentieth century belief that there are many paths to truth. In so doing, he also reaffirmed the Romantic principle that each person must find his own role in life and that salvation is finally an individual matter.

Summary

Theodore Roethke provides a link with the poetic tradition of the past while remaining very much a man of the twentieth century and a poet with his own unique vision. He demonstrates that the Romantic philosophy of imaginative, transcendent, and fulfilling unity with nature is not a relic of the dead past but an approach to life that is still valid today. His invocation of more recent poetic tradition shows that he was aware of the problems of his own time, and his use of poetry to grapple with his own emotional and psychic distress reaffirms the role of poetry as a regenerative and healing agent.

Bibliography

Blessing, Richard Allen. *Theodore Roethke's Dynamic Vision*. Bloomington: University of Indiana Press, 1974.

Heyen, William, ed. *Profile of Theodore Roethke*. Columbus, Ohio: Charles E. Merrill, 1971.

Kalaidjian, Walter B. *Understanding Theodore Roethke*. Columbia: University of South Carolina Press, 1987.

La Belle, Jenijoy. *The Echoing Wood of Theodore Roethke*. Princeton, N.J.: Princeton University Press, 1976.

Malkoff, Karl. *Theodore Roethke: An Introduction to the Poetry*. New York: Columbia University Press, 1966.

Parini, Jay. *Theodore Roethke: An American Romantic*. Amherst: University of Massachusetts Press, 1979.

Seager, Allan. *The Glass House: The Life of Theodore Roethke*. New York: McGraw-Hill, 1968.

Stein, Arnold, ed. *Theodore Roethke: Essays on the Poetry*. Seattle: University of Washington Press, 1965.

Stiffler, Randall. *Theodore Roethke: The Poet and His Critics*. Chicago: American Library Association, 1986.

Sullivan, Rosemary. *Theodore Roethke: The Garden Master*. Seattle: University of Washington Press, 1975.

James Baird

PHILIP ROTH

Born: Newark, New Jersey
March 19, 1933

Principal Literary Achievement

Roth is recognized, along with Saul Bellow and Bernard Malamud, as one of the foremost contemporary Jewish-American novelists.

Biography

Philip Roth was born in Newark, New Jersey, on March 19, 1933, and grew up in a section of Newark that was then predominantly middle-class Jewish. Roth graduated from Weequahic High School in 1951 and attended Newark College at Rutgers University for a year before transferring to Bucknell University in Pennsylvania. Though the family could scarcely afford the expensive private college, Roth's father was determined to make the sacrifices necessary to let his son get the education he wanted.

At Bucknell, Roth wrote for the literary magazine, in which he published his earliest stories. He made Phi Beta Kappa and graduated with an A.B., magna cum laude, in 1954, after which he went to the University of Chicago as a graduate student and instructor in English literature. He received his M.A. in 1955 and then served in the United States Army in 1955 and 1956. By this time, his stories began appearing in literary magazines such as *The Chicago Review* and *Epoch*; in 1955, one of them was selected for Martha Foley's anthology, *Best American Short Stories*. While in the Army he continued writing, and in 1959 his first collection, *Goodbye, Columbus and Five Stories*, was published. It won the National Book Award for fiction in 1960. Roth was only twenty-six.

Much of his early life is presented in *The Facts: A Novelist's Autobiography* (1988), in which he describes in detail what it was like growing up in Newark in the 1930's and 1940's among lower-middle-class Jews. Family life was close and intense; whatever internal friction or strife there might be, everyone recognized that "family indivisibility" was "the first commandment." Although Roth modeled the life of Alexander Portnoy in *Portnoy's Complaint* (1969) somewhat upon his own experiences, the reader must be careful not to make exact identifications between the real Philip Roth and his fictional counterpart—a major concern especially in his later fiction. Roth idolized his mother, who from all accounts was vastly different from Sophie Portnoy, just as his hard-working, devoted father differed from harried, constipated Jack Portnoy, Alex's father. Although both were employed by large insurance compa-

nies and were discriminated against for being Jewish, their personalities are scarcely identical. Unlike Alex Portnoy, but like Nathan Zuckerman in "Salad Days" (one of the "useful fictions" in *My Life as a Man*, published in 1974), Roth has an older brother, Sandy, who studied art at the Pratt Institute in New York after serving in the Navy. It was through his brother that Roth began reading works such as Sherwood Anderson's *Winesburg, Ohio* (1919) and James Joyce's *A Portrait of the Artist as a Young Man* (1916) while still in high school.

Like other boys of his social class and religion, Roth attended Hebrew School after public school and received at least a rudimentary training in Judaism. That aspect of his life may be glimpsed in stories such as "The Conversion of the Jews" and "'I Always Wanted You to Admire My Fasting': Or, Looking at Kafka." The energy, vitality, and iconoclasm of his schoolmates contrasted vigorously with the biblical stories of Jews living in tents or building the pyramids, and in his later life Roth admitted to missing that kind of person when he moved for awhile to London (he has since returned to the United States). Young Roth was also an avid baseball fan and loved to play the sport. His powerful interest in baseball appears in several of his novels, but in *The Great American Novel* (1973) it takes over the scene and situation completely.

College confirmed his interest in literature. His stories written while still an undergraduate were not at all about Jews or Newark, and they were not humorous. He admits to the influence of Thomas Wolfe, J. D. Salinger, and Truman Capote. With several of his fraternity brothers, he helped to found *Et Cetera*, the campus literary magazine, which he edited in 1952-1953.

At the University of Chicago, Roth was a popular graduate student; his gift for mimicry made him the hit of many graduate-student parties. In Chicago he met and became friends with Theodore Solotaroff, later an editor for *Commentary* and subsequently of *The New American Review*, and an important literary critic. At this time, Roth was seriously interested in the work of Henry James, whose influence on his first full-length novel, *Letting Go* (1962), is profound. Returning to Chicago after his Army service to work on a Ph.D. in English, Roth began dating Margaret Martinson, a divorcée with two children. They were married in 1959 after a tumultuous relationship. Far from a happy marriage, theirs was fraught with quarrels and antagonism, which Roth fictionalized in *My Life as a Man* (the trick that Margaret's counterpart uses to get her lover to marry her is factual).

Encouraged by the success of *Goodbye, Columbus*, Roth had by then abandoned his doctoral studies and was writing *Letting Go*, set largely in Chicago. From 1960 to 1962, he was visiting writer at the University of Iowa. In 1962, Roth won a legal separation from Margaret and went to Princeton University as writer-in-residence. Afterward, he lived in New York City and continued writing full time. Margaret refused to grant him a divorce, and the stringent laws of New York State then made it impossible for him to obtain one any other way.

Roth lived in a small apartment, where he studiously wrote his next novels and had a long romance with someone he calls "May Aldridge" in *The Facts*; he chose not to marry her, however, after Margaret was killed in an automobile accident in 1968. From 1967 to 1980, he was a popular part-time lecturer at the University of Pennsylvania, where he taught the works of Franz Kafka, Fyodor Dosteoevski, and other great novelists. He became interested in contemporary Eastern European writers and edited a series for Penguin Books called "Writers from the Other Europe," in which books by such authors as Milan Kundera appeared in English translations. When he began sharing his life with the British actress Claire Bloom, Roth divided his time between London, where he keeps a flat and a studio for working, and his home in rural Connecticut. He married Bloom on April 29, 1990, and now lives mostly in the United States, where he has been a member of the American Academy since 1970.

Analysis

Often called a psychological realist by literary critics, Roth uses a variety of techniques in his fiction that make it difficult to classify his work under only one category. His early stories and novels, including *Goodbye, Columbus, Letting Go*, and *When She Was Good* (1967), were heavily influenced by the great nineteenth century psychological realists such as Henry James and Gustave Flaubert and by later ones such as Theodore Dreiser and Sherwood Anderson. *Portnoy's Complaint*, however, while drawing for its themes and structure upon therapeutic psychoanalysis, represents a breakthrough to new forms of fiction. Since then, Roth has written satire, such as *Our Gang (Starring Tricky and His Friends)*, 1971, fantasy (*The Great American Novel*), *Bildungsroman* (the *Zuckerman Bound* trilogy, 1985), and other types of fiction that demonstrate his versatility and originality as a writer.

Roth has also been called a social critic, and he has definitely earned the title. Taking on the conservative Jewish establishment in both his fiction and nonfiction, he exposes the foibles, coarseness, hypocrisies, and materialism of middle-class Jewish families, as in his portrayal of the Patimkin clan in *Goodbye, Columbus*. At the same time, he shows the intensity, closeness, and warmth that are also part of their lives. Attacked for his story "Epstein," in which a decent, hard-working Jewish businessman gets caught in the trammels of an adulterous relationship, Roth has defended himself against rabbis and others who feel he has defamed the Jewish people. He presents his views in essays such as "Writing About Jews" (1963) and "Imagining Jews" (1974), collected in *Reading Myself and Others* (1975), where he argues on the behalf of the writer's freedom and the autonomy of the imagination against those who insist on greater discretion and diplomacy. Where formerly he brilliantly portrayed middle-class Jewish life as it was in the neighborhoods where he grew up, Roth subsequently moved on to other aspects of contemporary Jewish life, as in his vivid descriptions of kibbutz life and the controversy over West Bank settlements in Israel in *The Counterlife* (1986) and the problems of anti-Semitism he encountered while living in England in *Deception* (1990).

Above all, Roth is an amusing and witty writer, with a good ear for the cadences and inflections of actual speech and a stand-up comedian's sense of timing. His humor has been attributed to influences such as comedians Lenny Bruce and Henny Youngman, but Roth also acknowledges the influence of the "sit-down" comedy of Franz Kafka, about whom he writes in " 'I Always Wanted You to Admire My Fasting': Or, Looking at Kafka" (1973, collected in *Reading Myself and Others*). He models his novella *The Breast* (1972; revised, 1980), partly on one of Kafka's short stories, "Metamorphosis." The humor and tall tales that grew out of the great American Southwest inform *The Great American Novel*, which also indulges in send-ups of famed American writers Ernest Hemingway, Nathaniel Hawthorne, Herman Melville, and others.

In *Portnoy's Complaint*, Roth has said, he tried to bring obscenity to the level of a subject. He may or may not have succeeded, but it is true that in that novel, as in his later works, he has taken full advantage of the current freedom to explore sexual involvements in an open and direct way. Yet, for all his apparent licentiousness, as in his stunning take-off on Irving Howe as the pornography king, Milton Appel, in *The Anatomy Lesson* (1983), Roth remains what he always was, a serious writer with a strong moral strain that remains under even the wildest humor or most grotesque fantasy. For all of his extravagant sexual exploits, Portnoy is a pathetic creature, a man desperately trying to become whole with the help of a psychiatrist. For all of his craziness in getting involved with Maureen Ketterer, Peter Tarnopol is someone who goes through countless agonies trying to determine the noblest courses of action he should take. The jokes are there in Roth's novels, but it would be a mistake to read them for their humor alone. Like the best of the humorists who have preceded him, Roth writes with a more serious agenda underlying the comedic elements in his fiction.

GOODBYE, COLUMBUS

First published: 1959
Type of work: Novella

A young Newark man falls in love with a Radcliffe student from a nouveau riche Jewish family in suburban New Jersey and discovers how spoiled she is.

In *Goodbye, Columbus*, Neil Klugman meets and falls in love with Brenda Patimkin, the spoiled, attractive daughter of a middle-class Jewish family. The family has recently moved from Newark to the suburbs in Short Hills, New Jersey, where they have a large, comfortable home, typical of the nouveau riche class to which they belong. For Neil, however, Brenda and Short Hills represent an enticing version of a pastoral ideal. When he met her for the first time at a country club swimming pool, she was for him "like a sailor's dream of a Polynesian maiden, albeit one with prescription sun glasses and the last name of Patimkin." She has an older brother, Ron, a basketball star just graduating from Ohio State University, whose favorite record, "Goodbye, Columbus," gives the story its title. She also has a kid sister, Julie, a younger version of Brenda, equally as smart and equally as spoiled. By contrast, Neil's more humble family consists of his parents, permanently absent in Arizona because of their asthma, and his Aunt Gladys, with whom he lives and who cooks his meals as well as her husband's, her daughter's, and her own—all different and all served at different times. Aunt Gladys is modeled on the stereotyped Jewish mama and has a funny accent, but she also demonstrates the most common sense and genuine humanity of any of the characters in the novella.

As their affair progresses, Neil and Brenda spend more and more time together at her family's home in Short Hills, where at the end of the summer Neil is invited to spend a week of his vacation; they make love clandestinely in her room every night. The family is suddenly plunged into a frenzy of activity when Ron announces his engagement to Harriet, his Ohio State sweetheart, and they decide to get married over Labor Day weekend. In all the turmoil that ensues, Brenda gets Neil an extension on his visit as well as an invitation to Ron's wedding.

Neil is not sure whether he feels more love or lust for Brenda, and he debates with himself whether to ask her to marry him. Fearing rejection, he proposes instead that she get a diaphragm. At first, she demurs, but Neil argues that their lovemaking will be not only safer but also more enjoyable, at least for him. Still she demurs, and it becomes a contest of wills, like many of the other games played in the story. Finally, under Neil's insistence, Brenda capitulates, and they go to New York together for her to be fitted with the device. While she is in the doctor's office, Neil enters St. Patrick's cathedral and questions himself and his feelings. He recognizes his carnality, his acquisitiveness, and his foolishness in coveting all that Brenda is and represents: "Gold dinnerware, sporting-goods trees, nectarines, garbage disposal, bumpless noses"—and the list goes on.

Ron's wedding is a typical Jewish celebration, with too much food and champagne. The occasion provides Roth with further opportunities for satire, as Neil meets the rest of the family and Ron's college friends. He gets considerable free advice from Leo Patimkin, one of Brenda's uncles, who tells Neil that he has a good thing going with Brenda and he should not louse things up. Actually, in demanding that she get the diaphragm to please him, he already has begun to louse things up.

The sad end of the story comes when Brenda asks Neil to come to Boston for the Jewish holidays in the fall. Although he is not an observant Jew and has difficulty getting time off from his work at the Newark Public Library, Neil goes to the hotel that Brenda has booked for them. When he arrives, however, Brenda is deeply distressed. She has foolishly left her diaphragm at home, where her mother has found it and thereby discovered the affair. Her parents each write separate letters to her, telling her in their different ways of their shame and unhappiness. When Neil learns all this, he is shocked at Brenda's carelessness but then realizes that leaving the device where it could be found may have been the result of an unconscious desire on her part to end the affair. Since she has invited Neil to Boston ostensibly to continue their lovemaking and insists that he make every effort to get there, she obviously has some ambivalence (or perhaps Roth does) toward Neil. He finds it impossible now to go on with her, and he takes the train back to Newark, where he arrives just in time to begin work on the Jewish New Year.

Neil Klugman, whose surname translated from Yiddish means "clever man," is typical of Roth's early heroes. Sophisticated, bright, and educated, he is nevertheless a schlemiel, a loser, someone who bungles golden opportunities that come his way. He is the prototype for Gabe Wallach in *Letting Go*, another loser, whose divided self prevents him from having satisfying and permanent relationships with others. Both have the knack, as Neil puts it, of turning winning into losing, so that "Klugman" comes to have an ironic implication. Nevertheless, Roth is hardly an advocate for the values represented by the Patimkin family, who are the principal and most obvious target for his ridicule.

THE DEFENDER OF THE FAITH

First published: 1959
Type of work: Short story

Sergeant Nathan Marx, a World War II combat veteran, struggles with his conscience over the favors demanded from him by a new Jewish recruit.

After the Allies are victorious in the battle against the Axis in Europe, Sergeant Nathan Marx, in "Defender of the Faith," is rotated back to the States, to Camp Crowder, Missouri. A veteran and a war hero with medals to prove it, Sergeant Marx is modest enough—and totally unprepared for confrontations with Private Sheldon Grossbart from the Bronx, whom he is assigned to train along with other recruits for the continuing war against Japan. Quickly recognizing in Marx a "landsman"—that is, a fellow Jew from New York—Grossbart begins to play on the sergeant's hidden sympathies. Although he is far from an observant Jew himself, Marx cannot bring himself to reject totally the pleas for special favors that Grossbart repeatedly brings to him, such as being excused from a "G.I. Party" (that is, a barracks cleaning) on Friday nights (the start of the Jewish sabbath). Marx is uncomfortable about this, but Grossbart is persuasive, not only on his own behalf, but also on behalf of Fishbein and Halpern, two other Jewish men in the company.

One success leads to another, as Grossbart wheedles favor after favor from Marx. He apparently goes too far when he complains about the non-kosher food and writes a letter to his congressman over his father's signature. When the commanding officer of his company finds out, he questions Grossbart in front of Marx, holding the sergeant up to him as a model. At this point, Grossbart backs off, and another letter arrives, again purportedly from Grossbart's father to his congressman, praising Sergeant Marx for helping his son over the hurdles he has to face in the Army. In a note attached to the letter, passed down through the chain of Army command to Marx, the congressman also praises the sergeant as "a credit to the U.S. Army and the Jewish people." After that, Grossbart seems to disappear from his life for awhile and Marx is relieved.

The reprieve, however, is short-lived. Grossbart turns up one day in Marx's office with two matters on his mind. The first concerns their eventual assignment; Marx surmises, rightly, that it will probably be the Pacific. Grossbart hopes it might be New York so he could be near his immigrant parents. The other matter concerns a pass for Passover dinner with relatives in St. Louis. Marx reminds him that passes are not possible during basic training, but Grossbart perseveres, using a variety of ploys and tactics, until he gets passes for himself and his two friends as well. When they return from St. Louis, they bring Marx a gift—Chinese egg rolls, not Passover fare.

Marx is disgusted, and his fury mounts; he calls Grossbart a liar, a schemer, and a crook. When he discovers soon afterward that Grossbart has manipulated another Jewish non-commissioned officer to get himself sent to Fort Monmouth, New Jersey, instead of the Pacific with the rest of the company, Marx decides to use Grossbart's tactics against him. He asks a friend in Classification and Assignment to alter the orders, sending another man to Fort Monmouth in place of Grossbart. He invents a story about Grossbart's longing to fight against the enemy because his brother was killed and he would feel like a coward staying Stateside. Marx explains that Grossbart is Jewish and that he would like to do him this favor.

A final confrontation ends the story, as Grossbart accuses Marx of anti-Semitism, of really wanting to see him dead. At first, Marx ignores him, but a bitter, fruitless argument ensues. Both of them know, however, that Grossbart will be all right, and so will Fishbein and Halpern, as long as Grossbart can continue to find ways to use them for his own advantage. Weeping, Grossbart eventually accepts his fate, as Marx accepts his, rejecting the strong impulse to turn and ask Grossbart's pardon for his vindictiveness.

The story shows Roth's ability early in his career to develop vivid and convincing characters and use themes not designed to be popular with Jewish audiences. Other stories in the collection *Goodbye, Columbus,* such as "The Conversion of the Jews" and "Eli the Fanatic," develop similar themes and characters with the kind of irony that Roth uses here. In those stories, Roth shows realistically what makes people behave in the ways they do—self-interest may be an irresistible motive, as it is in Grossbart's case. The motives are not always admirable and, as Marx demonstrates, not always simple. When conflict occurs, resolution is seldom easy, and it always comes at a cost.

PORTNOY'S COMPLAINT

First published: 1969
Type of work: Novel

A man seeks help from his psychiatrist for the anxieties and other difficulties he attributes to the conflict between his Jewish upbringing and his strong sexual urges.

Portnoy's Complaint is not only the title of this novel, it is also the illness defined in an epigraph that precedes the book: "A disorder in which strongly-felt ethical and altruistic impulses are perpetually warring with extreme sexual longings, often of a perverse nature." Alexander Portnoy, after whom the disease is named, is a young Jewish professional, the Assistant Commissioner for Human Opportunity in New York City. After a recent trip to Israel in which he discovers to his dismay that he has become impotent, he seeks the help of a psychiatrist, Dr. Otto Spielvogel. The novel, in fact, is in the form of a long monologue, or a series of psychiatric sessions, in which Portnoy describes his past life, beginning with his earliest years growing up in Newark, New Jersey, as the son of Sophie and Jack Portnoy, to his present life as an important official in the New York bureaucracy. The monologue is punctuated by much dialogue, as he recalls conversations, quarrels, and arguments with his family and a number of lovers, culminating in his disastrous sexual experience in Israel.

The dominant figure in his early life is his mother, whose behavior as a stereotyped Jewish mother is the subject of much satire and humor. Little Alex is astonished at her omnipotence and her apparent omnipresence. A good little boy, he is nevertheless punished at times for faults he cannot understand how—or if—he committed. His rebellions are futile, and his perplexity is immense. His mother's threats puzzle him as does his poor, constipated father's reluctance to stop her. As Alex enters puberty, he finds solace in masturbation, which, like everything else in this novel, becomes excessive. In a whimsical allusion to the amoral protagonist of Dostoevski's *Prestupleniye i nakazaniye* (1866; *Crime and Punishment*, 1886), Portnoy calls himself at one point the Raskolnikov of "whacking off."

Ashamed of his parents and to some extent of his Jewishness, Portnoy yearns for a more typical American family life. From an early age he tries to woo Gentile girls, disguising himself when he can as a non-Jew himself. His nose is his greatest impediment, he believes, hence, he imagines excuses and explanations for it and for his name (saying that it is from the French, *porte-noir*). A hilarious episode occurs when he joins two of his friends to visit the notorious Bubbles Girardi, known to have sex with boys, and he wins the chance to be the only one on that occasion that she will see. Like so much else in his life, however, the event turns into disaster. At first he cannot even get an erection, and later he climaxes too quickly and ejaculates directly into his own eye. Thinking he has gone blind, he fantasizes returning home with a seeing-eye dog, much to the horror of his parents—especially his mother, who becomes upset because she has just cleaned the house and her son has brought home a dog.

Other sexual escapades include the romance with his college sweetheart, Kay Campbell, nicknamed "The Pumpkin," who invites him to spend Thanksgiving in Iowa with her and her family. He is amazed at his reception and the civility he witnesses; it is so different from the outlandish melodramas that daily characterize his family. The romance cools when, half-jokingly, Alex suggests her conversion to Judaism after they are married, and Kay responds indifferently. Another Gentile lover several years later is "The Pilgrim," Sarah Abbott Maulsby, the daughter of a

New England family. Alex realizes that his desire for her is fueled as much by his determination to wreak vengeance against her family, typical of those anti-Semites who discriminate against his hard-working father, as by any other appeal she may have for him.

Portnoy apparently finds everything his hedonistic heart desires in Mary Jane Reed, "The Monkey," a sexual adept and sometime model, who is trying to overcome her hillbilly childhood. Mary Jane does everything that Portnoy wants, but unfortunately in the process falls in love with him—unfortunately because he is far from ready to accept marriage with anyone, least of all her. Another *shikse* (non-Jewish woman), she has too checkered a career, although for a brief moment while they impersonate a married couple on a weekend holiday in Connecticut, he almost believes that it might be possible. Portnoy's sexual adventures end in Israel where, after abandoning Mary Jane in Greece, he meets his match in Naomi, a six-foot Israeli woman whom he tries to seduce and even rape, only to discover that he is unable to get an erection.

Throughout the novel, Portnoy's "extreme sexual longings" conflict with his "ethical and altruistic impulses," invariably to comic effect. For example, he wants to educate The Monkey and tries hard to do so, with ludicrous results. He complains to his psychiatrist that he is the Jewish son in a Jewish joke and wants to find a way out of it, because to him it is not funny; it "hoits." His expression is funny, however, partly through its excessive diction, his inherited tendency to melodrama, and the ridiculous plight that he himself describes. He concludes his monologue with what amounts to a long primal scream, after which Dr. Spielvogel delivers his famous punch line: "So. Now vee may perhaps to begin. Yes?"

MY LIFE AS A MAN

First published: 1974
Type of work: Novel

Peter Tarnopol struggles to write a novel about his traumatic marriage, introducing fictitious character Nathan Zuckerman as his alter ego.

In *My Life as a Man*, Roth invents a fictitious character, Peter Tarnopol, whose life closely parallels his own, just as the life of Tarnopol's fictitious character, Nathan Zuckerman, closely parallels his. The result is what Roth calls a "useful fiction." Such fictions help the writer explore alternative ideas of one's fate—in this instance, alternative versions of Roth's early years and particularly of his marriage to Margaret Martinson.

The novel begins with two such "useful fictions." The first, "Salad Days," recounts Zuckerman's early childhood, not unlike Portnoy's, although here it is the father who dominates rather than the mother. Light-hearted and funny, especially in Zuckerman's seduction of Sharon Shatzky, it is different in tone from the darker humor of "Courting Disaster," the "useful fiction" that follows it, in which Tarnopol describes his strange courtship and unhappy marriage to Lydia Ketterer.

In "My True Story," Tarnopol drops his alter ego, Zuckerman, and attempts to tell what really happened. He writes while secluded in Quahsay, an artists' colony similar to Yaddo, Roth's favorite retreat. He describes meeting Maureen while an instructor at the University of Chicago. Not her beauty so much as her prior experience, especially with men who had mistreated and abused her, is her main attraction. Eventually, although their affair has been anything but tranquil, Maureen tricks Tarnopol into marrying her, and when the marriage proves to be bad, she will not let him go. She is determined, she says, to make a man of him, to force him to accept his responsibilities. Several years later, Tarnopol gets a legal separation and flees to New York City to try to develop his career as a writer.

Maureen follows and even attempts to compete with him as a writer. Meanwhile, Tarnopol meets and falls in love with Susan Seabury McCall, a charming, rich, and devoted young woman. From the storms and stresses of his marriage to Maureen, Susan provides a calm and welcome shelter. Tarnopol eventually gives her up, however, knowing that she wants children and believes she should have them; he does not want marriage and a family. She attempts suicide. Tempted to return to her, Tarnopol resists the urge. Meanwhile, he has sought help from a therapist, none other than Dr. Otto Spielvogel, and Maureen is killed in an automobile wreck.

The novel ends where it began, with nothing resolved, except that Tarnopol is now freed at last from his marriage. He has also been able to write the story of his life with Maureen—the novel with which Roth struggled for years after his own wife's death in a similar accident. After five years, he has given up therapy, partly as the result of an article Spielvogel wrote entitled "Creativity: The Narcissism of the Artist," in which Tarnopol appears very thinly disguised as an Italian-American poet. Like *Portnoy's Complaint*, *My Life as a Man* uses interesting and original fictive devices and techniques, eschewing straight lineal narrative for more discursive, nonchronological accounts that are not, however, at all confusing. On the contrary, Roth's juxtapositions are witty and meaningful, pointing up many aspects of the absurdity of human existence.

ZUCKERMAN BOUND: A TRILOGY AND AN EPILOGUE

First published: *The Ghost Writer*, 1979; *Zuckerman Unbound*, 1981; *The Anatomy Lesson*, 1983; *The Prague Orgy*, 1985
Type of work: Novels

The series of novels traces the development of Nathan Zuckerman as a young writer through the successful publication of his notorious novel, "Carnovsky," and its aftermath.

The Ghost Writer opens as young Nathan Zuckerman comes to visit the distinguished stylist E. I. Lonoff at his home in the Berkshires. Zuckerman is filled with admiration and awe for the older writer, with whom he enjoys discussing literature. He is struck, moreover, by the young woman, Amy Bellette, a former student of Lonoff, who is helping Lonoff assemble his papers for deposit in the Harvard library where she works. He is also struck by Lonoff's wife, Hope, the descendant of New England families different from Lonoff's own Russian-Jewish heritage. At several points, she expresses extreme frustration with the life her husband leads and asks him to "chuck her out" in favor of Amy Bellette, who is obviously in love with him. Lonoff has no intentions of doing any such thing; although he recognizes the young woman's attractions and devotion to him, he is loyal to his wife and rejects all of her exhortations to the contrary.

Amazed by the situation he finds, but flattered by Lonoff's praise of his work so far—four published short stories—Zuckerman is easily persuaded to spend the night on a daybed in Lonoff's study. While trying to write a letter to his father, he finds and reads *The Middle Years* by Henry James. Lonoff has excerpted an intriguing passage from it about the "madness of art" and pinned it to a bulletin board near his desk. Later, after Amy returns for the evening, Zuckerman hears an argument in the bedroom above him, in which Amy tries to persuade Lonoff to leave Hope and go off with her to a villa in Florence. Lonoff refuses, and afterward Zuckerman has a long fantasy in which he imagines that Amy Bellette is in reality Anne Frank, miraculously saved from the death camps.

The next morning, all illusions disappear after another scene between Lonoff and Hope, when Zuckerman can find no trace of a tattooed number on Amy's forearm. As he returns to the artists' colony at Quahsay, Zuckerman receives some words of advice from Lonoff, who also anticipates with interest what Zuckerman will make in his fiction of everything he has seen and heard during his visit.

In *Zuckerman Unbound*, Nathan is no longer a young, somewhat callow writer, anxious about making his way in the world, but an accomplished novelist whose fourth book, *Carnovsky*, has become notorious (just as *Portnoy's Complaint* became notorious in Roth's own life and career). By this time it is apparent that the trilogy is a *Bildungsroman*, or portrait novel, based, like *My Life as a Man*, on Roth's own experiences. It thus presents another "idea of one's fate," but without the mediation of Peter Tarnopol. The reader must be constantly careful, however, not to draw exact equivalences between Roth and his surrogates. For example, Zuckerman's father becomes very upset by his treatment of the family in *Carnovsky*, quite unlike Roth's own father, who took pride in everything his son wrote. Roth fictionalizes his experiences to see how they might otherwise have come out, to explore alternative, imaginative versions of them, and thereby gain further insights.

In *Zuckerman Unbound*, Nathan is beset by people, such as Alvin Pepler, the Jewish Marine, who recognizes him as the author of *Carnovsky* and believes that the book is autobiographical. A mysterious caller telephones and tries to extort money from him, threatening to kidnap his mother in Miami if he does not pay up. When

Zuckerman gets a message from his aunt in Florida, he is sure that his mother has been abducted, but it is his father who is in trouble. He has had a serious heart attack, which proves fatal soon after Zuckerman arrives with his brother Henry.

His father's last word is ambiguous. Nathan believes that he said "bastard," but Henry reassures him on the flight home after the funeral that he said "batter," referring to the days when they all played baseball together. When they get to the Newark airport, after exchanging some further confidences on the plane, Henry suddenly turns on Nathan, and they become estranged. Nathan is left to drive alone through the neighborhood he once knew so well but which has now changed drastically. He feels like he is no one—no man's son, no woman's husband, no longer his brother's brother. He does not come from anywhere any longer, either. He is utterly alone.

He is not quite alone, however, in *The Anatomy Lesson*. Afflicted by a strange pain in the neck and back that no doctor has been able to diagnose, let alone treat successfully, Zuckerman is attended by four women who look after his various needs, including his sexual needs. Among them are his financial adviser's wife, the most sexually adroit of them all; a young college student from nearby Finch College, who also works as his secretary; another young woman who lives in Vermont and occasionally comes to town to visit and encourage Zuckerman to come and live in the mountains with her; and finally, Jaga, the Polish émigré who works at the trichologist's clinic where Zuckerman goes to have his increasing baldness treated.

Nothing works, so Zuckerman decides to give up writing, which he has not been able to do anyway, and return to the University of Chicago, his alma mater, and become a doctor. His college friend, Bobby Freytag, now a prominent anesthesiologist, tries to talk him out of it, but disaster strikes from an unexpected direction. Zuckerman takes Bobby's father to the cemetery where his wife has recently been buried, and while there Zuckerman goes berserk. Having taken too much Percodan and drunk too much vodka for the pain in his neck, and feeling antagonized by the old man's sentimentalism, he attacks him, then falls on a tombstone and fractures his jaw. Learning what pain is really like now, in the hospital after surgery, Zuckerman spends his days recuperating and helping patients more unfortunate than he is.

The theme of fathers and sons, pervasive in the trilogy, takes a different twist in *The Prague Orgy*, which forms the epilogue. Zuckerman is persuaded by a Czech émigré and writer to rescue his father's short stories, written in Yiddish, from the writer's sex-crazy wife. In Prague, Zuckerman meets other writers and intellectuals, as well as Olga Sisovsky, who finally turns over the stories to him. Although well known as the author of *Carnovsky* to some, who admire his work, he is not allowed to leave the country with the stories, which are confiscated. Instead, he is escorted to the airport by Novak, the minister of culture, who delivers a lecture to him on the values of socialism, particularly as they pertain to cultural deviance and filial respect. The patriotism of Novak's father, however, is little more than political expediency, and the cultural deviance is simply a code word for divergence from the party line. Zuckerman realizes this and realizes, too, that it apparently was not his fate to become a "cultural eminence" or hero by performing extraordinary literary deeds such as rescuing the Sisovsky manuscripts.

THE COUNTERLIFE

First published: 1986
Type of work: Novel

In a series of contrasting episodes, Nathan and Henry Zuckerman trade places as victims of serious heart disease, ending in their deaths.

In *The Counterlife*, Roth more forthrightly and ingeniously than ever before exploits the technique of developing alternative versions of one's fate. Thus, in the first section, "Basel," Henry Zuckerman, a successful dentist, husband, and father of three children, suffers from a serious heart ailment that is properly treated by use of a beta-blocker, which renders him impotent. Finding his sex life reduced to nothing and desperate to resume an extramarital affair with his dental assistant, he decides to undergo surgery, and dies. Before the surgery, feeling the need to talk to someone, he confides in his brother, Nathan, from whom he has been long estranged. At Henry's funeral, however, Nathan is unable to deliver the eulogy, since the three thousand words he has written are hardly suitable for the occasion. Always the novelist, he knows that they are more suitable to his craft than for his brother's funeral.

In the next section, "Judea," Henry has not died but is alive and well and living in Israel. The surgery, while successful, left him deeply depressed, and he experiences a kind of ethnic conversion during a visit to the Orthodox quarter in Jerusalem. His wife asks Nathan, now married to an Englishwoman, Maria, and living in London, to find Henry and try to get him to come home to his family. More interested in what has happened to his brother than in actually returning him to New Jersey, Nathan agrees. He finds Henry in a kibbutz on the West Bank under the influence of an extreme right-winger, Mordecai Lippman. During his visit, Nathan is several times put on the spot, not only by Henry, but by others, who question his politics, his loyalty to Israel, and his Jewishness. In "Aloft," he returns to London without Henry and becomes comically implicated in an abortive hijack attempt by a crazy young man from West Orange, New Jersey.

The fourth section, "Gloucestershire," is the most complex. Now Nathan is afflicted with the heart ailment and wants to get off the beta-blocker so that he can marry Maria and have children. She is his upstairs neighbor, married to a man who fails to appreciate her. She tries to talk Nathan out of the operation, but he goes ahead with it, and he dies. At his funeral, Henry is unable to give the eulogy, which is delivered by Nathan's editor and is mostly about *Carnovsky* and the role of the novelist. Henry is outraged by everything he says. When he goes to Nathan's apartment, he finds "Draft #2," including chapters of *The Counterlife* that the reader has read as well as an additional chapter, "Christendom," that follows. Henry is further outraged by his brother's fictionalizing—his "lies." Henry has never had an affair with his dental assistant or gone to Israel. To avoid any possible embarrassment to himself or his family, he takes 250 pages of the manuscript and destroys them on his way home.

Maria also enters the apartment and finds "Christendom," which she criticizes, as Henry had done the earlier chapters. She does not destroy the manuscript, however compromising it appears (it includes passages about their love affair); instead she determines to brazen her way out of whatever problems may arise with her husband. When the reader comes to "Christendom," he or she finds that it is about Nathan and Maria's imagined married life together, their happiness (Maria is pregnant) and their problems (Maria is from an anti-Semitic family). The novel ends with a quarrel over English attitudes toward Jews, and Nathan imagines a farewell letter that Maria has written to him.

The Counterlife is a postmodernist tour de force. Despite the convolutions of its plot and the ways the novel loops back upon itself and alters events, characters, and impressions, the reader is never confused for long as to what is happening. Roth exercises to the fullest his novelistic imagination, juxtaposing counterlives upon counterlives with wit, humor, and excellent technical skills.

Summary

Philip Roth's development as a novelist shows both a deepening of his comedy and an expanding range of skills. Preoccupied by the idea of "counterlives," or variations upon self-portraits, he examines various versions of his experience with telling effect and enormous insights. His preoccupation notwithstanding, he rarely repeats himself; instead, he constantly attempts to expand the boundaries of his essentially comic art, whose depths he tirelessly and wittily explores, with bountiful rewards.

Bibliography

Jones, Judith Paterson, and Guinevera A. Nance. *Philip Roth*. New York: Frederick Ungar, 1981.

Lee, Hermione. *Philip Roth*. London: Methuen, 1982.

Milbauer, Asher Z., ed. *Reading Philip Roth*. New York: St. Martin's Press, 1988.

Pinsker, Sanford. *The Comedy That "Hoits": An Essay on the Fiction of Philip Roth*. Columbia: University of Missouri Press, 1975.

_____, ed. *Critical Essays on Philip Roth*. Boston: G. K. Hall, 1982.

Rodgers, Bernard F., Jr. *Philip Roth*. Boston: Twayne, 1978.

_____. *Philip Roth: A Bibliography*. 2d ed. Metuchen, N.J.: Scarecrow Press, 1984.

Schechner, Mark. *After the Revolution: Studies in the Contemporary Jewish American Imagination*. Bloomington: Indiana University Press, 1987.

Jay L. Halio

J. D. SALINGER

Born: New York, New York
January 1, 1919

Principal Literary Achievement
Although primarily a writer of short stories, Salinger is best known for his novel *The Catcher in the Rye*, which had an enormous influence on young readers of the 1950's and succeeding generations.

Biography

Because of Salinger's insistence on preserving his privacy, and the willingness of his family and friends to assist him in doing so, little biographical information on Salinger is available, especially regarding his later life. Moreover, Salinger's habit of deliberately misleading would-be biographers with false information further complicates the picture; nevertheless, some elements of Salinger's biography are generally accepted as true.

Jerome David Salinger was born in New York City on January 1, 1919, to a Jewish father, Sol Salinger, a successful importer of hams and cheeses, and a Christian mother, Miriam Jillich Salinger. He was the second of two children; his sister, Doris, was eight years his senior. Salinger attended public schools on the upper West Side of Manhattan and seems to have been an average student. His first sign of distinction came at age eleven when he was voted "most popular actor" at Camp Wigwam in Maine. At age thirteen, Salinger was enrolled in the prestigious Mc-Burney School in Manhattan, but he was dismissed with failing grades after a year. He was then sent to Valley Forge Military Academy in Pennsylvania, which was to become the model for Pencey Prep in *The Catcher in the Rye* (1951). At Valley Forge, Salinger was the literary editor of the school yearbook, and there he wrote his first stories.

After he was graduated from Valley Forge, Salinger attended the summer session at New York University, then accompanied his father to Vienna to learn the Polish ham business. He soon returned to the United States, however, and entered college again, this time at Ursinus College in Pennsylvania. He wrote a column called "The Skipped Diploma" for the *Ursinus Weekly*, but he dropped out in the middle of his first semester there. He then enrolled in a short story writing class at Columbia University taught by Whit Burnett, editor of *Story* magazine. Salinger's first published story, "The Young Folks," appeared in the March/April, 1940, issue of *Story*.

Salinger subsequently published stories in *Collier's* and *Esquire* magazines, and more stories in *Story*, before being drafted into the Army in 1942. He attended officer training school, achieved the rank of staff sergeant, and was sent to Devonshire, England, for counter-intelligence training. On D Day, June 6, 1944, Salinger landed on Utah Beach in Normandy with the Fourth Army Division. As a security officer, he was assigned to interrogate captured Germans and French civilians to identify Gestapo agents. While in France, Salinger met Ernest Hemingway, to whom he later wrote an admiring letter.

After the war ended, Salinger was hospitalized for psychiatric treatment in Nuremberg, Germany, but continued to write and publish stories, as he had done throughout the war. He returned to New York in 1947 and signed a contract to write stories for *The New Yorker*. In 1950, Salinger's story "For Esmé—with Love and Squalor" was designated one of the distinguished American stories of the year. Salinger spent much of this period in Greenwich Village, where he associated with other young writers and artists, and reportedly dated a wide variety of women in order to collect dialogue for his stories. He also began to exhibit a keen interest in Zen Buddhism, which would greatly influence his later work.

Another Salinger characteristic that began to manifest itself at this time was a desire for isolation. Salinger left Greenwich Village for a cottage in Tarrytown, New York (although he is said to have finished writing *The Catcher in the Rye* in a room near the Third Avenue El in New York City). When *The Catcher in the Rye* was published in 1951, Salinger went to Europe to avoid publicity and the following year traveled to Mexico. In 1953, he bought ninety acres of land on the Connecticut River in Cornish, New Hampshire. During that year, he agreed for the first and last time to be interviewed by a reporter—a sixteen-year-old high school girl writing for a local newspaper.

In 1955, Salinger married Claire Douglas, an English-born graduate of Radcliffe College. Salinger is said to have written the story "Franny" (1955) as a wedding present for Claire, and the heroine of the story is supposed to be based on Claire. The couple had two children before divorcing in 1967.

Salinger's last published work was a short story called "Hapworth 16, 1924," which appeared in *The New Yorker* in 1965. Since then, Salinger has said he will allow no further publication of his work. In 1988, an unauthorized biography of Salinger by British literary critic Ian Hamilton became the occasion of a major court battle when Salinger sued to prevent Hamilton from quoting or even paraphrasing Salinger's unpublished letters. Salinger won the case, but even some of his supporters believed that the decision raised troublesome First Amendment questions.

Salinger has refused all requests for interviews or commentary on his published work, saying, "The stuff's all there in the stories; there's no use talking about it."

Analysis

Several characteristic themes are evident throughout Salinger's work: the innocence of childhood versus the corruption of adulthood; honesty versus phoniness;

estrangement, isolation, and alienation; and the quest for enlightenment and understanding of such fundamental issues as love, suffering, and the problem of evil. Several characteristic techniques recur as well: the use of dialogue, gesture, and personal objects to reveal character and relationships; the repetition of characters from one story to another; the reliance on puzzles, paradoxes, and riddles in a way similar to that used by teachers of Zen Buddhism; and frequent allusions to religious teachers and texts, philosophers, and authors and their works.

The importance of children to Salinger becomes obvious upon reading even a few of his stories: Sybil in "A Perfect Day for Bananafish," Esmé in "For Esmé—with Love and Squalor," and Phoebe and several other children in *The Catcher in the Rye* are examples of a certain wise innocence which the older protagonists of the stories seem to have lost and struggle to recapture. It is also noteworthy that many of these children are extremely precocious; indeed, *Franny and Zooey* (1961), as well as *Seymour: An Introduction* (1963) and *Raise High the Roof Beam, Carpenters* (1963), deal with a whole family of precocious "whiz kids" who have been regular contestants on a radio quiz program called *It's a Wise Child*. The use of precocious children and the title of the program itself reflect Salinger's sense that children possess some kind of innate understanding only rarely and with great difficulty retained in growing up. This idea is closely linked to the theme of honesty versus phoniness. "Phony" is Holden Caulfield's favorite epithet for any kind of behavior that strikes him as insincere (in *The Catcher in the Rye*), and phoniness appears to Holden as one of the chief evils of the world. Thus the attraction children have for Holden and other Salinger spokesmen—they are rarely, if ever, "phony." Sincerity, honesty, and innocence are the features of the ideal state to which Salinger's characters aspire and whose absence, scarcity, or remoteness causes them such pain.

The quest for these lost qualities is ultimately a religious quest for Salinger, and his writing relies heavily on terms and concepts taken from a wide variety of religious teachings to describe this quest. Christian references are frequent in *The Catcher in the Rye*. Another religious tradition that is equally important to an understanding of Salinger's work but less familiar to most readers is the tradition of Zen Buddhism.

Zen is a branch of Buddhist philosophy that emphasizes the impossibility of arriving at enlightenment by logical means. For this reason, teachers of Zen make use of paradoxes and riddles (called koans) to illustrate the futility of logic as a means of acquiring religious understanding. One of the most well-known of these koans serves as the epigraph for Salinger's *Nine Stories* (1953): "We know the sound of two hands clapping/ But what is the sound of one hand clapping?" Just as this question has no rational answer, so many of Salinger's stories seem to have no rational explanation—particularly "A Perfect Day for Bananafish," which ends with the unexpected and unexplained suicide of the main character. By using such Zen techniques, Salinger may be adopting the role of a Zen teacher in inviting (or forcing) the reader into a non-rational mode of experiencing the story. If each reader experiences the story in a unique way, it then becomes impossible to establish an agreed-upon "meaning" or "message" for the story, but this may be just what Salinger intended. In Zen, enlightenment can never be imparted to one person by another—each seeker must arrive there on his or her own.

As important as Zen may be as a means toward enlightenment, it makes no attempt to answer the profound questions troubling many of Salinger's characters: how to deal with the problems of evil, suffering, estrangement, and alienation. Esmé is obsessed with "squalor"; Holden is haunted by obscenity. Few of Salinger's characters can speak directly with those to whom they are supposed to be closely related, those whom they are supposed to love. They talk over the telephone, through bathroom doors, or by means of letters, but rarely look one another in the eye; they are afflicted with the essential estrangement and alienation that plagues modern life. The task of Salinger's characters is to overcome these barriers through love, but it is a task infrequently and imperfectly achieved.

The most widely admired of Salinger's writing techniques is his ability to create convincing dialogue, especially for Holden Caulfield in *The Catcher in the Rye*. Holden's speech is slangy enough to be believable, yet eloquent enough to make profound and intellectually challenging observations. Salinger also shows a particular gift for creating realistic telephone conversations in several stories, as well as minutely detailed descriptions of revealing personal gestures, such as Muriel's painting of her fingernails in "A Perfect Day for Bananafish." Salinger describes significant personal objects with the same effect: Allie's baseball glove, covered with poems written in green ink, in *The Catcher in the Rye* is a good example. Critics sometimes fault Salinger for excessive attention to dialogue and seemingly trivial details (particularly in *Franny and Zooey*), but Salinger consistently prefers to let his characters reveal themselves through their words and actions, rather than perform that operation for them.

Many of Salinger's characters are introduced in abbreviated form in his earlier stories, only to reappear for fuller development later on. Holden Caulfield appears several times (although sometimes called by other names) in stories published before *The Catcher in the Rye*, and Seymour, Walt, and Boo Boo Glass are first introduced in three separate stories published in *Nine Stories*, written well before the Glass family was first presented in its entirety in *Franny and Zooey*. This repetition of characters could be explained as merely the fondness authors often feel for the products of their imaginations or as representing various facets of Salinger himself, but their effect is one of further uniting Salinger's work, as if it were one long story composed of a number of distinct but interrelated chapters.

Finally there are Salinger's frequent and wide-ranging references to religious, philosophical, and literary figures and works: Christ, Buddha, Lao-tzu, Chuang-tzu, Epictetus, Sri Ramakrishna, the *Bhagavad Gītā*, T. S. Eliot's *The Waste Land* (1922), Fyodor Dostoevski, *The Great Gatsby* (1925), and Ring Lardner are only a few. Some of these, particularly the religious and philosophical references, may be intended to point to the universality of the quest for enlightenment in which Salinger's characters are engaged. The literary references sometimes seem to be a form of literary criticism put by Salinger into the mouths of his characters, and other times merely examples of the honesty and sincerity for which his characters yearn. It is impossible to say just what expectations Salinger may have had for his audience, since he has never said, but if he had any intention of directing his readers on their own quests for enlightenment, he may have left these references as signposts of a sort.

THE CATCHER IN THE RYE

First published: 1951
Type of work: Novel

Having been kicked out of a prestigious prep school, a sensitive adolescent makes a disturbing odyssey through New York City.

The Catcher in the Rye, Salinger's only full-length novel, is the work that made him famous and for which he is remembered by high school and college students throughout America and much of the world. It has been translated into nearly every major language and continues to be assigned reading in many high school and college classrooms (though it has also been banned from many high school classrooms for allegedly obscene language). Its utterly convincing portrayal of the thoughts, words, and feelings of a troubled adolescent has permanently influenced entire generations of young people, as well as writers throughout the world.

The book opens with Holden saying,

> If you really want to hear about it, the first thing you'll probably want to know is where I was born, and what my lousy childhood was like . . . and all that David Copperfield kind of crap, but I don't feel like going into it, if you want to know the truth. . . . I'll just tell you about this madman stuff that happened to me around Christmas just before I got pretty run-down and had to come out here and take it easy.

The opening paragraph is emblematic of the book in several ways: First, it introduces the reader immediately to Holden's essential character—his cynicism, irreverence, and complicated mixture of frankness and evasiveness. Eventually the reader comes to learn that "out here" is actually a psychiatric hospital in California and that Holden has been sent there for observation and treatment, not merely to "take it easy." Second, the language Holden uses to begin his story gives further insight into his character. Several phrases appear here which will serve as refrains for the novel: "If you really want to hear about it," "I don't feel like . . . ," "if you want to know the truth," and "madman." Holden's language is both representative of the typical adolescent of his time and place and indicative of his personal fears and frustrations. "If you really want to hear about it" and "if you want to know the truth" reflect Holden's despair that most people really do not want to know the truth. "I don't feel like . . ." demonstrates the emotional paralysis that contributes to Holden's breakdown, and "madman" expresses his fear of going crazy, not only going crazy himself, but the world going crazy as well. "This madman stuff" is everything that led up to Holden's collapse, beginning with his ejection from Pencey for "failing everything but English."

Holden begins his account with a description of the school and the "phonies" in it—administrators, teachers, and students. Phoniness is one of the many things that Holden says "drive me crazy" or "make me puke," another example of a slang expression pointing to an underlying truth—that the corruption of the world makes him physically ill. Holden despises his fellow students for being physically repulsive, like Ackley, the pimply faced boy with bad teeth in the room next door, or for being too attractive, like Stradlater, Holden's "handsome, charming bastard" of a roommate. Strangely enough, Holden ends up missing these same people, and practically everyone he has met, by the end of the book—typical of the mixture of attraction and repulsion life holds for him. Following a fight with Stradlater about a girl both boys have dated, Holden decides to leave Pencey in the middle of the night and, after shouting "Sleep tight, ya morons!" by way of farewell, walks to the station to catch a train to New York City.

Once in the city, Holden is unsure what to do. He is afraid to go home and let his parents know he has been kicked out of school, so he ends up taking a room at the sleazy Edmont Hotel. He spends the night watching "perverts" in the opposite wing of the hotel, thinking about calling up old girlfriends (but deciding he's "not in the mood"), and going to bars seeking companionship. In the bars he finds only pitiful, boring, or "phony" people, so he eventually returns to the hotel, where an encounter with a teenaged prostitute and her pimp gets him beaten up. He then leaves the hotel and goes to Grand Central Station to eat breakfast, where he meets a pair of nuns on their way to teach school and discusses *Romeo and Juliet* with one of them. (Religion and literature are frequent subjects for Holden's commentary.)

Holden spends the rest of the day wandering along Broadway and around Central Park. It is on Broadway that he observes the scene which gives the book its title: A family is walking home from church—"a father, a mother, and a little kid about six years old." The boy is walking in the street, next to the curb, singing a song that Holden hears as "if a body catch a body coming through the rye": "The cars zoomed by, brakes screeched all over the place, his parents paid no attention to him, and he kept on walking next to the curb and singing 'If a body catch a body coming through the rye.'" It is not until Holden sneaks home to visit his sister Phoebe, near the end of the book, that he explains the significance of the scene:

> I keep picturing all these little kids playing some game in this big field of rye and all. Thousands of little kids, and nobody's around—nobody big, I mean—except me. And I'm standing on the edge of some crazy cliff. What I have to do, I have to catch everybody if they start to go over the cliff—I mean if they're running and they don't look where they're going I have to come out from somewhere and *catch* them. That's all I'd do all day. I'd just be the catcher in the rye and all. I know it's crazy, but that's the only thing I'd really like to be. I know it's crazy.

It is here that Holden expresses most clearly what is bothering him: the inevitable loss of innocence involved in growing up. Other than children, the only people Holden respects completely (outside of books) are the two nuns, who have managed to remain unstained by the world. Holden realizes that it is nearly impossible for a child to grow up in the world and remain innocent, so his greatest wish is somehow to protect all children from the danger of going over the "crazy cliff" of adulthood. For Holden, the passage to adulthood proves to be a crazy cliff indeed.

FRANNY AND ZOOEY

First published: 1961
Type of work: Novella

An introduction to the Glass family, in which the youngest member recovers from an emotional breakdown with the help of her brother's explication of love.

Franny and Zooey is actually a compilation of two long stories first published separately in *The New Yorker*, and it indicates an increasing tendency of Salinger to create stories more as vehicles for the expression of religious and philosophical ideas than as pieces of dramatic fiction. The first story, *Franny*, describes the emotional collapse of the youngest member of the Glass family, several other members of which appear repeatedly in Salinger's work. Franny Glass, an honors student in English and drama at a New England women's college, goes to visit her boyfriend Lane at his Ivy League school on the weekend of the Yale game. Lane takes Franny to a fashionable restaurant for lunch, but as soon as they sit down she begins criticizing English professors, poets, actors, and almost everyone she and Lane know. When Lane seeks an explanation for her sudden peevishness, Franny begins talking about a book she has been reading called *The Way of a Pilgrim*, in which a nineteenth century Russian peasant learns to "pray without ceasing" by discovering the secret of the "Jesus Prayer." Lane dismisses the story as "mumbo jumbo," whereupon Franny leaves the table and collapses in the middle of the restaurant floor. At the end of the story, Franny is lying in the manager's office staring at the ceiling, "her lips . . . forming soundless words"—evidently practicing the Jesus Prayer.

Zooey picks up Franny's story at the Glass family home, where she has been brought to recuperate in the care of her mother Bessie and brother Zooey. Zooey is five years older than Franny, and both he and Franny, as well as their five older siblings, were regular contestants as children on a radio quiz show called "It's a Wise Child." Both were also influenced by their older brothers Seymour and Buddy to study a wide variety of religious and philosophical literature at a very early age. Zooey is now a successful television actor, however, and is convinced that Seymour's and Buddy's program of education has ruined him and Franny for the purposes of living in the actual world. (Franny got *The Way of a Pilgrim* from Seymour's old desk, which has remained undisturbed in the Glass apartment since his suicide.)

In contrast to Franny, Zooey, Buddy, and Seymour, Bessie Glass is every bit a creature of the actual world. She always appears in the story dressed in an old kimono with pockets sewn on front to serve as "the repository for the paraphernalia of a very heavy cigarette smoker and an amateur handyman." These pockets are stocked with a hammer and screwdriver "plus an assortment of screws, nails, hinges, and ball-bearing casters—all of which tended to make Mrs. Glass chink faintly as she moved about." Bessie's idea of a cure for Franny's breakdown is chicken broth. Zooey responds to Bessie's suggestions with sarcasm and ridicule, but in her plodding way Bessie gets to the root of Franny's and Zooey's problem: They do not "know how to talk to people you don't like. . . . Don't love, really." Though Zooey fails to acknowledge Bessie's insight here, at the end of the book he confirms Bessie's diagnosis with a prescription of an all-encompassing love as the solution to Franny's cynicism and despair.

Zooey leads up to his prescription by relating how Seymour used to tell him to shine his shoes "for the Fat Lady" before going on *It's A Wise Child*. Zooey had formed a mental picture of the Fat Lady "sitting on the porch all day, swatting flies, with her radio going full-blast from morning till night." Franny remembers that Seymour had told her to "be funny for the Fat Lady" and she had formed an almost identical mental picture. Zooey then proclaims, "I'll tell you a terrible secret—Are you listening to me? *There isn't anyone out there who isn't Seymour's Fat Lady. . . .* And don't you know—*listen* to me, now—*don't you know who that Fat Lady really is? . . .* It's Christ himself. Christ himself, buddy." Zooey is here rephrasing Seymour's advice to him in a letter written years earlier to "Act . . . when and where you want to, since you feel you must, but do it with all your might," with the added thought that any act must be done out of love to be worthwhile and that any act done out of love toward a human being is an act of worship, an act offered up to Christ himself. Franny's response to Zooey's message is to lie quietly "smiling at the ceiling," before falling into a "deep, dreamless sleep," a sure sign, in Salinger, that a cure has been effected.

A PERFECT DAY FOR BANANAFISH

First published: 1948
Type of work: Short story

> While vacationing with his wife at a Florida resort, a disturbed World War II veteran commits suicide after an enigmatic conversation with a little girl.

A Perfect Day for Bananafish, published first in *The New Yorker* and later in the collection *Nine Stories*, is one of Salinger's best-known and most puzzling stories. Although a few generally accepted themes can be identified, critics are widely divided as to the significance of the title, symbolism, and climax of the story.

The story opens with Muriel Glass, the wife of Seymour, oldest of the Glass children, waiting for a telephone call to be put through to New York. When the phone rings, the party on the other end of the line is Muriel's mother, who is extremely concerned about Seymour's state of mind and Muriel's safety. Muriel's mother is afraid that Seymour will "lose control of himself" — evidently with good reason. Seymour has recently driven a car into a tree, among other alarming acts that Muriel's mother relates: "That business with the window. Those horrible things he said to Granny about her plans for passing away. What he did with all those lovely pictures from Bermuda . . . what he tried to do with Granny's chair." During the course of the conversation the reader learns that Seymour was in Europe during the war and afterward was placed in an Army hospital, presumably as a psychiatric case. The Army apparently decided that Seymour was well enough for release, but his behavior remains erratic, at least by Muriel's mother's account. Muriel herself does not seem overly concerned, but she promises to call her mother "the *instant* he does, or *says*, anything at all funny" (as her mother puts it) before she hangs up.

The scene then shifts to the beach outside the hotel, where Seymour is lying on his back in his bathrobe. Sybil Carpenter, a little girl Seymour has befriended, approaches him and says, "Are you going in the water, see more glass?" Sybil is fascinated with Seymour's name, and she keeps repeating it like some kind of incantation: "Did you see more glass?" After some seemingly disconnected banter about the color of Sybil's bathing suit and the lack of air in Seymour's rubber float, Seymour takes Sybil down to the water. As they begin to wade in, Seymour tells Sybil, "You just keep your eyes open for any bananafish. This is a *perfect* day for bananafish." Bananafish, explains Seymour,

> lead a very tragic life. . . . They swim into a hole where there's a lot of bananas. They're very ordinary looking fish when they swim *in*. But once they get in, they behave like pigs. Why, I've known some bananafish to swim into a banana hole and eat as many as seventy-eight bananas. . . . Naturally, after that they're so fat they can't get out of the hole again. Can't fit through the door.

Sybil asks what happens to the bananafish after that. "Well, I hate to tell you, Sybil. They die . . . they get banana fever. It's a terrible disease." Just then a wave passes, and Sybil says, "I just saw one." "My God, no!" Seymour exclaims, "Did he have any bananas in his mouth?" Yes, says Sybil: "Six." Delighted with Sybil's answer, Seymour kisses her foot. He then returns her to the beach, goes back to his room where Muriel is sleeping, pulls "an Ortgies calibre 7.65 automatic" from his suitcase, and "fire[s] a bullet through his right temple." There the story ends.

As previously mentioned, critics have suggested a wide range of interpretations of *A Perfect Day for Bananafish*, but some of the most convincing look at the story in its relationship to Zen Buddhism. The epigraph to *Nine Stories* is the Zen koan, or paradox, "We know the sound of two hands clapping. But what is the sound of one hand clapping?" There are numerous allusions in the story to the Buddhist concept of the "wheel of life," the ceaseless round of daily existence from which it is the goal of Buddhism to escape. During Seymour's conversation with Sybil, the girl asks him if he has read "Little Black Sambo," in which six tigers chase one another around a tree until they melt into butter; Sybil also informs Seymour that she lives in "Whirly Wood, Connecticut," another possible reference to the wheel of life. Sybil's reading of Seymour's name as "see more glass" may reflect the Zen emphasis on self-knowledge and insight. And the bananafish themselves, whatever else they represent, seem to symbolize the danger of being trapped in the world of physical appetite, from which the only escape appears to be death.

Seymour's death is the most puzzling element of the story, coming as it does immediately after what appears to be a moment of great joy. This paradox has caused some critics to see Seymour's suicide as a moment of triumph, of having finally escaped from the wheel of life to some sort of nirvana. Others see it as an act of surrender, in which Seymour is destroyed by the oppressiveness of daily existence, a victim of "banana fever." Salinger has left no definitive clues by which either interpretation can be proved or disproved—in this sense the entire story may be seen as a Zen koan, intended to aid the reader in approaching truth, rather than to present the truth itself. In Zen, truth cannot be imparted by one person to another; one must achieve enlightenment on one's own. Whether or not Seymour achieved it Salinger leaves to the individual reader to decide.

Summary

The stories of J. D. Salinger present complex characters—brilliant, sensitive, and prone to nervous breakdowns and suicide—struggling to retain a belief in innocence, goodness, and truth in an increasingly corrupt and artificial world. Through a combination of vividly realistic dialogue and meticulous description of personal characteristics and mannerisms, the people in Salinger's stories take on a life of their own and occupy a permanent place in the minds of readers who come to know them.

Bibliography

Belcher, William F., and James W. Lee, eds. *J. D. Salinger and the Critics.* Belmont, Calif.: Wadsworth, 1962.

French, Warren T. *J. D. Salinger.* Rev. ed. Indianapolis: Bobbs-Merrill, 1976.

Grunwald, Henry Anatole, ed. *Salinger: A Critical and Personal Portrait.* New York: Harper, 1962.

Lundquist, James. *J. D. Salinger.* New York: Frederick Ungar, 1979.

Miller, James E., Jr. *J. D. Salinger.* Minneapolis: University of Minnesota Press, 1965.

Salzberg, Joel, ed. *Critical Essays on J. D. Salinger's "The Catcher in the Rye."* Boston: G. K. Hall, 1990.

Sublette, Jack R. *J. D. Salinger: An Annotated Bibliography, 1938-1981.* New York: Garland, 1984.

Alan Blackstock

CARL SANDBURG

Born: Galesburg, Illinois
January 6, 1878
Died: Flat Rock, North Carolina
July 22, 1967

Principal Literary Achievement

Sandburg celebrated democracy and the common man using the idiom of the American Midwest. Although he also wrote fiction and biography, he is revered for capturing the essence of America in poetry.

Biography

Charles August Sandburg was born in a modest clapboard cottage on January 6, 1878, in Galesburg, Illinois, to Swedish immigrants August Sandburg and Clara Anderson Sandburg. August worked for the Chicago, Burlington, and Quincy Railroad; Clara Anderson had been a hotel chambermaid before they were married. August Sandburg could read a Swedish Bible, but that was all. He signed his name with an X. Clara Sandburg could write in colloquial Swedish and could phonetically spell English and encouraged her son's learning. Charles, or Carl, as he was later to call himself, enjoyed school but deviated from the prescribed curriculum. He quit school after the eighth grade to help his father support the family. Sandburg stated that his true education began then, when he learned that crime and politics mixed and that justice belonged to the rich. At eighteen, Sandburg made for the open road, doing odd jobs and living with hoboes. When the Spanish-American War broke out, he enlisted. By the time his regiment was ready for action, however, the war was nearly over, so Sandburg saw no fighting.

Because he was a "war veteran," Sandburg was admitted to Lombard College without a high school degree. There the distinguished professor Philip Green Wright encouraged his writing. In college, Sandburg was active in academics and extra-curricular activities but left without a degree, probably because he failed to take some required courses. Despite this, Sandburg experienced the satisfaction of seeing his words in print: Professor Wright privately printed his first three books of poetry.

Sandburg wandered from Galesburg from time to time, supporting himself by peddling and by writing for a Chicago magazine. While in Chicago, he became associate editor of another Chicago magazine and active in the Social Democratic

Party. His loyalties to the poor, the oppressed, and the exploited, which found voice in his writings, became a permanent part of his psyche while he campaigned for Populist and Socialist causes. In fact, it was at the Milwaukee Socialist headquarters that Sandburg met his future wife, Lillian Steichen, sister of Edward Steichen (who became a world famous photographer). They were married after several months' courtship; it was a union that proved happy and lasted until Sandburg's death. By Lillian, Sandburg had three daughters, one of whom, Helga, became a novelist.

Sandburg broke with the Socialist Party after the outbreak of World War I, but still he wrote articles and editorials for socialist magazines. Despite his busy involvement in newspaper work, he also still wrote poetry. *Chicago Poems* (1916), began his reputation. The key poem, "Chicago" launched his literary fame, and some critics believe that "Chicago" is Sandburg's finest poem. From *Chicago Poems* followed two other volumes of poetry, *Cornhuskers* (1918) and *Smoke and Steel* (1920). These books illustrate Sandburg's concern for the working man; the first book is sometimes considered raw, the second more mellow.

His next book was not poetry but a collection of children's stories, *Rootabaga Stories* (1922). Afterward, he contracted with Harcourt and Holt to write a biography of Abraham Lincoln for teenagers. This modest project grew into an obsession for Sandburg, who adored Lincoln. Sandburg produced a two-volume work entitled *Abraham Lincoln: The Prairie Years* (1926). This biography was financially successful, and its popular acclaim encouraged him to continue Lincoln's biography through his presidency. At last financially secure, Sandburg could concentrate on his goal of writing a complete Lincoln biography.

Because Sandburg's future was assured, he was unaffected, except by his constant sympathies with the poor, by the Great Depression. During this time he published *The People, Yes* (1936), which asserted his faith in the people. In 1939, Sandburg published his four-volume continuing biography of Lincoln, *Abraham Lincoln: The War Years*. This was well received both by critics and by lay readers. It won the Pulitzer Prize in 1940 and may well be considered his most lasting work.

Ironically, Sandburg's wholehearted commitment to America resulted in one of his most flawed books. As a gesture of support for the United States' efforts in World War II, Sandburg wrote the novel *Remembrance Rock* (1948), a too-obvious symbolic representation of heroic people and heroic action. Critics agree that, whereas his intentions are noble, the book fails as art because of its patriotic overzealousness. The year the war ended, 1945, Sandburg and his family moved from his beloved Midwest to Flat Rock, North Carolina, where he lived until his death in 1967 at eighty-nine years of age.

Sandburg's *Complete Poems* (1950) earned another Pulitzer Prize but received mixed critical reviews. The new poems in this volume were often overlooked by critics who had stereotyped him as too "folksy" and too popular to be literary; however, Sandburg's public success had increased steadily since his later volumes of poetry. This was in part attributable to his talent as a public performer, both as a reader and folk singer. His poetry, performances, and Lincoln biographies combined to make him an American institution. In 1953, Sandburg published his autobiography, *Always the Young Strangers.* This was widely acclaimed as a sensitive, unpretentious portrait of a boy's growth in the Midwest.

Analysis

Sandburg wrote of the American common people; his work glorified both the everyday man and everyday life. "Moonlight and mittens," he believed, were the stuff of art. In addition, he made poetry of the harsh realities of immigrant urban life. Like nineteenth century American poet Walt Whitman, he broke with poetic convention by addressing "unpoetic" subjects, such as butchering and railroads. Also like Whitman, he broke with conventional rhyme schemes and forms; his verse is often called "prosy" in that he uses much dialogue and employs long lines. Sandburg defended free verse by quoting Oliver Wendell Holmes: "Rhythm alone is a tether, and not a very long one. But rhymes are iron fetters." Sandburg had an excellent ear for speech rhythms and the musical cadences of words. His form grew naturally out of his content, not only because of his skill in hearing the musical connotations of words but also because of his ability to balance and counterbalance phrases and clauses.

Critics sometimes regarded Sandburg as "subliterary." The polished literary fashion of his time considered form, structure, imagery, tension, and irony more important than content. Sandburg's poetry was a vehicle for his message of faith in "the people." He did not brood over poetry and what constitutes art, but instead had an almost irreverent attitude toward aesthetic theories. The question remains, however, whether Sandburg invented adequate poetic structures to replace those he spurned. Sandburg was not without poetic theory, but his definitions of poetry were impressionistic ("poetry is a shuffling of boxes of illusion buckled with a strap of facts") more than analytical. He wanted to synthesize the ethereal and the concrete, "hyacinths and biscuits," by juxtaposing one with the other. His poetry itself, however, reveals more care than his vague definitions would indicate.

William Carlos Williams made a classic case against Sandburg by charging that he had no unifying imaginative vision; since he had no formal poetic theory, he could write no coherent poetry. His poetry simply catalogued realistic detail in a sprawl of words. Other critics, however, found this uniting vision in the very inclusiveness of Sandburg's work and in his faith in the people, a faith that the slang and hardships of the people were the materials as well as the subjects of art.

Sandburg's poetry touched on the variety of American life, particularly that of the working man. Although he made his reputation on the brassy poem "Chicago," he also wrote of simple moments of joy, poignancy, and despair. A Jewish fishmonger has "a joy identical with that of Pavlova dancing"; a runaway girl is "Gone with her little chin." His populist views appear in countless images of struggle, such as a woman so worn out from making mittens that she sees evergreens by moonlight as a pair of mittens. That Sandburg should be obsessed with Abraham Lincoln is no surprise. Lincoln exemplified the working man who made good, the American Dream, a practical man who retained Midwest ideals in the face of one of America's most complex periods.

Sandburg has been faulted for not dealing with the evils of life, but this is a superficial criticism at best. True, there are no villains or monsters either in his poetry or in his children's tales, but evil exists, usually in the form of poverty, despair, and recurring defeats. The little man is saved not by circumstances, but by his resilience, humor, and common sense.

Although Sandburg has often been linked with Whitman, they differ in major respects, such as their attitudes toward death. Whitman celebrates death as undergirding and completing life; Sandburg views it merely as a terminus. Whereas Whitman believes in a pantheistic kind of immortality, Sandburg asks the eternal questions throughout his work but fails to find answers. Only in his last volume does he think he sees something of a "purpose" in life's randomness.

A typical Sandburg poem, however, does employ literary devices that are similar to Whitman's. Like Whitman, Sandburg is a master of the long, "prosaic" line, and he catalogues, glorifies, and repeats details from daily life. Sandburg's repetitions, however, also owe much in style to the Bible. He makes heavy use of dialogue in his work, and the verse is so free that it would be almost formless were it not for Sandburg's keen ear for the musical sequence of words. Sandburg's best work combines colloquial speech and homely imagery with an energy and force which come from unconventional line lengths. His long lines are saved from being prose by his handling of the sounds of words and his skill in paralleling words, phrases, and clauses, thus creating rhetorical rhythm.

Sandburg takes his images from the rural and urban Midwest, grounding them in physical reality. There are no fairy kingdoms or mystical revelations; instead, his work tells of strawberries, lattice shadows of doorways, cornhuskers, and men with their shirts off. Often he piles detail upon detail until the effect is kaleidoscopic.

Although Sandburg is noted for his celebration of exuberance and unthinking animal spirits, he has a melancholy side that mourns the transience of life. His better-known poems, such as "Chicago," are optimistic, but he also wrote meditative, weary lyrics that question life's meaning. His long poem *The People, Yes* achieves something of a balance between these two facets of Sandburg's personality.

CHICAGO

First published: 1916
Type of work: Poem

In sprawling Chicago, one sees young America, a vital people who can laugh at their destiny through sheer exuberance.

"Chicago" started Sandburg's literary rise, and many critics consider it one of his best poems. Certainly it is one of the most anthologized. "Chicago" contains most of the characteristics that made Sandburg famous: It breaks with conventional poetic versification, deals with the "unpoetic," and expresses his lifelong faith in the American people's resilience.

The opening verse imperatively addresses the city with brutal imagery and staccato lines. Sandburg personifies Chicago as a laborer by calling it "Hog Butcher for the World" and "City of the Big Shoulders." The following long and prosy lines challenge the city on its reported evils, cataloguing instances of cruelty and injustice. The speaker then defends Chicago for its pride, strength, and energy, implying that the aforementioned evils are by-products of its heartiness. Unconventional images describe the city's vitality: a dog eager for action, an ignorant, undefeated prizefighter.

In "Chicago," Sandburg demonstrates his love affair with the United States and its working class. This is evident in the image of Chicago as a brash prizefighter. The images of corruption of farm boys by prostitutes and of hunger on the faces of women and children also affiliate the city with the working man and the poor. Nowhere in its salute to Chicago's vitality does it refer to its rich or elite.

Supporting the themes of raw energy in America's working class is free verse and the use of several literary devices. Sandburg not only uses his excellent ear for words but also builds his lines as if building a skyscraper to achieve the effect of a bustling, amoral city. The first verse has short lines of salutation, then long-lined accusations followed by a rebuttal in the same form. The next statement abruptly lists the city's qualities. Parallelism speeds a tempo which has been slowed by long-lined accusations and defense. The following long lines reflect the lazy insolence of a bragging man, Sandburg's central image of the city. The one-word verse "Laughing!" expresses shock at Chicago's daring, and the final long descriptive lines express grudging approval.

"Chicago" shocked a public used to pretty poems. Some critics still refer to it as shrill and abrasive. Others consider it Sandburg's most brilliant poem. It captures like no other Sandburg poem the author's respect for his country's brawling nature. Sandburg's work is sometimes unfairly stereotyped by "Chicago," however; he is seen only as the versemaker of the lower classes, the poet who honors unthinking animal exuberance. He is much more.

GRASS

First published: 1918
Type of work: Poem

In this poem on the war dead, Sandburg links America with the rest of the world in resignation over death's inevitability and nature's indifference to man.

"Grass," first published in *Cornhuskers*, presents a side of Sandburg often overlooked, his melancholy in the face of death. Unlike "Chicago," "Grass" is conventional in subject, language, and tone. It is a "typical" Sandburg poem in its reference to train passengers and conductors in the Midwest and its stress upon the American war dead, but the link between Americans and people of other nations in the first line suggests a common fate.

"Grass" opens with the imperative to pile bodies high at Austerlitz and Waterloo, then to bury them so that the grass can get on with its work of covering the ground. The second verse calls for the same procedure at American Civil War battle sites: Bury the dead so the grass can grow, and after two years train passengers will ask the conductor where they are. Because of the grass's work, all who fell in battle will be forgotten. It is the grass's destiny to express nature's indifference by obliterating memories of the war dead.

This poem achieves its melancholy by simple words and images, conventional diction and repetition. Words such as "pile," "shovel," "bodies," and "under" connote death, as do the names of specific battle sites. Graveyards, trains, and conductors provide homely images, but there are no colorful colloquialisms. Instead, simple but standard English provides a formality similar to a chant or funeral dirge. The long lines are instructions to pile the bodies and shovel them under; the short lines are thematically significant, repeating that the passengers' questions and the relentless work of the grass prove that all is forgotten.

Even though it exhibits Sandburg's penchant for repetition, "Grass" is understated and concise. Unlike his better-known poems, "Grass" does not express faith in the people's ability to transcend life's difficulties. Its matter-of-fact tone is more reminiscent of Emily Dickinson than Walt Whitman, as it faces a mournful but unchangeable fact of life. In his mention of American battles and trains and conductors, Sandburg implies that even brash Americans with their outrageous democratic ideals are not exempt from war, death, and the silence of an unresponsive nature.

Although not given as much publicity, Sandburg's somber side is almost as prevalent in his work as his buoyant optimism toward "the people." He continued to ask large spiritual questions but never found solace in conventional religions. Although Sandburg has been accused of being "nonpoetic," his preoccupation with loss and melancholy place him in the tradition of English meditative verse, particularly the English graveyard poets.

Summary

Carl Sandburg was the first modern poet to use the language of the American people extensively in his work. For this reason alone, he deserves a place in American literary history. Although his work is not always polished, he achieved at times an enduring art. His best poems convey the vigor and brokenness of industrialization, the quaintness of small towns, and the transience of nature and love. His vision encompassed both the light and the dark. His best poems captured a part of the essence of his time and enlarged the potentials of language and subjects for other modern poets.

Bibliography

Allen, Gay Wilson. *Carl Sandburg.* Minneapolis: University of Minnesota Press, 1972.

Callahan, North. *Carl Sandburg: Lincoln of Our Literature.* New York: New York University Press, 1970.

Cowley, Malcolm. *After the Genteel Tradition.* New York: W. W. Norton, 1937.

Crowder, Richard. *Carl Sandburg.* New York: Twayne, 1964.

Golden, Harry. *Carl Sandburg.* Cleveland: World, 1961.

Hallwas, Jon E., and Dennis J. Reader, eds. *The Vision of This Land.* Macomb, Ill.: Western Illinois University Press, 1976.

Hoffman, Daniel. *"Moonlight Dries No Mittens": Carl Sandburg Reconsidered.* Washington, D.C.: U.S. Government Printing Office, 1979.

Mary H. Barnes

WILLIAM SAROYAN

Born: Fresno, California
August 31, 1908
Died: Fresno, California
May 18, 1981

Principal Literary Achievement

Briefly in the front rank of American dramatists, Saroyan is mostly valued for his pre-World War II plays and fictional sketches that espoused an infectious optimism and sanguine view of humankind during a period of great social and economic turmoil.

Biography

William Saroyan was born in Fresno, California, on August 31, 1908, the son of Armenak and Takoohi Saroyan, poor Armenian immigrants. In 1911, when his father died, Saroyan was put into an Oakland orphanage with his brother, Henry, and his two sisters, Cosette and Zabel, but in 1915 returned to Fresno with his family. Over the next decade, Saroyan attended school in Fresno and held various after-school jobs, including work as a telegraph messenger boy, an experience which he would later reflect in his fiction.

In 1926, after repeated expulsions from school for disciplinary reasons, Saroyan left Fresno without a high school diploma, first going to Los Angeles, where he served briefly in the California National Guard, then to San Francisco, where, after working as a telegraph operator, he eventually became manager at a branch office of the Postal Telegraph Company. By 1928, when he made his first trip to New York, Saroyan had made up his mind to make writing his career. Soon depressed, homesick, and discouraged, he returned to San Francisco, taking a series of brief jobs and spending most of his time learning his craft at the library and the typewriter.

Recognition and success first came in 1934, when *Story* magazine published two pieces that would also appear in his first collection of sketches, *The Daring Young Man on the Flying Trapeze and Other Stories* (1934). Once discovered, Saroyan quickly found markets for his backlog of pieces as well as his new works. In 1936, after travels abroad, Saroyan began work as a screenwriter in Hollywood. There he continued to write stories and sketches, published in several collections. Three years later, in 1939, he made his first serious venture into dramatic form with *My Heart's in the Highlands*, which opened in New York as a Group Theatre project. It was

1817

soon followed by his best-known play, *The Time of Your Life* (1939), for which, in 1940, Saroyan won both the New York Drama Critics Circle Award and the Pulitzer Prize, which, with characteristic obstinacy, he refused to accept. In 1941, frustrated by conditions imposed by Broadway entrepreneurs, Saroyan directed and produced his own play, *The Beautiful People*, and in the following year did the same for two of his one-acts, *Across the Board on Tomorrow Morning* and *Talking to You*, establishing, as an impresario, a reputation for his unconventional methods of casting and directing. His best-known one-act play, *Hello Out There*, was staged in 1942, the year that marked the end of his most vital development as a dramatist.

Success brought Saroyan his share of problems. In fact, soon after the enthusiastic reception of *My Name Is Aran* (1940), fictionalized sketches based on his boyhood, Saroyan began to experience serious financial reversals, in part because of his addiction to gambling. Needing money, he agreed to write a screenplay for Metro-Goldwyn-Mayer, turning out *The Human Comedy*, which he would later rewrite as a novel under the same title. Published in 1943, *The Human Comedy* remains Saroyan's most reputable fictional work.

Drafted into the Army in 1942, Saroyan served to the end of World War II and, in the interval, married Carol Marcus, whom he would later divorce, remarry, and then divorce again. Upon his release from service, Saroyan attempted to reestablish himself as a premier playwright and writer of fiction, but with only partial success. His propaganda novel, *The Adventures of Wesley Jackson* (1946), was met with hostile reviews that even questioned his patriotism. The film version of *The Time of Your Life*, released in 1948, proved to be a financial disaster. Gambling losses continued to plague him and contributed to his marital difficulties. With the publication of *The Assyrian and Other Stories* (1950), however, critics pronounced that he had returned to form. He also gained some popularity as a lyricist when his song, "Come on-a My House," coauthored with his cousin, topped the Hit Parade in 1951.

From 1952 to 1958, after his second divorce from Carol Marcus, Saroyan lived in Malibu Beach, California. During that period, in addition to other works, he wrote his first nonfictional autobiographical work, *The Bicycle Rider in Beverly Hills* (1952); a bitter novel based in part on his troubled marriage, *The Laughing Matter* (1953); and his first play to be staged in New York in fourteen years, *The Cave Dwellers* (1957).

In 1959, proclaiming himself a tax exile, Saroyan left the United States for Europe, producing plays in London before returning to teach at Purdue University in 1961. Thereafter, Saroyan met with little success as a playwright and turned almost exclusively to fiction and autobiography. He did author a teleplay, "The Unstoppable Gray Fox" (1962), which was broadcast on *The General Electric Theater*, but over the last twenty years of his life Saroyan concentrated on personal memoirs. The most important works of this period include an autobiography, *Here Comes, There Goes, You Know Who* (1961); a novelized memoir, *Boys and Girls Together* (1963); an anthology of occasional pieces, *I Used to Believe I Had Forever: Now I'm Not So Sure* (1968); and several memoirs, including *Obituaries* (1979), for which, in 1980, he was nominated for the American Book Award. Another autobiographical work, *My Name Is Saroyan*, was published posthumously in 1983, two years after he died of cancer.

Analysis

From 1934, when *The Daring Young Man on the Flying Trapeze* appeared, to the wartime era of the early 1940's, Saroyan enjoyed a literary reputation rivaling those of William Faulkner and Ernest Hemingway. After the war, however, he was unable to achieve enough critical recognition and popularity to regain it. To later generations of readers, the vigor and originality that marked his writing in the 1930's and early 1940's was gone, and, with some exceptions, his successive works seemed too familiar, self-centered, and routine. As a result, his postwar era audience steadily dwindled.

Ironically, it was partly Saroyan's success that accounted for his ebbing popularity. The literary voice he fashioned was well-suited to the bad times of the Great Depression and the anxious situation of the prewar era, but conditions changed, and, like many other writers, Saroyan was unable to make a full adjustment to either his fame or the changing times. His later literary career seems largely spent in self-justification.

The solipsistic self-centeredness of Saroyan's later work is to some measure foreshadowed by the earlier work on which his reputation rests. His first collection of stories, *The Daring Young Man on the Flying Trapeze*, contains several pieces in which the narrative voice is unabashedly the author's own, despite the narrator's fictional identification as a character of a different ethnic or national origin than Saroyan's.

Although some critics demurred, the conspicuous presence of the author did not repel Saroyan's early readers. What they found in his work was a freshness in style and theme offering a welcome tonic for the harshness of the times. Breaking with the tradition of the "well-made" or formulaic story, Saroyan presented a series of stories centered on character rather than plot. Some of them seem to be little more than transliterations of notebook observations, without conflict, plot, or theme, more rightly considered sketches than stories. Still, despite a rather sophomoric audacity that marks the preface, and the authorial intrusions in some pieces, the work has an engaging, highly individual, lyrical style.

To a nation standing in bread lines, Saroyan (himself poor but optimistic) offered an affirmation of life in his insistence that, even in starvation, man has a dignity and grace of which no external conditions can deprive him. This idea infuses all of his early work, including the two works for which he is best known: *The Time of Your Life* and *The Human Comedy*. Throughout these and his shorter fiction, Saroyan insists that there is an irrepressible joy in living and hope even in death. Within that general thematic frame, Saroyan focuses mostly on have-not characters who struggle against bad odds with simple faith and compassion. Saroyan's best delineated characters are males, many undergoing an internal rite of passage from adolescence to adulthood with a self-consciousness that is, itself, the story. In nine pieces of *The Daring Young Man on the Flying Trapeze*, the central character is a writer who is, in fact, Saroyan, rallying his lust for life under a thin fictional veil.

Although full of ironic contradictions, *The Daring Young Man on the Flying Trapeze* iterates Saroyan's notion that fiction should not be contrived and artificially plotted, but should be an expression of the writer's inner self, presented free of dogmatic principles of composition. The lyric and impressionistic quality of much of Saroyan's prose derives from this artistic credo. In a narrow, less all-consuming way, Saroyan shares the involvement in humankind that is the focus of Walt Whitman's poetry. He repeatedly confirms his determination, through himself, to investigate humans, to reveal their inner core, to understand and honor them.

In his more mature work, especially *The Time of Your Life* and *The Human Comedy*, Saroyan achieves greater objectivity, but the dominant themes remain. In the exchange of ideas and in their thoughts, Saroyan's wholly sympathetic characters explore most of the essential notions advanced in his first stories. Perhaps a bit facile and naïve, the characters are nevertheless warm and engaging. Saroyan's world is one in which the poor and the weak can find riches in human love and compassion and strength in hope and simple decency. It is also a world in which innocence can be restored to the fallen, and human greatness has nothing to do with the public recognition of it.

Although even Saroyan's best works have been faulted for their lack of a principal conflict and a corresponding lack of a strong plot line, many of his episodes and vignettes are memorable. Saroyan, of course, explicitly rejected plot as a vital concern in his fiction. Many of his short pieces are sketches, even personal essays and letters, rather than stories, and his plays, including *The Time of Your Life*, tend to be diffuse and lacking in dramatic urgency. As a result, Saroyan characters are more memorable than their contexts.

At his best, Saroyan creates highly original, atypical, and occasionally quixotic characters. For example, he floods *The Time of Your Life* with a variety of genial and zany losers and misfits, all of whom are highly individualized. Particular character poignancy is achieved in motifs that occur in several works, especially in the spiritual bonding of male characters. His better characters tend to transcend their simple, humdrum lives in their basic goodwill and kindness, and it is principally for these, his beautiful people, that Saroyan will be remembered.

THE HUMAN COMEDY

First published: 1943
Type of work: Novel

A lad of fourteen in wartime America learns to accept death through the affirmation of life.

The Human Comedy, dedicated to Takoohi Saroyan, was first written as a screenplay under a contractual arrangement with Metro-Goldwyn-Mayer, but in 1943, with the film version in production, Saroyan used the script scenario as the basis of his first and most popular novel. Set in Ithaca, a fictional name for Fresno, the work is based on some of Saroyan's boyhood experiences and familiar reminiscences. In fact, the Macauley family, central in the plot, has parallels to Saroyan's real family, without, however, a similar heritage.

The novel's main character, Homer Macauley, is a fourteen-year-old adolescent with a job and some experiences that relate to actual events in the author's life. With his father deceased and his older brother in the Army, Homer must assume adult responsibilities beyond his years, as a surrogate father to his younger brother, Ulysses, and the provider for his whole family. At the outset of the novel, he has secured a part-time job as a telegraph messenger boy, which takes him into a variety of homes and businesses to encounter the richly delineated and variegated characters that people the novel.

Apart from Homer, the most engaging characters are Mr. Grogan, the old rummy telegraph operator; Spangler, the telegraph office manager; Homer's mother, Kate Macauley; Miss Hicks, Homer's teacher; and Ulysses, his younger brother. These and a few others, such as Marcus, Homer's older brother, are rather representative of the vintage Saroyan character who, though well enough individualized, shares with the rest a simple faith, love for life, and inherent goodness.

Although there is a central, persistent concern with the disruptive impact of the war on the lives of these characters, the novel, like Saroyan's early sketches, provides a series of vignettes that are only loosely connected. Some have no inherent connection to the central focus of the novel or causal relationship to scenes juxtaposed to them. Nevertheless, most offer charming, human-interest interludes and comic leavening to the novel's more serious themes and maudlin moments. Two examples are the episodes in which Ulysses gets caught in the trap in Covington's Sporting Goods Store and his later confrontation with Mr. Mechano, a mechanical man on display in a drug-store window.

Despite the thematic similarities and use of characters who seem familiar from Saroyan's earlier stories, *The Human Comedy* departs from his earlier work both in style and in technique. The novel is basically more objective, the style more direct and less effusive. The point of view is that of an omniscient and unidentified third person, and although there are incursions into the thoughts of some characters, the impressionistic reverie that marks several of the sketches is virtually gone. Saroyan's earlier concern with his travails as artist is totally obliterated, and his authorial presence is largely masked and mute.

Perhaps the result of writing for the stage, Saroyan also makes very effective use of dialogue in the novel, something sparingly used in his very first sketches. In focusing on character interaction, Saroyan may sacrifice the lyricism of his internal monologues, but he in turn gains an admirable economy and tough simplicity of expression reminiscent of Hemingway's prose.

Despite its convoluted development, the novel prepares the reader for its final, inevitable revelation: the death of Marcus and its impact on Homer and the rest of the Macauleys. From the outset, it is clear that death is never far away for the Macauley family. The much-beloved deceased father is frequently alluded to, with an insistence that his spirit lives in those who remain alive. It is Homer, though, who most often confronts the fact of death throughout the novel. He bears the burden of delivering the War Department telegrams to the surviving families of servicemen killed in battle. Homer does not know the families, but it is a hateful duty that he comes to dread. Near the novel's end, death suddenly becomes more personal for Homer, first with the death of Mr. Grogan, then with the death of Marcus. Homer, death's envoy and bringer of pain, finally has the devastating duty of carrying home to his mother the telegram informing her of her oldest son's death.

What Homer learns is that death, if accepted as a necessary part of life, is largely an illusion, as Mrs. Macauley had earlier explained to Ulysses. The spirit of Marcus lives in the remaining family members; it also lives in his special friend and fellow soldier, Tobey George, who coincidentally appears in Ithaca on the very day the War Department telegram announcing the death of Marcus arrives. In an earlier episode, Marcus and Tobey engage in a ritual of spiritual bonding that prepares the reader for the novel's conclusion. He is accepted into the Macauley family and welcomed home as if he were, in truth, Marcus himself. Although it strains credibility, it is a touching scene that evades sentimentality through its terse, direct, and unadorned style. It is also a good example of Saroyan's ebullient view of human beings and his ability to evince a zest for life under the most devastating circumstances.

THE TIME OF YOUR LIFE

First produced: 1939 (first published, 1940)
Type of work: Play

A group of destitute drifters and misfits invades a waterfront dive in San Francisco and discovers the fundamental goodness of humanity in others and themselves.

The Time of Your Life, Saroyan's most critically acclaimed play, was received with warm praise for its great originality. As in his early fiction, Saroyan seemed determined to break with tradition, developing the comedy in his own, inimitable fashion and playing havoc with standard theatrical conventions. Set in Nick's, a San Francisco waterfront honky-tonk, the play focuses on Joe, his friend Tom, and an engaging prostitute named Kitty Duval, but there are a host of other destitute but benign characters who drift in and out. Nick's place offers a haven of hope for all who enter, unless, like Blick, an abrasive detective, they are persecutors of the downtrodden.

Nick's is also a sort of microcosm of Saroyan's ideal of America. It is clearly a melting pot, for among its various denizens are a melancholy Arab, a young, starving black, an Irish cop, the gruff Italian proprietor, a prostitute of Polish ancestry, a

Greek newsboy, and a crusty old mule skinner who seems to embody an offbeat variety of every trait ascribed to the legendary frontier hero of the dime novel. More important, Nick's is a place of great tolerance and freedom, bordering more on fantasy than reality. It is a place where the dreams of the characters begin to come true, where the starving find sustenance, the deprived get a break, and the lonely and disheartened find love and hope.

Other than Nick, only Joe has any money. Throughout the play, as if he possesses a magic pocket, Joe pulls out whatever cash is needed to fulfill his momentary whim. Surely one of Saroyan's most enigmatic characters, Joe is merely evasive and mysterious about his money's origin. He has no job and seems simply to reside at Nick's, seldom even rising from his chair. At most, he hints that the money is somehow tainted because his possession of it has entailed grief for others. About him, too, there is the aura of the Hollywood gangster. He is taciturn, shrewd, steady, and impassive, in obvious contrast to his errand runner, Tom, who is eager, effusive, and earnest in a tongue-tied sort of way. Yet, except in his penchant for bossing Tom around, there is no meanness in the man. As Joe himself claims, he is simply trying to see if it is possible to live in such a way as to bring no harm to anyone. At worst, he is somehow trying to expiate past sins.

Detached from the welter of activity in Nick's, Joe sits and steadily drinks, almost mechanically, until, without apparent forethought, he sends Tom off on what seems another trivial errand—to fetch him magazines, gum, and toys, things to keep him amused. It is, however, other humans that really interest and amuse Joe, especially Kitty Duval, the whore, in whom Joe sees an innocence and beauty, despite her profession.

In Nick's, Saroyan's happy place, the characters who find refuge provide a human carnival in their various chaotic activities. If Joe is impassive and at times remote, most of the others are irrepressible and ardent. The monologues of Kit Carson, encapsuling his eccentric life, gush forth breathlessly. Harry, the self-styled comedian, breaks into his sadly unfunny comic stories with little prodding, then whirls away in a dance routine when another character drops a coin in the jukebox. Willie, the pinball addict, drops nickel after nickel in the machine, beating away on it until he finally wins. Nick, the animated owner of the bistro, is loud and brassy, though hiding, through his gruffness, a golden heart. Wesley, once discovering the piano, plays the blues incessantly, providing a counterpoint to the more joyous, upbeat mood generated by the others. Only the sullen, gloomy, nearly silent Arab sits at the bar, unaffected by anything.

Like the idealized green worlds of Shakespearean comedy, Saroyan's honky-tonk is a place where the wonderful becomes the possible. It is a place of realized dreams, a place where instant love is possible, where a prostitute can regain her lost innocence, where bullies are destroyed, where the machine bends to man's will and repeatedly registers with whistles and waving flags his victory over it.

In mood and technique, *The Time of Your Life* is surrealistic. Many of the characters, like Joe, seem detached from any sort of past; they appear from the dark world outside as if from a void. Kit Carson is more an anachronistic figure from a tall tale than a valid character, needed to do in the dastardly Blick as a sort of heroic ringer for Joe. He shoots Blick offstage, as if to confirm that in Saroyan's happy world violent death is really not allowed. Character motivation, so carefully investigated in the drama of psychological realism, is often lacking. Joe seems to aid and abet Tom's love for Kitty with the same capriciousness with which he buys the newsboy's remaining papers.

There is a tumultuous quality to the play. Several actions go on simultaneously, like several vaudeville routines all being staged at once, and focus in the play keeps shifting from one character to another with no particular rationale. It is a three-ring technique that could easily become distracting, but Saroyan's skillful control makes it all work. For sheer ingenuity of design and experimental method, the play ranks with pieces such as Thornton Wilder's *The Skin of Our Teeth* (1942) as a classic of the American theater.

THE DARING YOUNG MAN ON THE FLYING TRAPEZE

First published: 1934
Type of work: Short story

A destitute writer, unable to find work, starves to death.

"The Daring Young Man on the Flying Trapeze," the story giving Saroyan's first collection of stories and sketches its title, initially appeared in *Story* magazine. The piece is basically an impressionistic reverie. Although told in the third person, it works through the recording consciousness of the unnamed protagonist, an impoverished writer who is literally starving to death. The writer's thoughts are disjointed and incoherent, as is characteristic of the stream-of-consciousness technique used by French novelist Marcel Proust, whose work the writer reads in the story.

The hunger gnawing at the writer's body presumably accounts for the randomness of his thoughts. Aware that his strength is slipping away, he sets out to look for work, fortified, as on many previous days, with only coffee and cigarettes. Little actually happens during his sojourn outside. He finds a penny in a gutter and speculates on its possible use, moves through the city (looking at his reflection in the window glass of stores and restaurants) and goes for an interview at an employment agency. He goes to the Y.M.C.A. and to the library to read Proust before returning to his room, where, at last, he falls face down on his bed and dies a peaceful, almost welcomed death. During these mostly mechanical actions, his mind races through a welter of disconnected ideas. The song of the title keeps humming in his brain, as do thoughts about public figures, writers, food, places, and his plan to write *An Application for Permission to Live*. His only interaction with another character occurs in his interview with the cold and efficient woman at the employment agency.

Saroyan's style in the story is poetic in its lyric statement and rich allusions to people and things. Like images of a life going quickly by, the names cascade through the character's mind, seemingly out of his control to shape them into a logical pattern. His desperation at times directs his thoughts to food and shelter, but his weakness does not allow him to hold or develop any singular thought for long. At the last, his thoughts drift up, away from his body, with his life, in death, becoming "dreamless, unalive, perfect." That dissolving of life into nothingness offers a quiet, dignified apotheosis of the human spirit that Saroyan makes almost enviable.

THE MAN WITH THE HEART IN THE HIGHLANDS

First published: 1936
Type of work: Short story

An old drifter is fed by a poor family and returns their kindness by winning food from others with his enchanted bugle.

"The Man with the Heart in the Highlands," later to evolve into the full-length play *My Heart's in the Highlands*, first appeared in a collection of Saroyan's short fiction entitled *Three by Three*, issued in 1936. It is a charming fantasy focusing on an old vagabond actor named Jasper MacGregor and his magical bugle, the use of which results in a minor miracle.

The narrator, Johnny, recalls the story as an experience he had in 1914, when he was six years old. Old MacGregor appears in front of Johnny's house on San Benito Avenue, presumably in Fresno, playing a solo on his bugle. In the exchange that follows, MacGregor insists that his heart is in the highlands of Scotland, where it grieves, though for what remains a mystery. The thirsty bugler begs for water, and Johnny takes him inside to give him some. When MacGregor asks for food, Johnny's father, a poet, sends Johnny to a local grocer, Mr. Kosak, to get cheese and bread on credit. At first adamant in his refusal, Kosak finally relents and sends Johnny home with the requested items and advice that the boy's father find work. The trio quickly down the food, but MacGregor remains unsatisfied. He begins searching the house for more to eat. When Johnny refuses to allow him to stew up a pet gopher snake, MacGregor resorts to using his bugle. His blowing is so loud that people from miles around gather by the house to listen. In exchange for playing music for each of them, MacGregor asks them to go and return with food. All comply, and the family and its guest feast grandly on the food from the newly stocked larder. MacGregor remains with Johnny and his father for more than two weeks, but he is then asked to go to an old people's home to serve as lead actor in an entertainment for the inmates. He complies, whereupon the poet once more sends his son to Kosak's store to get food on credit. Johnny returns with bird-seed and some maple syrup, which makes his father ponder his chances of writing great poetry fed on such fare.

The tale is fablelike and otherwise typical of Saroyan in its cheerfulness and buoyancy. Yet in its style and technique, it departs sharply from the earlier impressionistic sketch "The Daring Young Man on the Flying Trapeze." It develops largely through dialogue, with its narrative description held to an essential minimum, at times serving no other purpose than to identify the speaker of a line of the dialogue. It was this dramatic method that prompted the editor of *The One-Act Play Magazine* to suggest that Saroyan turn the piece into a one-act play, which became, in fact, the first form that the play *My Heart's in the Highlands* took.

The first portion of the story has Johnny functioning as an insistent inquisitor, interrogating MacGregor almost unmercifully. The staccato exchange of one-liners is direct and abrupt and is interrupted only when Johnny's father comes out to the porch. Then there is a similar exchange between father and son. Many of the lines, like theatrical dialogue, are elliptical sentence fragments. Questions and commands are dominant, with simple, monosyllabic words like "get" and "go" beginning the speeches and being repeated in tight patterns. Similar dialogue, though modified by more description as the story progresses, is used throughout the piece, notably in the exchanges between Johnny and Mr. Kosak. Coupled with diction that is very simple, the style is tough, brusque, and brittle. Furthermore, there is no probing of any character's thoughts, so the narrative point of view is wholly objective.

The relationship of Johnny and his father is particularly amusing. The father is crusty and demanding, cursing freely as he orders Johnny about, but Johnny more than holds his own, talking back and arguing with his father spiritedly. The father's cantankerousness is being visited on the son, but in an entirely humorous and harmless way. Neither the father nor the son is anything other than a Saroyan good guy in a gruff disguise.

Summary

In his 1966 critical study of William Saroyan, Howard Floan claimed that the writer's reputation would ultimately rest on the plays and fiction that he wrote prior to World War II. That view, issued when Saroyan was still actively writing, has since been validated.

The quintessential Saroyan pieces are unquestionably his early works. It is they that bear his peculiar stamp—the charm, good will, and delight in experimentation for which he will be remembered. Perhaps it was the war that robbed him of his youthful, wide-eyed acceptance and love of life that is the hallmark of his best work; perhaps it was the misfortune of success and his stormy marriage. In any case, from the war's end to his death, except for brief flashes of his former brilliance, Saroyan never again achieved the high critical esteem he once enjoyed.

Bibliography

Clurman, Harold. *Lies Like Truth*. New York: Macmillan, 1958.

Floan, Howard R. *William Saroyan*. New York: Twayne, 1966.

Lee, Lawrence, and Barry Gifford. *Saroyan: A Biography*. New York: Harper & Row, 1984.

McCarthy, Mary. *Sights and Spectacles, 1937-1956*. New York: Farrar, Straus and Cudahy, 1956.

Nathan, George Jean. *The Magic Mirror*. New York: Alfred A. Knopf, 1960.

_____. *The Theater Book of the Year, 1943-1944*. New York: Alfred A. Knopf, 1944.

Saroyan, Aram. *William Saroyan*. San Diego: Harcourt Brace Jovanovich, 1983.

Trilling, Diana. *Reviewing the Forties*. New York: Harcourt Brace Jovanovich, 1978.

John W. Fiero

NTOZAKE SHANGE

Born: Trenton, New Jersey
October 18, 1948

Principal Literary Achievement

Through her poetry, novels, and writing for the theater, Shange has given a distinctive voice to the experience of African-American women.

Biography

Ntozake Shange was born Paulette Williams in Trenton, New Jersey, on October 18, 1948, the eldest of four children. Her father, Paul T. Williams, was a surgeon, and her mother, Eloise Williams, was a psychiatric social worker and educator. During her childhood, her family moved from Trenton to upstate New York, then to St. Louis, Missouri.

Although many of the characters she writes about in her literary works are rural, poor, or members of the urban underclass, Shange grew up in a privileged, upper-middle-class environment. Because her father was a musician and painter as well as a ringside surgeon, the Williams household was frequently visited by well-known African-American musicians, writers, and sports figures. Cultural and artistic achievement was emphasized within the family environment; the members of the Williams family would entertain one another on Sundays with readings, music, and dance.

Despite this protective environment, Shange was spared neither the experience of racial discrimination nor that of sexual discrimination. As a young teenager in St. Louis, she was bused, as part of a desegregation program, to a mostly white school, where she felt out of place and was mistreated by her fellow students. She was also told that her career goals (she wanted to be a war correspondent or a jazz musician) were not appropriate to a woman. Experiences of these kinds are the roots of the interest in feminism and African-American issues that informs Shange's literary work.

Shange attended Barnard College in New York City, where she earned a bachelor's degree in American studies, emphasizing African-American poetry and music, in 1970. She married a lawyer; depression over his leaving her prompted several suicide attempts. (A later marriage, to jazz musician David Murray, would also dissolve.) She became active in political and social movements, concluding later, however, that they were not receptive to women. She went on to graduate study in Los Angeles, at the University of Southern California, where she earned a master's de-

gree in American studies in 1973. She changed her name in 1971 as part of her effort to establish her African-American identity. The name Ntozake means "she who comes with her own things," while Shange means "who walks like a lion." The new name clearly represents the strength and independence that Shange, like many of the characters in her writings, was seeking.

While living in Oakland, California, and teaching in the women's studies program of a nearby college, Shange began giving readings of the poems she had been writing, often collaborating with dancer Paula Moss, who would develop dances based on the poems. On occasion, Shange and Moss also collaborated with musicians. These experiments developed into the theatrical text *for colored girls who have considered suicide/ when the rainbow is enuf* (1976). Shange and Moss moved to New York City in 1975, where they performed the work in a variety of venues. Ultimately, their work attracted the attention of theatrical producers, first Woodie King, the preeminent producer of African-American theater in New York, then the New York Shakespeare Festival's Joseph Papp. Papp first produced the play at the festival's Public Theatre, then transferred it to a commercial theater in 1976, where it enjoyed a two-year run.

For colored girls who have considered suicide/ when the rainbow is enuf, which received almost uniformly favorable reviews, though it was also criticized for some of its feminist sentiments and its depiction of African-American men, catapulted Shange into the public eye. She continued to write plays, and Papp continued to produce them at the Public Theatre. Her next play was *A Photograph: Lovers in Motion* (1977). Subsequent plays include *Boogie Woogie Landscapes* (first produced in 1979) and *Spell No. 7: Geechee Jibara Quik Magic Trance Manual for Technologically Stressed Third-World People* (1979). Her adaptation of Bertolt Brecht's *Mutter Courage und ihre Kinder* (1941; *Mother Courage and Her Children*) was produced at the Public Theatre in 1980. In 1985, she adapted her novel *Betsey Brown* (1985) for the musical stage in collaboration with playwright Emily Mann and composer Baikida Carroll; the musical premiered in 1989.

In addition to acting in *for colored girls who have considered suicide/ when the rainbow is enuf,* Shange continued to perform her poetry. Her first published collections of poems were *Nappy Edges* (1978) and *Natural Disasters and Other Festive Occasions* (1979). Shange's first effort at writing fiction was the novella *Sassafrass* (1976), which she later expanded into the novel *Sassafrass, Cypress, & Indigo* (1982). Her major publications of the 1980's include *A Daughter's Geography* (1983), a collection of poems, and *See No Evil: Prefaces, Essays, and Accounts 1976-1983* (1984), a collection of prose pieces. Returning to an interest in the visual arts inspired by her father's activity as a painter, Shange collaborated with visual artist Wopo Holup for *From Okra to Greens: A Different Kinda Love Story* (1985), a collection of poems and illustrations based on a piece first performed in 1978, and wrote *Ridin' the Moon in Texas: Word Paintings* (1987), a collection of responses in prose and poetry to works of visual art by a variety of artists. Shange's poetry has received more consistently favorable critical response than her work in other forms.

Her writing does not fall easily into the traditional categories of drama, poetry, and fiction, however; it is noteworthy that she won the *Los Angeles Times* Book Prize for Poetry in 1981 for *Three Pieces* (1981), actually a collection of plays in poetry. She has received a number of other prestigious literary and theatrical awards, including two Obie (Off-Broadway) awards and the Pushcart Prize. Although her recent work for the theater has not attracted the attention lavished on *for colored girls who have considered suicide/ when the rainbow is enuf,* Shange has continued to write plays and to direct her own plays and those of others, often in experimental theater spaces or outside New York. She is an associate professor of drama at the University of Houston.

Analysis

Although Shange writes poetry, drama, essays, and fiction, she thinks of herself primarily as a poet. In an essay entitled "Unrecovered Losses/ Black Theatre Traditions" (the foreword to *Three Pieces*), she writes: "I am interested solely in the poetry of a moment" rather than in traditional dramatic structure, which she rejects. A Shange poem, play, or story typically is best understood as an accumulation of moments rather than as a sustained action or narrative. Many of her early works, especially, are structured as groupings of thematically related poems and lyric passages to be read or performed together. Her best-known play, *for colored girls who have considered suicide/ when the rainbow is enuf* is a series of poems spoken by a group of women. *Spell No. 7* (first produced in 1979) begins as a minstrel show, a collection of individual acts and routines.

Shange is concerned primarily with the inner lives of her characters—her work tends toward the lyrical exploration of that inner life, even in the context of a realistic, autobiographical novel such as *Betsey Brown*, where the main character's thoughts, imaginings, and reveries are as central to the impact of the story as her actions. The play *Boogie Woogie Landscapes* consists entirely of the thoughts of one central character, a young woman. Other figures who appear on the stage are her memories and dreams.

The episodic structure, lyricism, and intensely personal tone of Shange's work, however, do not exclude the expression of larger political and social concerns. Quite the contrary—Shange is concerned with the impact of political and social structures on the inner life of African Americans, particularly African-American women. Her description of her characters in one play as "afflicted with the kinds of insecurities and delusions only available to those who learned themselves thru the traumas of racism" could apply to all of her characters. Thematically, Shange's work reflects an ongoing concern not only with the implications of being black in a white world and female in a male world but also with the forms of discrimination that exist within African-American communities (based on skin color, cultural sophistication, urban or rural origins, and so forth) and the difficulties those pressures create for the individual attempting to arrive at a sense of self and a sense of racial identity. Shange refers frequently to the folk culture of rural, Southern African Americans. Although many of her more urbane characters look down upon that culture, it figures in Shange's work as a source of spirituality and a positive influence on the lives of the characters touched by it. Her works also contain frequent allusions to urban African-American culture, especially jazz and rhythm and blues music, and to the African-American literary heritage.

Important aspects of Shange's effort to find a distinctly African-American voice that reflects the positive values of African-American culture are her diction and orthography. She generally writes in a nonstandard English that reflects the grammatical characteristics of African-American dialects (the use of "they" for "their," for example). She uses this dialect not only to individuate characters who might speak that way but also as the narrator's or authorial voice in her poems and stories. In this way, she posits so-called "Black English" as a valid and expressive literary language rather than simply as a nonstandard dialect. Her early writings and most of her poems are rendered in lower case, using irregular spellings of some words and using both common and unusual abbreviations and symbols (the ampersand, for example) in place of others. In addition to asserting the nonstandard nature of her language, these devices make her writing a form of visual, as well as literary, art. For Shange, her orthography connects her writing with music and dance, which she considers the essential forms of African-American culture. Her unconventional spelling and orthography make the visual aspect of her writing akin to dance and make reading her work "not just a passive act and more than an intellectual activity," but an act that "demands rigorous participation."

FOR COLORED GIRLS WHO HAVE CONSIDERED SUICIDE/ WHEN THE RAINBOW IS ENUF

First produced: 1976 (first published, 1976)
Type of work: Play

Seven African-American women describe the pains and joys particular to being black and female in the United States.

For colored girls who have considered suicide/ when the rainbow is enuf is Shange's first, and most acclaimed, theater piece. It is not really a play in that it has no continuous plot or conventional development; it consists, rather, of a series of poetic monologues to be accompanied by dance movements and music—a form Shange calls the "choreopoem." Shange originally wrote the monologues as separate poems in 1974, then began performing them in California with choreography and musical accompaniment under their collective title. After moving to New York City, Shange continued work on the piece, which opened on Broadway to an enthusiastic reception in 1976.

The play is performed by seven women, each dressed in a different color. In the introduction, the Lady in Brown describes the purpose of the piece as to "sing a black girl's song/ bring her out to know herself." The majority of the poetic monologues describe relationships between black women and black men. The Lady in Yellow describes her loss of virginity the night after her high school graduation; the Lady in Brown tells of the first boyfriend she had, at the age of eight. Harboring a secret crush on Toussaint-Louverture, the eighteenth century Haitian patriot, the eight-year-old girl finds herself attracted to a young boy, also named Toussaint. The Lady in Red describes "the passion flower of southwest los angeles"—a woman who seduces men, then rejects them. In a contrapuntal passage, three of the women describe the violence and abuse suffered by women who are raped by male acquaintances. Several speeches concern the women's feelings of having been rejected by men, despite their love for them. The last, and longest, story, recounted by the Lady in Red, is of Beau Willie, a Vietnam veteran, and Crystal, with whom he has two children. Crystal leaves Beau Willie because of his drug-induced violence and his inability to provide for the children; ultimately, he returns and threatens to kill the children if she will not marry him.

Although the poetic monologues in the play are unquestionably fueled by rage at the mistreatment of black women by their own community, the rage is balanced by compassion and joy. Even Beau Willie, illiterate and adrift after serving his country, is portrayed as a victim as well as a victimizer. Even as the women speak out against their mistreatment, they find pleasure in music, dance, love (when it succeeds), and African-American history and heritage, the points of reference in all Shange's work. Shange's diction and style are, as always, ripe and exuberant, themselves testimonies to the joys of creation and expression available to the women on stage. The ultimate point of the theater piece is that the African-American woman must learn to accept herself and her ethnic identity and learn to find strength in herself through them, rather than depending on her relationship with a man for identity. The fact that there are only black women on stage, describing their experience in the first person, is itself an expression of Shange's thesis. In the final passage, the women talk of feeling that they are "missin somethin" even when in love. The Lady in Red describes an epiphany in which she finds the missing thing: "I found god in myself/ & i loved her." This line combines the sense of self, self-identity, and self-love that Shange's "choreopoem" is intended to create for black women. The image of the rainbow, enacted by the women dressed in different colors, derives from Shange's experience of seeing a rainbow and thinking that it represents for African-American women "the possibility to start all over again with the power and the beauty of ourselves."

A PHOTOGRAPH: LOVERS IN MOTION

First produced: 1977 (first published, 1981)
Type of work: Play

Five young African-American artists and professionals contend with the difficulty of achieving their aspirations and with changes in the relationships among them.

A Photograph: Lovers in Motion, first produced by the New York Shakespeare Festival in 1977, is a more conventionally structured play than *for colored girls who have considered suicide/ when the rainbow is enuf*. The characters exist as individually developed entities rather than as the storytellers of the earlier play: They interact through dialogue and action and advance a plot. Two of the characters, Sean and Michael, are struggling artists; he is a photographer, she is a dancer. Earl and Nevada are both attorneys; Earl is also a longtime friend of Sean. The fifth character, Claire, is a model who poses for Sean's photography.

The plot concerns Sean's relationships with the three women—Michael, Nevada, and Claire. All three are or have been his lovers; initially, he wants to maintain all these relationships, saying to Michael: "There are a number of women in my life/ who i plan to keep in my life." Nevada and Michael, however, each want an exclusive relationship with Sean, a situation that results in several confrontations among the characters, including a physical fight between Michael and Claire. Sean, who has decided he is most attracted to Michael, attempts to persuade Earl to take up with Nevada. The final scene is a confrontation among all five characters, from which three withdraw, leaving Sean and Michael together.

Although the emotional entanglements are played out fairly realistically, Shange retains her commitment to Poetic drama. In addition to realistic exchanges among the characters, the characters speak in lyrical passages describing their feelings and aspirations. Some of these lyrical sections are performed by a single character, alone on stage. Even when placed in the context of dialogue, the passages seem more like solo expressions than genuine exchanges. In the first scene, Sean has a long lyrical passage on his artistic hero, the nineteenth century French novelist Alexandre Dumas, to which Michael responds with a long poem on the image of a man she had heard of that has governed the choices she has made in her own relationships with men.

Michael and Sean also have poetic speeches concerning their feelings about and ambitions for their respective art forms, photography and dance. They describe these two arts in similar terms, as activities that enable them to fix a moment in time. Michael describes dance as allowing her to "be free in time/ a moment is mine always." Sean says that "a photograph is like a fingerprint/ it stays & stays forever."

A Photograph touches on a number of Shange's major themes. The issues concerning relationships between African-American women and men are addressed through the attitudes expressed by the characters, including Sean's view that he can be involved with as many women as he chooses, Nevada's desperate need for Sean, Claire's indiscriminate seductiveness, and Michael's attraction to a kind of man she knows to be dangerous. Shange raises racial issues through Nevada, who considers herself racially superior to the other characters, even though all are African-Americans, because her slave ancestors were freed earlier than those of the other characters. She looks down on the others and refers to them in disparaging racial terms, yet she is attracted to the very qualities she disparages in Sean.

As artists, Sean and Michael must also address the issues confronted by Shange's creative characters. Sean views his art as a means of satisfying personal needs. He sees the story of Alexandre Dumas' rejection of his illegitimate son as an allegory for his own unsatisfying relationship with his father, and also for the position of the black man in American culture. He fantasizes that he will receive the Nobel Prize for photographs that reveal the truth of African-American life. Michael questions his ambitions, suggesting that he is more interested in personal success than in the integrity of his art, or the lives of the human subjects he photographs.

The women in the play represent different options for Sean. Nevada is a snobbish, wealthy, professional woman who wants to support Sean's career but looks down on his artistic life-style. Claire, the model, represents the sensual side of Sean's work — his photographs of her are provocative, but they lack the seriousness of purpose to which he aspires. By choosing Michael as his true love, Sean chooses the one woman who understands and shares in the nature of the creative artist, and who challenges Sean to remain faithful to his higher aspirations.

SASSAFRASS, CYPRESS, & INDIGO

First Published: 1982
Type of work: Novel

Three sisters discover themselves through explorations of their ethnicity, sexuality, and creativity.

Sassafrass, Cypress, & Indigo incorporates Shange's earlier novella *Sassafrass* (1976). Apparently set during the Vietnam War era, it tells the story of Hilda Effania and her three daughters, African-American natives of Charleston, South Carolina, descendants of a family of weavers who did piecework for a wealthy white family. Hilda Effania has conventional aspirations for her daughters, hoping that each will marry well and happily, preferably to a doctor's son. She gives them the means to follow an upwardly mobile path: She sends Sassafrass to an exclusive Northern prep school, and Cypress to New York City to study ballet. She offers Indigo the opportunity to study the violin. Her daughters, however, are not content merely to follow the paths she suggests to them.

The daughters' stories are told separately. Indigo's story concerns her arrival at sexual maturity at the age of twelve and the resulting changes in her life. Her constant companions have been dolls she has made, and she sees herself as inhabiting a world of magical people and events. When she is on the verge of giving up her dolls, Uncle John the ragpicker, one of the mysterious figures she has befriended, gives her a violin. She becomes adept at improvising on the instrument, producing unconventional but compelling music. Initially resisting her mother's desire that she learn to play properly, she ultimately does learn to play conventionally.

For a while, Indigo uses the magical power of her fiddle as part of a motorcycle gang, the Geechee Capitans. Her epiphany occurs when she is being chased during a misadventure through vaults where African slaves were once imprisoned. At that point, she renounces her flirtation with a life of violence: "Indigo knew her calling. The Colored had hurt enough already." Ultimately, she goes to live with her aunt on a coastal Carolina island, where she learns the aunt's trade of midwifery.

Despite her education, Sassafrass eschews college in favor of the artistic life. A weaver like her mother, she has turned the craft of weaving into an art form, weaving expressive hangings rather than utilitarian cloth. In Los Angeles, she becomes involved with Mitch, a tenor saxophonist and drug addict, with whom she has a tempestuous relationship. Mitch wants Sassafrass not to be a weaver but to express herself through writing. They finally move together to an artistic commune in Louisiana, where Sassafrass finds herself through religion and leaves Mitch behind definitively.

Sassafrass's story is interwoven to an extent with Cypress's—during a stormy episode with Mitch, Sassafrass goes to visit her sister in San Francisco. Cypress has become a dancer in an African-American idiom rather than ballet, with a dance troupe called The Kushites Returned. She supports herself largely by selling drugs and surrounds herself with a bohemian entourage. She travels with The Kushites Returned back to New York City. Disgusted with the behavior of the male dancers around her, she enters the orbit of Azure Bosom, a radical feminist dance company by which she feels comforted and protected for a time. Feeling betrayed by one of the dancers in Azure Bosom, however, she falls into a relationship with Leroy, an alto saxophonist, with whom she finds happiness.

Sassafrass, Cypress, & Indigo combines third-person narration with other literary forms—it includes letters, journal entries, even recipes and magical spells. Although each sister's story is told separately, they are punctuated by letters to them from their mother which frame each story in terms of the mother's values and ambitions for them. This diversity mirrors the multiple pressures and issues the three women must face as they discover themselves. Each woman must, in her own way, reconcile the need for autonomy with her family and ethnic history, and with the urge to create. Indigo negotiates her mother's disapproval of her interest in magic and desire to leave the mythological aspect of their heritage behind by immersing herself in Geechee culture, where she is accepted as a midwife and woman of magic, while simultaneously studying the violin. Her fiddle playing, spell casting, and desire to help her race fit comfortably into the folk culture of the island. Through her immersion in non-Western religion, Sassafrass also finds a context that gives her natural creative outlet, weaving, a higher significance. Cypress explores several possibilities, expressing aspects of herself through her work with African-American and feminist dance companies. Through her relationship with Leroy, she is freed from the attempts of others to define her creativity and also freed to express her rage at the historical mistreatment of African Americans. Ultimately, all three women return to Charleston to attend to the birth of Sassafrass' child—each has found her own path and place in life, her own way of reconciling their common conflicts, and her own way of permitting her particular sense of personal and racial identity to create a context for her need to create.

BETSEY BROWN

First published: 1985
Type of work: Novel

Betsey Brown, a thirteen-year-old girl in St. Louis, negotiates the pressures of growing up in a racially charged atmosphere.

Although all Shange's works contain elements of autobiography, *Betsey Brown* is the most overtly autobiographical, clearly deriving from Shange's own experiences as a young teenager in St. Louis, Missouri, during the 1950's. Like Shange, Betsey is a member of an upper-middle-class black family originally from the North. Her father, Greer, is a physician, while her mother, Jane, is a social worker. Many of the book's episodes are universal adolescent experiences: Betsey contends with her physical maturation, her desire for a boyfriend, and her need for privacy and a sense of her own identity. She also, however, confronts issues that are specific to the African-American experience.

Stylistically, *Betsey Brown* is more conventional than *Sassafrass, Cypress, & Indigo*. The narrative follows Betsey through a series of experiences from an omniscient third-person point of view that makes the reader privy to Betsey's thoughts and emotions in addition to her behavior. The point of view shifts periodically, so that the thoughts and motivations of the adults in Betsey's life (her parents and her grandmother, for example) are made available to the reader as well. In this way, the reader is able to share Betsey's adolescent perspective on the world around her while also gaining some perspective on her through the thoughts of those responsible for her environment.

The Brown household is distinctive—Greer, who is intensely concerned that his children grow up with an appreciation of African-American culture, wakes them each morning by beating on a conga drum (Shange's own father was a percussionist) and by playing jazz and rhythm and blues on the household radio. Jane is somewhat disapproving of this raucous behavior, but accepts it out of her love for Greer; Greer's mother-in-law, Vida, looks down upon him as too overtly African for her tastes. This intraracial discrimination causes the major conflicts in the narrative. Betsey identifies with her father's appreciation for the sensual side of African-American culture—her ambition is to sing with Ike and Tina Turner as an "Ikette." Her identification with African-Americanism is only heightened by her being bused to a white school, where she feels alienated and out of place. Her mother's tacit disapproval of Betsey's particular sense of her race causes Betsey to attempt to run away to a place where she can be the kind of African American she wants to be, away from the pressures of white society and her own mother's desire for gentility. The tension between Greer's and Jane's respective senses of themselves as black people also creates a rift between them, which causes Jane to leave her family for a period after Greer insists to her that he wants their children to participate in a demonstration against segregation.

Another set of events that address social issues within the African-American community has to do with the Brown family's efforts to secure domestic help. The people they hire are other African Americans who have come to St. Louis from rural areas of the South and are somewhat looked down upon by the urbanites. After Betsey and her three siblings terrorize one such character, Betsey is made to feel ashamed by a friend of hers whose own mother does domestic work. A subsequent domestic has better luck with the family, only to lose her job after committing a crime.

Although the tensions governing the story between an insular black community and the surrounding white world, between growing children and the adults trying to maintain order, and between different understandings of African-American cultural and social aspirations are not fully resolved at the end of the story, they are sufficiently resolved to allow the family to continue as a unit and to permit Betsey some sense of having her own place in her world.

Summary

Ntozake Shange's effort to give expression to the African-American experience, particularly the experience of African-American women, has led her to innovation at every level of her writing—from her choices of subject matter, to the unconventional forms of her plays and novels, to her distinctive diction and orthography. Her interests in African-American culture, both urban and rural, and in music, dance, and the visual arts are evident throughout her literary output. The dominant trend in her work has been toward a more personal kind of writing. In her earlier works, she embodies her concerns in those of archetypal characters; subsequently, she has acknowledged the basis of her work in her own experience and biography more directly.

Bibliography

Chinoy, Helen Krich, and Linda Walsh Jenkins, eds. *Women in American Theatre.* New York: Crown, 1981.

Christ, Carol P. *Diving Deep and Surfacing: Women Writers on Spiritual Quest.* Boston: Beacon Press, 1980.

Flowers, Sandra Hollin. " 'Colored Girls': Textbook for the Eighties." *Black American Literature Forum* 15 (Summer, 1981): 51-54

Richards, S. L. "Conflicting Impulses in the Plays of Ntozake Shange." *Black American Literature Forum* 17 (Summer, 1983): 73-78

Rushing, A. B. "For Colored Girls, Suicide or Struggle." *The Massachusetts Review* 22 (Autumn, 1981): 539-550.

Squier, Susan Merrill, ed. *Women Writers and the City: Essays in Feminist Literary Criticism.* Knoxville: University of Tennessee Press, 1984.

Timpane, John. "The Poetry of a Moment": Politics and the Open Form in the Drama of Ntozake Shange." *Studies in American Drama, 1945-Present* 4 (1989): 91-101.

Philip Auslander

SAM SHEPARD

Born: Fort Sheridan, Illinois
November 5, 1943

Principal Literary Achievement

Shepard's is one of the most individualistic voices on the American stage, and his work is considered the most enduring postmodern dramatic literature of the 1970's and 1980's.

Biography

Born on an Army base in 1943, growing up mainly on a California ranch, arriving in New York City in the 1960's, living for three years in London, gifted in timpani, devoted to sports, and an outdoorsman of the working kind, Sam Shepard is almost a living example of the kind of characters he puts on the stage. After high school graduation (in Duarte, California, in 1960), Shepard experimented with several life-styles and occupations, including ranchhand, sheep shearer, and rock-and-roll musician. The early successes of one-act plays such as *Cowboys* (1964) and *Rock Garden* (1964) (part of Kenneth Tynan's 1969 Broadway revue, *Oh! Calcutta!*), especially in the Off-Off-Broadway theaters of New York in the 1960's, gave him the incentive to continue in drama (other genres, as well as music and art, drew him and still invest his plays with variety and a unique creative signature). His marriage to O-lan Johnson in 1969 produced a son; he also has a daughter by Jessica Lange.

His serious interest in writing drama began in 1964, with the production of *Cowboys* in New York, which was quickly followed by several other one-act plays, the most familiar being *Chicago* (1965). His long canon of plays from that time is attributable in part to his prolific imagination and in part to his indifference about editing or polishing his work, preferring to get it produced and letting it stand or fall in its original form. He once remarked, "I like to start with as little information about where I'm going as possible." Some critics have found fault with this tendency on his part, noting that his plays lack the cohesion and sense of closure usually found in successful stage work.

His first full-length success, *Operation Sidewinder* (1970), was performed as part of the inaugural season of the new producer/directors of Lincoln Center, Jules Irving and Herbert Blau. The play, combining American Indian folklore with high-technology weaponry, drew strong critical response in both directions, but it clearly marked Shepard's debut as an important new writer of the American cultural present.

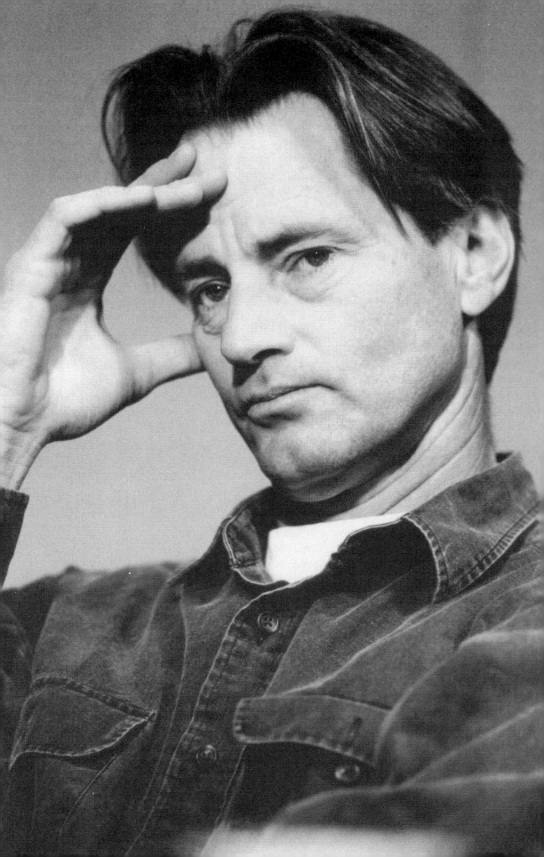

Awards have come his way with alarming ease and regularity: A Yale University fellowship (1967), Obies (ten since 1967), and a Pulitzer Prize in 1979 for *Buried Child* (1978) are among two dozen honors bestowed on him by the theater world and by cultural foundations such as the Guggenheim and Rockefeller foundations. Continuing to write for the stage despite his financial success as screenwriter and actor, his *A Lie of the Mind* (1986), another anguished examination of the disfigured family, brings to the stage once again the conflict among passion, family, and a strangely American sense of lost dignity. Most of his plays since 1976 have debuted at the Magic Theatre, San Francisco, where he is playwright in residence.

Shepard moves equally well in the world of American film. His own screenplays are distinctly Shepard: visual, asymmetrical, and obtuse, full of creative bravado, not entirely interested in telling the story in a coherent way. As a film actor, Shepard has been unable to keep from the public spotlight. *Days of Heaven* (1978) won for him critical acclaim; he also played Eddie in the film version of his own play *Fool for Love* (play, 1983; film, 1985) opposite Kim Basinger. He played Dolly Parton's husband in *Steel Magnolias* in 1989. His partnership with Jessica Lange, after her relationship with Mikhail Baryshnikov, brought him more tabloid space than any playwright could ever expect to receive; they starred together in *Country* (1984). His screenplay for *Paris, Texas* won a Palm d'Or in 1985, the prestigious Cannes Film Festival prize.

Analysis

Sam Shepard has something of the American cowboy in him—the dreamer, the drifter, the outdoorsman, the individualist, the misfit. Yet these traits are coupled with a deft linguistic touch, a visual imagination based on observation, and a sophisticated view of the value of myth in articulating the modern human condition. His works tend to be enigmatic; they seem almost right but somehow off the mark, as though too much reality would get in the way of Shepard's describing the chaos of actual day-to-day existence. Shepard is obsessed with a "loss" of some kind, often identified by critics as the failure of the American spirit, of "America in flames," or as the dilemma of the rugged individual consumed by high technology in a world too complex for individual achievement and success. Shepard's heroes are, if not sociopaths, at least angry and isolated loners, always bordering on the violent; when this violence is turned against women, the plays get frighteningly sadistic. There is an edge of Old Testament righteousness gone sour, as though too strict an upbringing has evoked a rebel response—but with an underlying need for rules just under the dialogue.

The structure of the plays is imperfect. Superficially realistic in the later plays, but stylized and theatrical in the earlier work, the plays move quickly into what has been called "supra-realism," an enlarged version of realistic, detailed life that somehow transcends itself to speak, however vaguely, of larger orders and disorders in the playwright's universe. Robert Cohen, in his discussion of *Buried Child*, defines supra-realism as "a device that seeks patterns beneath the surface of everyday reality, and meanings in the silences that punctuate everyday speech." Far from being a symbolic writer or an allegorist, Shepard manages to speak of reality while at the same time tapping into universal combats with his specified opponents. For example, Hoss and Crow in *The Tooth of Crime* (1972), besides fighting their own fight to the death, are fighting the eternal battle of the successful figure struggling to keep his reputation versus the newcomer, full of energy and undaunted by the reputation of the current champion. In this work, as in *Geography of a Horse Dreamer* (1974), the artist himself is the subject of the action.

The same Jack London or James Dean attitude that can make the male American seem romantic and inaccessible at the same time is present in Shepard's work. There is also a taint of incest, a hint of forbidden love, in the character studies as the plots unravel, never spoken directly but implied by the narrative voice (as in *Fool for Love*) or inferred from the dialogue (as in *Buried Child*). If the work is autobiographical in any way, it is in Shepard's obsession with inter-family affections and emotions, both tender and violent. While it would be too facile to say that Shepard is searching for his father, the characters in his work are all struggling with the reality of a father who fell under the demands of American individuality. The obsessive, often violent, attraction of male to female protagonist cannot be ignored when examining his work, but it would be a mistake to simplistically identify those themes with the playwright's own biography. The attraction takes on its violent stage form as a signal to the depth and importance of essential relationships such as male/female love or family ties. No social philosopher, Shepard stays well inside the personal worlds of his own experience, neither casting about for historically viable motifs nor seeking commercial success. His ideas and images are distinctly his own.

Shepard's plays are probably parts of a whole imaginative construction, as were the works of Eugene O'Neill, with whom Shepard is often compared, and whose family served as grist for his mill as well. The whole epic, whose parts will emerge as Shepard continues his work, develops the chaotic impulses that work within him. His single subject is an examination of what went wrong, somewhere, somehow, in his life as well as in the American Dream. His concentration on family distortions allows ready comparisons with other American playwrights, such as Arthur Miller and Clifford Odets, who also found their themes inside the family life.

Shepard's major themes are the loss of the American Dream, the romance of the West, the artist's exploitation by commerce, the "musical" significance of contemporary dramatic rhythms, the breakdown of the family unit because of unspoken imperfections on the part of the parents, and the ongoing search for place and identity in a fragmented world. In the final analysis, however, themes are not as important as lyrics for Shepard. Ruby Cohn names her chapter on Shepard "The Word is my Shepard," and Bonnie Marranca speaks at length of Shepard's poetic voice. In a sense, all his plays are songs, written to a rhythm and beat that is entirely his own. They make sense only in near-rhymes, and the parallels to myth are imperfect, sketched in, barely recognizable. Neither a thinking playwright nor an intellectual analyst, but an instinctive observer of human beings, Shepard is writing song lyrics for the stage, caring not so much about the content as the amorphous, yet distinctive, form and rhythm of human relationships.

LA TURISTA

First produced: 1966 (first published, 1968)
Type of work: Play

In mirrored acts, a pair of tourists fights the hallucinating effects of disease, assisted by a voodoo doctor and his son.

Shepard wrote his first two-act play while living in Mexico; the mirroring acts give him a structure for his ideas that would work in several subsequent plays, including *The Tooth of Crime*, *Geography of a Horse Dreamer*, and *Operation Sidewinder*. Shepard takes advantage of the automatic tendency on the part of the audience to compare and contrast the events of each act, thereby informing both parts in the examination.

Kent and Salem are traveling in Mexico (in act 1) when Kent becomes very sick with "La Turista," the Mexican slang name for diarrhea. In a crazed, fevered state, Kent is "treated" by a native doctor and his son; Salem interrupts the dialogue with long monologues of the past, a device that Shepard had employed in earlier, short plays. Salem's speeches add color and shadow to the bare plot. In act 2, which takes place earlier in time than act 1, Kent suffers from sleeping sickness (judging from the symptoms). Again, a doctor and his son are called in to help; Kent becomes violent in his hallucinations, eventually crashing through the wall of his room.

"La Turista" is both the tourist and his disease—a displacement of the artist, with concomitant suffering. Two figures, echoed in each act, on one level the doctor and his son, are on another level the appeal of the hero to a cosmic cure to a universal sickness. The two invade the privacy of the tourist with a curative, but at the expense of forcing Kent and Salem into the mythic structure of the alien place, transforming "tourist" mentalities (removed and temporary) into serious participating members of an old cult. The acts are reversed in time, the second act coming before the trip to Mexico of the first act.

The first act's disease is replaced in the second act by a kind of sleeping sickness, to counteract which Kent is walked up and down until he can find the strength to leave the theater entirely. His rambling, inchoate monologue, underscored by "Doc," tells the story of Doc himself, in the present tense, seeking "the beast" in a Western setting. In the second act, the "cult" participation involves the storytelling and the crying out of the fevered victim, a freeing of the soul from the body. The disease invading Kent is insidious, destructive from the inside, and one of its symptoms is delirium, here vocalized in ranting speeches whose content seems arbitrary, almost a jazz improvisation around a theme. As the monologue climaxes in pain and absurd sacrifice, Kent swings from a rope, crashing through the upstage wall, leaving his silhouette in the drywall, like a cartoon character in an absurdist universe.

Critics point out several important features of this play: the mirrored acts, each of which contains a reflection of the other; the cigarette brand names of the characters (although no critic explicates this detail to satisfaction); and the Western pioneer motif, especially of Kent's final speeches; the enigmatic characters of the Mexicans; the cold, almost brutal love relationship. Easy connections with cigarette brands, Kent and Salem, can be made, as an indictment of American myth, for example, but in this early work, any speculation as to real meaning takes more effort from the critic than the playwright put into the play's subcontext.

THE TOOTH OF CRIME

First produced: 1972 (first published, 1974)
Type of work: Play

Two rock-and-roll hoodlums duel with words and bravado for the commercial turf of musical stardom.

The Tooth of Crime is a large idea, a play imbued with the energy and chaos of jazz and rock, a 1960's look at the future alterations in the nature of the duel, and the challenge of sexual and power-oriented dominance as found in competitiveness. This play attempts to combine street-gang dueling traditions with the commercial competition of the rock-and-roll industry: Hoss ("Rip Torn only younger") opens the first act with a "flyting," or bragging of his superiority; Crow ("just like Keith Richard") opens the second act as the young upstart ready to duel the famous but aging Hoss.

The result, despite its shouting violence and rapacious arena, is a strangely touching portrait of the aging artist, torn between continuing popularity and an admission of his own mortality. The cycle of leadership and popular appeal drives the plot forward, from Hoss's early claims to superiority, through his moments of doubt (in which he is encouraged by Becky, his "moll," and his gang of singing hoods), to the second-act duel itself, a stand-off. The finale, an imperfect and inconclusive scene in which Hoss kills himself, ostensibly to take Crow's victory from him by choosing to "lose to the big power," implies that the cycle will continue, with Crow eventually finding the same hollowness, only temporarily concealed by the "image" of his commercial and popular success.

Shepard adds songs to this piece, the lyrics in the country and western style, the music in the rock-and-roll idiom. Hoss's gang (called Four Guys when singing together) acts as commentary to the action, underscoring the violence and combativeness of the scenes. Taken alone, the combined western/rock musical numbers do not make much sense, but as background to the almost dancelike violence of the players, they serve as a kind of film score to the nonverbal combat: "We're fighting ourselves. . . . He's my brother and I gotta kill him."

The central act, a rock duel between Crow and Hoss, substitutes for physical violence a competition using language instead of weapons; the metaphor makes this play more a musical combat than a story with a through line. The dialogue, often a forced slang, part authentic and part fabricated, moves the play forward slowly. This is a futuristic world, where violence is delimited by power combats on "turf," and each player tries to get "kills" as a way of keeping score. In the process, the "duel" takes on thematic substance—the role of jazz in the emancipation of the slaves is one particularly artificial and awkward example of the intrusion of styles into the dramatic action.

Hoss's "moll," Becky Sue, handles his weapons and serves as messenger to the other sinister participants in the game. In one scene she acts out both the role of sexual victim and sexual assailant, stripping herself with her own hands while protesting to an invisible assaulter, assumed to be Hoss. Difficult to cast and stage, *The Tooth of Crime* does not receive the same number of productions as other, more realistic, Shepard works. Nevertheless, it deserves consideration as a rock-and-roll musical drama, along with such musicals as *Hair* (1968) and the film *Tommy* (1975).

GEOGRAPHY OF A HORSE DREAMER

First produced: 1974 (first published, 1974)
Type of work: Play

A prophetic dreamer of horse race results, kidnapped by hoodlums, changes his predictions to dog races and is rescued by his brothers.

In this portrait of the artist exploited by big business (a recurrent theme with Shepard, who nevertheless found a commercial outlet for his talents quite early in his career), the artist is a dreamer and his dreams are his art. The hero, Cody, has been kidnapped by thugs, who cull race winners from his dreams, moving him from place to place. As in all Shepard's two-act plays, the two acts bear likenesses that underscore their differences. In act 1, it is horse racing that Cody dreams about, but in act 2, he has switched to dog racing. Once the thugs understand the switch, they continue to let the dreamer do his work. Cody's brothers rescue him from the Doctor (a sinister figure representing cold-blooded murder) in a violent ending, which unfortunately seems almost tacked on to the mood of the rest of the piece.

A displacement from one's locale, another standard Shepard theme, is what makes the dreams so vivid and so destructive. When Cody is removed from his (Western) homeland, he suffers. Shepard is saying that the artist has been displaced from his "geography," in this case the American West, where much of Shepard's own personal youth was spent. From the play's opening, Cody has been dreaming of the past rather than the present (the opening act is called "The Slump"). The thugs will be in trouble with their boss, Fingers, if Cody ("Mr. Artistic here") does not come up with some winners soon. The whole operation has fallen on hard times since Cody's failures; they have gone from fancy hotels to this cheap motel, where even the wallpaper goes against the grain of dreaming.

The hero-artist, handcuffed to a bed, is a commodity in one of its sinister forms; when the dreams turn from horses to dogs, the artist is exploited even more. The disorientation caused by the boarded-up windows and the blindfolded travel have caused him to lose his sense of place. The fact that the brothers save him, rescuing him in the only really violent scene in the play, is important. The goons of society, milking and draining the artist, will eventually be overcome by the irresistible force of brotherly comradeship.

As in Shepard's other two-act plays, the mirror images of the two acts help the reader to understand each of the images themselves. Cody needs a sense of geography to keep his dreams intact; when he dreams of dog races, the implication is that he has been moved, possibly to Florida. (Shepard worked on this piece while in London; he raised and bred racing dogs during this period.)

If there is significance to the pair of hoodlums watching Cody, it lies in the contrast between them; there is the hard-shell Santee, against whom the more sympathetic Beaujo offers relief. They are there for exposition more than for plot, because neither character serves as more than an instrument; there are no significant changes in their personalities. The drama is not about them. Fingers, a sinister offstage figure until the end of the play, is the real antagonist, and Cody remains in his power until freed by his brothers. The Doctor, a symbol of death as much as an integral part of the crooked gang, has the real power, however, as shown by the deference paid to him by Fingers. Until the entrance of Fingers and the Doctor, the reader is led to believe that Fingers is the main force, but in fact it is the Doctor who figures as the main evil.

As ingenious as the basic plot idea is, the possibilities of the situation do not seem to be fully exploited; the piece remains stationary until the climax. It is essentially the staging of a large metaphor: The artist, who dreams of possibilities, is held captive by money interests, displaced and disoriented, until rescued by a return to his roots.

BURIED CHILD

First produced: 1978 (first published, 1979)
Type of work: Play

The return of grandson Vince to the family homestead churns up a past that has been buried for years in the cornfield.

A family drama, a strange parody of the warm families of many previous American plays, the three-act *Buried Child* is perhaps the best known of Shepard's work. From the striking images of the old man on the couch to the moment when his son carries in the buried child from the cornfield, the play embodies all that is best about

Shepard's combining of realistic family drama with larger mythic patterns. Either as "American Gothic" or as a modern-day version of Greek tragedy, the play invites examination on many levels.

The opening of the play sets the tone of the entire piece; Dodge is lying asleep or drunk on the couch, "a sedentary cougher solaced only by television and whiskey," as Ruby Cohn describes him. He holds the center of the stage while his family— wife Halie, an aging flirt in league with the local clergyman; half-wit Tilden, silently returning again and again to the family secret; vicious Bradley, crippled but powerful, full of sexually destructive energy—lives a half-life in the shattered family home. When a young grandson brings home his girl to meet the family, the worst in them is called out, and one can see the decay of the American family in general, caused in part by the wanderlust of the previous generation (brought about by war) and in part by the avoidance of unhappy truths—family secrets hidden away in the cornfield.

Grandson Vince, traveling adventurously through the country with his girlfriend, drops in on the family for some reminiscences; his father Tilden does not recognize him, nor do his grandparents. The prevailing sense of the awkward, unwelcome meeting is that the youth of the house—its promise, its reputation, its future—has been "buried" along with a real corpse, the buried child, the secret in the corn. Although far from explicit, the plot seems to suggest that the buried child is the result of an incestuous union of the mother and one of the sons.

As in all Shepard's "family cycle" plays, which include *True West* (1980) and *Curse of the Starving Class* (1976), the ostensible battle of the family is enlarged by the oddly symbolic details. The most important of these is the buried child of the title (reminiscent of the absent child in Edward Albee's 1962 play, *Who's Afraid of Virginia Woolf?*, dug up from the corn rows and tragically reintroduced; the child is the buried secret of the family that must be dealt with in order for the family finally to find rest in the present. The details of the play—such as Tilden pouring corn husks over Dodge, with the corn husks sticking in his hair and hat; Bradley, the older brother, crippled but powerful, his artificial leg a prop dominating the action as Bradley dominates Vince's girl, forcing his finger into her mouth; the suggestion that Haltie has spent the night with the minister (she comes home in a different dress from the one she wore when she left)—add up to a very dark family portrait indeed. The mother, cheating on the old man, is a shadow of the lust that once dominated the family. Tilden's simple madness, contrasted with his former football glory, transforms his character from the pathetic mold of Lenny in John Steinbeck's *Of Mice and Men* (1937) into a brooding giantlike Tiresias (the seer in Sophocles' *Oedipus Tyrannus* from the fifth century B.C.); Bradley's artificial leg may remind one of the lame king in the Arthurian legends and the quest for the Holy Grail. Finally, the last image of the play leaves the entire story only partly told, perhaps hinting that Shepard will return to this destructive family in subsequent work.

This is not the chronicle of a real family, despite the play's realistic trappings, but the universal struggle of every family to reconcile itself to the imperfections, the "humanness" of the parents, whose offspring, losing their youth day by day, have romanticized them beyond recognition. The play is not so much about revealing secrets as it is about forgiving or understanding the parents as people; however, Shepard allows no reconciliation or forgiveness to enter into the play's climactic scene.

The tone of *Buried Child* marks a turning point for Shepard. While still far from a realistic play, it depicts an actual family dwelling, with recognizable characters acting in a "real" world. It is a family gone wrong somewhere in its past. Critics have offered various explanations for the central symbol, the "buried child"—the secret that has disintegrated the family. Is the "child" a real one, possibly the product of an incestuous union? How did it die? Who was responsible for the burial itself; was it agreed upon by the family or was it the act of an individual (Tilden carries the little body wrapped in rags onstage at the end of the play)? How does the return of Vince precipitate the play's action?

These and other questions will remain, but critics agree that a deeply mythic, symbolic "death" is implied in the action. Whether Shepard meant to depict a real "child" or was returning to his theme of a lost American spirit is a matter of theatrical interpretation. As a stage event, *Buried Child* is a powerful experience, full of tensions and puzzles, gripping as it unfolds. Such acts as Tilden slowly showering the sleeping figure of his father with corn husks linger in the mind long after the play is over. When the play is done carelessly, the flaws in its exposition get in the way of the theatrical experience, which turns into an exasperating and unfulfilling evening. When performed effectively, it never leaves the imagination.

TRUE WEST

First produced: 1980 (first published, 1981)
Type of work: Play

Two brothers, rivals in a writing contest, debate their views of the lost American West and compete for their mother's affection.

Part of a "family trilogy," *True West* differs from Shepard's other plays in its almost lighthearted bantering dialogue between the two protagonists. Austin, one brother of a pair, is conservative and formal, fitting into society with reasonable comfort. Lee, on the other hand, is the cowboy misfit character that Shepard uses in virtually every drama. They are both writing a film scenario about the true West, and their conversation, wildly funny in the beginning of the play, but deepening as the play moves forward, is actually a debate about what (if anything) made America great. Shepard is, in a way, having a conversation with himself in this play, taking the two sides in the form of the two brothers.

The kitchen setting is appropriate, especially in the light of the late arrival of the mother, the actual adjudicator between the two brothers and the person whose affection they both seek. The two brothers are central to Shepard's mythology. The brief appearance of the mother at the end demonstrates what the competition was really about. The kitchen is her domain, despite the fact that the two brothers have temporarily claimed it for their lives and their debate. Again, the family in disarray, the siblings at odds and representing diverging life-styles, the homage to a lost American tradition represented by the cowboy's life—all the trademarks of Shepard are here. What sets this play apart from the others is the humor with which Shepard deals with the subject. The dialogue, relatively realistic and conversational here, plays the two brothers off each other both in content and in linguistic style. The proliferation of physical objects, in the manner of Eugène Ionesco, underlines the immovability and intractability of the "real" world as opposed to the world of the imagination that both brothers are seeking to portray in their screenplays.

The two brothers here bear virtually no resemblance to Tilden and Bradley from the earlier *Buried Child*. Their articulation, their energy, and their obvious partnership (despite their differences) is antithetical to the family of Dodge and Haltie; here is found a masculine bonding within the combat, a family unit despite all the superficial antagonisms.

FOOL FOR LOVE

First produced: 1983 (first published, 1983)
Type of work: Play

Eddie and May, lovers and half-siblings, fight out their jealousies while the otherworldly absent father drinks and comments on their past.

Shepard begins the stage directions of *Fool for Love* with an admonition that could be applied to his whole artistic life: "This play is to be performed relentlessly without a break." Stepping aside from the two-act form that worked in his past few plays, but in no way retreating to the short "sketches" of his first Off-Off Broadway successes, *Fool for Love* is a long single-minded battle; in dance terms, it is an "apache," or violent combat between lovers. Frank Rick refers to this play as "a western for our time," seeing Eddie and May as "gunslingers."

The scene is a seedy motel room "on the edge of the Mojave Desert," lit by neon from the window covered with Venetian blinds—a place of transition, flight, and homelessness. May, a beautiful woman in her late twenties, has fled here to escape her half-brother, Eddie, whose pursuit has reduced itself to an obsessive search of the countryside for his lover and half-sister.

This play is another of Shepard's combats between two related forces. The stylized and energetic choreography of the fights is distinctive, and it brings a kind of ritualistic dancelike universality to the piece. Eddie has tracked down his fleeing half-sister May and tries, with words, memories, and physical force, to persuade her to come back home with him. Half-brother and half-sister, desperately and destructively in love, confront the impossibility of their situation in this seedy, transitory place, a metaphor for the inability of the two lovers to find a permanent place for themselves in the world.

Again, the combat motif substitutes for a truly dramatic situation—the audience is not so much concerned with whether Eddie will win May as with whether May will survive the anger and vengeance of the jealous lover who has found her and will apparently do anything to force her to return with him. A mild-mannered suitor, Martin, acts as a foil for the powerful and destructive force of Eddie, a cowboy who ropes the bedposts during the whole show. At one point Eddie stands against the wall, digging his heels into the woodwork, a kind of silhouette not unlike the final image in *La Turista*—man, flattened out, two-dimensional, a presence by the strength of his outline on the wall.

The extreme down-left stage is occupied by a rocking chair and an old man in grays and subdued tones; he is the father of both Eddie and May, telling his story in disjointed monologue, drinking and dreaming, neither in the world of the motel or entirely out of it—on several occasions he shares the bottle of liquor with Eddie and May, either by placing it on the "real" table in the motel room or by pouring a drink into Eddie's cup.

The old man is the closest that Shepard gets to identifying and articulating the father figure that dominates his work. In the father's monologues, a sort of dream remembrance, one hears the father's side of the story, culminating in the realization that the father was a bigamist whose children are now in love with each other in a destructive way. Eddie was the son of one family that he maintained in one town; May was the daughter of another family. The moment of their meeting, which Eddie remembers vividly, was the moment their love was born.

The set, in one sense a simple, scaled-down motel room and in another sense a surreal fighting pit with amplified walls, puts the play into the "supra-real" category. As an ever-present counterbalance to the hyperrealism of the main scene, the old man is visible in a black, undefined space, suspended in time, talking as though from the shadows; he is neither in Eddie's head nor in May's head, but is a presence representing the past.

The story proceeds by impassioned argument between Eddie and May, Eddie roping the bedposts in a vaguely sinister, threatening gesture, May preparing for her "date," moving in and out of the bathroom during the course of the argument. The only relief in the story is the introduction of Martin, a mild-mannered local suitor to May, representing not so much a real threat to the Eddie-May relationship as an example of the kind of safe, even timid, life May would face without the energy of Eddie's love. Yet, at his entrance, Martin tackles and overpowers Eddie, a temporary physical advantage quickly countered by the psychological advantage that Eddie has: He knows what his relationship is to May and his power over her. Another complication, this time an offstage presence, is apparently a rich woman who follows Eddie from place to place; she arouses a jealousy that shows May to be equally obsessed by this destructive relationship, and she forms a menacing presence outside the temporarily safe motel room. An offstage figure, signalled onstage by flashing and whirling headlights shining through the blinds of the window, she actually shoots out Eddie's windshield in a moment of dangerous intrusion.

Far more than an incestuous love story, *Fool for Love* can be seen as a psychological examination of the duality in the human psyche. It is about the obsession of one part of a person trying to find the other part. The themes of search and pursuit of the separated ideal, and the combat between those halves, will be told again in the screenplay *Paris, Texas* and in Shepard's *A Lie of the Mind*, in which the female figure suffers such a severe beating that she requires hospitalization. Thus, Shepard takes to its extreme the question of whether the male/female split in every human being is a permanent and self-destructive schism or is a temporary separation to be eventually reconciled.

Summary

Sam Shepard, as much a poet as a playwright, prevails as a major literary and theatrical voice because his themes speak to a sense of lost dignity in American culture and society. What the American West means to Shepard and his characters is so successfully expressed in the plays that he will always be seen as a critic of the present day, despite his own natural abilities to survive in it. All Shepard's plays are cries for another time, whether expressed in the ultramodern idiom of rock and roll or in the voices of lost American heroes misplaced on the concrete sidewalks of the big city.

Bibliography

Auerbach, Doris. *Sam Shepard, Arthur Kopit, and the Off-Broadway Theater.* Boston: Twayne, 1982.

Cohen, Robert. *Theatre.* Palo Alto, Calif.: Mayfield, 1981.

Cohn, Ruby. *New American Dramatists: 1960-1980.* New York: Grove Press, 1982.

Hart, Lynda. *Sam Shepard's Metaphorical Stages.* Westport, Conn.: Greenwood Press. 1987.

Marranca, Bonnie, ed. *American Dreams: The Imagination of Sam Shepard.* New York: Performing Arts Journal Publications, 1981.

Marranca, Bonnie, and Gautam Dasgupta. *American Playwrights: A Critical Survey.* New York: Drama Book Specialists, 1981.

Mottram, Ron. *Inner Landscapes: The Theater of Sam Shepard.* Columbia: University of Missouri Press, 1984.

Oumano, Ellen. *The Life and Work of an American Dreamer.* New York: St. Martin's Press, 1986.

Patraka, Vivian M., and Mark Siegel. *Sam Shepard.* Boise, Idaho: Boise State University Press, 1985.

Thomas J. Taylor

LESLIE MARMON SILKO

Born: Albuquerque, New Mexico
1948

Principal Literary Achievement

Recognized initially as one of the leading female contributors to the renaissance in Native American literature, Silko has established a place for herself in the accepted canon of contemporary American literature.

Biography

Leslie Marmon Silko was born with a diverse heritage derived from her mixed ancestry (Laguna Pueblo, Mexican, and white). Much of her work examines the culture of Native Americans as it conflicts and combines with those of Mexican Americans and Anglo-Americans in the Southwest. Her biography, mostly revealed through her own stories, resonates with the pain of cultural collisions and racism. Yet it also acknowledges, in a self-assured tone, the value of multiplicity, of perceiving things in more than one way as a method of surviving in the contemporary world.

Vital to Silko's upbringing was her great-grandmother, Marie Anaya. Married to Silko's paternal great-grandfather, Robert G. Marmon, a pioneer who moved from Ohio to settle in New Mexico, Marie was known to Silko as Grandma A'Mooh ("A'Mooh" is a Laguna expression of love). A'Mooh, who cared for Silko when she was a baby and lived into her eighties while Silko grew up, told Silko many stories of earlier, difficult times, of the ancient traditions that had sustained the Laguna people.

Equally important are Silko's memories of her great-grandfather Stagner, his wife, Helen, and their daughter Lillie, who was Silko's grandmother. Helen, of the Romero family near Los Lunas, New Mexico, represents the Mexican influence on Silko's life and work, making Spanish as important to her as English and the Indian language of Laguna. Silko acknowledged the vital connections between generations of her family when she dedicated *Ceremony* (1977) to both her grandmothers, Jessie Goddard Leslie and Lillie Stagner Marmon, and her sons, Robert William Chapman and Cazimir Silko.

Perhaps the most significant contributor to Silko's early perceptions and later work was her father, Lee H. Marmon. A talented amateur photographer, he experienced

racism as a young boy when he was denied entrance to an Albuquerque hotel while his light-skinned father was told he was welcome anytime (Hank Marmon, Silko's grandfather, refused to patronize the hotel for the rest of his life). Like the protago- nist of *Ceremony*, Lee Marmon fought in World War II; his photographic records of the life to which he returned—the Laguna and Paguate villages, the Marmon Trad- ing Post, his daughters, the deer hunts, the desert stretches of New Mexico and Arizona—contribute to the richly patterned texture of *Storyteller* (1981).

In addition to her ethnic heritage, the landscapes of Silko's life have profoundly in- fluenced her writing. Most of her work incorporates the distinctive geography around Albuquerque, where she was born, and the Laguna Pueblo Reservation, where she grew up. In contrast to the mountains and mesas of her childhood, Silko, in some of her stories, beautifully describes the stark environment of Alaska, a landscape she became familiar with after spending 1974 as artist-in-residence at the Rosewater Foundation-on-Ketchikan Creek.

Silko has achieved much recognition for her work, publishing many stories and poems in numerous journals and widely read anthologies. She has garnered praise and support from other Native American writers, notably N. Scott Momaday, whose novel, *House Made of Dawn* (1968), is widely credited with beginning the resur- gence of contemporary Native American literature. Throughout *Storyteller*, Silko acknowledges the influence of her Acoma Pueblo colleague Simon Ortiz, who in turn included her story "Private Property" in his edited collection of Native Ameri- can fiction, *Earth Power Coming* (1983).

A poet, short story writer, novelist, and teacher (both as a faculty member at the University of Arizona and as artist-in-residence), Silko has received support from the National Endowment for the Arts and was the recipient of a highly prestigious five-year MacArthur Foundation grant.

Analysis

Leslie Marmon Silko is not a writer whose style is easily defined. Mixing the genres of fiction and poetry, and blurring the lines between reality and fantasy, Silko's works *Ceremony* and *Storyteller* portray a vision of rich complexity. Inter- ested in cultural collision and the violence it sometimes engenders, Silko also ex- plores the possibilities of cultural connectedness. Her primary artistic concern is to celebrate the power of storytelling and ceremony in human life, and the forms of her poetry and fictions parallel to a great extent the oral traditions of her Indian ancestors.

Silko's work is also open to feminist interpretation. The opening story of *Cere- mony* is about Ts'its'tsi'nako, or Thought-Woman, who has created the universe with her two sisters. Thought-Woman is the creator who names things; whatever she thinks about appears. Additionally, one of the characters who is most useful in bringing about the protagonist's healing is a mysterious woman who becomes his lover and warns him of evil he will encounter in his future. The strength of these mythic figures is echoed in many of the narratives related by human women that are part of

Storyteller. In the title story, an Eskimo girl not only lures her parents' killer to his death on an icy river (an occurrence that white lawyers want to define as an accident) but also takes over the tribal storytelling function of the old man who has reared her. This demonstration of her power gains her the respect of the villagers, who formerly scorned her.

The culture-bearing function of women is further apparent in the stories that Silko has heard from her own relatives. She received much of her practical and moral instruction through the tales told by her grandmother and aunts. Many of the heroines are women who accomplish exceptional tasks, often by accepting the possibility of the supernatural intervening in their lives. In "Yellow Woman," also in *Storyteller*, the ordinary heroine is abducted by Silva, apparently an outlaw rancher, but possibly a Pueblo deity in disguise. Uncertain, but willing to believe that she is living out the stories told to her in childhood by her grandfather, she becomes the beloved Yellow Woman and temporarily escapes her dull life as a housewife to lead a sensuous existence in the mountains. The important ability of women both to create and to accept the truth of storytelling is emphasized repeatedly in Silko's work, suggesting the valuable contributions Native American women make to the continuation of their cultures.

Silko's concerns are also contemporary and political. She examines racism and the violence it engenders and reveals the devastating consequences of war, both for the individuals who participate in it and the earth itself. Her love and respect for the earth are evident in her many lyrical descriptions of the New Mexico landscape; part of contemporary humans' plight, she suggests, is alienation from the earth that sustains them.

Racism is developed as the counterpart to the selfish misuse of the natural world; it is the force that alienates people from one another. Silko's primary concern is the racism that has allowed the systematic oppression of Native Americans by descendents of white Europeans, but in *Ceremony*, especially, she examines the way that racist attitudes can foster and prolong violence against any group or individual defined as different by the majority. Only by recognizing the essential connectedness of human beings and by choosing to refrain from violence can humans break the brutal cycles of hatred. Silko acknowledges that such recognition is not easy—it requires ceremonial, ritualistic healing, as if all suffer from a psychological illness.

That such healing is possible, however, suggests Silko's fundamentally positive view of human nature and its recuperative powers. In *Ceremony*, enough knowledge of the ancient ways remains to perform the necessary life-giving ceremonies. More ancient knowledge can be recovered and sustained through storytelling. Silko is trying to capture, in writing, the power and rhythms of oral tradition, a task that fulfills at least two functions. First, it makes accessible to people outside Native American culture the rich myths and beliefs that were fostered by the North American landscape. Second, it preserves those myths for future generations at a time when the integrity of Native American culture is threatened by assimilation into mainstream

American society. Already, many languages are lost; by writing primarily in English, with smatterings of Laguna and Spanish, Silko conveys the essential meaning of many of her tribal myths while helping to preserve the tribal language. Working with three languages further suggests the strengths of assimilation; each culture can enhance and enrich the others. Such connectedness may be the only hope for a productive future; undivided by racism, less alienated from the natural world, the human community has a greater chance of survival, both physically and psychologically.

CEREMONY

First published: 1977
Type of work: Novel

Experiencing deep depression after fighting in World War II, a young man finds health and new meaning after his return to the Laguna reservation.

Ceremony, Silko's first published novel, won the attention of critics and other Native American writers, particularly N. Scott Momaday. Interestingly, the basic situation of Silko's novel parallels that of Momaday's *House Made of Dawn*. Both writers create protagonists who have been psychologically wounded by service in the Army during World War II and who encounter racism and brutality when they attempt to return to reservation life afterwards. Although Momaday's character eventually experiences a partial return to health, Silko's main character, a half-breed named Tayo, fully overcomes his impulses toward violence by undergoing the traditional healing ceremonies of the past.

The novel continually pits the world of the white race against Indian culture, a contrast that is highlighted by Tayo's experience as a soldier. Seen only as an American when he is in uniform, Tayo is treated well by white women and storeowners, who are anxious to help the boys at the front. Out of uniform, Tayo is relegated to the position of second-class citizen, either ignored or insulted by the same people who had been kind previously. Tayo's position is further complicated by the fact that he is not fully accepted in the Indian community either, because he has a Mexican father. The racism that contributes to his confused sense of identity also precipitates his breakdown: When he suddenly perceives a Japanese enemy to be no different than his Indian uncle, he collapses on the battlefield. His precarious mental condition is further jeopardized when his cousin, Rocky, who has worked hard to assimilate himself into the mainstream culture, is killed in the war. Tayo returns to his aunt's home on the reservation, convinced that he, not Rocky, is the one who should have died.

Racism is also seen as a major contributor to the self-destructive behavior of other Indian veterans. Tayo's friends retreat into alcoholism and repetitive recitations of their sexual exploits with white women; eventually they can only feel good about themselves when they commit violent acts of domination, reenacting the atrocities of war. Tayo himself falls victim to this temptation and stabs another veteran before embarking on his ceremonial journey toward psychological wholeness.

The process of healing provides another cultural juxtaposition: Tayo's illness originally is defined and treated by white doctors, who attempt psychological explanations and scientific cures. Tayo's stay in a mental hospital is described in images of whiteness; most tellingly, he feels immersed in a white fog. It is not until he goes through the ritual healing ceremonies of the Laguna that he realizes that his "craziness" may actually be a the result of special perception, the ability to realize the interconnectedness of seemingly unrelated events.

Through ceremony and story, Tayo comes to accept not only the power of traditional Indian ways but also the truth of ancient beliefs. Embarking on a journey to find his uncle's stolen cattle, Tayo gradually senses his oneness with the earth and acknowledges that the earth gives of itself to humans out of love. Through this realization, he is able to overcome his hatred of humans—particularly the white people who are destroying the earth and one another—and his impulses toward violence. Faced with the difficult test of stopping a brutal attack only by performing worse brutality himself, Tayo decides not to act and thus frees himself from the fear that he is as others have defined him: a drunken, lawless, incapable half-breed. With his choice, Tayo not only gains a sense of himself as an independent, strong individual but also recognizes the kinship among all peoples. His earlier confusion of the Japanese soldier with his uncle is transformed into the startling awareness that people are artificially divided and made to hate one another. Symbolically, this recognition occurs near the site of played-out uranium mines in New Mexico; the weapon that defeated the Japanese had its origins on traditional Indian lands. Both Japanese and Native American have been victimized by the white race and have been deceived into fighting each other, but Tayo realizes that, ultimately, white people have injured the earth and themselves beyond repair or redemption. In realizing this, he affirms his Native American heritage and sees himself as the inheritor of Laguna traditions, traditions that teach him how to live fully after his dehumanizing military experience.

STORYTELLER

First published: 1981
Type of work: Short stories

A collection of narrative and poetic tales focusing on the author's Laguna heritage.

The unifying theme of the short stories and poems of *Storyteller* might be considered Leslie Silko's life itself. Punctuated with photographs of the Laguna reservation and surrounding landscape, often taken by her father, *Storyteller* seeks to assert the importance and vitality of an oral culture. Many of the tales included were told to Silko by her relatives; although not always understanding their import at the time, Silko came to realize that such stories include practical or moral instruction. Other tales and poems are imaginative reconstructions of ancient myths or are Silko's responses to her immediate environment. Throughout, the connective thread is Silko's experience of life as a Native American woman.

Silko assumes many guises as a storyteller and becomes many narrators, each with an individual voice. With equal versatility, she is the Eskimo girl who tricks her parents' killer to his death, the mythic Yellow Woman riding into the mountains with her lover, or herself as a child, tormenting her uncle's goat. As she demonstrates so forcefully in *Ceremony*, she capably creates male characters, catching the rougher resonances of their voices as well. Two striking stories narrated by male characters are "Tony's Story" and "Coyote Holds a Full House in His Hand."

In the first, Silko focuses on the killing of a New Mexico state patrol officer, seen from the point of view of one of the participants. Brutalized by the patrol officer, who seeks out Indians in order to beat them, Antonio Sousea kills the officer in front of his friend Leon and then sets fire to the body in the squad car. Leon, who has responded to an indiscriminate beating from the officer by talking about his civil rights and appealing to the Pueblo meeting, is appalled. Tony, however, has perceived the officer to be something worse than a violent racist; he believes the man to be a force of evil, the focal point of a bad spell that perpetuates the drought conditions on the reservation.

Tony believes that to exorcise the evil, the killing and burning are necessary and justified from the perspective of ancient beliefs. His view is in sharp contrast to Leon's, which has been affected by his service in the military and his desire to assimilate into the cultural mainstream.

"Coyote Holds a Full House in His Hand" is much more lighthearted. The final story in the collection is the tale of an old Laguna man who poses as a medicine man in order to take advantage of a gathering of Hopi women. Coyote is a traditional trickster of Laguna legend who is foiled by his own cleverness as often as he succeeds in getting what he wants. In this tale, however, he is victorious, securing for himself a photograph of the women, who have believed his lie and submitted to his cure, which involves caressing their thighs with juniper ashes. The humor of this tale, especially contrasted with the seriousness of "Tony's Story," demonstrates the versatility of Silko's art, not only in her creation of multiple voices but also in her treatment of diverse subject matters. *Storyteller* is a brilliant exhibition of her range and imaginative powers.

Summary

Historically, Leslie Marmon Silko's significant contribution may be the retrieval and recording of stories that are part of an oral culture not accessible to many Americans. Yet, aesthetically, her art provides much more: Politically and socially aware, Silko offers a critique of American culture that emphasizes the importance of Native American values to the mainstream population. Without the Native American ability to accept multiple points of view, to embrace ambiguity, American society becomes sterile and divisive. Further, without the Native American respect and love for the land, the very future of American society is threatened. Through her gift of storytelling, Silko offers her readers ways to embrace a holistic, healing perspective by understanding the import of ancient beliefs and ceremonies.

Bibliography

Aithal, S. K. "American Ethnic Fiction in the Universal Context." *American Studies International* 21 (October, 1983): 61-66.

Antell, J. A. "Momaday, Welch, and Silko: Expressing the Feminine Principle Through Male Alienation." *American Indian Quarterly* 12 (Summer, 1988): 213-220.

Blicksilver, E. "Traditionalism Versus Modernity: Leslie Silko on American Indian Women." *Southwest Review* 64 (Spring, 1979): 149-160.

García, Reyes. "Senses of Place in *Ceremony.*" *MELUS* 10 (Winter, 1983): 37-48.

Hirsh, B. A. "The Telling Which Continues: Oral Tradition and the Written Word in Leslie Marmon Silko's *Storyteller.*" *American Indian Quarterly* 12 (Winter, 1988): 1-26.

Gweneth A. Dunleavy

NEIL SIMON

Born: New York, New York
July 4, 1927

Principal Literary Achievement
Simon's humorous plays have made him the most commercially successful playwright in the history of theater.

Biography

Born in the Bronx, New York, on July 4, 1927, Marvin Neil Simon was the second of two sons in a middle-class Jewish family. His father, Irving, was a garment salesman who abandoned the family several times before the marriage ended in divorce. Because of his parents' domestic difficulties, Simon's childhood was not particularly happy, but he nevertheless developed his affinity for comedy at an early age. As a schoolboy, he earned his nickname "Doc" for his ability to imitate the family doctor, and he reported in a *Life* magazine interview:

> When I was a kid, I climbed up on a stone ledge to watch an outdoor movie of Charlie Chaplin. I laughed so hard I fell off, cut my head open and was taken to the doctor, bleeding and laughing. I was constantly being dragged out of movies for laughing too loud. Now my idea of the ultimate achievement in a comedy is to make a whole audience fall onto the floor, writhing and laughing so hard that some of them pass out.

Simon's plays are often quite nearly that amusing, but his gift for provoking riotous laughter has ultimately been a burden, because it has prevented most critics from taking him seriously as a comic dramatist.

Simon demonstrated his ability to make people laugh even as a teenager, when he teamed with his older brother Danny to write material for stand-up comics and radio shows. After briefly attending New York University (he was never graduated from college) and serving in the Army at the end of World War II, Neil teamed with Danny again as they began, in 1946, to create material for one of the radio era's most successful comedy writers, Goodman Ace. The Simon brothers prospered as radio comedy writers but shifted in the early 1950's to television as the new medium developed. Writing for such television notables as Phil Silvers and Tallulah Bankhead, they were each earning huge weekly salaries of sixteen hundred dollars by the mid-1950's. During his television writing in the 1950's, Simon worked alongside many young writers who would later make successful careers of their own, most

notably Mel Brooks and Woody Allen. Danny left the writing team in 1956 to pursue a career as a television director, but Neil continued writing for such stars as Sid Caesar, Garry Moore, Jackie Gleason, and Red Buttons, earning two Emmy Awards (in 1957 and 1959) for his comedy writing.

Simon believed that writing for television did not allow him enough independence, so while writing for *The Garry Moore Show*, he teamed with Danny to develop his first play, *Come Blow Your Horn* (1960), which eventually ran eighty-four weeks on Broadway. The success of this play encouraged Simon to leave television for good. Working solo this time, Simon first wrote the book for a musical comedy, *Little Me* (1962), and then wrote his second Broadway comedy, *Barefoot in the Park* (1963). The latter, starring a young actor named Robert Redford, was an enormous success, running for four years and 1,532 performances. As the first of many television and film offers followed, Simon soon became rich and famous. While *Barefoot in the Park* was still running on Broadway, Paramount bought the film rights to Simon's next play, *The Odd Couple* (1965), on the basis of a forty-word synopsis, and he soon sold the television rights to the American Broadcasting Company, although for only a small percentage of the millions of dollars the television series eventually earned.

By the mid-1960's, then, Neil Simon was already a household name, his popularity and wealth virtually assured. Although he experienced some setbacks (*The Star-Spangled Girl* in 1966 was not a Broadway hit), he recovered almost immediately with the successes of *Promises, Promises* (1968), *Plaza Suite* (1968), and *Last of the Red Hot Lovers* (1969). Simon has suffered occasional disappointments—for example, with *The Gingerbread Lady* (1970), *The Good Doctor* (1973), *God's Favorite* (1974), and *Fools* (1981)—but overall, his comedies have been very successful at the box office, his name on the marquee assuring a receptive audience.

In 1973, Simon's personal life was dealt a severe blow when his wife of twenty years, dancer Joan Baim, died of cancer. He eventually recorded his grief in *Chapter Two* (1977), the story of a man who loses his wife and then immediately remarries, fending off the subsequent feelings of guilt. *Chapter Two* was hailed by some critics as a new kind of triumph for Simon, a comedy that could be taken seriously, that was more than a series of one-liners. Then, in 1983, the first of a trilogy of semi-autobiographical plays confirmed this assessment in the eyes of even more critics. *Brighton Beach Memoirs* (1983), *Biloxi Blues* (1984), and *Broadway Bound* (1986) did not convince everyone that he was a serious playwright, but they convinced enough people for those plays to be considered a turning point in Simon's career.

In addition to his comedies, Simon has written four musicals—*Little Me* (1962; revised, 1982), *Sweet Charity* (1966), *Promises, Promises* (1968), and *They're Playing Our Song* (1978). He has also written extensively, although not as successfully, for the screen. Starting with *After the Fox* in 1966, Simon's original film scripts include *The Heartbreak Kid* (1972), *Murder by Death* (1976), and *The Goodbye Girl* (1977). He has also adapted most of his own plays for the screen. Simon's habit is to write daily from 10:00 A.M. to 5:00 P.M. in either his Manhattan apartment or his Bel Air, California, home. He usually starts ten or more plays for every one he finishes. If he passes page thirty-five of a play, Simon usually completes it, although he reports that the revision process always lasts much longer than the original composition.

Analysis

A natural gift for wit and humor and a decade of writing television comedy in the 1950's enabled Neil Simon to create enormously amusing plays from the very beginning of his career. Even in *Come Blow Your Horn* and *Barefoot in the Park*, Simon had mastered the one-liner, the clever and witty reply that catches an audience by surprise and compels it into explosive laughter.

Take, for example, Victor Velasco's quip upon entering the nearly barren one-room apartment of Paul and Corie Bratter in *Barefoot in the Park*. Their furniture has not yet arrived, but Corie announces that "we just moved in"; looking around the barren room, Velasco replies, "Really? What are you, a folksinger?" Initially, the audience is surprised by the apparent incongruity of the remark; then, within milliseconds, the audience realizes that there is a certain aptness in the reply, given the circumstances. The laughter is boisterous because surprise triggers it, and then the laughter is sustained because aptness justifies it. Simon had polished this technique in his early writing for such television comedians as Phil Silvers, Sid Caesar, and Jackie Gleason. In the introduction to volume 2 of his *Collected Plays* (1979), Simon recalls that writing humorous dialogue for his film *The Goodbye Girl* was much easier than trying to write "a funny lead-in to Jo Stafford's next song" on the old Garry Moore Show.

Although his ability to create uproarious laughter endears Simon to the general populace, it has done little to endear him to many critics, who see comedy as a thought-provoking genre and who associate steady, boisterous laughter with mind-numbing television situation comedies. Simon himself has been sensitive to this critical disparagement of his work and has attempted throughout his career to make his comedies more "serious" without sacrificing the laughter that he loves to create and that his audiences pay to enjoy. As early as *The Odd Couple*, Simon was attempting to go beyond the gag-comedy, one-liner format of *Come Blow Your Horn* and *Barefoot in the Park*. As reported in a 1979 *Playboy* interview, Simon's original conception for his famous play about Oscar and Felix was to make it a "black comedy."

Transcending his one-liner format and gaining more respect from the critics did not come easily. By 1979, Simon was secure in his commercial success, having turned out popular hits on Broadway and in Hollywood for nearly twenty years. Yet in the introduction to volume 2 of his *Collected Plays*, Simon admitted that he was still suffering from insecurity as a writer, and he openly confessed to neurosis, an ulcer, and envy over his good friend Woody Allen's success with the motion picture *Manhattan* (1979), which had led reviewers to call Allen "the most mature comic mind in America."

Simon acknowledged in that same introduction that people ranked his plays in terms of aesthetic extremes, judging them anywhere from "a delightful evening" to "worthy of Molière." Those who ranked his plays as "a delightful evening" were essentially admitting that the plays, although very amusing, could only be considered entertainment. Those who ranked his plays as "worthy of Molière" were asserting that his comedy should be taken as seriously as the plays of such classic comic writers as Aristophanes, William Shakespeare, and George Bernard Shaw. Very few mature and responsible critics would go that far, and a much more fruitful comparison for Simon's work is with that of contemporary playwright Alan Ayckbourn, who is often referred to as the "English Neil Simon." Both are prolific, writing very amusing plays about conventional middle-class people. The chief value in the comparison is that Ayckbourn's work has received a far more positive reception from the serious-minded critics, which may enable one to deduce what the critics find lacking in Simon.

The more positive critical assessment of Simon's work, however, which began with the response to *Chapter Two*, seems at least partially justifiable; his later, semi-autobiographical plays are indeed different from his earlier comedies. *Chapter Two* does not seem to depend so much on one-liners and boisterous laughter. Written as a response to the death of his first wife, *Chapter Two* finally turned the focus of Simon's plays toward dramatic narrative, toward the situations in which he put his characters. The play opens quite typically with a wisecracking character named Leo Schneider, but when Leo's brother George is introduced, the pain that George feels over the loss of his wife Barbara begins to dominate the opening scene and create genuine pathos. The play does have sections where the one-liners predominate, but overall, the play focuses on the courtship of George and his new girlfriend, Jennie, and the portrayal in the last act of their post-honeymoon conflict is as genuine and moving as the pathos in the first scene. Those more serious qualities also appear prominently in the plays of Simon's autobiographical trilogy—*Brighton Beach Memoirs*, *Biloxi Blues*, and *Broadway Bound*. As Simon entered the 1990's he continued to bask in the increased critical respect generated by these plays.

Yet critical opinion is seldom unanimous. Although the new plays were clearly different, critics such as the redoubtable John Simon of *New York* magazine suggested that Neil had simply substituted one commercial formula for another—that the gagwriter had merely been replaced by a sentimental writer. So, although the disparagement of Simon's work has abated somewhat, the controversy remains.

BAREFOOT IN THE PARK

First produced: 1963 (first published, 1964)
Type of work: Play

A newly married couple irons out superficial differences and agrees to live happily ever after, finding happiness for the bride's mother in the bargain.

In *Barefoot in the Park*, newlyweds Corie and Paul Bratter have completed their six-day honeymoon and are moving into their first apartment. Corie is romantic, impulsive, and enthusiastic, while her husband is a proper, careful, even "stuffy" young attorney who is more concerned with his budding legal career than he is with helping to build their love nest and perpetuating the honeymoon atmosphere. Soon Corie and Paul quarrel, Paul questioning Corie's judgment and Corie questioning Paul's sense of romance and adventure. Complicating their discord is Corie's attempt to enliven the life of her widowed mother, Ethel. Against Paul's advice, Corie tricks her mother into a blind date with their eccentric neighbor, Victor Velasco, who skis, climbs mountains, and is known as "The Bluebeard of 48th Street."

By the end of act 2, the question of the blind date has precipitated such a conflict between Corie and Paul that they agree to divorce, and in act 3, they fight over the settlement before Paul stalks out. Ethel and Velasco, however, reveal that they have found romance. Ethel had rediscovered her vitality, while Velasco has decided that he must act his âge and settle down. After the new lovers depart, Paul returns, outrageously drunk, having walked barefoot in the park in the middle of winter to prove that he is not a "fuddy-duddy." The newlyweds are reconciled and promise to live happily ever after.

Even in his first play, Simon had mastered the qualities that would make him enormously successful. First and foremost, *Barefoot in the Park* is clever and hilarious, filled with snappy dialogue and witty one-liners. One of the most famous of his "running gags" (a joke repeated for laughs) appears in this play. Because Paul and Corie's apartment is on the fifth floor of their building, nearly all the characters suffer extreme exhaustion in the climb. The joke is carried throughout the play but continues to elicit laughter because Simon always finds a different angle when he repeats it.

Nevertheless, the limitation that has haunted Simon throughout his career is present: The humor of the one-liners overwhelms the potentially literary elements of the play. There is a clear sense that the characters and plot are simply serving as a framework for the funny lines. As a result, the dramatic conflicts in the play do not seem real or deeply felt. In act 3, for example, when Paul and Corie are arguing about their divorce, Simon manages to maintain the rich humor of the play, but he is not able to create a convincing sense of conflict at the same time. Corie exclaims that she wants Paul to move out immediately, and as Paul angrily begins to pack his suitcase, Corie says, "My divorce. When do I get my divorce?" Paul replies, "How should I know? They didn't even send us our marriage license yet." The one-liner reestablishes the play's frivolous tone and creates the impression that there is really little at stake. There is no satiric attitude toward either point of view, no comic judgment of anyone's folly, and really no thought process, only the explosive laughter that comes from the line. The dominant tone created by the one-liners suggests that this marital discord is both trivial and temporary, a condition that will be resolved painlessly in a happy ending.

Simon does attempt to make a serious point in his play, asserting that moderation will make everyone happier and that marriage is too important an institution to take lightly, but his sentiments strike most critics as conventional and not thought-provoking. Ironically, Simon's penchant for safe sentiments traps him in this play. At a pivotal moment, when Corie's mother is counseling Corie about how to resolve the marital conflict and get Paul back, Simon gives the mother some marriage-saving "wisdom" that dates the play and made it seriously anachronistic within a decade. What seemed to Simon in the early 1960's to be conservative, conventional wisdom would soon become sexism in the 1970's:

> It's very simple. You've just got to give up a little of you for him. Don't make every-thing a game. Just late at night in that little room upstairs. But take care of him. And make him feel important. And if you can do that, you'll have a happy and wonderful marriage.

THE ODD COUPLE

First produced: 1965 (first published, 1966)
Type of work: Play

Two men, one divorced and sloppy, the other newly separated from his wife and very tidy, discover that they cannot live together.

The Odd Couple was not merely another Neil Simon hit: It might be considered the greatest hit of his career, if popularity is measured by the kind of impact a play has on American culture. *The Odd Couple* ran on Broadway for nearly one thousand performances, then was made into a film (1968), then into a very successful net-work television program (1970-1975), and then recast in a female version (1985), in which the two roommates are played by women. These facts alone would be signifi-cant indications of popularity, but Simon's play has had such an impact on American life that the phrase "odd couple" has become part of American folklore. Many may not remember the names of the two men or which was the messy one, but nearly every adult is familiar with the situation to which the phrase "odd couple" refers and can use the phrase to describe similar situations.

The Odd Couple refers to Oscar Madison and Felix Ungar. Oscar, the messy one, is divorced from his wife and lives alone in a spacious, eight-room apartment on Riv-erside Drive in New York City. Even when he entertains Felix and his other poker-playing buddies, Oscar's apartment is littered with dirty dishes, discarded clothes, and even garbage. When Felix's wife demands a trial separation, Felix comes to live with Oscar and soon wears out his welcome, even with their poker buddies, because he insists on keeping the apartment sparkling clean and tidy. Furthermore, Felix's despondency over his separation not only depresses Oscar but also ruins Oscar's plans to seduce the two British sisters, Cecily and Gwendolyn Pigeon, who live in the apartment above them. When Oscar can endure no more, he demands that Felix leave, and Felix moves upstairs temporarily with the Pigeon sisters, who find his sensitivity charming. The play ends in an uncomplicated way, with Oscar and Felix agreeing to separate.

In many ways, Simon demonstrates more skill as a playwright in *The Odd Couple* than in earlier works. He does not depend on simple "running gags" such as the exhausting set of stairs in *Barefoot in the Park*, and his one-liners are much more integrated into the play's action and characterization. As adept as Simon had been with theatrical gesture in *Barefoot in the Park*, it is clear in *The Odd Couple* that he has become even more expert at creating a captivating theatrical experience for his audience. For example, in the opening lines of the play, the poker players have gathered at Oscar's apartment for a game and the exasperated Speed is watching the painfully deliberate Murray shuffle the cards. This opening moment is spellbinding even before Speed's first word is spoken. The curtain rises on an arresting image: an obviously lavish apartment comically devastated by neglect, a diverse group of men engaged in a smoky masculine ritual around the poker table, and the group's focus immediately engaged on the comically slow Murray, shuffling the cards as if he were handling precious jewels. Speed then delivers the opening line and the first one-liner of the play:

> *Speed* (Cups his chin in his hand and looks at Murray) Tell me, Mr. Maverick, is this your first time on the riverboat?

Even in *The Odd Couple*, however, a masterpiece in many ways, Simon was still unable to achieve a convincing level of seriousness to accompany the rich laughter. This is most apparent at the end of the play, when it finally appears that there really has not been much of a point to the conflict between Oscar and Felix. Some critics claim that the play shows how incompatibility is as likely to occur between men as between spouses and that the spirit of compromise is necessary to marriage. Most critics argue, however, that this is not saying much beyond the painfully obvious. *The Odd Couple* ends inconclusively without being thought-provoking; it ends ambiguously without being suggestive. Oscar and Felix part as friends, Oscar has become more neat and more responsible about paying his alimony, and Felix will spend a few days with the Pigeon sisters before facing some unknown future.

LAST OF THE RED HOT LOVERS

First produced: 1969 (first published, 1970)
Type of work Play

A middle-aged man discovers that extramarital affairs are less satisfying than conventional matrimony.

Last of the Red Hot Lovers is one of the most amusing of Neil Simon's comedies. It focuses on Barney Cashman, a forty-seven-year-old owner of a seafood restaurant who is afraid that the sexual revolution of the 1960's is passing him by. Over the space of nine months, he invites three different women to his mother's Manhattan apartment in an attempt to have an afternoon of extramarital sex. None of the affairs is consummated, however, and Barney decides after the last one that he would prefer a romantic afternoon with his wife, Thelma.

Of the three women who meet Barney, the first two are caricatures of sexually liberated women from the 1960's. In act 1, Elaine Navazio comes to the afternoon tryst as a veteran of casual sex. In her late thirties and married, Elaine indulges frequently in extramarital affairs simply because they make her feel good. Flippant and irreverent, Elaine is openly contemptuous of Barney's maladroit, unsophisticated style (he is nervous, wanting the affair to be "meaningful") and bombards him with insults that hit like machine-gun fire. She is only interested in their sensual experience and is comically desperate for a cigarette throughout their meeting. When the encounter fails to produce sexual satisfaction, Elaine leaves, and Barney vows never to be tempted again. Yet eight months later, he repeats the experience with Bobbi Michele.

Bobbi Michele is an uninhibited and adventurous twenty-seven-year-old woman who entices Barney into smoking his first marijuana and regales him with wild stories about her prospects in show business, about men attempting to have sex with her, and about the lesbian Nazi vocal coach with whom she lives. The totally bizarre Bobbi Michele generates tremendous laughter as her high-energy, nonstop talk reduces Barney to bewilderment. The frenetic pace that was established in the first act with Elaine is maintained and perhaps even topped in this segment.

In act 3, less than a month later, Barney is attempting to seduce Jeanette Fisher, who is thirty-nine years old and the wife of a close friend. Unlike the promiscuous Elaine and Bobbi Michele, Jeanette is a reluctant visitor, joining Barney only because she thinks her husband Mel is having an affair of his own. Depressed and guilt-ridden, an unwilling participant in the prevailing sexual climate, Jeanette lectures Barney on moral issues and challenges him to prove that there are decent people in the world. The comic energy in this segment is generated by the reversal of Barney's role. In this act Barney has become the aggressor, having gained savoir-faire and confidence from his previous meetings, and rich laughter is generated by the conflict between Barney's new impatience and Jeanette's reticence. Barney finally sees the wisdom of not engaging in illicit sex, and when he and Jeanette part at the end of the play, Barney seems to be cured of his desire for promiscuity.

In addition to being a very funny play, *Last of the Red Hot Lovers* is a critique of the permissive 1960's from a conservative point of view. Simon's message is that the conventional values of marriage, home, and family are still sacrosanct, even though they seem old-fashioned in the prevailing cultural climate. Ironically, Simon's conservative thinking serves him well in this case. Looking back, one can see that the permissiveness of the 1960's was beginning to fade as Simon was writing this comedy. The increasingly moralistic climate of the 1980's would make this play look like an eloquent and prophetic swan song for an era. Thus, in *Last of the Red Hot*

Lovers, Simon added, perhaps inadvertently, a serious quality to his comic writing. It was not, however, a seriousness that all the critics considered profound, subtle, or artistic.

BRIGHTON BEACH MEMOIRS

First produced: 1983 (first published, 1984)
Type of work: Play

Problems are caused by having too many relatives live under one roof, but they are resolved, and a young boy comes of age during the process.

Brighton Beach Memoirs is about the Jeromes, a Brooklyn family in the late Depression era (1937), and the financial difficulties they face when three relatives join the household. For three-and-a-half years, Kate Jerome's sister Blanche Morton and Blanche's two teenage daughters, Laurie and Nora, have lived with the middle-class Jeromes. Although the arrangement is basically amicable, new financial tensions culminate in hard words between Kate and Blanche. Fortunately, the argument teaches Blanche about independence and the play ends happily, with Blanche making plans to move and with the two sisters closer than ever.

Brighton Beach Memoirs does not really focus on this story of sibling love, however; rather, it is what Simon calls his first "tapestry play." In all of Simon's previous plays, he focused on two or three characters and made the other characters peripheral. Here, there is a sense that each character's story is told with similar emphasis. Jack Jerome struggles to balance all of his familial roles, as husband, father, and surrogate parent for Laurie and Nora. Stanley Jerome, the eldest son, achieves adulthood by learning from his errors in judgment. Nora Morton, the eldest daughter, gives up illusions of easy fame and fortune as a Broadway showgirl, accepting a closer relationship with her mother and a more responsible familial role, while Laurie Morton, the sickly and highly pampered youngest daughter, will clearly profit from a less indulgent treatment of her illness. A slightly greater dramatic emphasis is perhaps given to fifteen-year-old Eugene Jerome, Simon's autobiographical alter ego, who serves as the play's charming narrator. Eugene comes of age in the play, leaving puberty behind as he confronts sexual feelings for his cousin Nora.

As the first play in Simon's autobiographical trilogy, *Brighton Beach Memoirs* decisively raised the critical opinion of Neil Simon's comedies because the play was not at all dependent on one-liners. Its laughter was less boisterous and explosive, becoming warmer, more gentle, more related to character and situation, and more sentimental. Take, for example, one of the first big laughs in the play. Eugene is banging an old softball against a wall, and his mother asks him to stop because Aunt Blanche is suffering from a headache. Eugene begs for a few more pitches because it is a crucial moment in his imaginary replaying of a Yankee World Series game. When he finally has to give in, he "slams the ball into his glove angrily" but then "cups his hand, making a megaphone out of it and announces . . . 'Attention, ladeees and gentlemen! Today's game will be delayed because of my Aunt Blanche's headache.'" This humor provokes a smile or chuckle rather than a guffaw; it directs warm and sentimental feelings back toward the character. While there are many one-liners in *Brighton Beach Memoirs*, they come after the tone of the play has been set and are absorbed by the play's emphasis on character development and narrative.

Building on the more delicate seriousness achieved in *Chapter Two, Brighton Beach Memoirs* displays a Neil Simon who is capable of creating moments of genuine tenderness, as in the scene between Laurie and Nora that begins with "Oh, God, I wish Daddy were alive" and ends with the image of Nora searching the deceased father's coat pocket for her usual gift. Many critics responded appreciatively, lauding Simon's new direction. For other critics, however, the overall effect of the play was still sentimental rather than convincingly serious. Blanche's fear of intimacy after the death of her husband was easily resolved, for example, and Eugene's obsession with sex, although cute, was hardly profound.

Summary

Neil Simon has always been able to make audiences laugh, although it has been debated whether he is more than a gag writer, a creator of situation comedies for the stage. *Chapter Two* and the three plays of his Brighton Beach trilogy have wrested additional respect from the critics, but the issue remains unresolved. Audiences, on the other hand, have been markedly less critical, usually flocking to Simon plays regardless of the level of seriousness he achieves. While it is not yet appropriate to place Neil Simon in the company of Shakespeare, Molière, or Shaw, his is no small achievement: to have become the most successful playwright in the history of theater.

Bibliography

"The Craft of the Playwright: A Conversation Between Neil Simon and David Rabe." *The New York Times Magazine,* May 26, 1985, p. 36.

Henry, William A., III. "Reliving a Poignant Past." *Time* 128 (December 15, 1986): 72-78.

Johnson, Robert K. *Neil Simon.* Boston: Twayne, 1983.

McGovern, Edythe M. *Neil Simon: A Critical Study.* New York: Frederick Ungar, 1979.

"(Marvin) Neil Simon." In *Contemporary Authors.* New rev. ser. Vol. 26, edited by Thomas Wiloch. Gale Research, 1989.

Meryman, Richard. "When the Funniest Writer in America Tried to Be Serious." *Life* 70 (May 7, 1971): 60-83.

Simon, Neil. Interview by Lawrence Linderman. *Playboy,* February, 1979, 58.

Terry Nienhuis

GARY SNYDER

Born: San Francisco, California
May 8, 1930

Principal Literary Achievement
A celebrated poet, essayist, and translator, Snyder weaves strands of American transcendentalism, American Indian culture, and Asian philosophy into writings that illuminate the spiritual and ecological connectedness of humans with the natural world.

Biography

Although he was born in San Francisco, Gary Snyder moved to the Pacific Northwest before he was two, and he spent his youth and college years there. His parents, Harold and Lois Snyder, eked out a living on small family farms—first near Seattle, then near Portland. Snyder and his sister Thea enjoyed the plants and animals of these rural areas and learned the challenges and satisfactions of hard physical work. Snyder also traces his political orientation through family roots: His grandfather was a labor organizer for Industrial Workers of the World, and Snyder often cites their motto of "forming the new society within the shell of the old"—of developing a healthy alternative culture rather than seeking to confront and destroy outmoded institutions.

During his high school years, and through college and several years after, Snyder worked at a variety of jobs. Some were cerebral (such as jobs in journalism, radio programming, and teaching), but more often they involved manual labor and craftsmanship in the outdoors—aspects of a life-style that Snyder has continued to embrace even after he could have supported himself solely as a writer. This physical work in his youth involved jobs as a ranger and fire lookout, logger, trail crew worker, and seaman.

In 1947, Snyder enrolled at Reed College, an intense liberal arts institution in Portland, which he says taught him valuable research and writing skills and encouraged critical thinking from a wide range of viewpoints. He earned a B.A. in literature and anthropology in 1951, and his honors thesis, *He Who Hunted Birds in His Father's Village: The Dimensions of a Haida Myth*, was published in book form in 1979. This thesis, a research study of an Indian myth from British Columbia, is both a remarkably mature piece of scholarship and an extraordinary early statement of the principles linking poet, community, and nature that would come to guide Snyder's poetic practice throughout the coming decades. Also while at Reed, he entered the

1873

first of his three marriages—to Alison Gass, a marriage that lasted only one year.

Snyder's first move toward an academic career was also short-lived: He began a graduate program in linguistics at Indiana University in 1951 but dropped out after a semester. Returning to the West Coast in the fall of 1952, Snyder lived in the San Francisco Bay Area for four years—a crucial period in his development as a poet. In 1953, he began a three-year stint in the graduate program in Oriental languages at the University of California at Berkeley. Even as a child, Snyder's imagination had been drawn to Asia. When he first saw Chinese landscape paintings at age nine, he noted close similarities between the wet, heavily forested mountains of Washington and Chinese "mountains of the spirit." Later he immersed himself in the poetry of China, which he viewed as "a high civilization that has managed to keep in tune with nature." Ezra Pound and Kenneth Rexroth served as models of older American poets who had also learned from the concentrated imagery of Asian poetry.

During these years in the Bay Area, Snyder also became part of the loosely knit community of writers who became known as the Beats. On October 13, 1955, a reading at Six Gallery in San Francisco publicly launched the Beat movement; though the event is best remembered for Allen Ginsberg's reading of *Howl*, Gary Snyder also contributed a memorable reading of his poem "A Berry Feast" (later published in *The Back Country* in 1967). In the frequent public readings that were an important part of the Beat movement, Snyder found reinforcement for his belief (drawn from Native American cultures) that poetry is primarily an oral art that energizes and binds a community. Snyder's poetry did not become nationally known until he began to publish it in book form in 1959, but his reputation as a charismatic oral poet and Asian scholar preceded him by way of the hyperbolic fictional portrait of him as Japhy Ryder in Jack Kerouac's novel *The Dharma Bums* (1958).

Just as the glare of national publicity and controversy began to bear down on the Beats in 1956, Snyder left for Japan, where he spent most of his time during the next dozen years. There he embarked on a challenging program of Zen Buddhist study and meditation with the *roshi* ("old teacher") Oda Sesso at the Daitoku-ji monastery in Kyoto. During these years, Snyder also traveled further into Asia, and he worked as a seaman on an oil tanker sailing to the Middle East. He returned repeatedly to the United States, to teach (at Berkeley in 1964) and to oversee the publication of seven books of poetry, journals, and essays—from *Riprap* (1959) through *Earth House Hold: Technical Notes and Queries to Fellow Dharma Revolutionaries* (1969). Snyder married poet Joanne Kyger in 1960, traveled with her to India during 1961 and 1962, and was divorced from her in 1964. In January of 1967, Snyder presided with Allen Ginsberg over the Great Human Be-In in San Francisco—an event that proved to be a historic apex of 1960's American counterculture.

During the late 1960's, the focus of Snyder's life and poetry shifted slightly but significantly, from that of an individual soul adventuring in quest of spiritual truth to that of a man singing in praise and protection of the family and communities to which he had become committed. *Earth House Hold* is a pivotal work in this regard, for in it Snyder gives increased emphasis to the themes of tribal community and global ecological responsibility. At the end of that book, he writes of his stay at the Banyan Ashram, an island commune in southern Japan, and of his marriage there to his third wife, Masa Uehara, in August, 1967. Snyder and his wife soon produced two sons, Kai in 1968 and Gen in 1969, and in 1970 they moved into the Sierra Nevada foothills north of Sacramento. There they have built their permanent home: Kitkitdizze, an eclectic primitivist-New Age homestead. Kitkitdizze has become the center for the Allegheny Star Route community, a group committed to living on the land and to supporting fundamental changes in society.

Snyder's life since 1970 has taken on a seasonal rhythm of work on his home and land during the spring and summer and writing and travel for public readings and lectures during the fall and winter. Between 1970 and 1990, he published three books of prose and four of poetry; among the latter, *Turtle Island* (1974) won the 1975 Pulitzer Prize for Poetry. Snyder has generously contributed his talents as a writer, scholar, and engaging public speaker to the support of the social, religious, and literary viewpoints he espouses. He presents poetry readings and lectures as an advocate of greater environmental awareness and responsibility. In the late 1970's, he was appointed to the California Arts Council and served as its first chairman. Through the years, he has also provided numerous introductions and prefaces to works of translation, scholarship, and poetry.

Analysis

In his recurrent themes and various styles, Gary Snyder could be considered the first truly international Pacific Rim writer. That is, his poetry and prose takes the westward impulse of American civilization and literature all the way west to Asia, and his work represents an original and exhilarating synthesis of the two cultures.

From the American West, Snyder derives his interest in Native American tribal culture and in wilderness adventure. With his backwoods experience as a forest look-out, logger, mountain climber, and foothills homesteader, he is the contemporary equivalent of the American frontiersman—seeking now not to conquer nature, but rather to live in harmony with it. His roots in American literature reach from the New England transcendentalism of Ralph Waldo Emerson, Henry David Thoreau, and Walt Whitman to the West Coast celebrations of nature in John Muir, Robinson Jeffers, and Kenneth Rexroth. Some of Snyder's poetry collections, such as *Myths and Texts* (1960) and *Mountains and Rivers Without End* (a sequence of poems, sections of which were published in 1965 and 1970), display the expansive am-bitiousness to encompass America—or even all Western culture—that one finds in such classic American long poems as Whitman's *Leaves of Grass* (1855-1892), T. S. Eliot's *The Waste Land* (1922), and Ezra Pound's *Cantos* (1917-1970).

On the other hand, Snyder's longtime commitment to Asian philosophy and aes-thetics has led him to the mastery of a very different sort of poetry. He was drawn very early to Chinese verse as translated by Arthur Waley and Ezra Pound, and his study of Chinese and Japanese language and literature (and of Zen Buddhism) has helped him to create masterful short lyrics. This side of Snyder's poetry can be seen in his devotion to simple, direct images that resonate in their clarity and depth.

This mystic Asian imagism is particularly characteristic of Snyder's early poetry, and the title of his first volume, *Riprap*, presents his controlling metaphor for this aesthetic. To "riprap," as a worker on a trail crew, is to embed rocks on a steep mountain trail to provide sure footing for horses. For Snyder, the placement of what he calls "tough, simple short words" establishes a necessary connection to natural facts—and to words felt as palpable objects—even as his mind and spirit expand through and beyond these objects to transcendent states of enlightenment. Though Snyder has published seven major collections of poetry since *Riprap*, it is a testimony to the enduring appeal of these early short lyrics that several are still among the most anthologized and analyzed of Snyder's poems: "Riprap," "Piute Creek," "Milton by Firelight," "Above Pate Valley," and "Water."

Myths and Texts, Snyder's second collection, also employs this riprap approach to poetry, and it in fact makes explicit the intended spiritual resonances of this aesthetic when, toward the end of the book, Snyder includes a definition of poetry as "a riprap on the slick rock of metaphysics." Whereas *Riprap* is a collection of shorter lyrics that makes no attempt at overall coherence, in *Myths and Texts* Snyder groups forty-eight lyrics into three long interrelated poems. The individual lyrics often display the anecdotal settings, concentrated imagery, and monosyllabic diction of the riprap style, but Snyder hopes through the course of the book to render not only isolated, disparate moments of enlightenment but also an overall critical perspective on Western civilization. Thus "Logging," the first long sequence poem, adds up to a critique of American logging practices and the destructive alienation from nature that these practices reveal. "Hunting," the second poem, presents an alternative approach to gaining one's livelihood from nature: The poem dramatizes the attempts made by tribal hunters to enter the consciousness of their animal prey. "Burning," the final poem, presents a series of dark visions of fire and falling—visions that ultimately lead to a sense of renewal and rebirth. Many academic critics rate *Myths and Texts* as Snyder's best book of poetry, praising the precise craftsmanship of its individual sections, the expansive comprehensiveness of its overarching structure, and the wide range of its cultural allusions. The book has been compared with T. S. Eliot's *The Waste Land*, a classic long poem also known for its craftsmanship, visionary structure, and allusiveness.

The other collection of Snyder's poetry that academic critics often rate as his best is *Mountains and Rivers Without End*—also a book of sequence poems, but of a different type from *Myths and Texts*. Snyder sets forth the most useful terms for discussing the difference in a journal entry in "Tanker Notes," in *Earth House Hold*:

> *Poems* that spring out fully armed; and those that are the result of artisan care. The contrived poem, workmanship; a sense of achievement and pride of craft; but the pure inspiration flow leaves one with a sense of gratitude and wonder, and no sense of "I did it"—only the Muse. . . . [O]ne can see where it goes: to all things and in all things.

In these terms, Snyder's riprap lyrics would be the poems of "artisan care," "workmanship," and "craft," while what he later calls his "shaman poems" would be the poems of "pure inspiration flow" that go "to all things and in all things." *Mountains and Rivers Without End*, according to Snyder, explores the "close correspondence between the external and internal landscape[s]" of his life. It is a growing work; six sections were published in the 1965 volume, another was added in the 1970 edition, and others have been published separately. Critics have been particularly impressed by the additions "The Blue Sky" and "The Hump-Backed Flute Player," which aspire to the magical powers of a healing chant or mantra. Though incomplete, versions of the work have nevertheless been compared to Whitman's *Leaves of Grass* and Pound's *Cantos*, two other cumulative poetic projects that occupied their authors over much of their lifetimes.

Snyder's shamanic style also informs the short poems of *Regarding Wave* (1970), but in a more compressed, less overtly allusive manner. The book is the first of Snyder's to bear a dedication, "For Masa"; the poems make clear how his third wife has fulfilled his ideals, expressed in the essay "Poetry and the Primitive" in *Earth House Hold*, of how a loving and creative relationship between man and woman can reflect and become attuned to the larger creative processes of nature. The shamanic effect of these poems depends on their silences as well as their sounds, on their repetitions of sound and idea, and on the multiple references of words that express the reflexive unity of poetic, sexual, and ecological harmonies.

In the years since the publication of *Regarding Wave*, Snyder has tried to lead a life more centered on his family, home, and local community. At the same time, he has graciously (though with some reluctance) accepted the role increasingly thrust on him of international spokesperson on environmental issues. This dual focus of his life is reflected in three volumes of his poetry published after 1970: *Turtle Island* (1974), *Axe Handles* (1983), and *Left Out in the Rain* (1986). Each volume contains impressive shamanic celebrations of nature, like those found in *Regarding Wave*, along with two other types of poems. One type is the colloquial anecdote, often humorous, sketching incidents in Snyder's daily life and often involving his wife and children; an entertaining example in *Turtle Island* is "The Bath." The other type is polemic, in which Snyder speaks in a more didactic voice on environmental or political issues; examples in *Turtle Island* are "Front Lines" and "The Call of the Wild." Often, Snyder shifts among these three voices—anecdotal, polemic, and shamanic—in a single poem, addressing the reader on personal, political, and religious levels. The directions that Snyder's style has taken in his anecdotal and polemic voices has made his reputation as a poet—always a matter of some contention among critics—even more controversial. Yet rather than become anxious himself that his anecdotal voice is becoming too relaxed and prosaic or his polemical voice too strident and propagandistic, Snyder seems content to reach out to a wider audience and to express the political zeal that he feels is appropriate to specific occasions.

EARTH HOUSE HOLD

First published: 1969
Type of work: Journals, essays, and translations

Snyder's first volume of collected prose traces his transition from a life of individual exploration to a life of community responsibility.

Gary Snyder derived the title for his first book of collected prose from word play on the root of the word "ecology." As he points out in the key essay in the book, "Poetry and the Primitive," "eco" comes from the Greek work *oikos*, meaning "house." Thus Snyder playfully renders "ecology" as "earth house hold"—as a perspective that compels humans to consider the entire "earth" as a "house" that they must "hold" with more tenderness and reverence.

The book gathers journals, essays, and translations from 1952 to 1969, a period of many changes in Snyder's life. Some of these pieces, such as reviews of two books of Native American folktales and a translation of the biography of a Buddhist master, are of interest mainly to serious Snyder scholars. For the general student and reader, however, the main interest of the book lies in the personal journals and the later essays, which show important transitions in Snyder's life, philosophy, and conception of poetry. In the course of *Earth House Hold*, Snyder evolves from a wandering, questing individualist to a man firmly rooted in specific commitments to wife, community, and a communal notion of poetry.

Three chapters drawn from Snyder's journals show his developing sense of commitment to family and community. In "Lookout's Journal" (1952), notes from his two summers as a ranger and forest lookout in the Washington Cascades, Snyder writes an entry that is surprisingly prophetic of his later marriage to Masa Uehara and their life at the Banyan Ashram. On the other hand, his prevailing attitude is expressed in a quotation from a friend: " 'Should I marry? It would mean a house; and the next thirty years teaching school.' LOOKOUT!" Similarly, in "Tanker Notes" (1957), journals from his period as a merchant seaman, Snyder's references to women express the exploitative attitude of sailors. By contrast, in the final chapter of the book, "Suwa-no-se Island and the Banyan Ashram," Snyder treats his relationship with Masa Uehara, and his marriage to her, as part of a communal life in close connection with nature. Snyder includes no description of Masa, or of their meeting and courtship, but describes in considerable detail the setting and rituals of their marriage ceremony and the ensuing community celebration.

Snyder's journals and essays in *Earth House Hold* show his conceptions of religion and poetry also developing more of a community orientation. Snyder's 1951 undergraduate dissertation shows that he had long understood, on an intellectual level, the role that he believed a poet should ideally play in the aesthetic and religious life of a community. The writings in *Earth House Hold* show that before

Snyder was able to enact such a role, he needed to work through other conceptions involving self, poetry, religion, and nature. A 1952 entry from "Lookout's Journal" considers poetry as a solitary activity, with primary emphasis on the poet's attempt to express a mystical relationship with nature that is, in Asian religions, considered essentially inexpressible: "If one wished to write poetry of nature, where an audience? Must come from the very conflict of an attempt to articulate the vision." On the other hand, in the early 1960's essay "Buddhism and the Coming Revolution," Snyder argues that Buddhism must move beyond its traditional focus on "liberating a few dedicated individuals" through its schools of meditation. In Snyder's view, persons who hold Buddhist values should move through meditation and personal liberation to a larger purpose of liberating all societies and "moving toward the true community (sangha) of 'all beings.'"

In the culminating essay of *Earth House Hold*, "Poetry and the Primitive: Notes on Poetry as an Ecological Survival Technique," Snyder presents a highly sophisticated analysis of how poetry should become part of oral community ritual. Through "the skilled and inspired use of the voice and language," the poet sings of "rare and powerful states of mind" that are "common to all who listen" and that unify individuals on a deep level with their inner selves, with other people, and with "all beings" with whom they share the planet. In a section called "The Voice as a Girl," Snyder explores concepts—crucial to an understanding of his later poetry—of how his poet's relation to this deeper voice, called "the Muse" in Western culture and "Vak" in Hinduism, is analogous to his relationship with his wife Masa.

RIPRAP

First published: 1959
Type of work: Poem

The craft of embedding rocks on a steep trail serves as a metaphor for the poet's placement of words as footing for journeys of the spirit.

"Riprap," the title poem in Snyder's first collection of verse, is an accomplished example of the craftsmanlike yet transcendent nature of his early poetry. He begins with short, percussive words, mostly monosyllabic, which follow the rhythm of the trail work that he had done in the Sierra Nevada:

> Lay down these words
> Before your mind like rocks.
>   placed solid, by hands
> In choice of place, set
> Before the body of the mind
>   in space and time:
> Solidity of bark, leaf, or wall
>   riprap of things.

Snyder's goal is not merely to reproduce the experience of trail work, but also to jolt the reader's mind into higher levels of consciousness through close attention to natural facts and to words experienced as palpable objects. In the practice of Zen religion, masters sometimes deliver unexpected physical blows to surprise their students into satori (enlightenment), and Snyder stated in a 1960 interview that he wrote the *Riprap* poems under the influence of "the five-and-seven-character-line Chinese poems I'd been reading at the time, which work like sharp blows to the mind." From this foundation of hard physical facts and sharp simple words, Snyder then launches the poem into cosmic realms:

> Cobble of milky way,
> > straying planets,
> These poems, people,
> > lost ponies with
> Dragging saddles—
> > and rocky sure-foot trails.
> The worlds like an endless
> > four-dimensional
> Game of *Go*.

In his playful references to the "milky way," "planets," "worlds," and the "game of *Go*," Snyder implies that the poet need not be limited to mundane physical facts for his choice of words, images, and concepts. Rather, through his placement of words, the poetic craftsman can embed seemingly ungraspable materials in the lines of a poem, just as nature can form into solid rock materials which once seemed too hot and fluid to control:

> Granite: ingrained
> > with torment of fire and weight
> Crystal and sediment linked hot
> > all change, in thoughts,
> As well as things.

Though "Riprap" is known as one of Snyder's carefully composed, craftsmanlike poems, in these concluding lines one can see Snyder prophesying other possibilities for his verse, affirming the heated and volatile flow of poetic imagination.

REGARDING WAVE

First published: 1970
Type of work: Poem

This poem sings of Snyder's love for his wife, for the processes of nature, and for the universal spirit of Dharma.

"Regarding Wave," the title poem in Snyder's remarkable 1969 collection of verse, contains references to Asian religion at the very beginning and end. The chief wonder of the poem, however, is more in the ways it performs, rather than alludes to, its religious and ecological ideas.

The title expresses in two simple words a large range of ideas that Snyder explores in the essay "Poetry and the Primitive" in *Earth House Hold*. According to that essay, in Indo-European etymology the word "Vak" is the name of the Muse-like wife of the Hindu god Brahma, and it is also the common root of the words "voice," "wife," "wave," and "vibration." Snyder considers his shamanic act of allowing a divine "voice" to flow through his poems to be analogous both to the act of making love to his wife and to the waves (the myriad rhythms, breaths, pulses, and vibrations) of natural processes that are flowing through a healthy ecosystem. The phrase "regarding wave" refers to an act of reciprocal and simultaneous perception that involves poet, wife, and world.

The opening lines of the poem call the reader to attention—attention to the waves of physical and spiritual energy that are moving like music through every being and object at every moment. "Dharma" in this context means "divine law":

> The voice of the Dharma
> > the voice
> > > *now*
>
> A shimmering bell
> > through all.
>
> . . . . . .
> Every hill,   still.
> Every tree alive. Every leaf.
> All the slopes flow.
> > old woods, new seedlings,
>
> . . . .
> Dark hollows; peaks of light.
>
> . . . .
> Each leaf living.
> > All the hills.

The words are simple, but the rhythms are subtle and powerful. Snyder makes language sing through many musical repetitions of words and syntax (such as "the voice" and "every"), by approximate and exact rhymes ("bell" and "all," "hill" and "still," "all" and "hill"), by assonance and consonance ("slopes," "flow," and "old"; "alive" and "every"; "each leaf"), and by alliteration ("leaf living"). The imagery of landscape (of "hollows," "slopes," and "hills") also refers to the contours of his wife's body, and it ties into a circular movement back to a reference to the voice from the beginning of the poem: "The Voice/ is a wife/ to/ him still." "Regarding Wave" is a moving and profound lyric, a ringing poem near the center of one of Snyder's most resonant collections.

THE BATH

First published: 1974
Type of work: Poem

A family bath becomes an expansive, joyous occasion that involves the interrelated "body" of the poet's family and the natural world.

"The Bath" illustrates how the experience of fatherhood has provided Snyder
with new perspectives on the interrelationship between the bodies of humans and the
ecological "body" of nature.

The poem begins with a vivid description of Snyder giving his older son Kai a
bath in the sauna at their backwoods home. The poet's mood is relaxed, yet also
attentive to details of his son's body and how that body relates to his own. When
Snyder washes his son's penis, it surprises him by becoming erect. Yet rather than
becoming embarrassed or anxious, Snyder is amused and delighted:

> Laughing and jumping, flinging arms around,
> I squat all naked too,
> > *is this our body?*

These italicized words become a refrain throughout the poem: first "*is this our
body?*," then "*this is our body*" as Snyder's wife Masa and his younger son Gen also
become involved in the scene.

In the second stanza, Masa joins Snyder and Kai in the bath, and the poet draws a
loving analogy between her body and that of the landscape where they make their
home: "The body of my lady, the winding valley spine." Snyder caresses and kisses
his wife, acts which stimulate him to draw further imaginative connections among
the sexual and nurturing powers of his family:

> Kai's little scrotum up close to his groin,
> > the seed still tucked away, that moved from us to him
> In flows that lifted with the same joys forces
> > as his nursing Masa later,
> > playing with her breast,
> Or me within her,
> Or him emerging.

Coming out of the bath, and out of the sauna enclosure, Snyder, Masa, and Kai
enjoy a variety of nature's sights, smells, and sounds. The poet's use of personifica-
tion ("murmuring gossip of the grasses,/ talking firewood") further contributes to
his theme that his family's interrelated body is part of the larger interrelated body of
nature. At the end of the poem, as he and his wife play with their children, Snyder

brings the refrain into his domestic narrative; this theme is now firmly grounded in reality and no longer needs to be treated as a separate "cosmic" thought.

> This is our body. Drawn up crosslegged by the flames
> > drinking icy water
> > hugging babies, kissing bellies,
>
> Laughing on the Great Earth
>
> Come out from the bath.

In many other poems in *Turtle Island*, Snyder gives vent to righteous environmentalist anger. In "The Bath," however, he allows the reader to share in a joyous domestic scene that reflects a surrounding joyous spirit in the natural world. With its humor and love, "The Bath" reminds readers in a gentle way of some of the reasons that nature is worth fighting for.

Summary

As an American cultural figure, Gary Snyder has gained the stature of a twentieth century Thoreau, living an exemplary life in accord with both the practical counsel and the visionary ideals that his writings express so eloquently. Snyder's place in the canon of great American poets is more problematic, particularly since much of his later poetry is more polemical or more relaxed than the most highly praised poems of his early career. Few would dispute, however, that the poetic voice of Gary Snyder often speaks with clarity, humor, and wisdom. Many would go further to contend that his poetry is powerful enough to transform the consciousness of those who read him, creating a shared vision that represents humanity's best chance to preserve the earth for future generations.

Bibliography

Almon, Bert. *Gary Snyder.* Boise, Idaho: Boise State University Press, 1979.

Altieri, Charles. *Enlarging the Temple: New Directions in American Poetry During the 1960's.* Lewisburg, Pa.: Bucknell University Press, 1979.

Kinzie, Mary. "Pictures from Borges." *The American Poetry Review* 12 (November/December, 1983): 40-46.

Molesworth, Charles. *Gary Snyder's Vision: Poetry and the Real Work.* Columbia: University of Missouri Press, 1983.

Steubing, Bob. *Gary Snyder.* Boston: Twayne, 1976.

Wright, James (under the pseudonym "Crunk"). "The Work of Gary Snyder." *The Sixties* 6 (Spring, 1972): 25-42.

Terry L. Andrews

MAGILL'S
SURVEY
OF
AMERICAN
LITERATURE

GLOSSARY

Absurdism: A philosophical attitude underlining the alienation that humans experience in what absurdists see as a universe devoid of meaning; literature of the absurd often purposely lacks logic, coherence, and intelligibility.

Act: One of the major divisions of a play or opera; the typical number of acts in a play ranges from one to four.

Agrarianism: A movement of the 1920's and 1930's in which John Crowe Ransom, Allen Tate, Robert Penn Warren, and other Southern writers championed the agrarian society of their region against the industrialized society of the North.

Allegory: A literary mode in which a second level of meaning (wherein characters, events, and settings represent abstractions) is encoded within the narrative.

Alliteration: The repetition of consonant sounds focused at the beginning of syllables, as in: "Large *m*annered *m*otions of his *m*ythy *m*ind."

Allusion: A reference to a historical event or to another literary text that adds dimension or meaning to a literary work.

Alter ego: A character's other self—sometimes a double, sometimes another side of the character's personality, sometimes a dear and constant companion.

Ambiguity: The capacity of language to sustain multiple meanings; ambiguity can add to both the richness and the concentration of literary language.

Angst: A pervasive feeling of anxiety and depression, often associated with the moral and spiritual uncertainties of the twentieth century.

Antagonist: The major character or force in opposition to the protagonist or hero.

Antihero: A fictional figure who tries to define himself and to establish his own codes, or a protagonist who simply lacks traditional heroic qualities.

Apostrophe: A poetic device in which the speaker addresses either someone not physically present or something not physically capable of hearing the words addressed.

Aside: A short passage generally spoken by one dramatic character in an undertone, or directed to the audience, so as not to be heard by the other characters onstage.

Assonance: A term for the association of words with identical vowel sounds but different consonants; "stars," "arms," and "park," for example, all contain identical "a" (and "ar") sounds.

Atmosphere: The general mood or tone of a work; it is often associated with setting, but can also be established by action or dialogue.

Autobiography: A form of nonfiction writing in which the author narrates events of his or her own life.

Avant-garde: A term describing works intended to expand the conventions of a genre through the experimental treatment of form and/or content.

Bardic voice: A passionate poetic voice modeled after that of a bard, or tribal poet/singer, who composed lyric or epic poetry to honor a chief or recite tribal history.

***Bildungsroman*:** Sometimes called the "novel of education," the *Bildungsroman* focuses on the growth of a young protagonist who is learning about the world and finding his place in life; typical examples are James Joyce's *A Portrait of the Artist as a Young Man* (1916) and Thomas Wolfe's *Look Homeward, Angel* (1929).

Biography: Nonfiction that details the events of a particular individual's life.

Black humor: A general term of modern origin that refers to a form of "sick humor" that is intended to produce laughter out of the morbid and the taboo.

Blank verse: Lines of unrhymed iambic pentameter; it is a poetic form that allows much flexibility, and it has been used since the Elizabethan era.

Caesura: A pause or break in a poem; it is most commonly indicated by a punctuation mark such as a comma, dash, semicolon, or period.

Canon: A generally accepted list of literary works; it may refer to works by a single author or works in a genre. The literary canon often refers to the texts that are thought to belong on university reading lists.

Catharsis: A term from Aristotle's *Poetics* referring to the purgation of the spectators' emotions of pity and fear as aroused by the actions of the tragic hero.

Character: A personage appearing in any literary or dramatic work.

Chorus: An individual or group sometimes used in drama to comment on the action; the chorus was used extensively in classical Greek drama.

Classicism: A literary stance or value system consciously based on classical Greek and Roman literature; it generally denotes a cluster of values including formal discipline, restrained expression, reverence for tradition, and an objective rather than a subjective orientation.

Climax: The moment in a work of fiction or drama at which the action reaches its highest intensity and is resolved.

Comedy: A lighter form of drama that aims chiefly to amuse and that ends happily; comedic forms range from physical (slapstick) humor to subtle intellectual humor.

Comedy of manners: A type of drama which treats humorously, and often satirically, the behavior within an artificial, highly sophisticated society.

Comic relief: A humorous incident or scene in an otherwise serious or tragic work intended to release the reader's or audience's tensions through laughter without detracting from the serious material.

Conceit: One type of metaphor, the conceit is used for comparisons which are highly intellectualized. When T. S. Eliot, for example, says that winding streets are like a tedious argument of insidious intent, there is no clear connection between the two, so the reader must apply abstract logic to fill in the missing links.

Confessional poetry: Autobiographical poetry in which personal revelation provides a basis for the intellectual or theoretical study of moral, religious, or aesthetic concerns.

Conflation: The fusion of variant readings of a text into a composite whole.

Conflict: The struggle that develops as a result of the opposition between the protagonist and another person, the natural world, society, or some force within the self.

Connotation: A type of meaning that depends on the associative meanings of a word beyond its formal definition. (*See also* Denotation.)

Conventions: All those devices of stylization, compression, and selection that constitute the necessary differences between art and life.

Counterplot: A secondary action coincident with the major action of a fictional or dramatic work. The counterplot is generally a reflection on or variation of the main action and is strongly integrated into the whole of the work.

Couplet: Any two succeeding lines of poetry that rhyme.

Cubism: In literature, a style of poetry, such as that of E. E. Cummings and Archibald MacLeish, which first fragments an experience, then rearranges its elements into some new artistic entity.

Dactyl: A metrical foot in which a stressed syllable is followed by two unstressed syllables; an example of a dactyllic line is "After the pangs of a desperate lover."

Deconstruction: An extremely influential contemporary school of criticism based on the works of the French philosopher Jacques Derrida. Deconstruction treats literary works as unconscious reflections of the myths of Western culture; the primary myth is that there is a meaningful world which language signifies or represents. The Deconstructionist critic is often concerned with showing how a literary text tacitly subverts the very assumptions or myths on which it ostensibly rests.

Denotation: The explicit, formal definition of a word, exclusive of its implications and emotional associations. (*See also* Connotation.)

Denouement: Originally French, this word literally means "unknotting" or "untying" and is another term for the catastrophe or resolution of a dramatic action, the solution or clarification of a plot.

Detective story: In the so-called "classic" detective story, the focus is on a crime solved by a detective through interpretation of evidence and clever reasoning. Many modern practitioners of the genre, however, have deemphasized the puzzle-like qualities, stressing instead characterization, theme, and other elements of mainstream fiction.

Determinism: The belief that a person's actions are essentially determined by biological and environmental factors, with free will playing a negligible role. (*See also* Naturalism.)

Deus ex machina: Latin, meaning "god out of a machine." In the Greek theater, it referred to the use of a god lowered by means of a mechanism onto the stage to untangle the plot or save the hero. It has come to signify any artificial device for the easy resolution of dramatic difficulties.

Dialogue: Speech exchanged between characters or even, in a looser sense, the thoughts of a single character.

Dime novel: A type of inexpensive book very popular in the late nineteenth century that told a formulaic tale of war, adventure, or romance.

Domestic tragedy: A serious and usually realistic play with lower-class or middle-class characters and milieu, typically dealing with personal or domestic concerns.

Donnée: From the French verb meaning "to give," the term refers to the premise or the given set of circumstances from which the plot will proceed.

Drama: Any work designed to be represented on a stage by actors. More specifically, the term has come to signify a play of a serious nature and intent which may end either happily (comedy) or unhappily (tragedy).

Dramatic irony: A form of irony that most typically occurs when the spoken lines of a character are perceived by the audience to have a double meaning or when the audience knows more about a situation than the character knows.

Dramatic monologue: A poem in which the narrator addresses a silent persona whose presence greatly influences what the narrator tells the reader.

Dramatis personae: The characters in a play; often it refers to a printed list defining the characters and their relationships.

Dramaturgy: The composition of plays; the term is occasionally used to refer to the performance or acting of plays.

Dream vision: A poem presented as a dream in which the poet-dreamer envisions people and events that frequently have allegorical overtones.

Dualism: A theory that the universe is explicable in terms of two basic, conflicting entities, such as good and evil, mind and matter, or the physical and the spiritual.

Elegy: The elegy and pastoral elegy are distinguishable by their subject matter, not their form. The elegy is usually a long, rhymed, strophic poem whose subject is meditation upon death or a lamentable theme; the pastoral elegy uses a pastoral scene to sing of death or love.

Elizabethan: Of or referring to the reign of Queen Elizabeth I of England, lasting from 1558 to 1603, a period of important artistic achievements; William Shakespeare was an Elizabethan playwright.

End-stop: When a punctuated pause occurs at the end of a line of poetry, the line is said to be end-stopped.

Enjambment: When a line of poetry is not end-stopped and instead carries over to the next line, the line is said to be enjambed.

Epic: This term usually refers to a long narrative poem which presents the exploits of a central figure of high position; it is also used to designate a long novel that has the style or structure usually associated with an epic.

Epilogue: A closing section or speech at the end of a play or other literary work that makes some reflection on the preceding action.

Episodic narrative: A work that is held together primarily by a loose connection of self-sufficient episodes. Picaresque novels often have an episodic structure.

Epithalamion: A bridal song or poem, a genre deriving from the poets of antiquity.

Essay: A nonfiction work, usually short, that analyzes or interprets a particular subject or idea; it is often written from a personal point of view.

Existentialism: A philosophical and literary term for a group of attitudes surrounding the idea that existence precedes essence; according to Jean-Paul Sartre, "man is nothing else but what he makes himself." Existential literature exhibits an awareness of the absurdity of the universe and is preoccupied with the single ethical choice that determines the meaning of a person's existence.

Expressionism: A movement in the arts, especially in German painting, dominant in the decade following World War I; external reality is consciously distorted in order to portray the world as it is "viewed emotionally."

Fabulation: The act of lying to invent or tell a fable, sometimes used to designate the fable itself.

Fantastic: The fantastic has been defined as a genre that lies between the "uncanny" and the "marvelous." All three genres embody the familiar world but present an event that cannot be explained by the laws of the familiar world.

Farce: A play that evokes laughter through such low-comedy devices as physical humor, rough wit, and ridiculous and improbable situations and characters.

First person: A point of view in which the narrator of a story or poem addresses the reader directly, often using the pronoun "I," thereby allowing the reader direct access to the narrator's thoughts.

Flashback: A scene in a fictional or dramatic work depicting events that occurred at an earlier time.

Foot: A rhythmic unit of poetry consisting of two or three syllables grouped together; the most common foot in English is the iamb, composed of one unstressed syllable attached to one stressed syllable.

Foreshadowing: A device used to create suspense or dramatic irony by indicating through suggestion what will take place in the future.

Formalism: A school of literary criticism which particularly emphasizes the form of the work of art—that is, the type or genre to which it belongs.

Frame story: A story that provides a framework for another story (or stories) told within it.

Free verse: A poem that does not conform to such traditional conventions as meter or rhyme, and that does not establish any pattern within itself, is said to be a "free verse" poem.

Genre: A type or category of literature, such as tragedy, novel, memoir, poem, or essay; a genre has a particular set of conventions and expectations.

Genre fiction: Categories of popular fiction such as the mystery, the romance, and the Western; although the term can be used in a neutral sense, "genre fiction" is often used dismissively to refer to fiction in which the writer is bound by more or less rigid conventions.

Gothic novel: A form of fiction developed in the eighteenth century that focuses on horror and the supernatural.

Grotesque: Characterized by a breakup of the everyday world by mysterious forces, the form differs from fantasy in that the reader is not sure whether to react with humor or with horror.

Half rhyme. *See* Slant rhyme.

Hamartia. *See* Tragic flaw.

Harlem Renaissance: A flowering of black American writing, in all literary genres, in the 1930's and 1940's.

Hero/Heroine: The most important character in a drama or other literary work. Popularly, the term has come to refer to a character who possesses extraordinary prowess or virtue, but as a technical term it simply indicates the central participant in a dramatic action. (*See also* Protagonist.)

Heroic couplet: A pair of rhyming iambic pentameter lines traditionally used in epic poetry; a heroic couplet often serves as a self-contained witticism or pithy observation.

Historical novel: A novel that depicts past events, usually public in nature, and that features real as well as fictional people; the relationship between fiction and history in the form varies greatly depending on the author.

Hubris: Excessive pride, the characteristic in tragic heroes such as Oedipus, Doctor Faustus, and Macbeth that leads them to transgress moral codes or ignore warnings. (*See also* Tragic flaw.)

Humanism: A man-centered rather than god-centered view of the universe that usually stresses reason, restraint, and human values; in the Renaissance, humanism devoted itself to the revival of the life, thought, language, and literature of ancient Greece and Rome.

Hyperbole: The use of gross exaggeration for rhetorical effect, based upon the assumption that the reader will not respond to the exaggeration literally.

Iamb: The basic metric foot of the English language, the iamb associates one unstressed syllable with one stressed syllable. The line "So long as men can breathe or eyes can see" is composed of five iambs (a form called iambic pentameter).

Imagery: The simulation of sensory perception through figurative language; imagery can be controlled to create emotional or intellectual effects.

Imagism: A school of poetry prominent in Great Britain and North America between 1909 and 1918. The objectives of Imagism were accurate description, objective presentation, concentration and economy, new rhythms, freedom of choice in subject matter, and suggestion rather than explanation.

Interior monologue: The speech of a character designed to introduce the reader directly to the character's internal life; it differs from other monologues in that it attempts to reproduce thought before logical organization is imposed upon it.

Irony: An effect that occurs when a writer's or a character's real meaning is different from (and frequently opposite to) his or her apparent meaning. (*See also* Dramatic irony.)

Jazz Age: The 1920's, a period of prosperity, sweeping social change, frequent excess, and youthful rebellion, for which F. Scott Fitzgerald is the acknowledged spokesman.

***Künstlerroman*:** An apprenticeship novel in which the protagonist, a young artist, faces the conflicts of growing up and coming to understand the purpose of his life and art.

Leitmotif: The repetition in a work of literature of a word, phrase, or image which serves to establish the tone or otherwise unify the piece.

Line: A rhythmical unit within a poem between the foot and the poem's larger structural units; the words or feet in a line are usually in a single row.

Lyric poetry: Poetry that is generally short, adaptable to metrical variation, and personal in theme; it may explore deeply personal feelings about life.

Magical realism: Imaginary or fantastic scenes and occurrences presented in a meticulously realistic style.

Melodrama: A play in which characters are clearly either virtuous or evil and are pitted against one another in suspenseful, often sensational situations.

Memoir: A piece of autobiographical writing which emphasizes important events in which the author has participated and prominent people whom the author has known.

Metafiction: Fiction that manifests a reflexive tendency and shows a consciousness of itself as an artificial creation; such terms as "postmodernist fiction," "antifiction," and "surfiction" also refer to this type of fiction.

Metaphor: A figure of speech in which two different things are identified with each other, as in the T. S. Eliot line, "The whole earth is our hospital"; the term is also widely used to identify many kinds of analogies.

Metaphysical poetry: A type of poetry that stresses the intellectual over the emotional; it is marked by irony, paradox, and striking comparisons of dissimilar things, the latter frequently being farfetched to the point of eccentricity.

Meter: The rhythmic pattern of language when it is formed into lines of poetry; when the rhythm of language is organized and regulated so as to affect the meaning and emotional response to the words, the rhythm has been refined into meter.

Mise-en-scène: The staging of a drama, including scenery, costumes, movable furniture (properties), and, by extension, the positions (blocking) and gestures of the actors.

Mock-heroic style: A form of burlesque in which a trivial subject is absurdly elevated through use of the meter, diction, and familiar devices of the epic poem.

Modernism: An international movement in the arts which began in the early years of the twentieth century; modernism in general was characterized by its international idiom, by its interest in cultures distant in space or time, by its emphasis on formal experimentation, and by its sense of dislocation and radical change.

Monologue: An extended speech by one character in a drama. If the character is alone onstage, unheard by other characters, the monologue is more specifically referred to as a soliloquy.

Musical comedy: A theatrical form mingling song, dance, and spoken dialogue which was developed in the United States in the twentieth century; it was derived from vaudeville and operetta.

Myth: Anonymous traditional stories dealing with basic human concepts and fundamentally opposing principles; a myth is often constructed as a story that tells of supposedly historical events.

Narrator: The character who recounts the story in a work of fiction.

Naturalism: The application of the principles of scientific determinism to fiction. Although it usually refers more to the choice of subject matter than to technical conventions, conventions associated with the movement center on the author's attempt to be precise and objective in description and detail, regardless of whether the events described are sordid or shocking. (*See also* Determinism.)

Neoclassicism: The type of classicism that dominated English literature from the Restoration to the late eighteenth century. Modeling itself on the literature of ancient Greece and Rome, neoclassicism exalts the virtues of proportion, unity, harmony, grace, decorum, taste, manners, and restraint; it values realism and reason.

New Criticism: A reaction against the "old criticism" that either saw art as self-expression, applied extrinsic criteria of morality and value, or gave credence to the professed intentions of the author. The New Criticism regards a work of art as an autonomous object, a self-contained universe. It holds that a close reading of literary texts will reveal their meanings and the complexities of their verbal texture as well as the oppositions and tensions balanced in the text.

New journalism: Writing that largely abandons the traditional objectivity of journalism in order to express the subjective response of the observer.

Nonfiction novel: A novel such as Truman Capote's *In Cold Blood*, which, though taking actual people and events as its subject matter, uses fictional techniques to develop the narrative.

Novel: A long fictional form that is generally concerned with individual characterization and with presenting a social world and a detailed environment.

Novel of ideas: A novel in which the characters, plot, and dialogue serve to develop some controlling idea or to present the clash of ideas.

Novel of manners: The classic example of the form might be the novels of Jane Austen, wherein the customs and conventions of a social group of a particular time and place are realistically, and often satirically, portrayed.

Novella, novelle, nouvelle, novelette: These terms usually refer to that form of fiction which is said to be longer than a short story and shorter than a novel; "novella" is the term usually used to refer to American works in this genre.

Ode: A lyric poem that treats a unified subject with elevated emotion and seriousness of purpose, usually ending with a satisfactory resolution.

Old Criticism: Criticism predating the New Criticism and bringing extrinsic criteria to bear on the analysis of literature as authorial self-expression (Romanticism), critical self-expression (Impressionism), or work that is dependent upon moral or ethical absolutes (new humanism).

Omniscient narration: A godlike point of view from which the narrator sees all and knows everything there is to know about the story and its characters.

One-act play: A short, unified dramatic work, the one-act play is usually quite limited in number of characters and scene changes; the action often revolves around a single incident or event.

Opera: A complex combination of various art forms, opera is a form of dramatic entertainment consisting of a play set to music.

Original Sin: A concept of the innate depravity of man's nature resulting from Adam's sin and fall from grace.

Paradox: A statement that initially seems to be illogical or self-contradictory yet eventually proves to embody a complex truth.

Parataxis: The placing of clauses or phrases in a series without the use of coordinating or subordinating terms.

Pathos: The quality in a character that evokes pity or sorrow from the observer.

Pentameter: A line of poetry consisting of five recognizable rhythmic units called feet.

Picaresque novel: A form of fiction that involves a central rogue figure, or picaro, who usually tells his own story. The plot structure is normally episodic, and the episodes usually focus on how the picaro lives by his wits.

Plot: The sequence of the occurrence of events in a dramatic action. A plot may be unified around a single action, but it may also consist of a series of disconnected incidents; it is then referred to as "episodic."

Poem: A unified composition that uses the rhythms and sounds of language, as well as devices such as metaphor, to communicate emotions and experiences to the reader or hearer.

Point of view: The perspective from which a story is presented to the reader. In simplest terms, it refers to whether narration is first-person (directly addressed to the reader as if told by one involved in the narrative) or third-person (usually a more objective, distanced perspective).

Postmodernism: The term is loosely applied to various artistic movements which have followed so-called high modernism, represented by such giants as James Joyce and Pablo Picasso. The term is frequently applied to the works of writers (such as Thomas Pynchon and John Barth) who exhibit a self-conscious awareness of their predecessors as well as a reflexive treatment of fictional form.

Prose poem: A type of poem, usually less than a page in length, that appears on the page like prose; there is great stylistic and thematic variety within the genre.

Protagonist: Originally, in the Greek drama, the "first actor," who played the leading role. The term has come to signify the most important character in a drama or story. It is not unusual for there to be more than one protagonist in a work. (*See also* Hero/Heroine.)

Psychoanalytic theory: A tremendously influential theory of the unconscious developed by Sigmund Freud, it divides the human psyche into three components—the id, the ego, and the superego. In this theory, the psyche represses instinctual and sexual desires, and channels (sublimates) those desires into socially acceptable behavior.

Psychological novel: A form of fiction in which character, especially the inner life of characters, is the primary focus. The form has characterized much of the work of James Joyce, Virginia Woolf, and William Faulkner.

Psychological realism: A type of realism that tries to reproduce the complex psychological motivations behind human behavior; writers in the late nineteenth and early twentieth centuries were particularly influenced by Sigmund Freud's theories. (*See also* Psychoanalytic theory.)

Pun: A pun occurs when words which have similar pronunciations have entirely different meanings; a pun can establish a connection between two meanings or contexts that the reader would not ordinarily make. The result may be a striking connection or simply a humorously accidental connection.

Quatrain: Any four-line stanza is a quatrain; other than the couplet, the quatrain is the most common type of stanza.

Rationalism: A system of thought which seeks truth through the exercise of reason rather than by means of emotional response or revelation.

Realism: A literary technique in which the primary convention is to render an illusion of fidelity to external reality. Realism is often identified as the primary method of the novel form; the realist movement in the late nineteenth century coincided with the full development of the novel form.

Regional novel: Any novel in which the character of a given geographical region plays a decisive role; the Southern United States, for example, has fostered a strong regional tradition.

Representationalism: An approach to drama that seeks to create the illusion of reality onstage through realistic characters, situations, and settings.

Revue: A theatrical production, typically consisting of sketches, song, and dance, which often comments satirically upon personalities and events of the day; generally there is no plot involved.

Rhyme: A full rhyme comprises two or more words that have the same vowel sound and that end with the same consonant sound: "Hat" and "cat" is a full rhyme, as is "laughter" and "after." Rhyme is also used more broadly as a term for any correspondence in sound between syllables in poetry. (*See also* Slant rhyme.)

Rhyme scheme: Poems which establish a pattern of rhyme have a "rhyme scheme," designated by lowercase letters; the rhyme scheme of ottava rima, for example, is abababcc. Traditional stanza forms are categorized by their rhyme scheme and base meter.

GLOSSARY

Roman à clef: A fiction wherein actual persons, often celebrities of some sort, are thinly disguised.

Romance: The romance usually differs from the novel form in that the focus is on symbolic events and representational characters rather than on "as-if-real" characters and events. Character is often highly stylized, serving as a function of the plot.

Romantic comedy: A play in which love is the central motive of the dramatic action. The term often refers to plays of the Elizabethan period, such as William Shakespeare's *As You Like It* and *A Midsummer Night's Dream*, but it has also been applied to any modern work that contains similar features.

Romanticism: A widespread cultural movement in the late-eighteenth and early-nineteenth centuries, Romanticism is frequently contrasted with classicism. The term generally suggests primitivism, an interest in folklore, a reverence for nature, a fascination with the demoniac and the macabre, and an assertion of the preeminence of the imagination.

Satire: Satire employs the comedic devices of wit, irony, and exaggeration to expose and condemn human folly, vice, and stupidity.

Scene: In drama, a division of action within an act (some plays are divided only into scenes instead of acts). Sometimes scene division indicates a change of setting or locale; sometimes it simply indicates the entrances and exits of characters.

Science fiction: Fiction in which real or imagined scientific developments or certain givens (such as physical laws, psychological principles, or social conditions) form the basis of an imaginative projection, frequently into the future.

Sentimental novel: A form of fiction popular in the eighteenth century in which emotionalism and optimism are the primary characteristics. The best-known examples are Samuel Richardson's *Pamela* (1740-1741) and Oliver Goldsmith's *The Vicar of Wakefield* (1766).

Sentimentalism: A term used to describe any emotional response that is excessive and disproportionate to its impetus or occasion. It also refers to the eighteenth century idea that human beings are essentially benevolent, devoid of Original Sin and basic depravity.

Setting: The time and place in which the action of a literary work happens. The term also applies to the physical elements of a theatrical production, such as scenery and properties.

Short story: A concise work of fiction, shorter than a novella, that is usually more concerned with mood, effect, or a single event than with plot or extensive characterization.

Simile: Loosely defined, a simile is a type of metaphor which signals a comparison by the use of the words "like" or "as." Shakespeare's line, "My mistress' eyes are nothing like the sun," establishes a comparison between the woman's eyes and the sun, and is a simile.

Slant rhyme: A slant rhyme, or half rhyme, occurs when words with identical consonants but different vowel sounds are associated; "fall" and "well," and "table" and "bauble" are slant rhymes.

Slapstick: Low comedy in which physical action (such as a kick in the rear, tripping, and knocking over people or objects) evokes laughter.

Social realism: A type of realism in which the social and economic conditions in which characters live figure prominently in their situations, actions, and outlooks.

Soliloquy: An extended speech delivered by a character alone onstage, unheard by other characters. Soliloquy is a form of monologue, and it typically reveals the intimate thoughts and emotions of the speaker.

Sonnet: A traditional poetic form that is almost always composed of fourteen lines of rhymed iambic pentameter; a turning point usually divides the poem into two parts, with the first part presenting a situation and the second part reflecting on it.

Southern Gothic: A term applied to the scenes of decay, incest, madness, and violence often found in the fiction of William Faulkner, Erskine Caldwell, and other Southern writers.

Speaker: The voice which speaks the words of a poem—sometimes a fictional character in an invented situation, sometimes the author speaking directly to the reader, sometimes the author speaking from behind the disguise of a persona.

Stanza: When lines of poetry are meant to be taken as a unit, and the unit recurs throughout the poem, that unit is called a stanza; a four-line unit is one common stanza.

Stream of consciousness: The depiction of the thought processes of a character, insofar as this is possible, without any mediating structures. The metaphor of consciousness as a "stream" suggests a rush of thoughts and images governed by free association rather than by strictly rational development; the term is often used loosely as a synonym for interior monologue.

Stress: When more emphasis is placed on one syllable in a line of poetry than on another syllable, that syllable is said to be stressed.

Subplot: A secondary action coincident with the main action of a fictional or dramatic work. A subplot may be a reflection upon the main action, but it may also be largely unrelated. (*See also* Counterplot.)

Surrealism: An approach to literature and art that startlingly combines seemingly incompatible elements; surrealist writing usually has a bizarre, dreamlike, or nightmarish quality.

Symbol: A literary symbol is an image that stands for something else; it may evoke a cluster of meanings rather than a single specific meaning.

Symbolism: A literary movement encompassing the work of a group of French writers in the latter half of the nineteenth century, a group that included Charles Baudelaire, Stéphane Mallarmé, and Paul Verlaine. According to Symbolism, there is a mystical correspondence between the natural and spiritual worlds.

Syntax: A linguistic term used to describe the study of the ways in which words are arranged sequentially to produce grammatical units such as phrases, clauses, and sentences.

Tableau: A silent, stationary grouping of performers in a theatrical performance.

Terza rima: A rhyming three-line stanza form in which the middle line of one stanza rhymes with the first line of the following stanza.

Tetrameter: A line of poetry consisting of four recognizable rhythmic units called feet.

Theater of the absurd: The general name given to plays that express a basic belief that life is illogical, irrational, formless, and contradictory and that man is without meaning or purpose. This perspective often leads to the abandonment of traditional theatrical forms and coherent dialogue.

Theme: Loosely defined as what a literary work means. The theme of W. B. Yeats's poem "Sailing to Byzantium," for example, might be interpreted as the failure of man's attempt to isolate himself within the world of art.

Thespian: Another term for an actor; also, of or relating to the theater. The word derives from Thespis, by tradition the first actor of the Greek theater.

Third person: Third-person narration is related from a point of view more distant from the story than first-person narration; the narrator is not an identifiable "I" persona. A third-person point of view may be limited or omniscient ("all-knowing").

Three unities. *See* Unities.

Tone: Tone usually refers to the dominant mood of a work. (*See also* Atmosphere.)

Tragedy: A form of drama that is serious in action and intent and that involves disastrous events and death; classical Greek drama observed specific guidelines for tragedy, but the term is now sometimes applied to a range of dramatic or fictional situations.

Tragic flaw: Also known as hamartia, it is the weakness or error in judgment in a tragic hero or protagonist that causes the character's downfall; it may proceed from ignorance or a moral fault. Excessive pride (hubris) is one traditional tragic flaw.

Travel literature: Writing which emphasizes the author's subjective response to places visited, especially faraway, exotic, and culturally different locales.

Trimeter: A line of poetry consisting of three recognizable rhythmic units called feet.

Trochee: One of the most common feet in English poetry, the trochee associates one stressed syllable with one unstressed syllable, as in the line, "Double, double, toil and trouble."

Unities: A set of rules for proper dramatic construction formulated by European Renaissance drama critics and derived from classical Greek concepts: A play should have no scenes or subplots irrelevant to the central action, should not cover a period of more than twenty-four hours, and should not occur in more than one place.

Verisimilitude: The attempt to have the readers of a literary work believe that it conforms to reality rather than to its own laws.

Verse: A generic term for poetry; verse also refers in a narrower sense to poetry that is humorous or merely superficial, as in "greeting-card verse."

Verse paragraph: A division within a poem that is created by logic or syntax rather than by form; verse paragraphs are important for determining the movement of a poem and the logical association between ideas.

Victorian novel: Although the Victorian period extended from 1837 to 1901, the term "Victorian novel" does not include works from the later decades of Queen Victoria's reign. The term loosely refers to the sprawling works of novelists such as Charles Dickens and William Makepeace Thackeray, which are characterized by a broad social canvas.

Villanelle: The villanelle is a French verse form assimilated by English prosody. It is usually composed of nineteen lines divided into five tercets and a quatrain, rhyming aba, bba, aba, aba, abaa.

Well-made play: A type of play constructed according to a nineteenth century French formula; the plot often revolves around a secret (revealed at the end) known only to some of the characters. Misunderstanding, suspense, and coincidence are among the devices used.

Western novel: The Western novel is defined by a relatively predictable combination of conventions and recurring themes. These predictable elements, familiar from television and film Westerns, differentiate the Western from historical novels and other works which may be set in the Old West.

Worldview: Frequently rendered as the German *weltanschauung*, it is a comprehensive set of beliefs or assumptions by means of which one interprets what goes on in the world.

LIST OF AUTHORS

LIST OF AUTHORS